The Ultimate Guitar
CHORD & SCALE BIBLE

National Guitar Workshop Method — Approved Curriculum

Over 5,000 Useful Chords and 130 Scales for Improvisation

Buck Brown & Mark Dziuba

Acquisition and editorial: Nathaniel Gunod, Burgess Speed

Cover, page layout (The Ultimate Chord Bible) and chord diagrams: Timothy Phelps

Page Layout (The Ultimate Scale Bible): Margo Farnsworth

Music typesetting: Mark Dziuba, Scott Smallwood and Gary Tomassetti

Fender Stratocaster courtesy of Fender Musical Instruments, Inc.

ISBN-10: 1-60347-000-X

ISBN-13: 978-1-60347-000-1

Exclusive distribution by Alfred Publishing Co., Inc.

P.O. Box 10003 • 16320 Roscoe Blvd. • Van Nuys, CA 91410-0003

Alfred

Introduction

You hold in your hands the most comprehensive resource for chords and scales available. Every chord or scale you will ever need to know can be found in these pages. For the first time ever, the best-selling books *The Ultimate Guitar Chord Bible* and *The Ultimate Guitar Scale Bible* have been combined to form *The Ultimate Guitar Chord and Scale Bible*—over 330 pages of information that can increase your musical knowledge and make you a better guitar player.

The Ultimate Guitar Chord Bible will show you the most useful variations and inversions of every major, minor, dominant 7th and altered dominant 7th chord on different sets of strings and in various inversions.

The fingerings shown are the easiest, and if you give them a chance you'll probably come to see why they were chosen. There are even some fingerings that include your thumb! Try them all out and see why they work. They are, however, just suggestions; you can make your own fingering decisions if you like.

This books starts with all the E chords and moves by key through the cycle of 4ths.

E   A   D   G   C   B$\flat$/A$\sharp$ E$\flat$/D$\sharp$ A$\flat$/G$\sharp$ D$\flat$/C$\sharp$ G$\flat$/F$\sharp$

The Ultimate Guitar Scale Bible is a vast scale and chord/scale relationship reference tool. To get the most out of this book, a basic knowledge of music theory and improvisation will be helpful. All the scales in this book were chosen because of their usefulness in improvisational or compositional contexts. Use this book to supplement your existing scale knowledge and further your melodic and harmonic universe. Remember, these scales don't make the music. You do!

The *Ultimate Guitar Chord and Scale Bible* is not only a groundbreaking combination of two best-selling books, it is the only resource for chords and scales you will ever need.

What are you waiting for? Dig in!

The Ultimate Guitar
CHORD BIBLE

Buck Brown

4

Contents

0

About the Author 7
Introduction 7
Chord Name Abbreviations and
   Reading Chord Diagrams................. 7

Easy Guide to Keys

E	8	G	53	B♭/A♯	98
A	23	C	68	E♭/D♯	113
D	38	F	83	A♭/G♯	128

D♭/C♯	143		
G♭/F♯	158		
B	173		

Chords Listed by Key

A 23
Maj, sus2, sus4, no 3rd, 6.......................... 23
Maj7, Maj9, 6/9.. 24
add9, Maj11, Maj13, Maj13add9,
  Maj13♯11, Maj7♭5................................ 25
Maj7♯11, Maj9♯11, aug............................. 26
min, min6, min7....................................... 27
minMaj7, min7♯5, minadd9, min6/9,
  minadd9/11....................................... 28
min9, min9Maj7, min9add11, min11 29
min13, min13add9, min7♭5,
  min9♭5.. 30
7, 9 31
9sus4, 11(7sus4), 13, 13add9................. 32
13sus4, 13add9sus4, 7♭5, 7♯5,
  7♭9, 7♯9 33
7♭9♭5, 7♯9♭5, 7♯5♭9, 7♯5♯9, 9♭5,
  9♯5, 11♭5 34
13♭5, 13♭9, 13♯9, dim9, dim11, dim 35
dim7 36
Three-Note Voicings
  Maj7, 7, min7, 6 37

B♭/A♯ 98
Maj, sus2, sus4, no 3rd, 6.......................... 98
Maj7, Maj9, 6/9.. 99
add9, Maj11, Maj13, Maj13add9,
  Maj13♯11, Maj7♭5...............................100
Maj7♯11, Maj9♯11, aug 101
min, min6, min7.......................................102
minMaj7, min7♯5, minadd9, min6/9,
  minadd9/11.......................................103
min9, min9Maj7, min9add11, min11 ... 104
min13, min13add9, min7♭5, min9♭5...... 105
7, 9 106
9sus4, 11(7sus4), 13, 13add9................. 107
13sus4, 13add9sus4, 7♭5, 7♯5,
  7♭9, 7♯9 108
7♭9♭5, 7♯9♭5, 7♯5♭9, 7♯5♯9, 9♭5, 9♯5, 11♭5 109
13♭5, 13♭9, 13♯9, dim9, dim11, dim........ 110
dim7 111
Three-Note Voicings
  Maj7, 7, min7, 6 112

B 173
Maj, sus2, sus4, no 3rd, 6......................... 173
Maj7, Maj9, 6/9....................................... 174
add9, Maj11, Maj13, Maj13add9,
  Maj13♯11, Maj7♭5............................... 175
Maj7♯11, Maj9♯11, aug............................ 176
min, min6, min7...................................... 177
minMaj7, min7♯5, minadd9, min6/9,
  minadd9/11....................................... 178
min9, min9Maj7, min9add11, min11 ... 179
min13, min13add9, min7♭5,
  min9♭5.. 180
7, 9 181
9sus4, 11(7sus4), 13, 13add9................. 182
13sus4, 13add9sus4, 7♭5, 7♯5,
  7♭9, 7♯9 183
7♭9♭5, 7♯9♭5, 7♯5♭9, 7♯5♯9, 9♭5, 9♯5, 11♭5.... 184
13♭5, 13♭9, 13♯9, dim9, dim11, dim........ 185
dim7 186
Three-Note Voicings
  Maj7, 7, min7, 6 187

C 68
Maj, sus2, sus4, no 3rd, 6.......................... 68
Maj7, Maj9, 6/9.. 69
add9, Maj11, Maj13, Maj13add9,
  Maj13♯11, Maj7♭5................................ 70
Maj7♯11, Maj9♯11, aug.............................. 71
min, min6, min7.. 72
minMaj7, min7♯5, minadd9, min6/9,
  minadd9/11... 73
min9, min9Maj7, min9add11, min11 74
min13, min13add9, min7♭5,
  min9♭5.. 75
7, 9 76
9sus4, 11(7sus4), 13, 13add9................. 77
13sus4, 13add9sus4, 7♭5, 7♯5,
  7♭9, 7♯9 78
7♭9♭5, 7♯9♭5, 7♯5♭9, 7♯5♯9, 9♭5, 9♯5, 11♭5...... 79
13♭5, 13♭9, 13♯9, dim9, dim11, dim.......... 80
dim7 81
Three-Note Voicings
  Maj7, 7, min7, 6 82

D♭/C♯ 143
Maj, sus2, sus4, no 3rd, 6......................... 143
Maj7, Maj9, 6/9....................................... 144
add9, Maj11, Maj13, Maj13add9,
  Maj13♯11, Maj7♭5............................... 145
Maj7♯11, Maj9♯11, aug............................ 146
min, min6, min7...................................... 147
minMaj7, min7♯5, minadd9, min6/9,
  minadd9/11....................................... 148
min9, min9Maj7, min9add11, min11 ... 149
min13, min13add9, min7♭5,
  min9♭5.. 150
7, 9 151
9sus4, 11(7sus4), 13, 13add9................. 152
13sus4, 13add9sus4, 7♭5, 7♯5,
  7♭9, 7♯9 153
7♭9♭5, 7♯9♭5, 7♯5♭9, 7♯5♯9, 9♭5, 9♯5, 11♭5.... 154
13♭5, 13♭9, 13♯9, dim9, dim11, dim........ 155
dim7 156
Three-Note Voicings
  Maj7, 7, min7, 6 157

D 38
Maj, sus2, sus4, no 3rd, 6.......................... 38
Maj7, Maj9, 6/9.. 39
add9, Maj11, Maj13, Maj13add9,
  Maj13♯11, Maj7♭5................................ 40
Maj7♯11, Maj9♯11, aug.............................. 41
min, min6, min7.. 42
minMaj7, min7♯5, minadd9, min6/9,
  minadd9/11... 43
min9, min9Maj7, min9add11, min11 44
min13, min13add9, min7♭5,
  min9♭5.. 45
7, 9 46
9sus4, 11(7sus4), 13, 13add9................. 47
13sus4, 13add9sus4, 7♭5, 7♯5,
  7♭9, 7♯9 48
7♭9♭5, 7♯9♭5, 7♯5♭9, 7♯5♯9, 9♭5, 9♯5, 11♭5...... 49
13♭5, 13♭9, 13♯9, dim9, dim11, dim.......... 50
dim7 51
Three-Note Voicings
  Maj7, 7, min7, 6 52

Contents—Chords Listed by Key

4

Contents—Chords Listed by Key

*TNV = Three-Note Voicings

Contents—Chords Listed by Type

	A	B♭/A♯	B	C	D♭/C♯	D	E♭/D♯	E	F	G♭/F♯	G	A♭/G♯
Maj	23	98	173	68	143	38	113	8	83	158	53	128
6	23	98	173	68	143	38	113	8	83	158	53	128
6(TNV)*	37	112	187	82	157	52	127	22	97	172	67	142
Maj7	24	99	174	69	144	39	114	9	84	159	54	129
Maj7(TNV)	37	112	187	82	157	52	127	22	97	172	67	142
Maj9	24	99	174	69	144	39	114	9	84	159	54	129
Maj11	25	100	175	70	145	40	115	10	85	160	55	130
Maj13	25	100	175	70	145	40	115	10	85	160	55	130
sus2	23	98	173	68	143	38	113	8	83	158	53	128
sus4	23	98	173	68	143	38	113	8	83	158	53	128
add9	25	100	175	70	145	40	115	10	85	160	55	130
6/9	24	99	174	69	144	39	114	9	84	159	54	129
Maj7♯5	25	100	175	70	145	40	115	10	85	160	55	130
Maj7♯11	26	101	176	71	146	41	116	11	86	161	56	131
Maj9♯11	26	101	176	71	146	41	116	11	86	161	56	131
Maj13add9	25	100	175	70	145	40	115	10	85	160	55	130
Maj13♯11	25	100	175	70	145	40	115	10	85	160	55	130
min	27	102	177	72	147	42	117	12	87	162	57	132
min6	27	102	177	72	147	42	117	12	87	162	57	132
min7	27	102	177	72	147	42	117	12	87	162	57	132
min7(TNV)	37	112	187	82	157	52	127	22	97	172	67	142
minMaj7	28	103	178	73	148	43	118	13	88	163	58	133
min9	29	104	179	74	149	44	119	14	89	164	59	134
min9Maj7	29	104	179	74	149	44	119	14	89	164	59	134
min11	29	104	179	74	149	44	119	14	89	164	59	134
min13	30	105	180	75	150	45	120	15	90	165	60	135
min7♭5	30	105	180	75	150	45	120	15	90	165	60	135
min7♯5	28	103	178	73	148	43	118	13	88	163	58	133
min9♭5	30	105	180	75	150	45	120	15	90	165	60	135
minadd9	28	103	178	73	148	43	118	13	88	163	58	133
minadd9/11	28	103	178	73	148	43	118	13	88	163	58	133
min9add11	29	104	179	74	149	44	119	14	89	164	59	134
min6/9	28	103	178	73	148	43	118	13	88	163	58	133
min13add9	30	105	180	75	150	45	120	15	90	165	60	135
7	31	106	181	76	151	46	121	16	91	166	61	136
7(TNV)	37	112	187	82	157	52	127	22	97	172	67	142
9	31	106	181	76	151	46	121	16	91	166	61	136
11(7sus4)	32	107	182	77	152	47	122	17	92	167	62	137
13	32	107	182	77	152	47	122	17	92	167	62	137
7♭5	33	108	183	78	153	48	123	18	93	168	63	138
7♯5	33	108	183	78	153	48	123	18	93	168	63	138
7♭9	33	108	183	78	153	48	123	18	93	168	63	138
7♯9	33	108	183	78	153	48	123	18	93	168	63	138
7♭9♭5	34	109	184	79	154	49	124	19	94	169	64	139
7♯9♭5	34	109	184	79	154	49	124	19	94	169	64	139
7♯5♭9	34	109	184	79	154	49	124	19	94	169	64	139
7♯5♯9	34	109	184	79	154	49	124	19	94	169	64	139
9♭5	34	109	184	79	154	49	124	19	94	169	64	139
9♯5	34	109	184	79	154	49	124	19	94	169	64	139
9sus4	32	107	182	77	152	47	122	17	92	167	62	137
11♭5	34	109	184	79	154	49	124	19	94	169	64	139
13add9	32	107	182	77	152	47	122	17	92	167	62	137
13sus4	33	108	183	78	153	48	123	18	93	168	63	138
13add9sus4	33	108	183	78	153	48	123	18	93	168	63	138
13♭5	35	110	185	80	155	50	125	20	95	170	65	140
13♭9	35	110	185	80	155	50	125	20	95	170	65	140
13♯9	35	110	185	80	155	50	125	20	95	170	65	140
aug	26	101	176	71	146	41	116	11	86	161	56	131
dim	35	110	185	80	155	50	125	20	95	170	65	140
dim7	36	111	186	81	156	51	126	21	96	171	66	141
dim9	35	110	185	80	155	50	125	20	95	170	65	140
dim11	35	110	185	80	155	50	125	20	95	170	65	140
no 3rd	23	98	173	68	143	38	113	8	83	158	53	128
	A	B♭/A♯	B	C	D♭/C♯	D	E♭/D♯	E	F	G♭/F♯	G	A♭/G♯

About the Author

Buck Brown plays guitar and keyboards with The Nils Lofgren Band and Robert Lee Castleman as well as performing his own solo act. He has been fortunate to be able to play with these great artists and many others, teach at the National Guitar Workshop, and write numerous instructional books for the National Guitar Workshop and Alfred.

As a composer, he has written music for America's Most Wanted, has won an Emmy Award in Cleveland, a Bronze medal at the New York Film Festival and has been nominated twice for Helen Hayes Awards in Musical Theatre.

When he is not on the road, Buck plays and teaches in the Washington D.C. area, is married to the fabulous chanteuse Rebecca Davis, plays with his son Will and their three dogs, bats right, throws right, plays loud.

Introduction

To become a better guitar player, it is important to spend some time learning how to play all chords in various places on the guitar. This book will show you the most useful variations and inversions of every major, minor, dominant 7th and altered dominant 7th chord on different sets of strings and in various inversions.

The fingerings shown are the easiest, and if you give them a chance you'll probably come to see why they were chosen. There are even some fingerings that include your thumb! Try them all out and see why they work. They are, however, just suggestions; you can make your own fingering decisions if you like.

The most common and useful chord voicings are highlighted and numbered according to their comparative usefulness. Otherwise, the chords are arranged from the lowest positive to the highest, making it easy for you to find the voicing best for the context in which it will be used.

This books starts with all the E chords and moves by key through the cycle of 4ths.

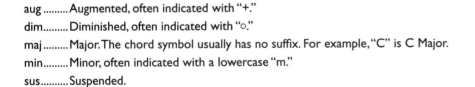

E   A   D   G   C   B♭/A♯   E♭/D♯   A♭/G♯   D♭/C♯   G♭/F♯   B

I hope this helps you get a good handle on chords. At the very least, you can use it as a reference for finding fingerings for any chords you might have to play.

See you at the gig.

Buck

Chord Name Abbreviations and Reading Chord Diagrams

aug ....Augmented, often indicated with "+."

dim.........Diminished, often indicated with "○."

maj ....Major. The chord symbol usually has no suffix. For example, "C" is C Major.

min.........Minor, often indicated with a lowercase "m."

sus..........Suspended.

For a thorough explanation of how all of the chords in this book are created, see *Theory for the Contemporary Guitarist*, by Guy Cappuzo (National Guitar Workshop/Alfred #16755).

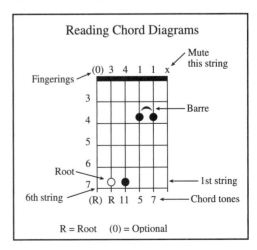

Reading Chord Diagrams

E

Maj
1, 3, 5

  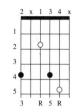  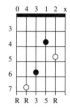 
    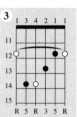 

sus2
1, 2, 5

  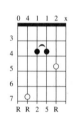   

sus4
1, 4, 5

  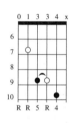 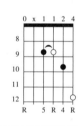 

no 3rd
1,5

 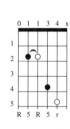  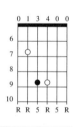 

6
1, 3, 5, 6

 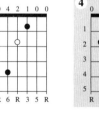  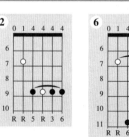
 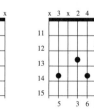 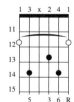

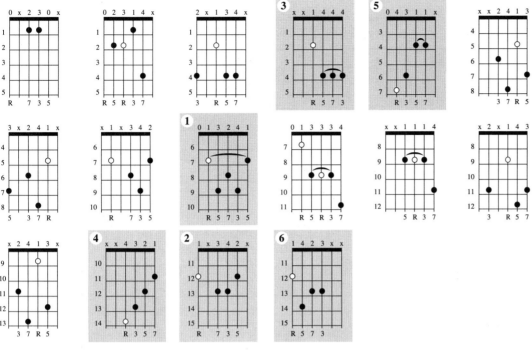

Maj7
1, 3, 5, 7

E

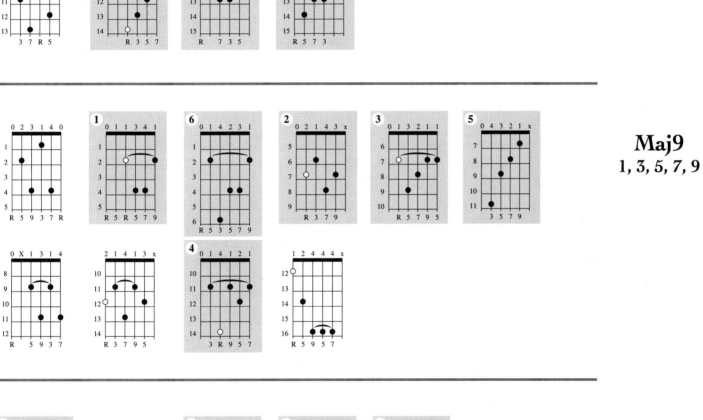

Maj9
1, 3, 5, 7, 9

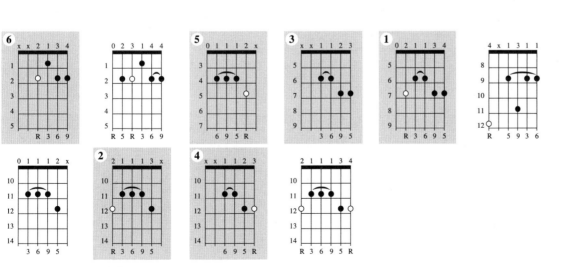

6/9
1, 3, 5, 6, 9

E

add9
1, 3, 5, 9

Maj11
1, 3, 5, 7, 11

Maj13
1, 3, 5, 7, 13

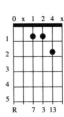

Maj13add9
1, 3, 5, 7, 9, 13

Maj13#11
1, 3, 7, #11, 13

Maj7#5
1, 3, #5, 7

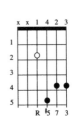

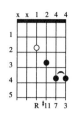 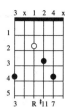 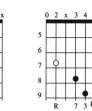   

Maj7#11
1, 3, 7, #11

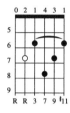 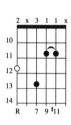 

Maj9#11
1, 3, 7, 9, #11

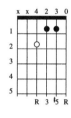  

Augmented
(aug)
1, 3, #5

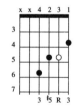 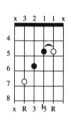 

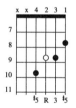 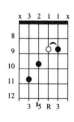  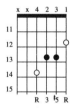

12

E

min
1, ♭3, 5

 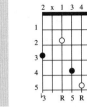   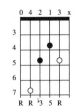 

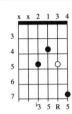    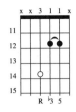 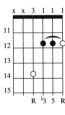

min6
1, ♭3, 5, 6

  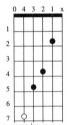 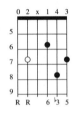 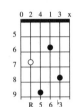 

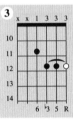 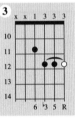 

min7
1, ♭3, 5, ♭7

  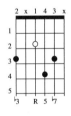 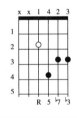 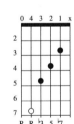 

 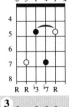 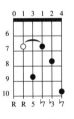  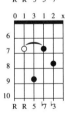 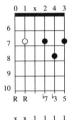

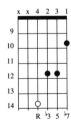  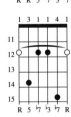 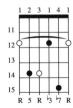 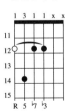 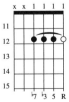

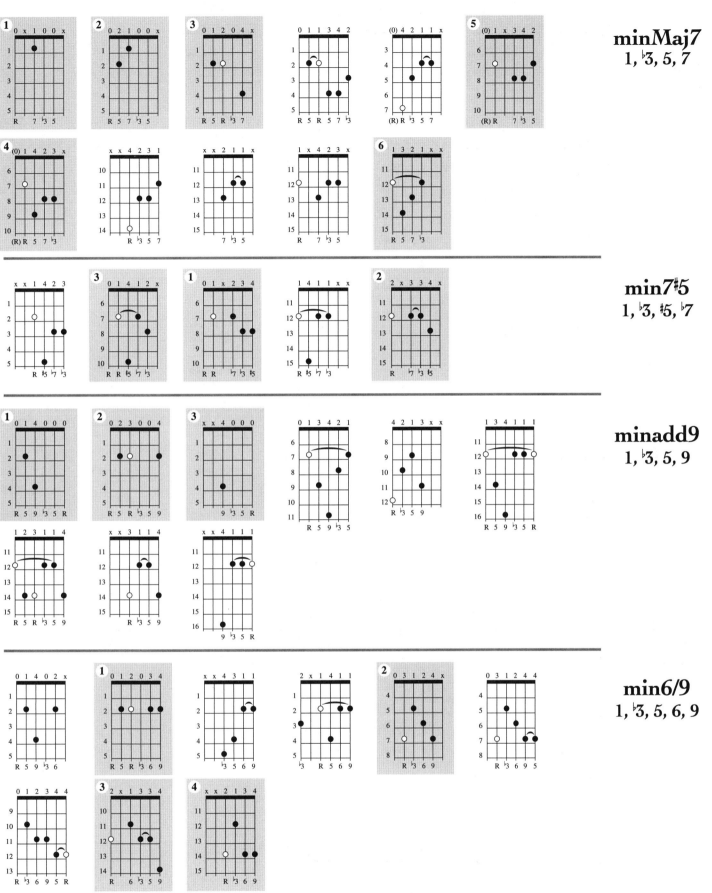

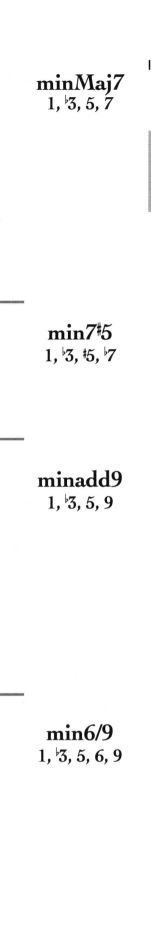

minMaj7
1, ♭3, 5, 7

min7♯5
1, ♭3, ♯5, ♭7

minadd9
1, ♭3, 5, 9

min6/9
1, ♭3, 5, 6, 9

E

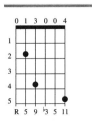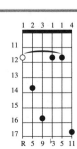

minadd9/11
1, ♭3, 5, 9, 11

E

min9
1, ♭3, 5, ♭7, 9

  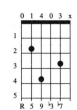  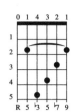 

   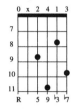 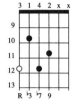 

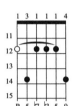 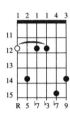 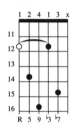 

min9Maj7
1, ♭3, 5, 7, 9

    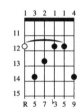 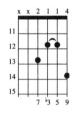

min9add11
1, ♭3, 5, ♭7, 9, 11

 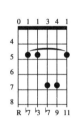  

min11
1, ♭3, 5, ♭7, 11

  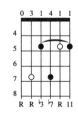  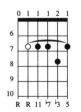 

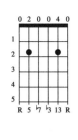  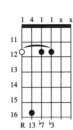 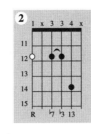 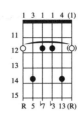

min13
1, ♭3, 5, ♭7, 13

E

  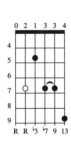 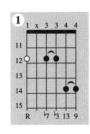 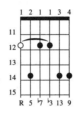

min13add9
1, ♭3, 5, ♭7, 9, 13

 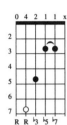 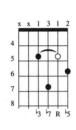 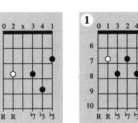 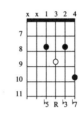

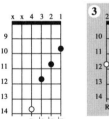  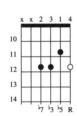

min7♭5
1, ♭3, ♭5, ♭7

 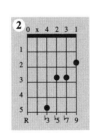    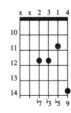

min9♭5
1, ♭3, ♭5, ♭7, 9

E

7
1, 3, 5, ♭7

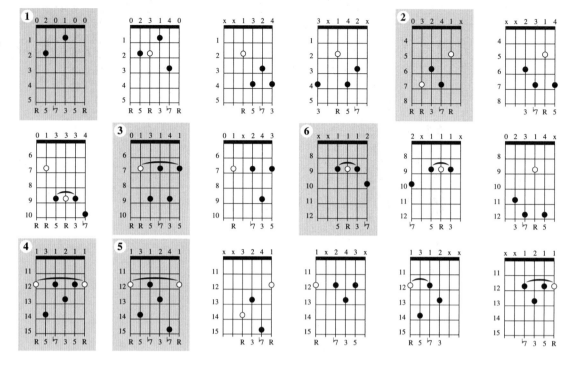

9
1, 3, 5, ♭7, 9

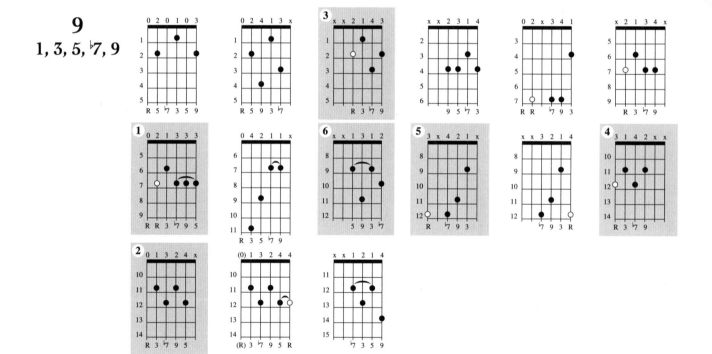

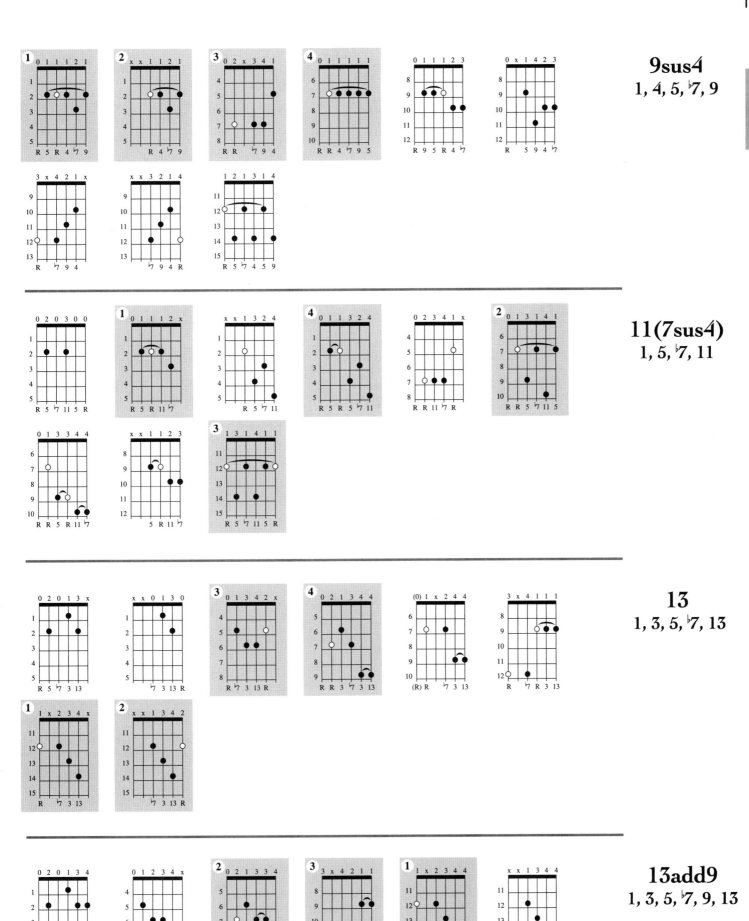

9sus4
1, 4, 5, ♭7, 9

E

11(7sus4)
1, 5, ♭7, 11

13
1, 3, 5, ♭7, 13

13add9
1, 3, 5, ♭7, 9, 13

18

E

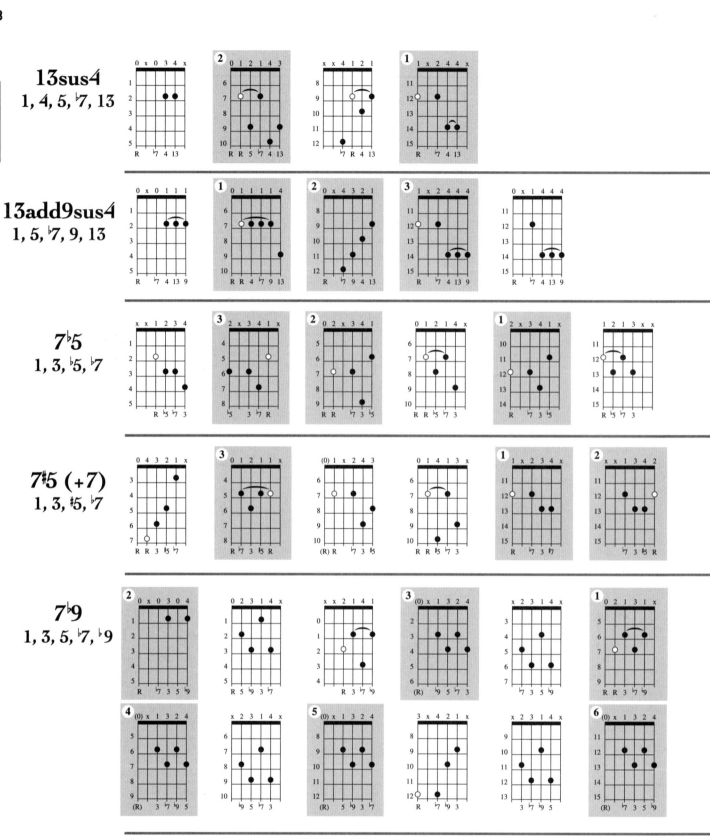

13sus4
1, 4, 5, ♭7, 13

13add9sus4
1, 5, ♭7, 9, 13

7♭5
1, 3, ♭5, ♭7

7♯5 (+7)
1, 3, ♯5, ♭7

7♭9
1, 3, 5, ♭7, ♭9

7♯9
1, 3, 5, ♭7, ♯9

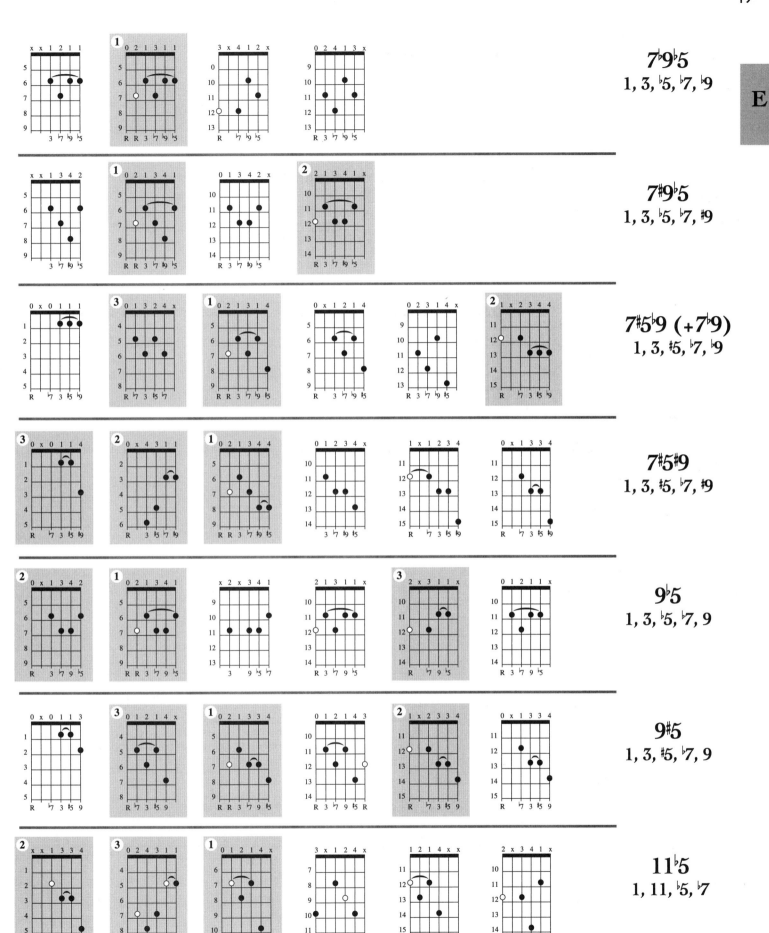

7♭9♭5
1, 3, ♭5, ♭7, ♭9

7♯9♭5
1, 3, ♭5, ♭7, ♯9

7♯5♭9 (+7♭9)
1, 3, ♯5, ♭7, ♭9

7♯5♯9
1, 3, ♯5, ♭7, ♯9

9♭5
1, 3, ♭5, ♭7, 9

9♯5
1, 3, ♯5, ♭7, 9

11♭5
1, 11, ♭5, ♭7

E

20

13♭5
1, 3, ♭5, ♭7, 13

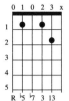
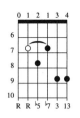
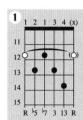

13♭9
1, 3, ♭7, ♭9, 13

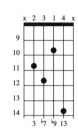

13#9
1, 3, ♭7, #9, 13

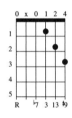
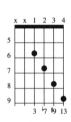

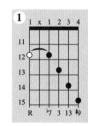
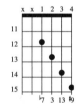

dim9
1, ♭3, ♭5, ♭♭7, 9

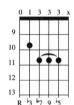

dim11
1, ♭5, ♭♭7, 11

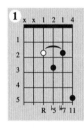

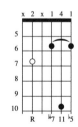
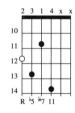
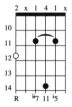

dim
1, ♭3, ♭5

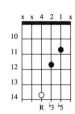

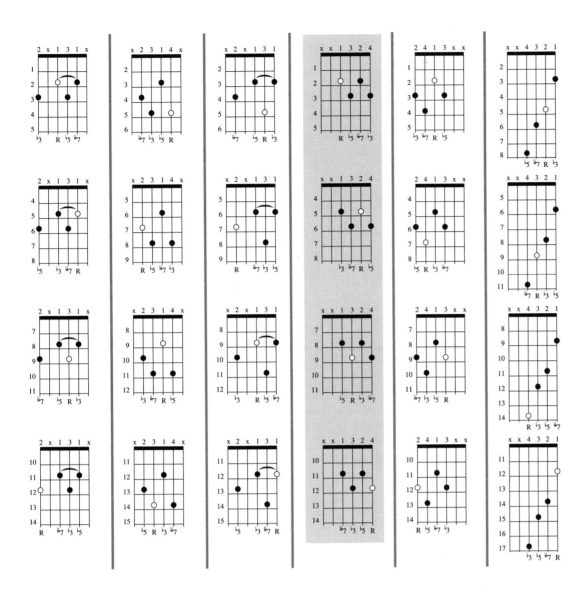

dim7 (°7)
1, ♭3, ♭5, ♭♭7

Three-Note Voicings

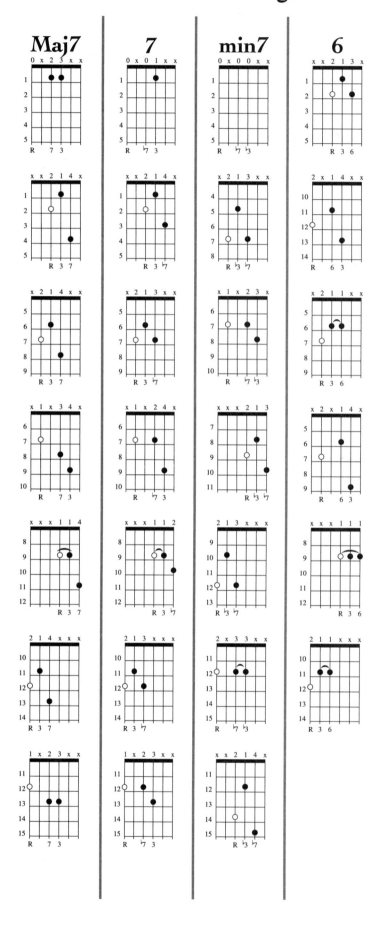

A

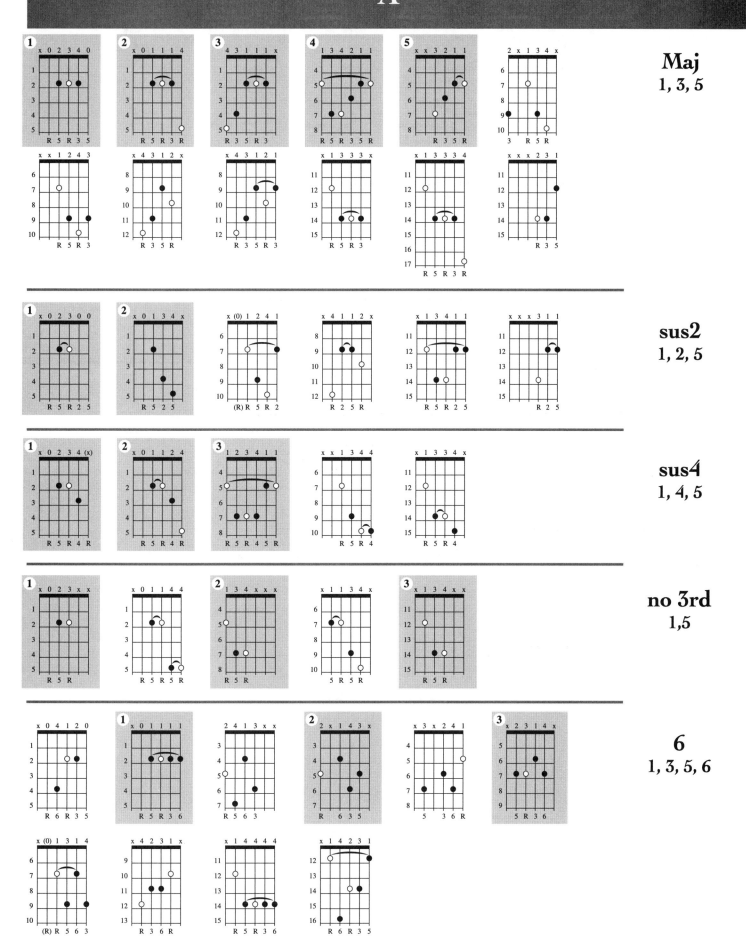

Maj
1, 3, 5

sus2
1, 2, 5

sus4
1, 4, 5

no 3rd
1,5

6
1, 3, 5, 6

A

Maj7
1, 3, 5, 7

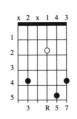

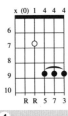
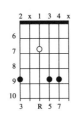
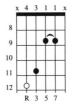
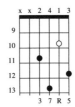
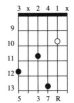
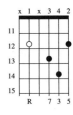

Maj9
1, 3, 5, 7, 9

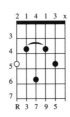

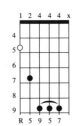

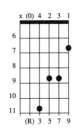
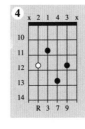

6/9
1, 3, 5, 6, 9

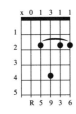

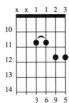

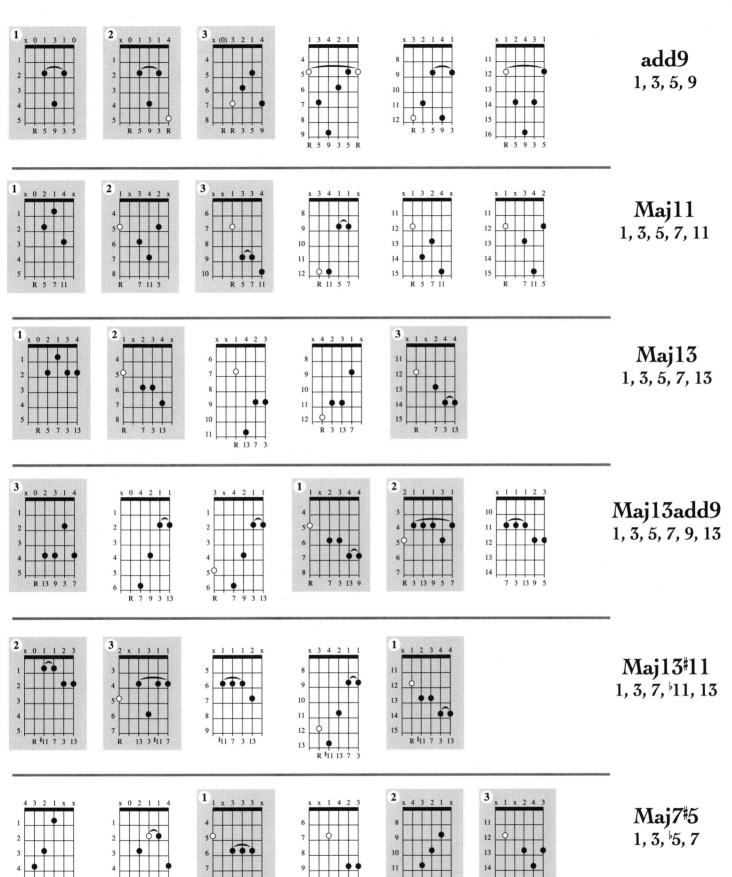

add9
1, 3, 5, 9

Maj11
1, 3, 5, 7, 11

Maj13
1, 3, 5, 7, 13

Maj13add9
1, 3, 5, 7, 9, 13

Maj13♯11
1, 3, 7, ♭11, 13

Maj7♯5
1, 3, ♭5, 7

A

A

Maj7#11
1, 3, 7, #11

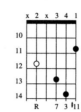

Maj9#11
1, 3, 7, 9, #11

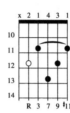

Augmented (aug)
1, 3, #5

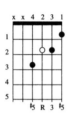
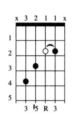

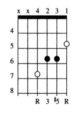
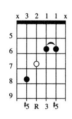

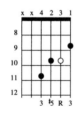
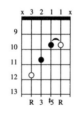

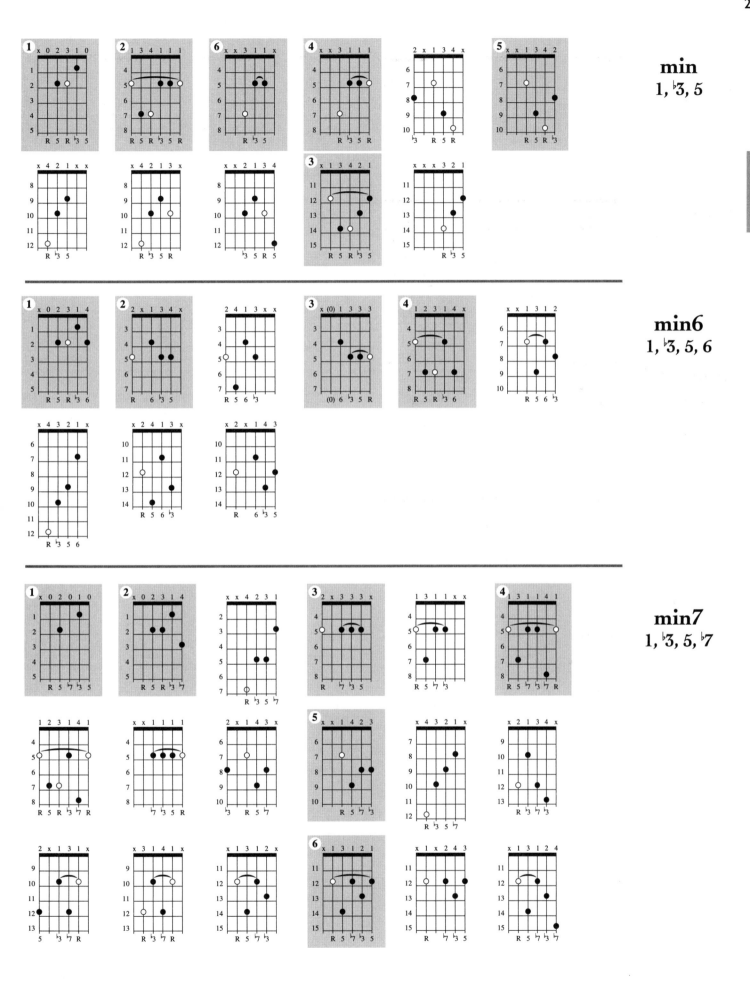

min
1, ♭3, 5

A

min6
1, ♭3, 5, 6

min7
1, ♭3, 5, ♭7

A

minMaj7
1, ♭3, 5, 7

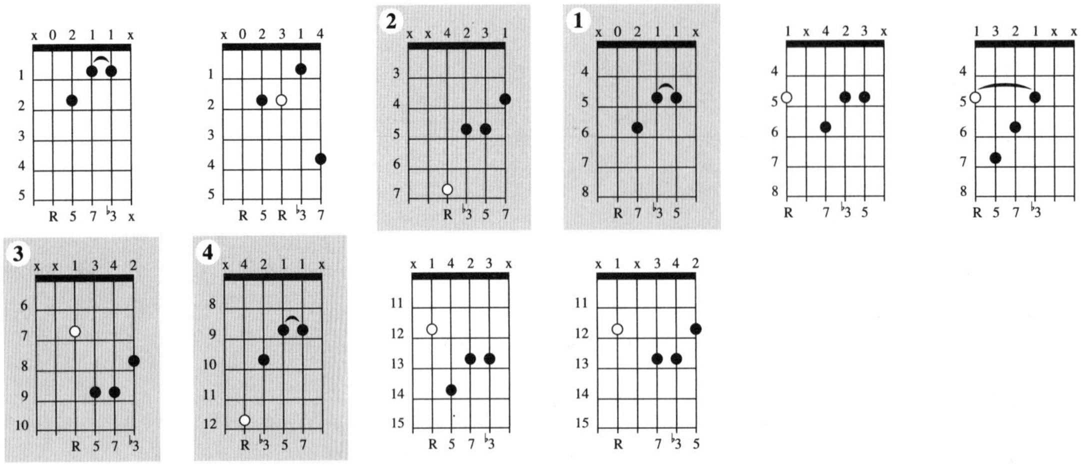

min7♯5
1, ♭3, ♯5, ♭7

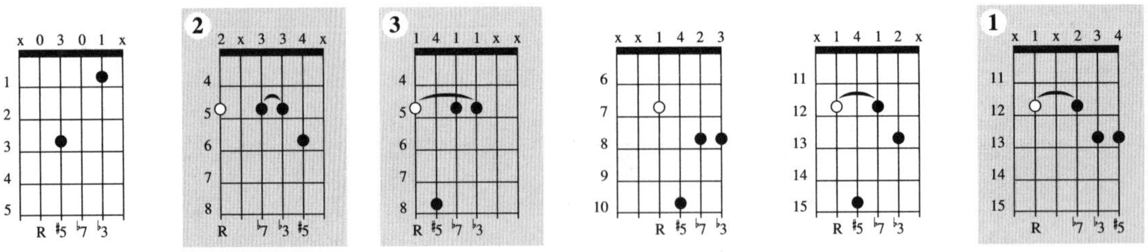

minadd9
1, ♭3, 5, 9

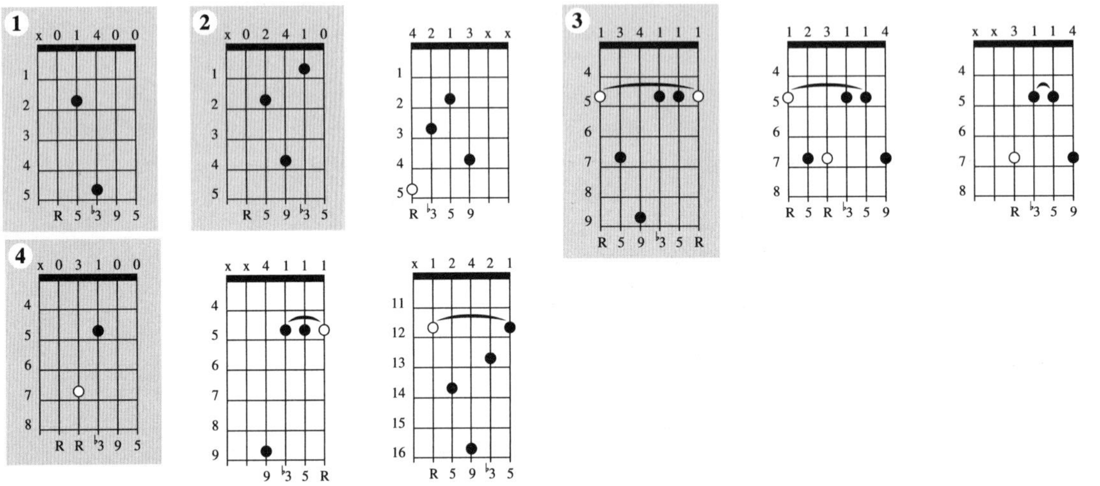

min6/9
1, ♭3, 5, 6, 9

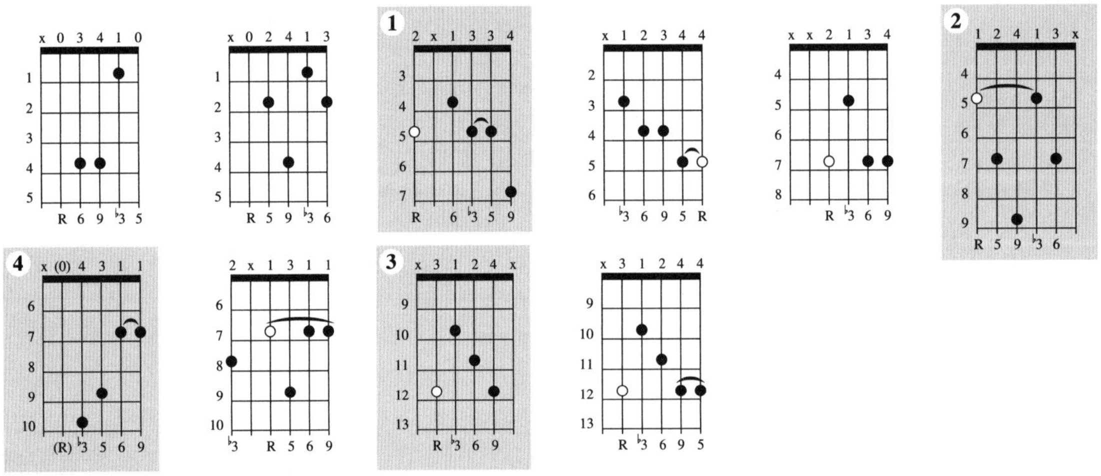

minadd9/11
1, ♭3, 5, 9, 11

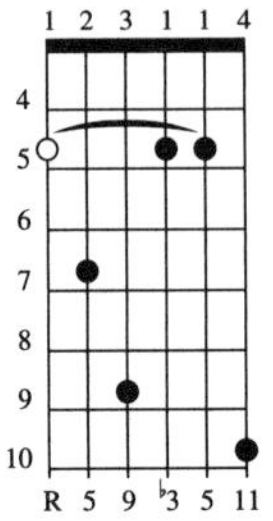

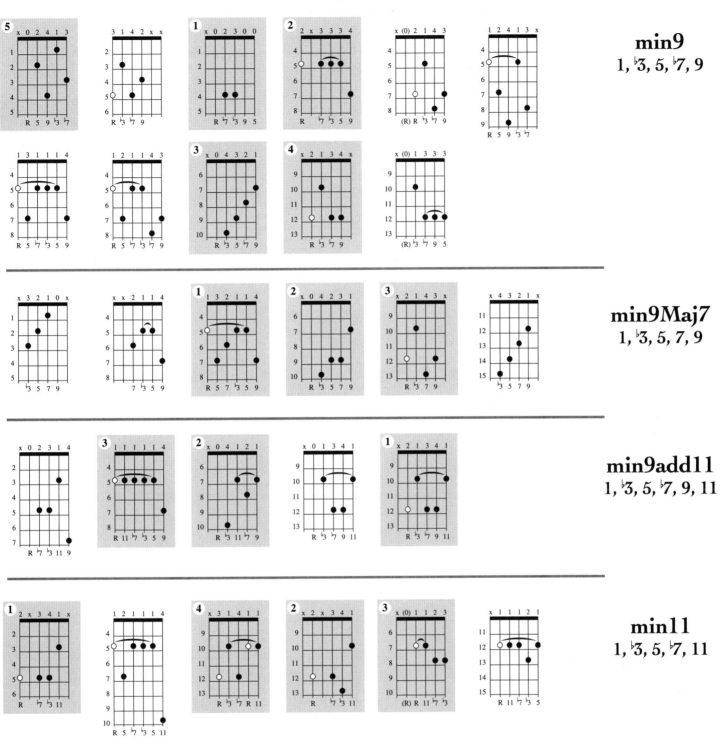

min9
1, ♭3, 5, ♭7, 9

min9Maj7
1, ♭3, 5, 7, 9

min9add11
1, ♭3, 5, ♭7, 9, 11

min11
1, ♭3, 5, ♭7, 11

A

A

min13
1, ♭3, 5, ♭7, 13

 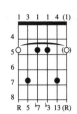 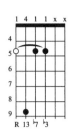 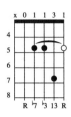 

min13add9
1, ♭3, 5, ♭7, 9, 13

  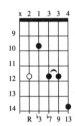

min7♭5
1, ♭3, ♭5, ♭7

 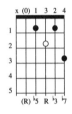 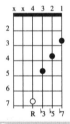  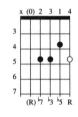 

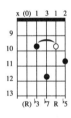  

min9♭5
1, ♭3, ♭5, ♭7, 9

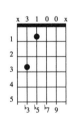    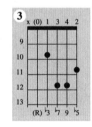 

7

1, 3, 5, ♭7

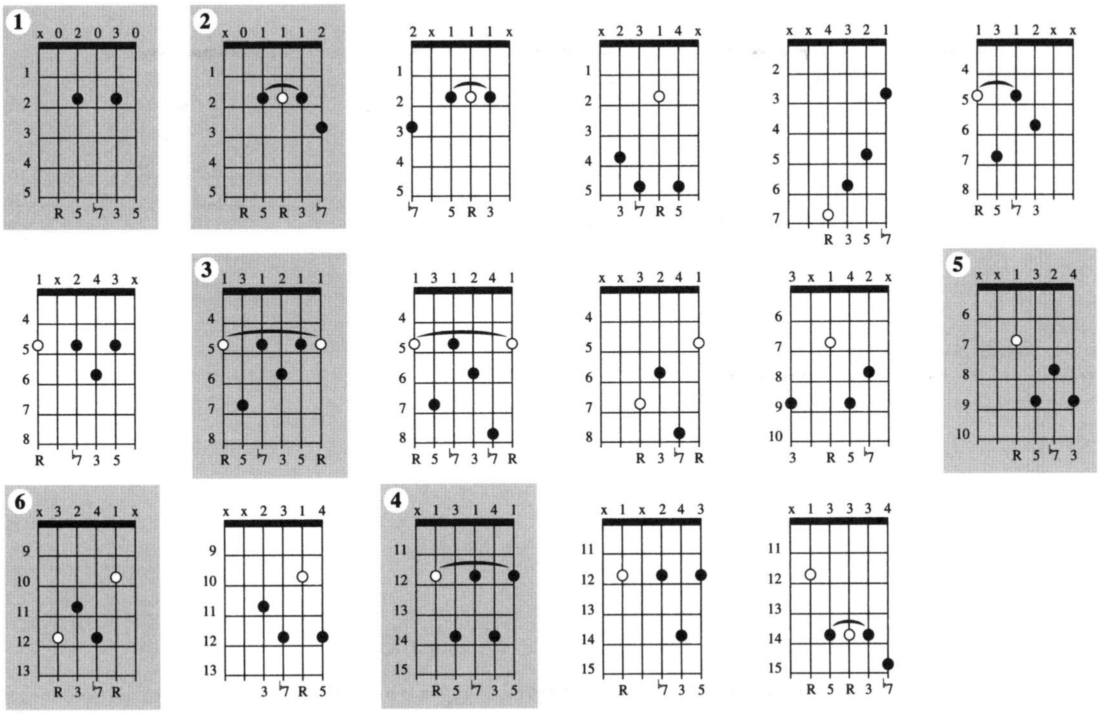

A

9

1, 3, 5, ♭7, 9

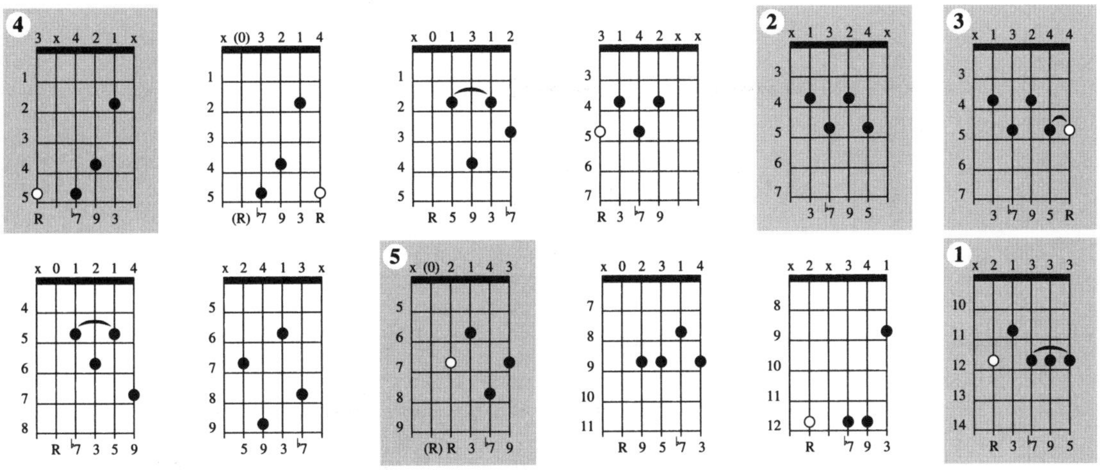

A

9sus4
1, 4, 5, ♭7, 9

 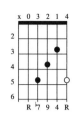  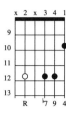

11(7sus4)
1, 5, ♭7, 11

  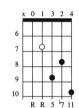 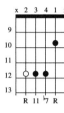

13
1, 3, 5, ♭7, 13

   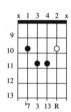 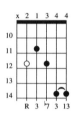

13add9
1, 3, 5, ♭7, 9, 13

   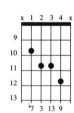 

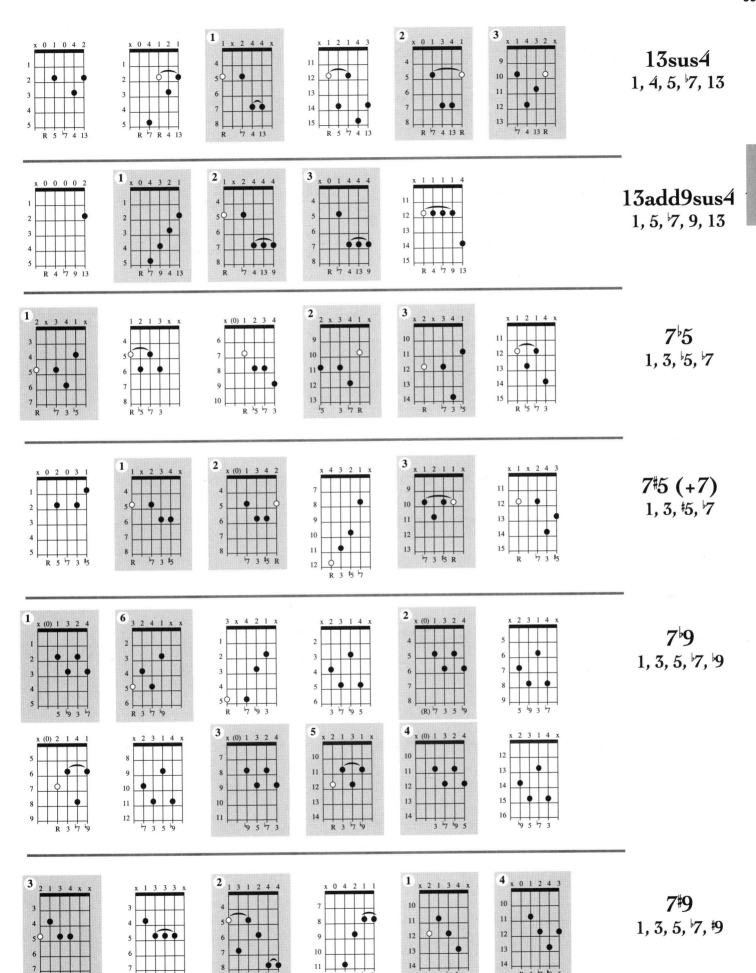

A

13sus4
1, 4, 5, ♭7, 13

13add9sus4
1, 5, ♭7, 9, 13

7♭5
1, 3, ♭5, ♭7

7♯5 (+7)
1, 3, ♯5, ♭7

7♭9
1, 3, 5, ♭7, ♭9

7♯9
1, 3, 5, ♭7, ♯9

A

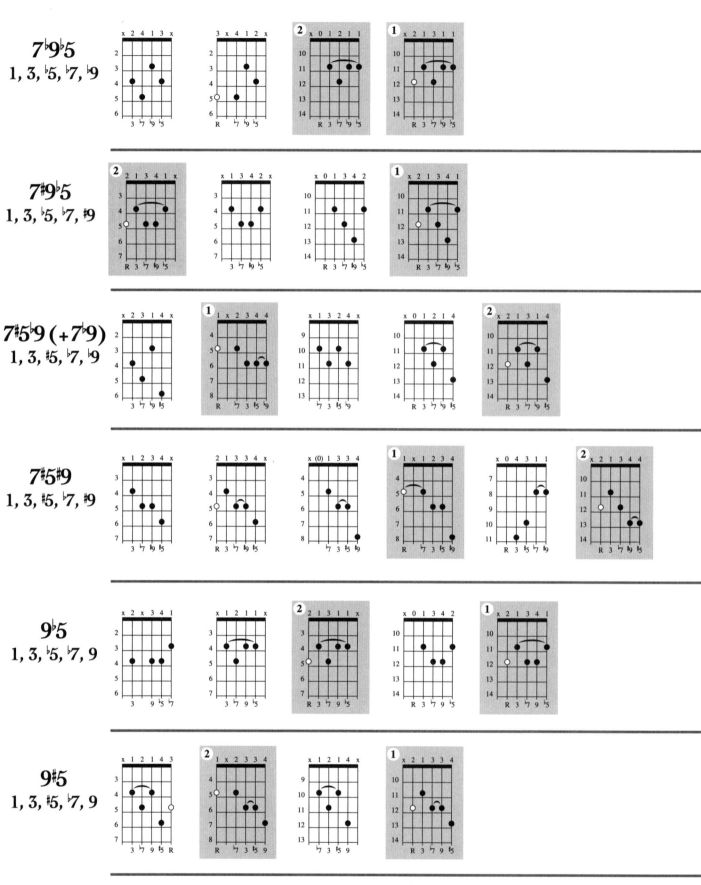

7♭9♭5
1, 3, ♭5, ♭7, ♭9

7♯9♭5
1, 3, ♭5, ♭7, ♯9

7♯5♭9 (+7♭9)
1, 3, ♯5, ♭7, ♭9

7♯5♯9
1, 3, ♯5, ♭7, ♯9

9♭5
1, 3, ♭5, ♭7, 9

9♯5
1, 3, ♯5, ♭7, 9

11♭5
1, 11, ♭5, ♭7

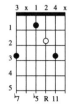
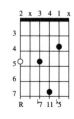
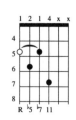

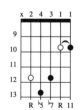
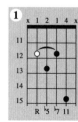

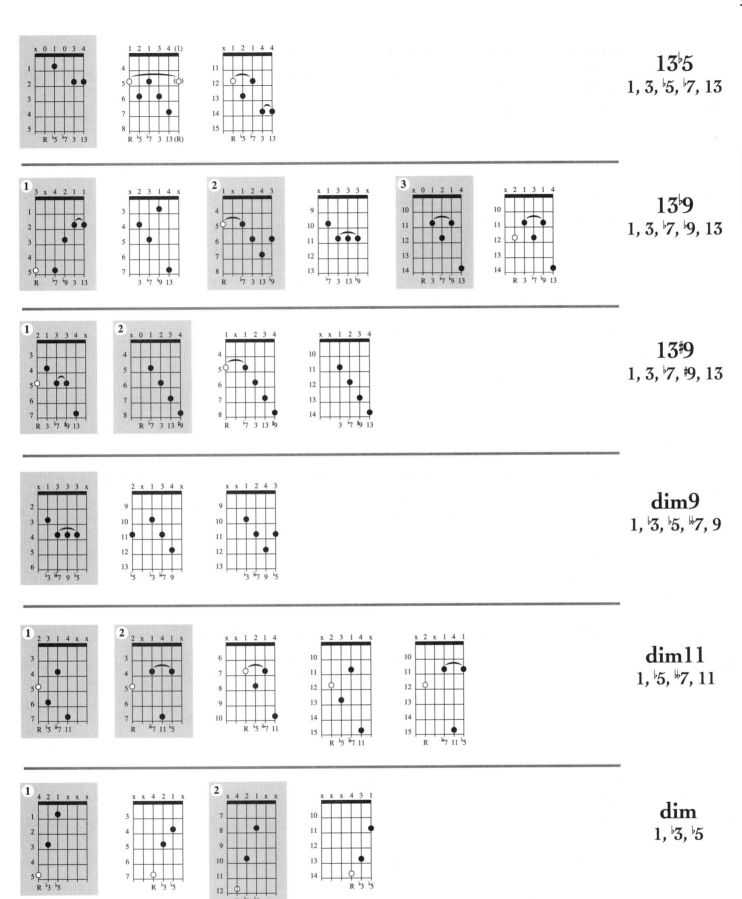

13♭5
1, 3, ♭5, ♭7, 13

13♭9
1, 3, ♭7, ♭9, 13

A

13#9
1, 3, ♭7, #9, 13

dim9
1, ♭3, ♭5, ♭♭7, 9

dim11
1, ♭5, ♭♭7, 11

dim
1, ♭3, ♭5

dim7 (°7)
1, ♭3, ♭5, ♭♭7

A

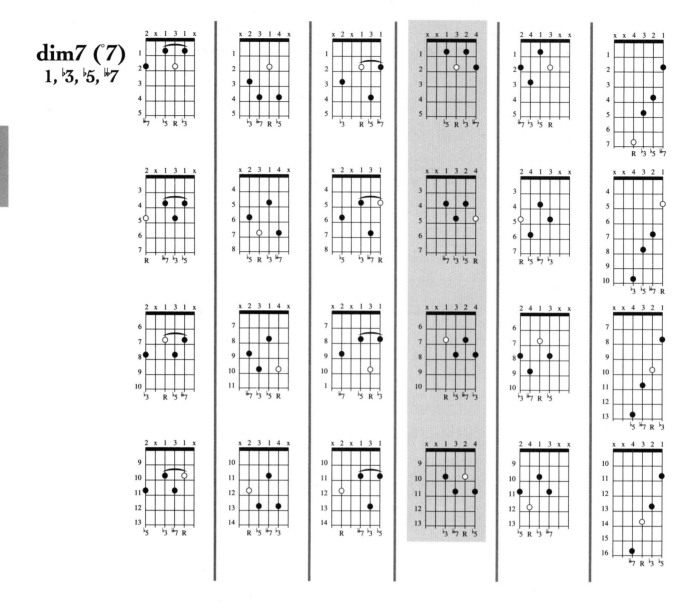

Three-Note Voicings

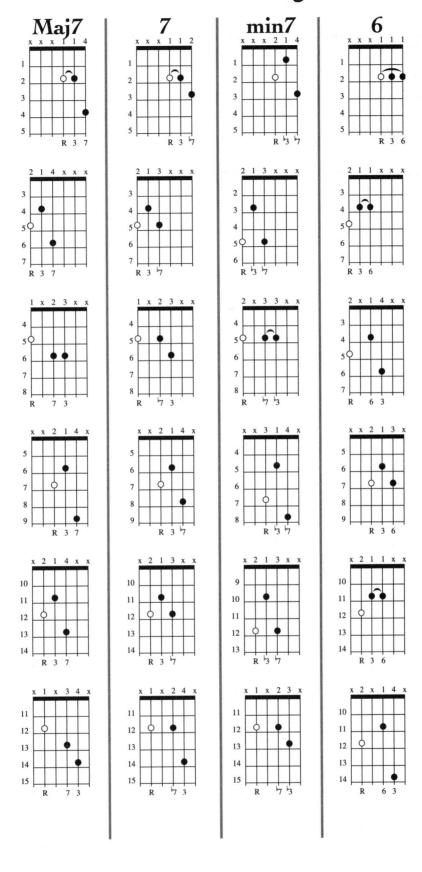

D

D

Maj
1, 3, 5

   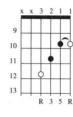 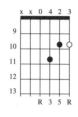 

sus2
1, 2, 5

   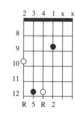 

sus4
1, 4, 5

   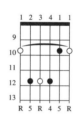 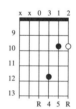 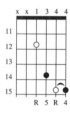

no 3rd
1, 5

  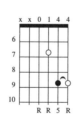  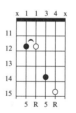

6
1, 3, 5, 6

  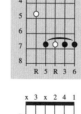 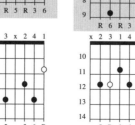 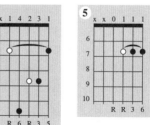 

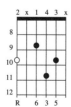 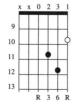 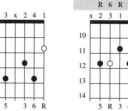

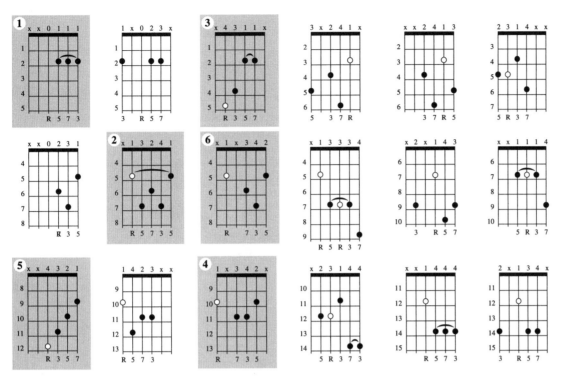

Maj7
1, 3, 5, 7

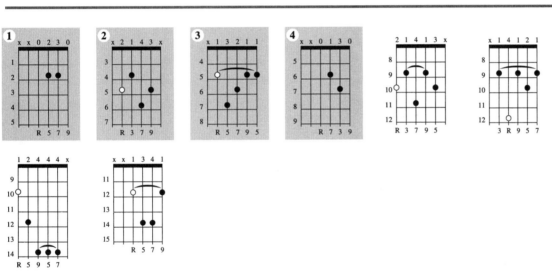

Maj9
1, 3, 5, 7, 9

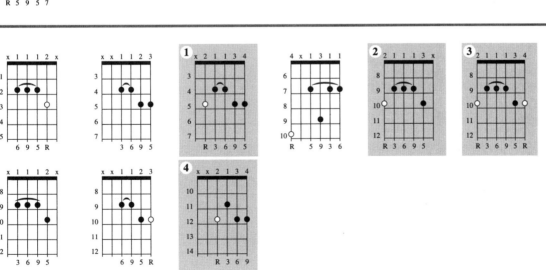

6/9
1, 3, 5, 6, 9

D

D

add9
1, 3, 5, 9

   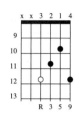 

Maj11
1, 3, 5, 7, 11

   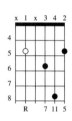 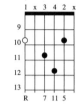 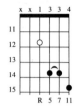

Maj13
1, 3, 5, 7, 13

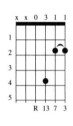    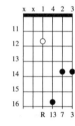

Maj13add9
1, 3, 5, 7, 9, 13

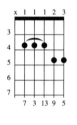 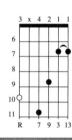  

Maj13#11
1, 3, 7, #11, 13

   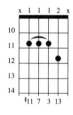

Maj7#5
1, 3, #5, 7

  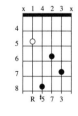  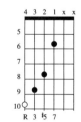 

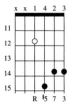

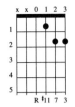 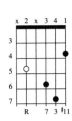  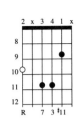  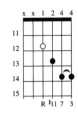

Maj7♯11
1, 3, 7, ♯11

 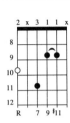 

Maj9♯11
1, 3, 7, 9, ♯11

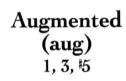

D

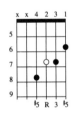 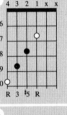

 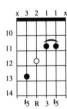

Augmented
(aug)
1, 3, ♯5

D

min
1, ♭3, 5

min6
1, ♭3, 5, 6

min7
1, ♭3, 5, ♭7

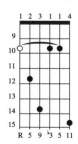

minMaj7
1, ♭3, 5, 7

min7♯5
1, ♭3, ♯5, ♭7

minadd9
1, ♭3, 5, 9

min6/9
1, ♭3, 5, 6, 9

minadd9/11
1, ♭3, 5, 9, 11

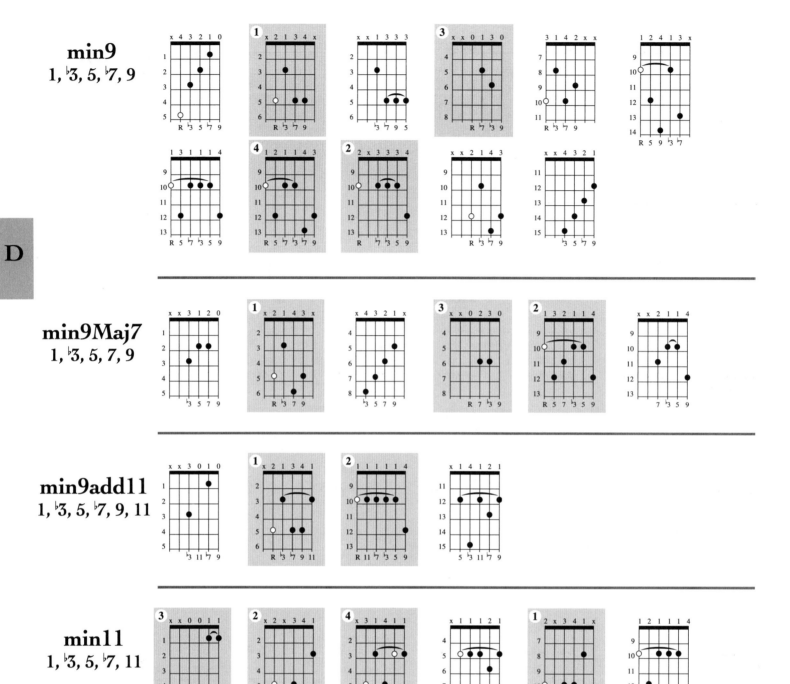

44

min9
1, ♭3, 5, ♭7, 9

min9Maj7
1, ♭3, 5, 7, 9

min9add11
1, ♭3, 5, ♭7, 9, 11

min11
1, ♭3, 5, ♭7, 11

D

min13
1, ♭3, 5, ♭7, 13

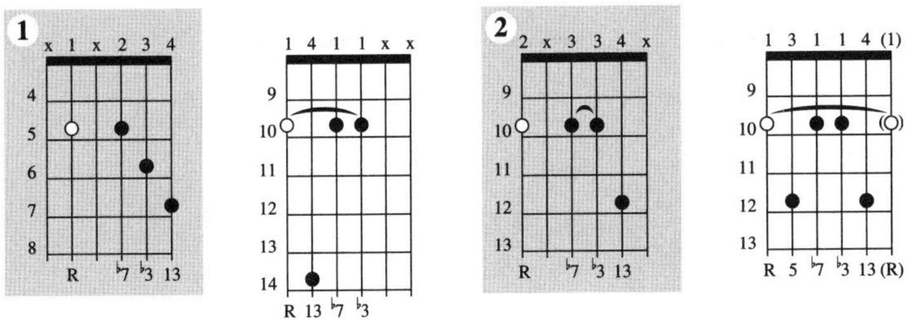

min13add9
1, ♭3, 5, ♭7, 9, 13

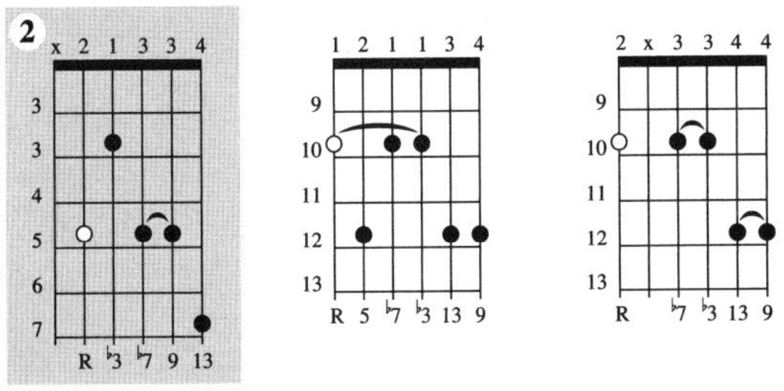

D

min7♭5
1, ♭3, ♭5, ♭7

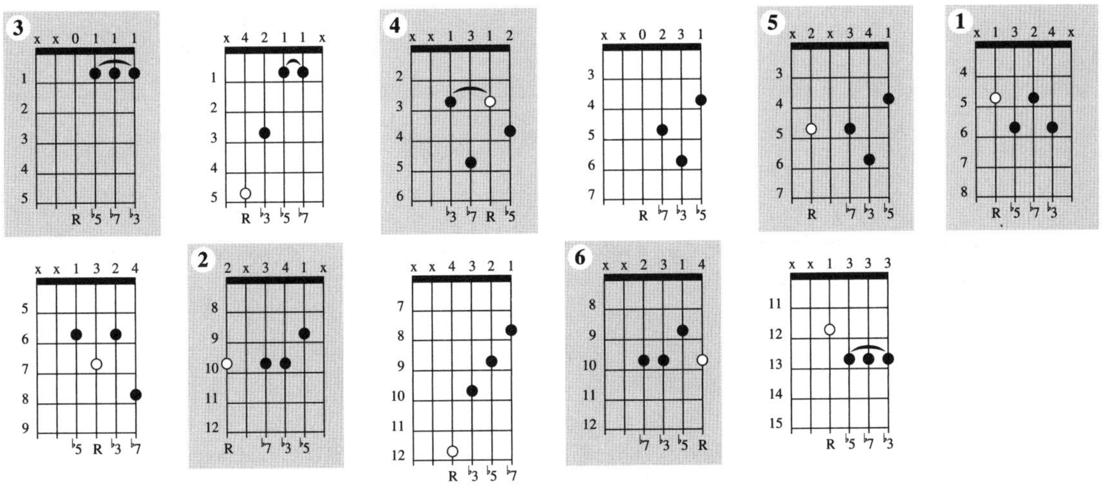

min9♭5
1, ♭3, ♭5, ♭7, 9

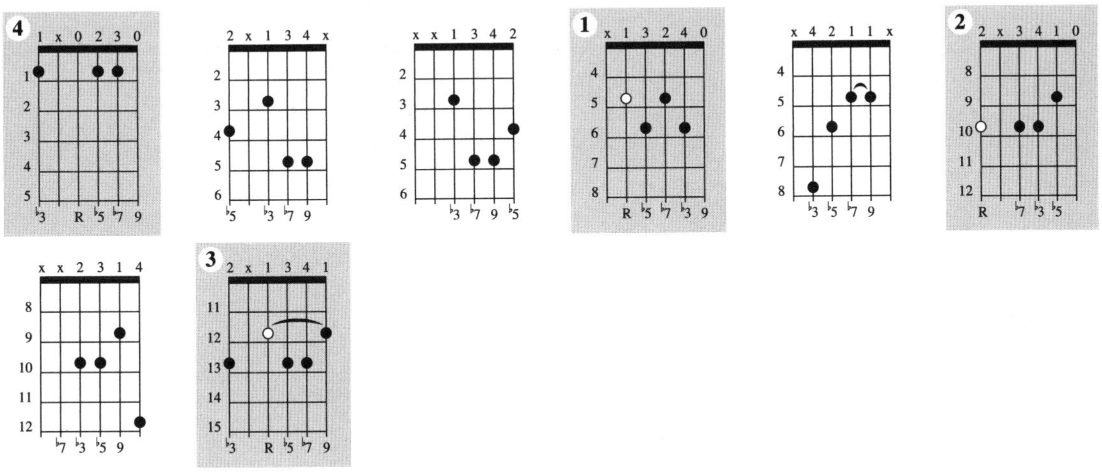

46

D

7
1, 3, 5, ♭7

9
1, 3, 5, ♭7, 9

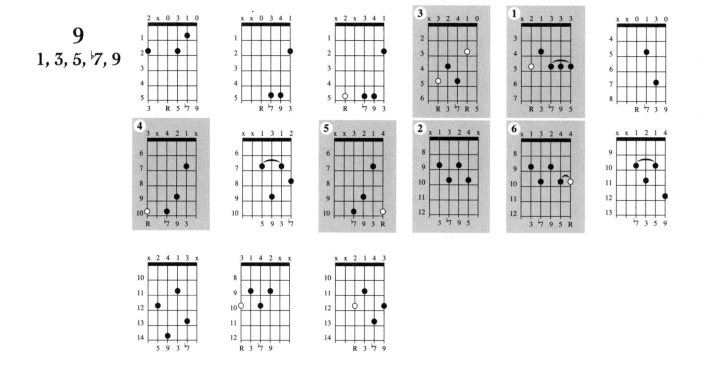

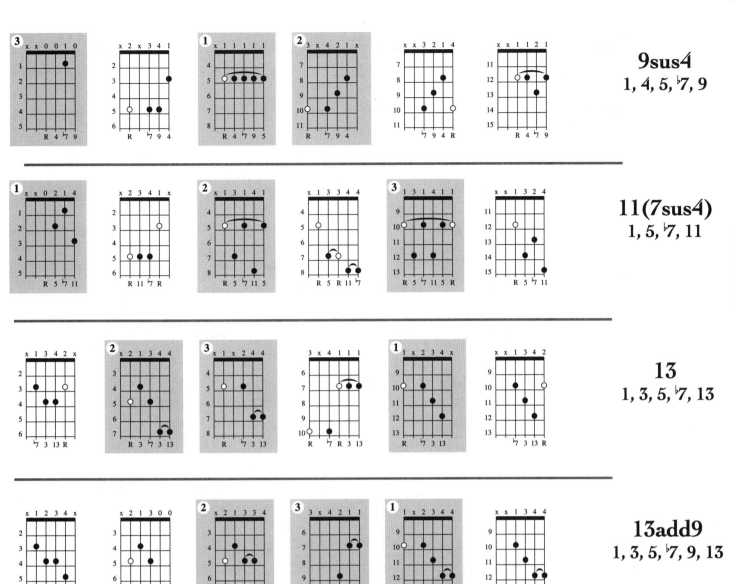

9sus4
1, 4, 5, ♭7, 9

11(7sus4)
1, 5, ♭7, 11

D

13
1, 3, 5, ♭7, 13

13add9
1, 3, 5, ♭7, 9, 13

48

13sus4
1, 4, 5, ♭7, 13

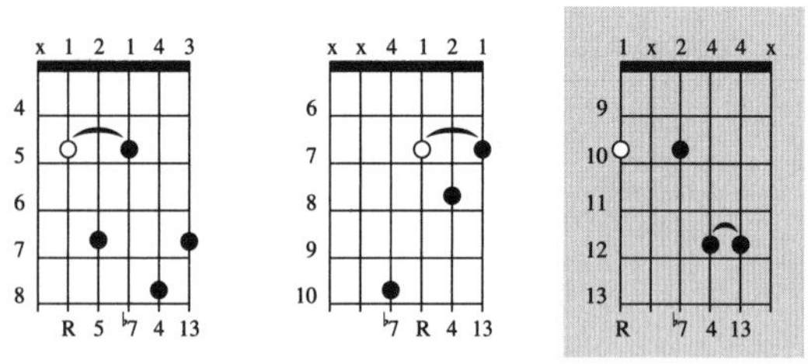

13add9sus4
1, 5, ♭7, 9, 13

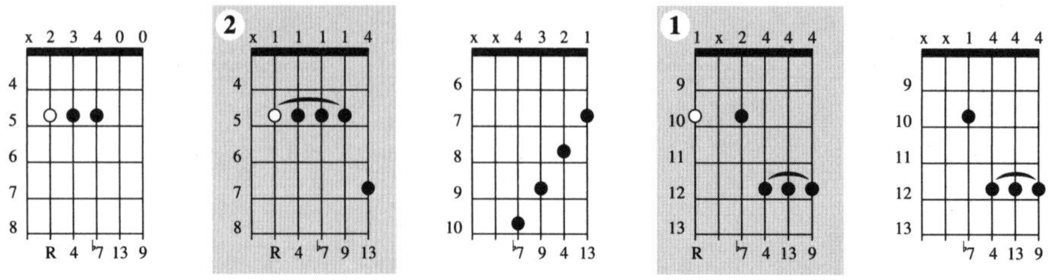

D

7♭5
1, 3, ♭5, ♭7

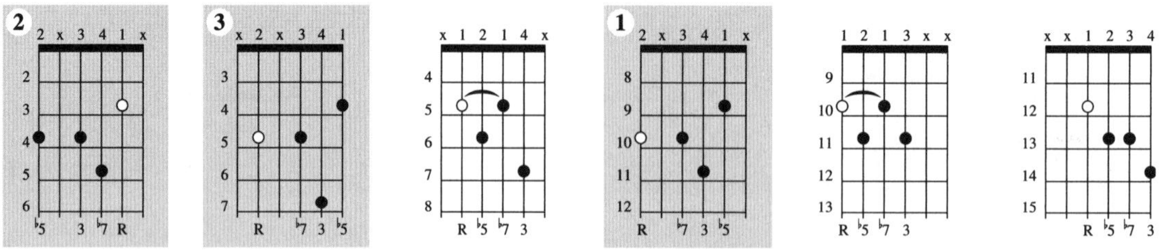

7♯5 (+7)
1, 3, ♯5, ♭7

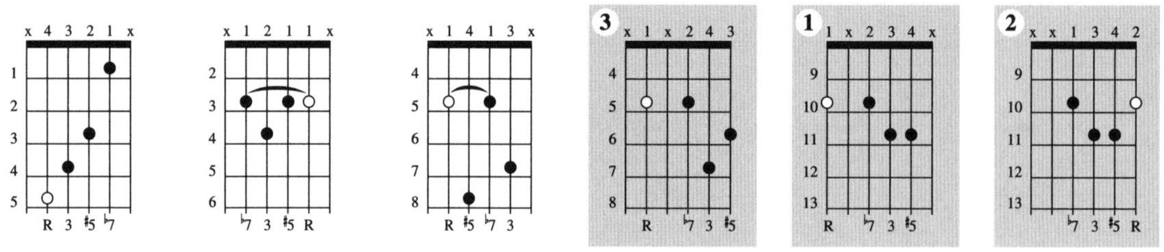

7♭9
1, 3, 5, ♭7, ♭9

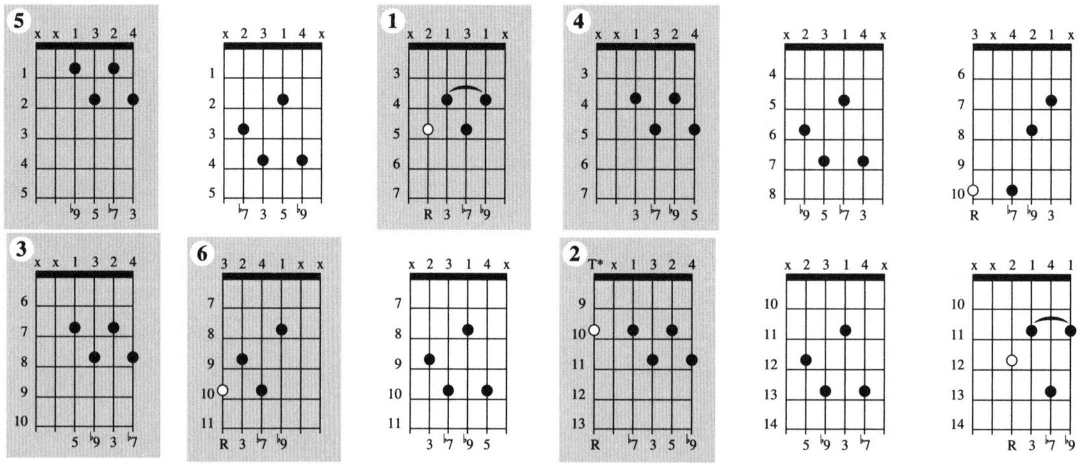

* T = Thumb

7♯9
1, 3, 5, ♭7, ♯9

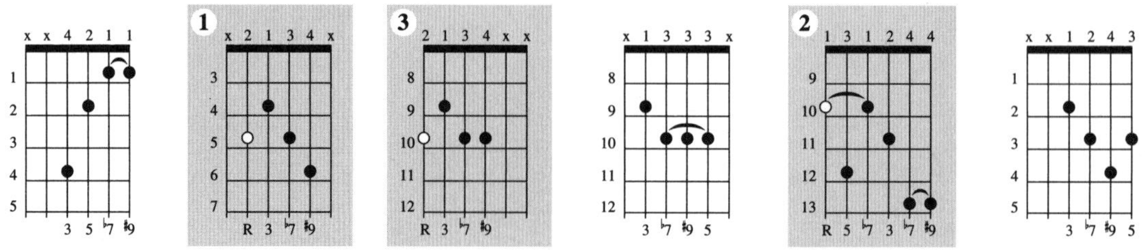

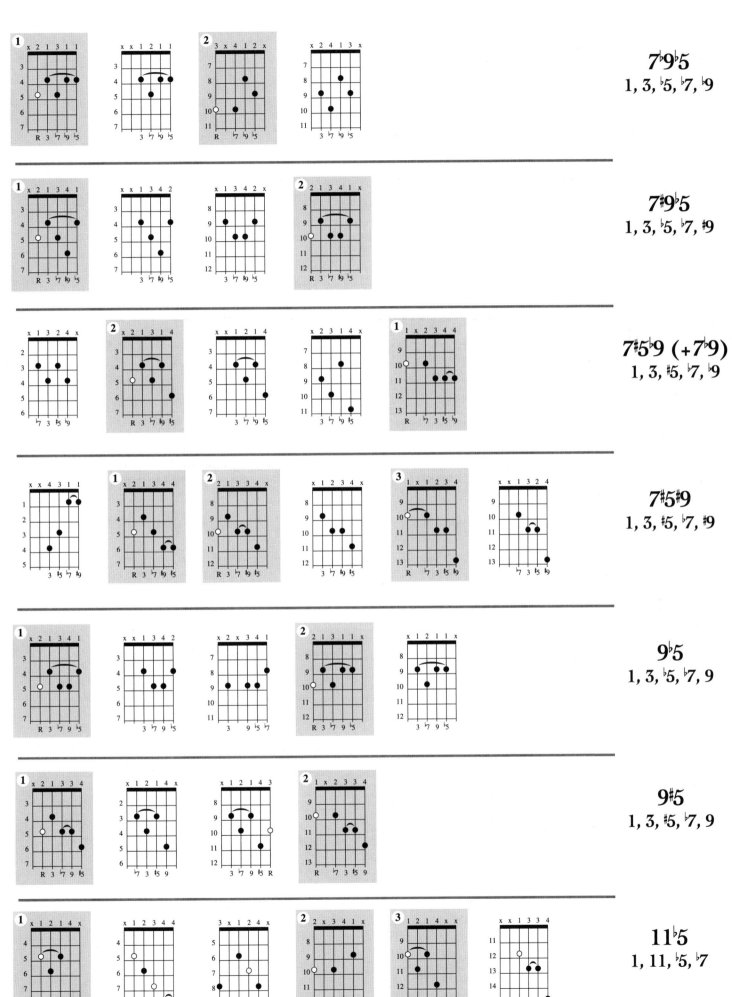

7♭9♭5
1, 3, ♭5, ♭7, ♭9

7♯9♭5
1, 3, ♭5, ♭7, ♯9

D

7♯5♭9 (+7♭9)
1, 3, ♯5, ♭7, ♭9

7♯5♯9
1, 3, ♯5, ♭7, ♯9

9♭5
1, 3, ♭5, ♭7, 9

9♯5
1, 3, ♯5, ♭7, 9

11♭5
1, 11, ♭5, ♭7

D

13♭5
1, 3, ♭5, ♭7, 13

13♭9
1, 3, ♭7, ♭9, 13

13♯9
1, 3, ♭7, ♯9, 13

dim9
1, ♭3, ♭5, ♭♭7, 9

dim11
1, ♭5, ♭♭7, 11

dim
1, ♭3, ♭5

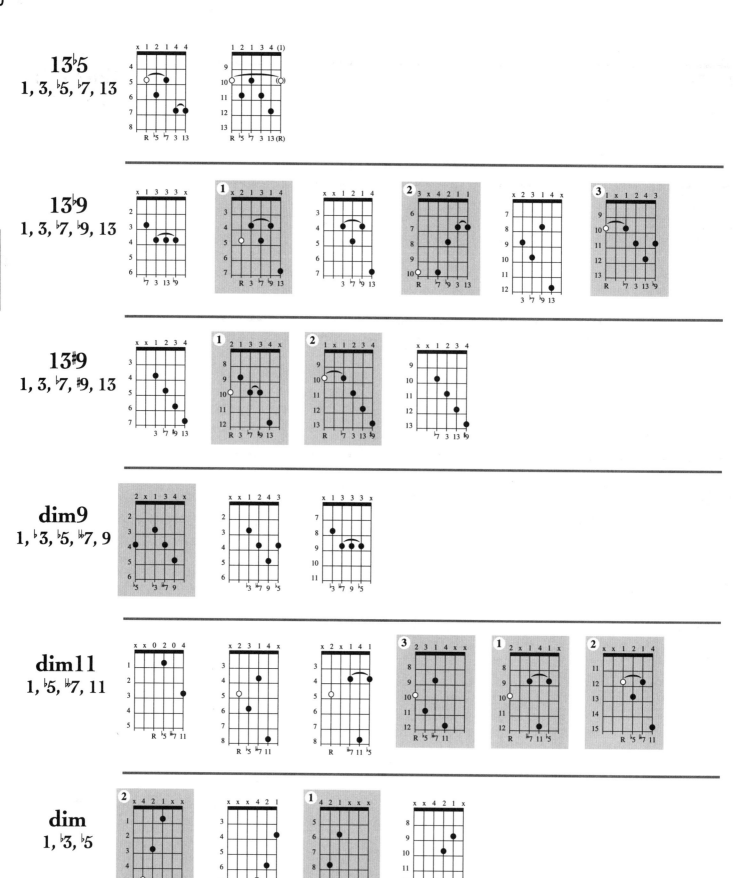

dim7 (°7)
1, ♭3, ♭5, ♭♭7

D

Three-Note Voicings

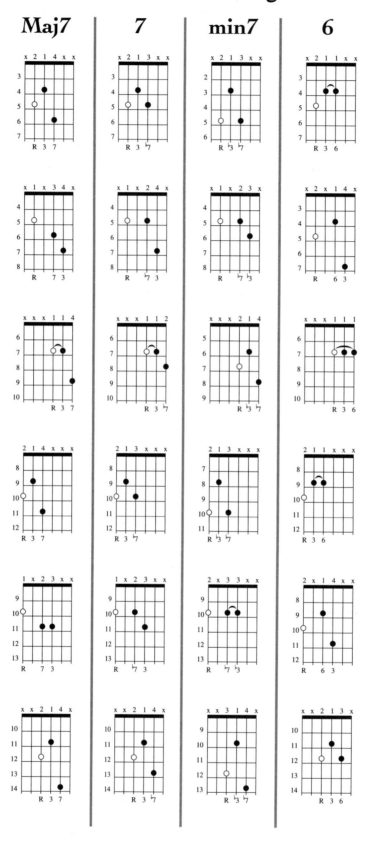

G

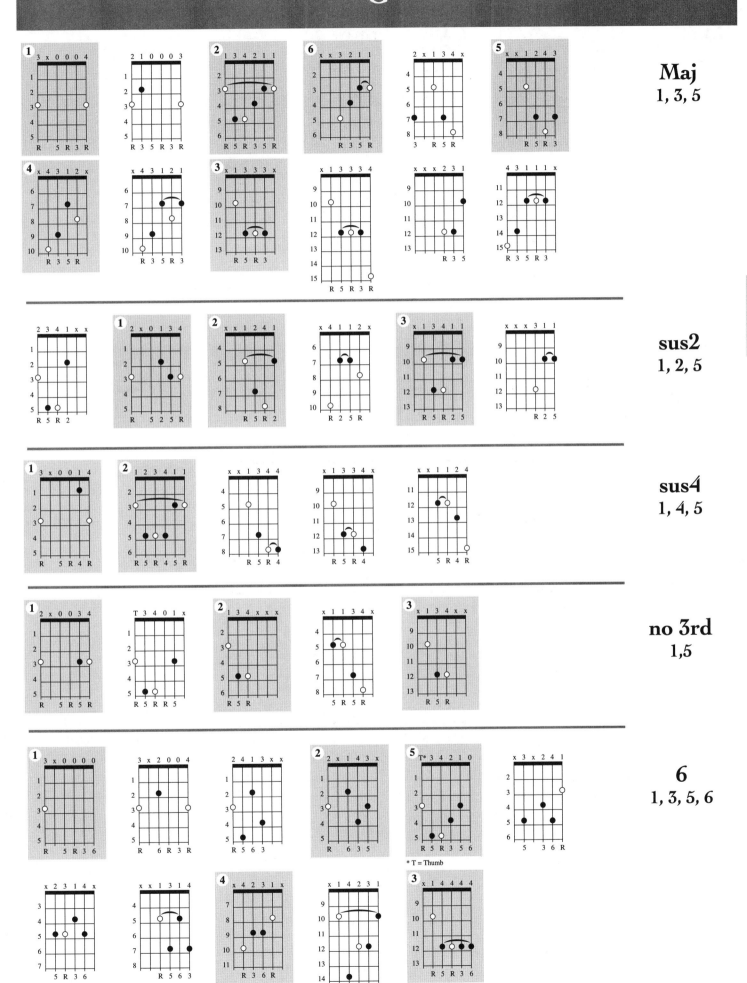

Maj
1, 3, 5

sus2
1, 2, 5

sus4
1, 4, 5

no 3rd
1,5

6
1, 3, 5, 6

* T = Thumb

G

Maj7
1, 3, 5, 7

Maj9
1, 3, 5, 7, 9

6/9
1, 3, 5, 6, 9

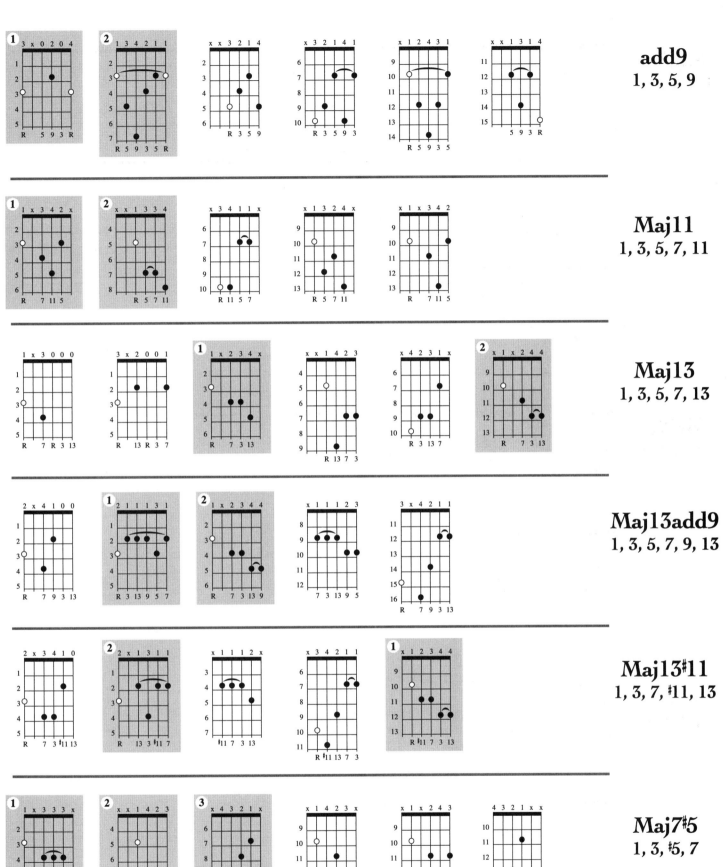

add9
1, 3, 5, 9

Maj11
1, 3, 5, 7, 11

Maj13
1, 3, 5, 7, 13

G

Maj13add9
1, 3, 5, 7, 9, 13

Maj13♯11
1, 3, 7, ♯11, 13

Maj7♯5
1, 3, ♯5, 7

Maj7#11
1, 3, 7, #11

Maj9#11
1, 3, 7, 9, #11

G

Augmented
(aug)
1, 3, #5

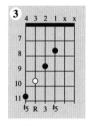

57

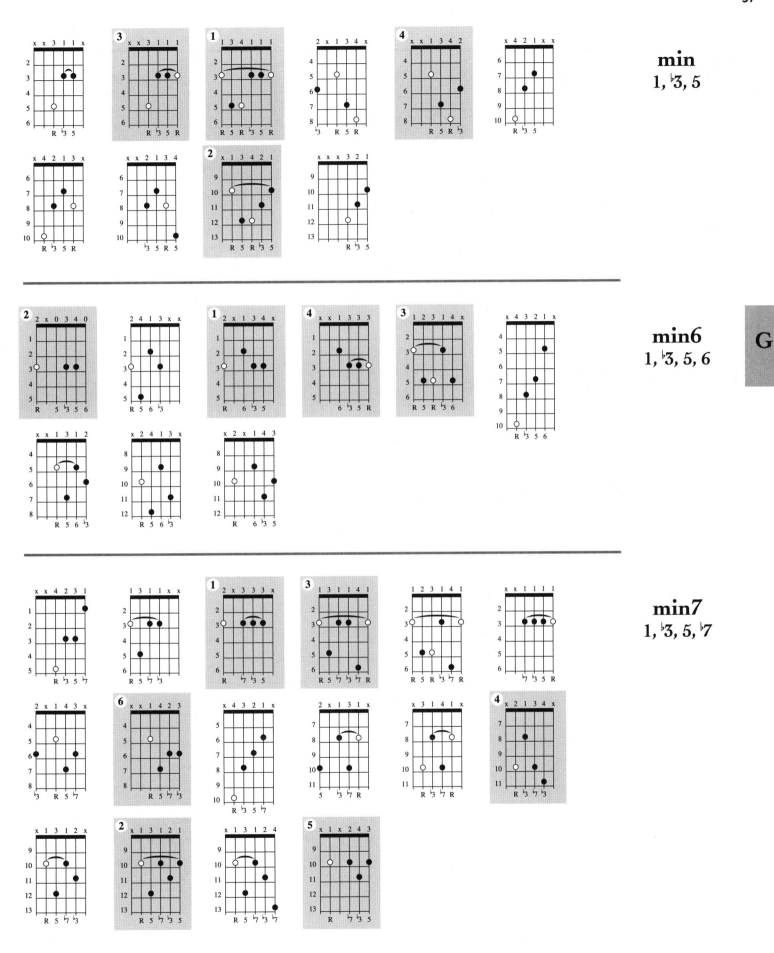

min
1, ♭3, 5

G

min6
1, ♭3, 5, 6

min7
1, ♭3, 5, ♭7

G

minMaj7
1, ♭3, 5, 7

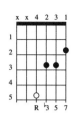   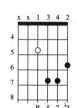 

min7♯5
1, ♭3, ♯5, ♭7

 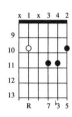 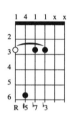  

minadd9
1, ♭3, 5, 9

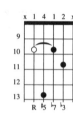    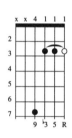 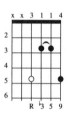

min6/9
1, ♭3, 5, 6, 9

 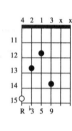 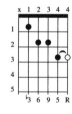     

minadd9/11
1, ♭3, 5, 9, 11

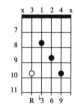 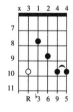 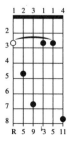

min9
1, ♭3, 5, ♭7, 9

min9Maj7
1, ♭3, 5, 7, 9

G

min9add11
1, ♭3, 5, ♭7, 9, 11

min11
1, ♭3, 5, ♭7, 11

G

min13
1, ♭3, 5, ♭7, 13

min13add9
1, ♭3, 5, ♭7, 9, 13

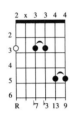  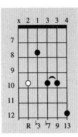

min7♭5
1, ♭3, ♭5, ♭7

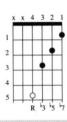  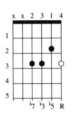  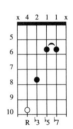 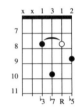

 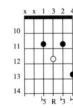

min9♭5
1, ♭3, ♭5, ♭7, 9

   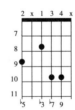 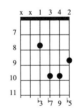 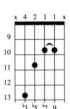

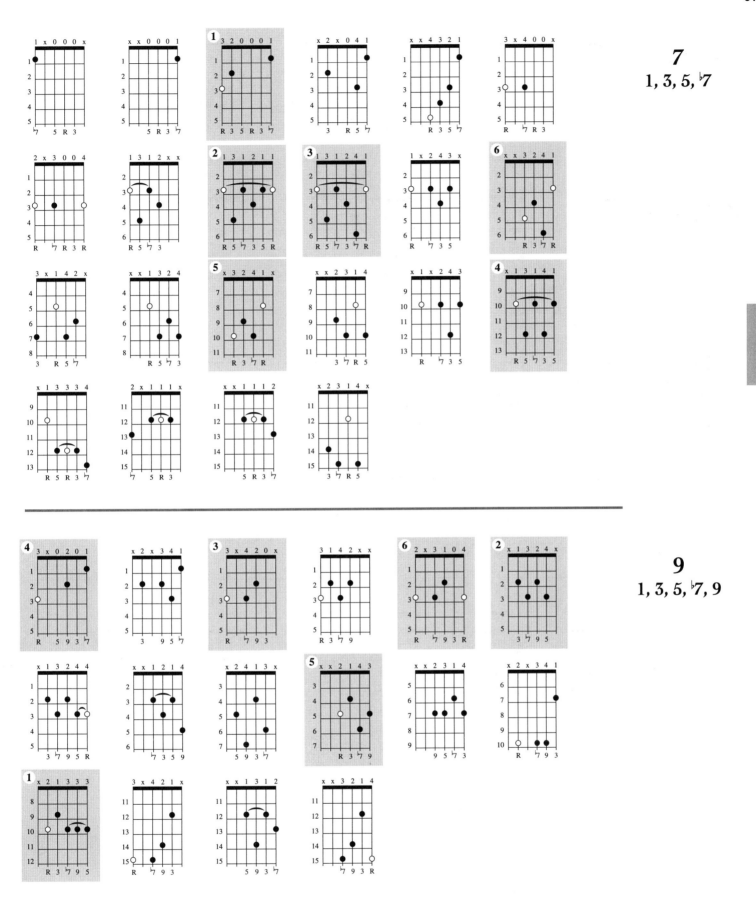

7
1, 3, 5, ♭7

G

9
1, 3, 5, ♭7, 9

62

G

9sus4
1, 4, 5, ♭7, 9

11(7sus4)
1, 5, ♭7, 11

  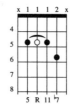  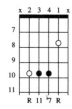
  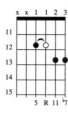

13
1, 3, 5, ♭7, 13

   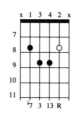 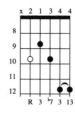 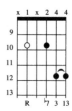

13add9
1, 3, 5, ♭7, 9, 13

  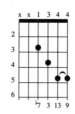 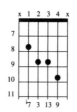  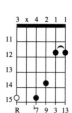

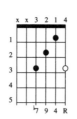 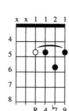 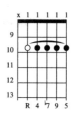

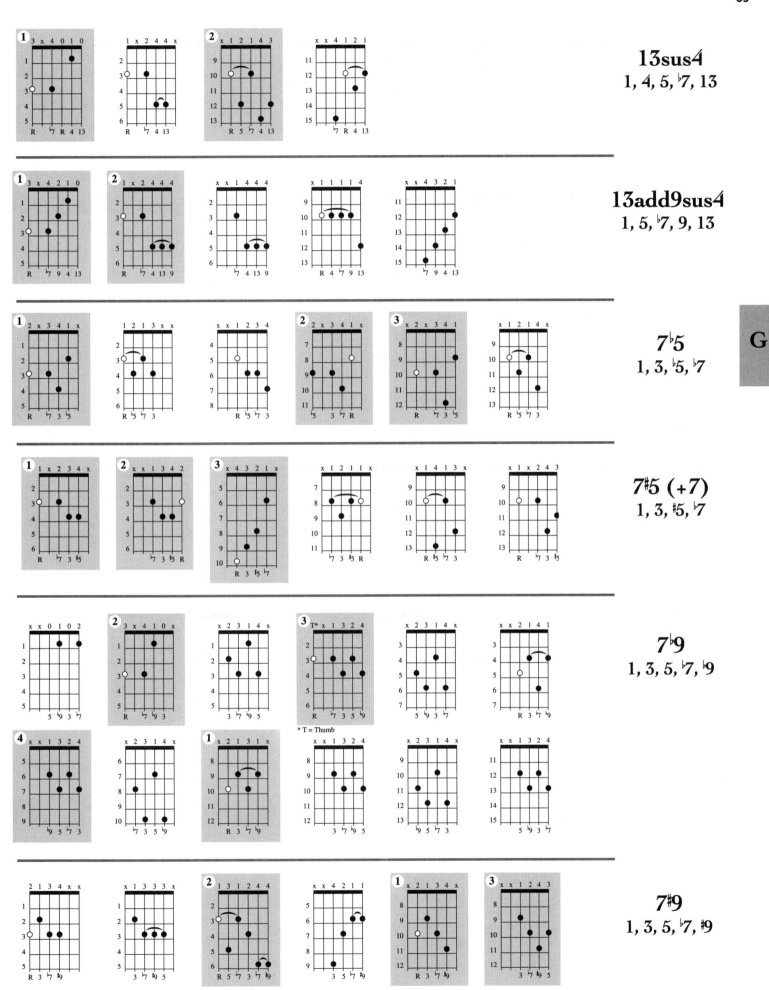

13sus4
1, 4, 5, ♭7, 13

13add9sus4
1, 5, ♭7, 9, 13

7♭5
1, 3, ♭5, ♭7

G

7♯5 (+7)
1, 3, ♯5, ♭7

7♭9
1, 3, 5, ♭7, ♭9

7♯9
1, 3, 5, ♭7, ♯9

* T = Thumb

G

7♭9♭5
1, 3, ♭5, ♭7, ♭9

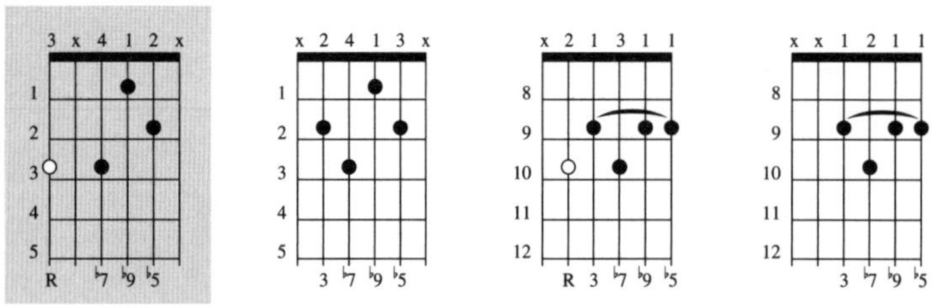

7♯9♭5
1, 3, ♭5, ♭7, ♯9

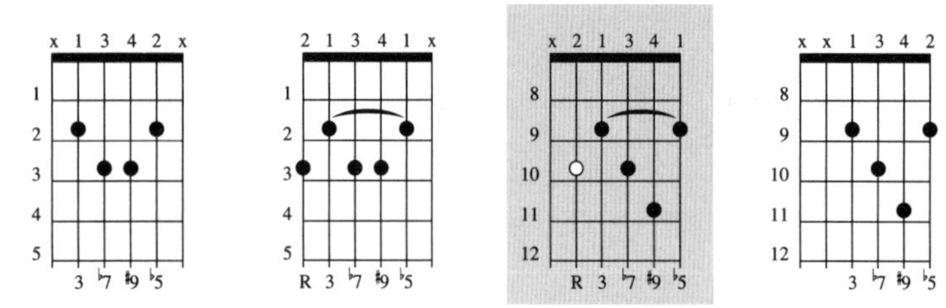

7♯5♭9 (+7♭9)
1, 3, ♯5, ♭7, ♭9

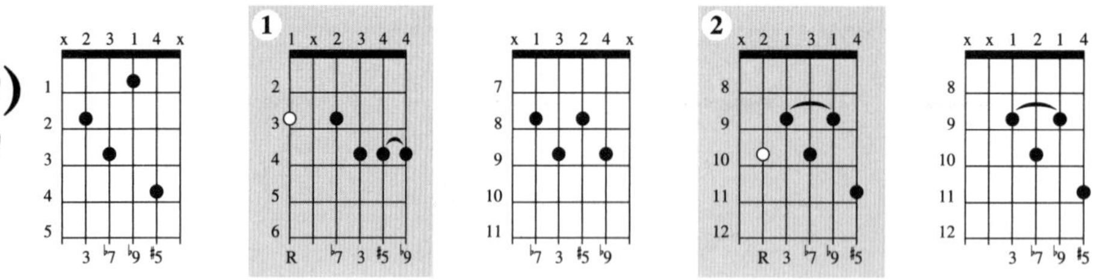

7♯5♯9
1, 3, ♯5, ♭7, ♯9

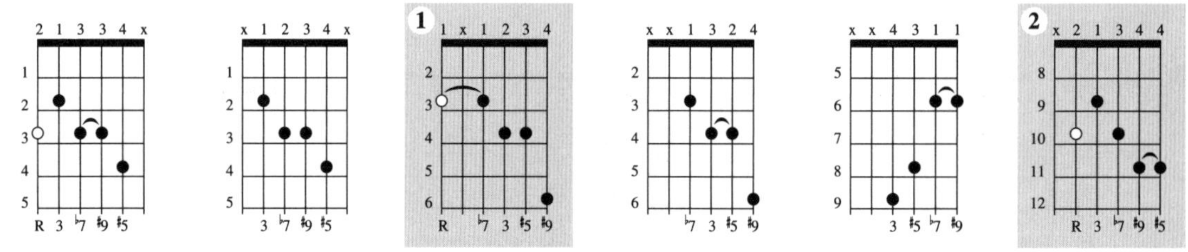

9♭5
1, 3, ♭5, ♭7, 9

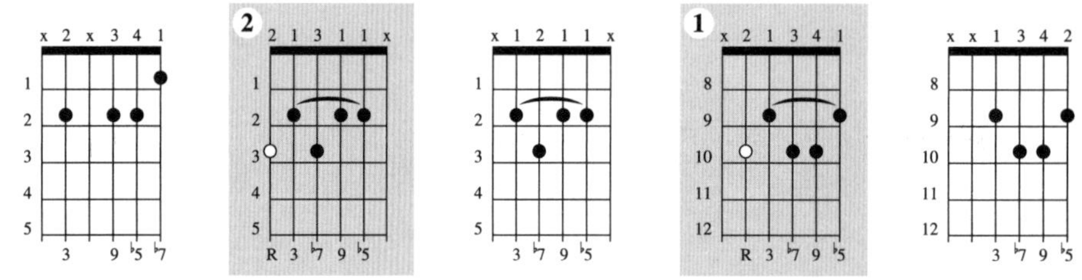

9♯5
1, 3, ♯5, ♭7, 9

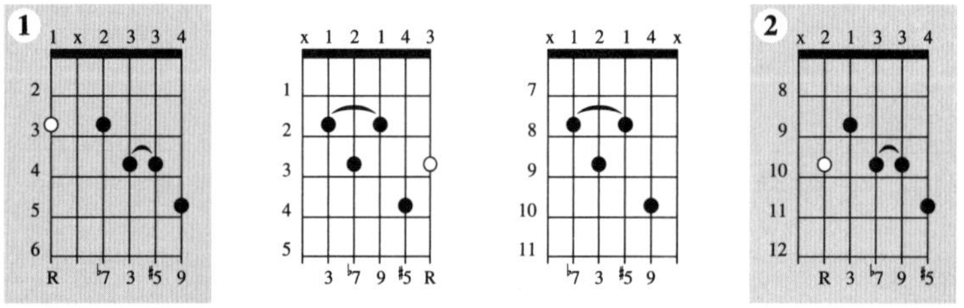

11♭5
1, 11, ♭5, ♭7

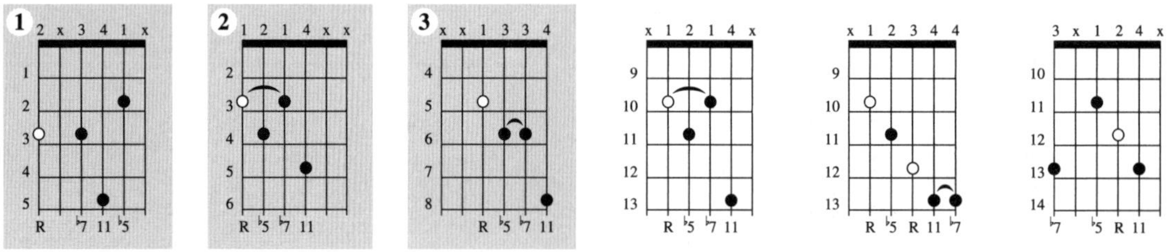

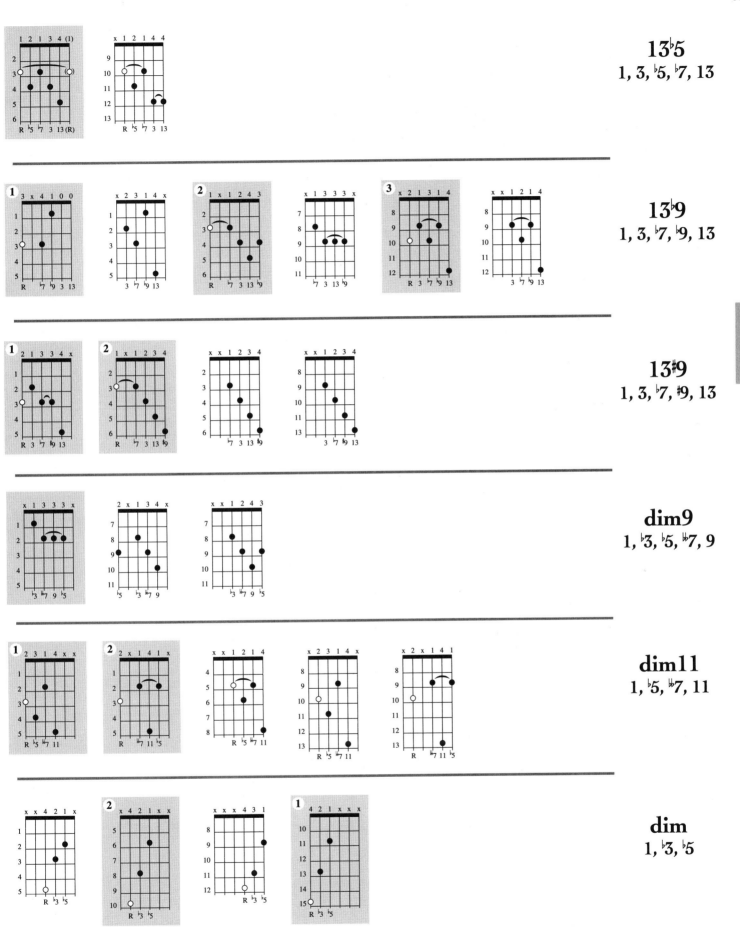

13♭5
1, 3, ♭5, ♭7, 13

13♭9
1, 3, ♭7, ♭9, 13

13♯9
1, 3, ♭7, ♯9, 13

dim9
1, ♭3, ♭5, ♭♭7, 9

dim11
1, ♭5, ♭♭7, 11

dim
1, ♭3, ♭5

G

dim7 (°7)
1, ♭3, ♭5, ♭♭7

Three-Note Voicings

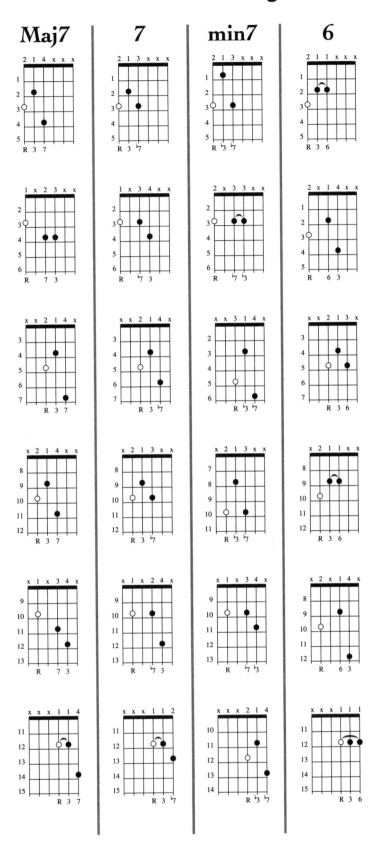

C

Maj
1, 3, 5

  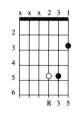

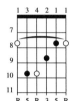 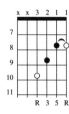 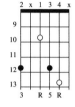 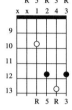 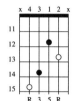 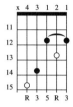

sus2
1, 2, 5

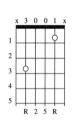   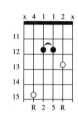 

sus4
1, 4, 5

 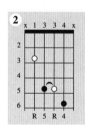 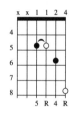 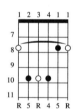 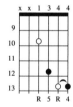

no 3rd
1, 5

 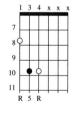 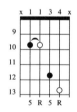

6
1, 3, 5, 6

 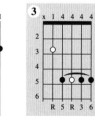 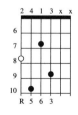  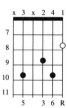

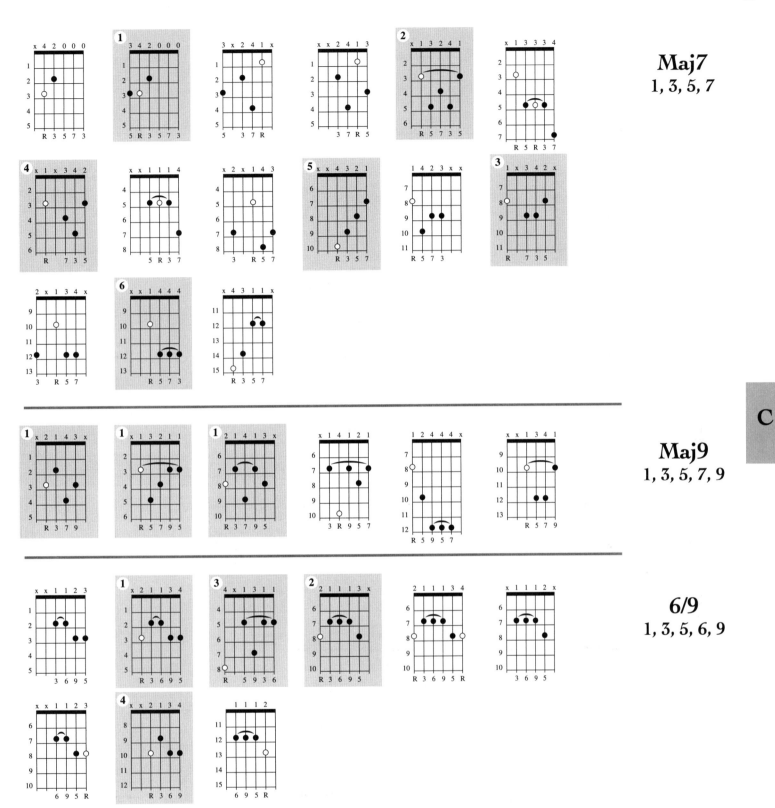

Maj7
1, 3, 5, 7

Maj9
1, 3, 5, 7, 9

6/9
1, 3, 5, 6, 9

C

C

add9
1, 3, 5, 9

  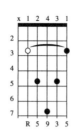 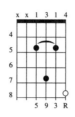 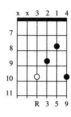 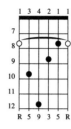

Maj11
1, 3, 5, 7, 11

 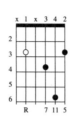 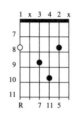 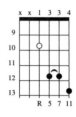 

Maj13
1, 3, 5, 7, 13

  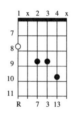 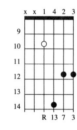 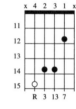

Maj13add9
1, 3, 5, 7, 9, 13

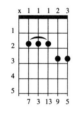   

Maj13#11
1, 3, 7, #11, 13

  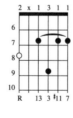 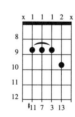 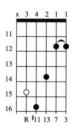

Maj7#5
1, 3, #5, 7

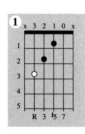  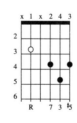 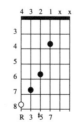 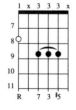 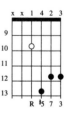

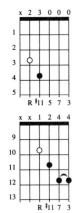

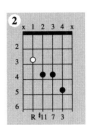
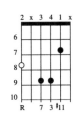

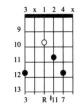

Maj7♯11

1, 3, 7, ♯11

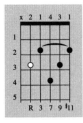

Maj9♯11

1, 3, 7, 9, ♯11

C

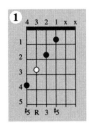
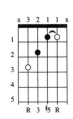
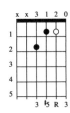

**Augmented
(aug)**

1, 3, ♯5

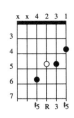

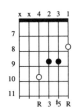

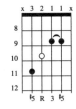
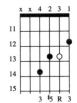

C

min
1, ♭3, 5

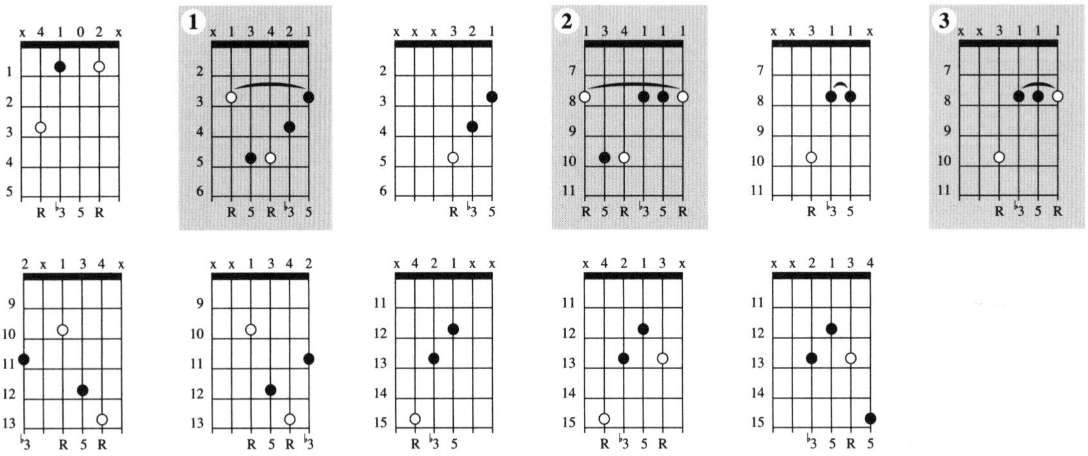

min6
1, ♭3, 5, 6

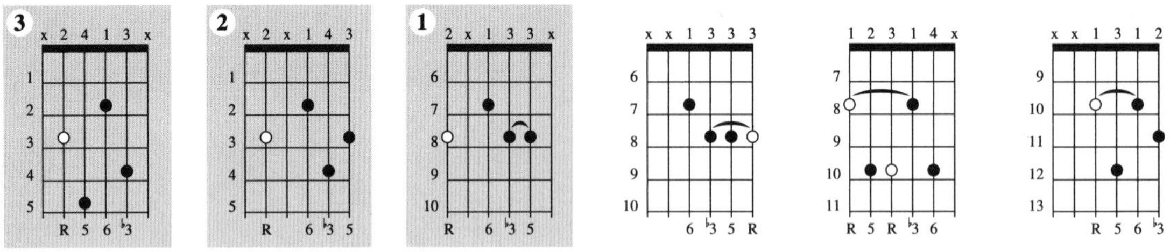

min7
1, ♭3, 5, ♭7

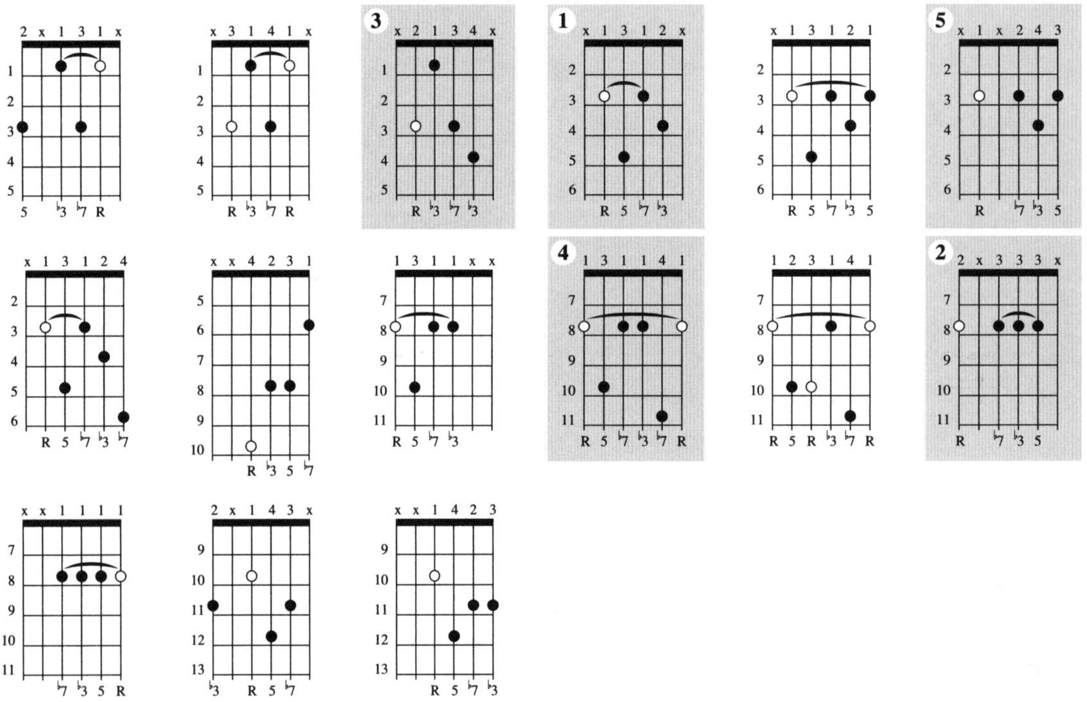

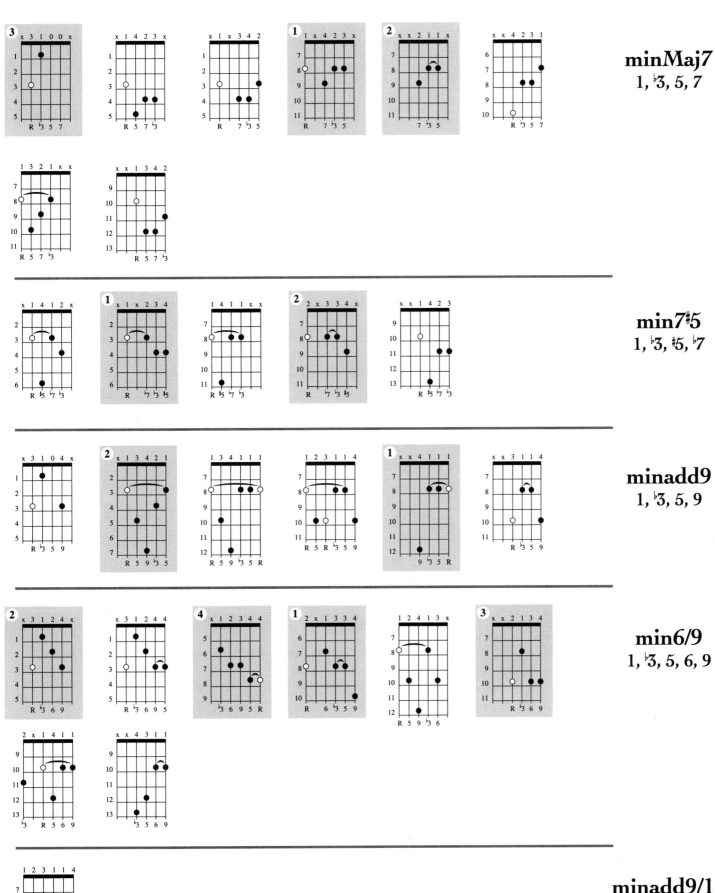

minMaj7
1, ♭3, 5, 7

min7♯5
1, ♭3, ♯5, ♭7

minadd9
1, ♭3, 5, 9

min6/9
1, ♭3, 5, 6, 9

minadd9/11
1, ♭3, 5, 9, 11

C

C

min9
1, ♭3, 5, ♭7, 9

min9Maj7
1, ♭3, 5, 7, 9

min9add11
1, ♭3, 5, ♭7, 9, 11

min11
1, ♭3, 5, ♭7, 11

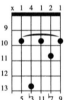

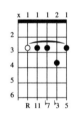
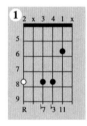
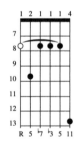
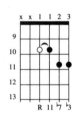

min13
1, ♭3, 5, ♭7, 13

min13add9
1, ♭3, 5, ♭7, 9, 13

min7♭5
1, ♭3, ♭5, ♭7

min9♭5
1, ♭3, ♭5, ♭7, 9

C

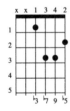
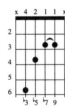

C

7
1, 3, 5, ♭7

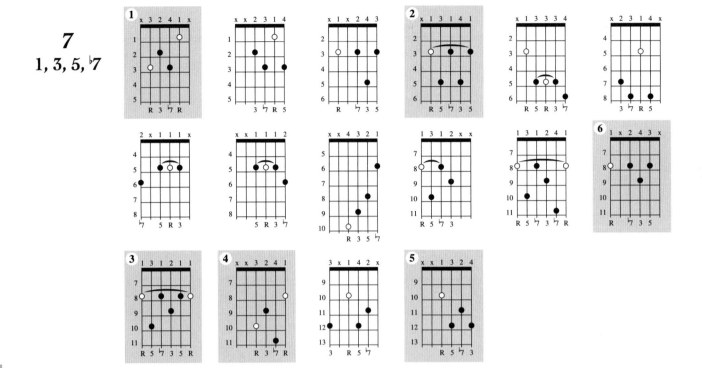

9
1, 3, 5, ♭7, 9

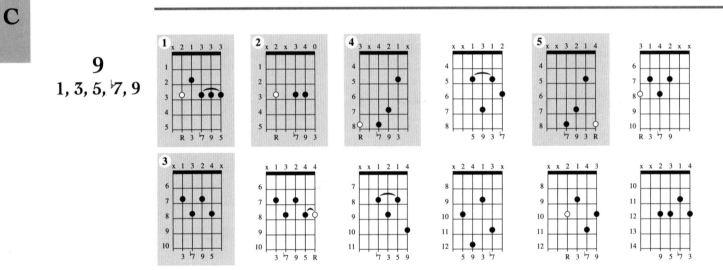

   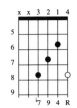 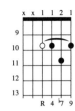

9sus4
1, 4, 5, ♭7, 9

  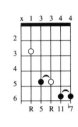 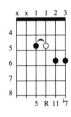  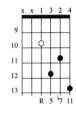

11(7sus4)
1, 5, ♭7, 11

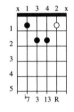  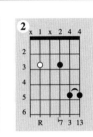 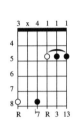 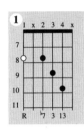 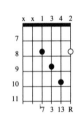

13
1, 3, 5, ♭7, 13

C

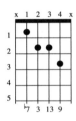 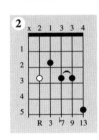 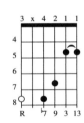  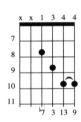

13add9
1, 3, 5, ♭7, 9, 13

78

C

13sus4
1, 4, 5, ♭7, 13

 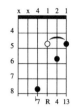

13add9sus4
1, 5, ♭7, 9, 13

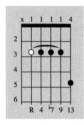 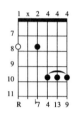 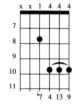

7♭5
1, 3, ♭5, ♭7

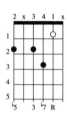 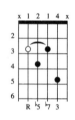 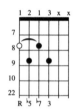 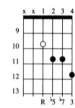

7♯5 (+7)
1, 3, ♯5, ♭7

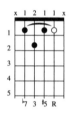 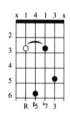 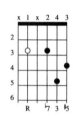   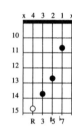

7♭9
1, 3, 5, ♭7, ♭9

  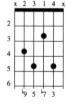 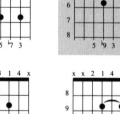 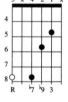 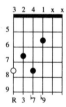

 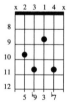 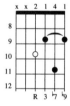 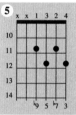

* T = Thumb

7♯9
1, 3, 5, ♭7, ♯9

 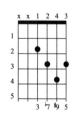  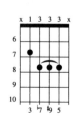 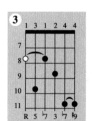 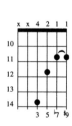

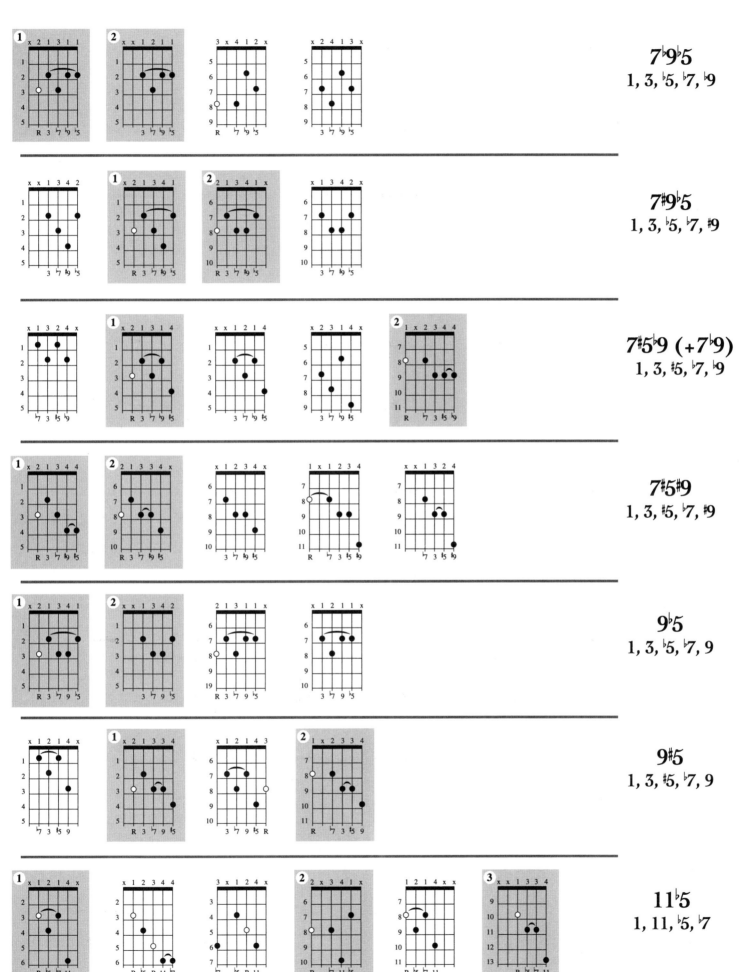

7♭9♭5
1, 3, ♭5, ♭7, ♭9

7♯9♭5
1, 3, ♭5, ♭7, ♯9

7♯5♭9 (+7♭9)
1, 3, ♯5, ♭7, ♭9

7♯5♯9
1, 3, ♯5, ♭7, ♯9

9♭5
1, 3, ♭5, ♭7, 9

9♯5
1, 3, ♯5, ♭7, 9

11♭5
1, 11, ♭5, ♭7

C

13♭5
1, 3, ♭5, ♭7, 13

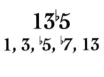 

13♭9
1, 3, ♭7, ♭9, 13

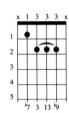    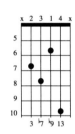 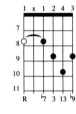

13#9
1, 3, ♭7, #9, 13

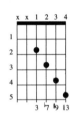   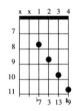

dim9
1, ♭3, ♭5, ♭♭7, 9

 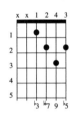 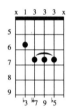

dim11
1, ♭5, ♭♭7, 11

  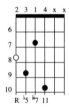 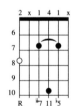 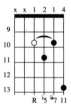

dim
1, ♭3, ♭5

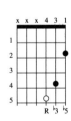  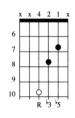 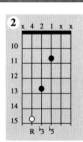

C

dim7 (°7)

1, ♭3, ♭5, ♭♭7

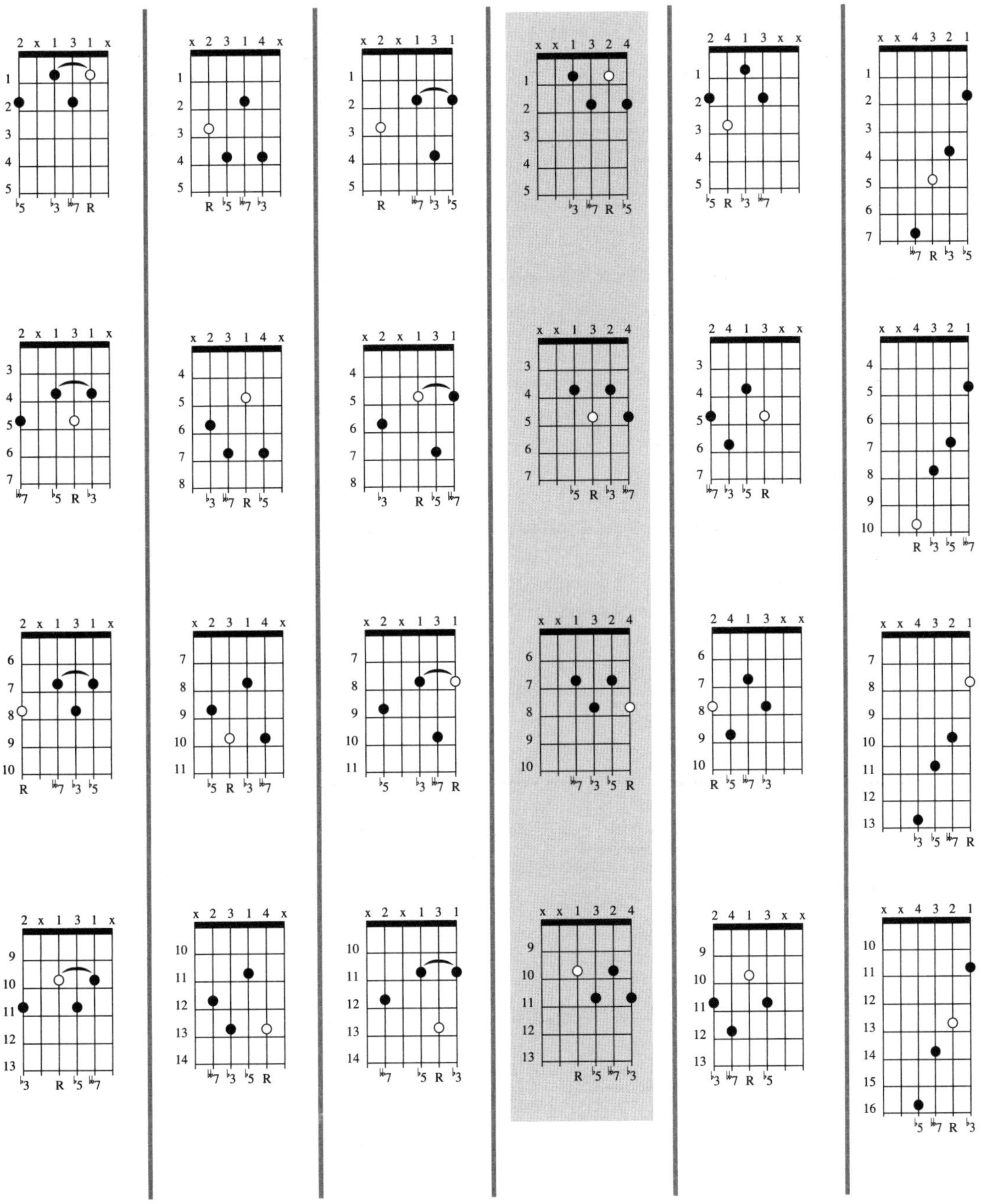

2 x 1 3 1 x
♭5 ♭3 ♭♭7 R
x 2 3 1 4 x
R ♭5 ♭♭7 ♭3
x 2 x 1 3 1
R ♭♭7 ♭3 ♭5
x x 1 3 2 4
♭3 ♭♭7 R ♭5
2 4 1 3 x x
♭5 R ♭3 ♭♭7
x x 4 3 2 1
♭♭7 R ♭3 ♭5
2 x 1 3 1 x
♭♭7 ♭5 R ♭3
x 2 3 1 4 x
♭3 ♭♭7 R ♭5
x 2 x 1 3 1
♭3 R ♭5 ♭♭7
x x 1 3 2 4
♭5 R ♭3 ♭♭7
2 4 1 3 x x
♭♭7 ♭3 ♭5 R
x x 4 3 2 1
R ♭3 ♭5 ♭♭7
2 x 1 3 1 x
R ♭♭7 ♭3 ♭5
x 2 3 1 4 x
♭5 R ♭3 ♭♭7
x 2 x 1 3 1
♭5 ♭3 ♭♭7 R
x x 1 3 2 4
♭♭7 ♭3 ♭5 R
2 4 1 3 x x
R ♭5 ♭♭7 ♭3
x x 4 3 2 1
♭3 ♭5 ♭♭7 R
2 x 1 3 1 x
♭3 R ♭5 ♭♭7
x 2 3 1 4 x
♭♭7 ♭3 ♭5 R
x 2 x 1 3 1
♭♭7 ♭5 R ♭3
x x 1 3 2 4
R ♭5 ♭♭7 ♭3
2 4 1 3 x x
♭3 ♭♭7 R ♭5
x x 4 3 2 1
♭5 ♭♭7 R ♭3

C

Three-Note Voicings

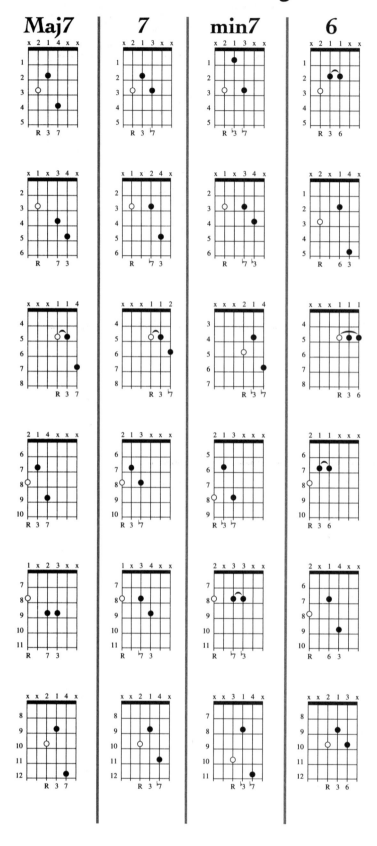

F

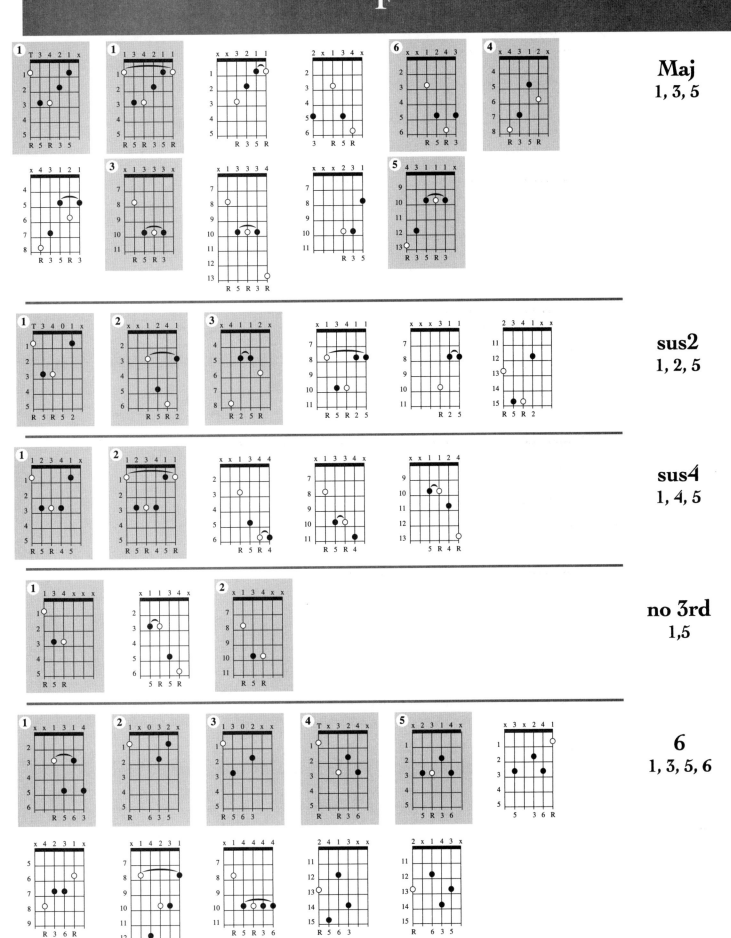

Maj
1, 3, 5

sus2
1, 2, 5

sus4
1, 4, 5

no 3rd
1,5

6
1, 3, 5, 6

F

Maj7
1, 3, 5, 7

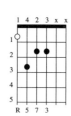 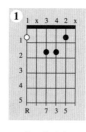  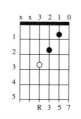  

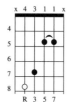 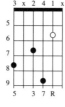 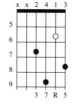 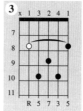  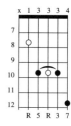

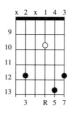 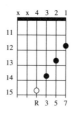

F

Maj9
1, 3, 5, 7, 9

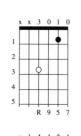  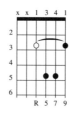   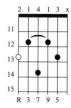

* T = Thumb

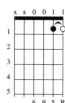 

6/9
1, 3, 5, 6, 9

  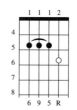  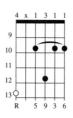 

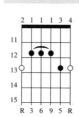 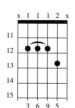 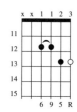

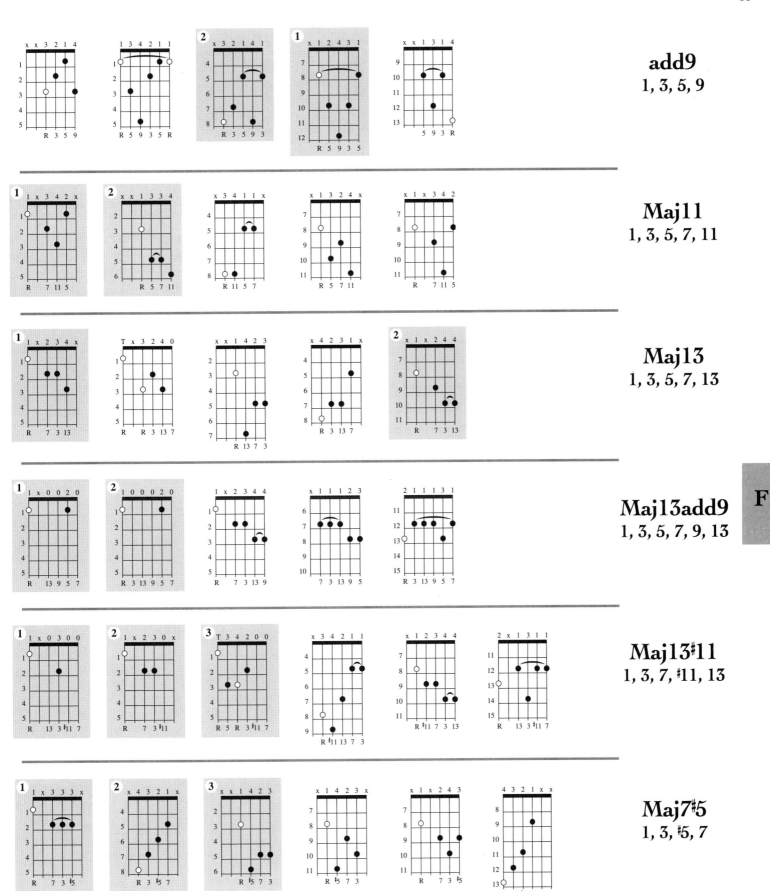

add9
1, 3, 5, 9

Maj11
1, 3, 5, 7, 11

Maj13
1, 3, 5, 7, 13

Maj13add9
1, 3, 5, 7, 9, 13

F

Maj13♯11
1, 3, 7, ♯11, 13

Maj7♯5
1, 3, ♯5, 7

Maj7#11
1, 3, 7, #11

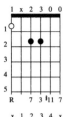    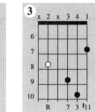

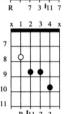  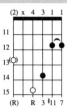

Maj9#11
1, 3, 7, 9, #11

  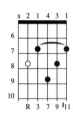 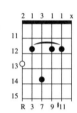 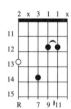

Augmented (aug)
1, 3, #5

F

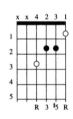  

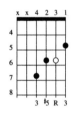  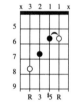

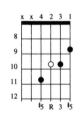 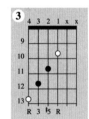 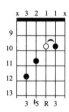

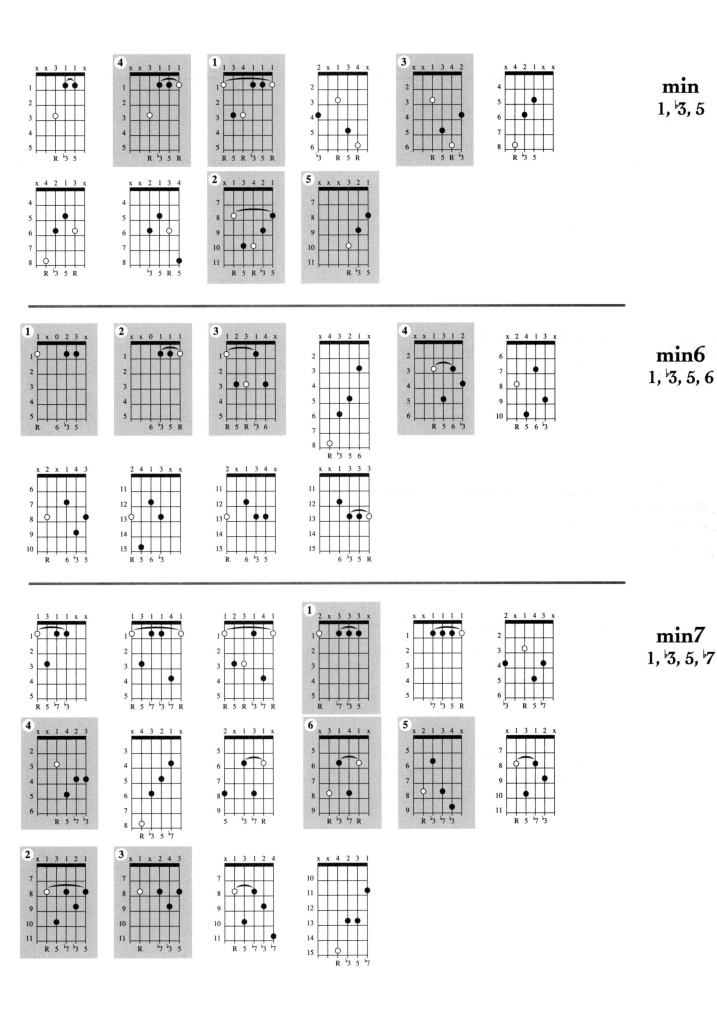

min
1, ♭3, 5

min6
1, ♭3, 5, 6

min7
1, ♭3, 5, ♭7

F

88

F

minMaj7
1, ♭3, 5, 7

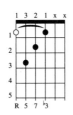

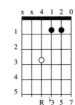
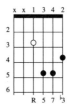
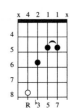

min7♯5
1, ♭3, ♯5, ♭7

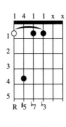
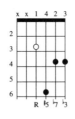
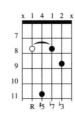

minadd9
1, ♭3, 5, 9

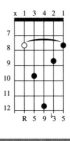

min6/9
1, ♭3, 5, 6, 9

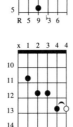

minadd9/11
1, ♭3, 5, 9, 11

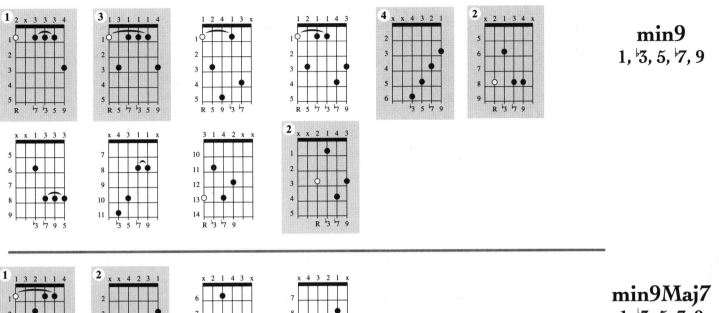

min9
1, ♭3, 5, ♭7, 9

min9Maj7
1, ♭3, 5, 7, 9

min9add11
1, ♭3, 5, 7, 9

F

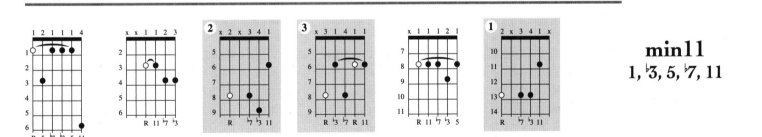

min11
1, ♭3, 5, ♭7, 11

min13
1, ♭3, 5, ♭7, 13

min13add9
1, ♭3, 5, ♭7, 9, 13

F

min7♭5
1, ♭3, ♭5, ♭7

min9♭5
1, ♭3, ♭5, ♭7, 9

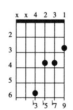
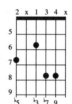

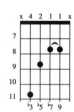

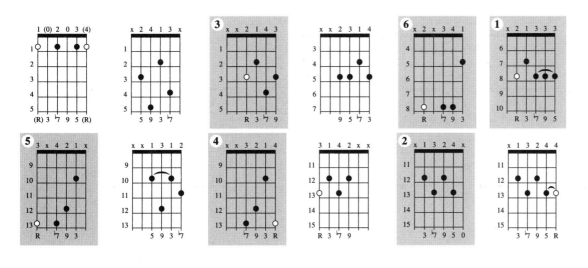

7
1, 3, 5, ♭7

9
1, 3, 5, ♭7, 9

F

9sus4
1, 4, 5, ♭7, 9

11(7sus4)
1, 5, ♭7, 11

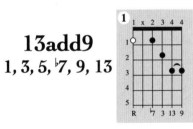
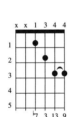

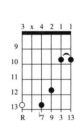

13
1, 3, 5, ♭7, 13

F

13add9
1, 3, 5, ♭7, 9, 13

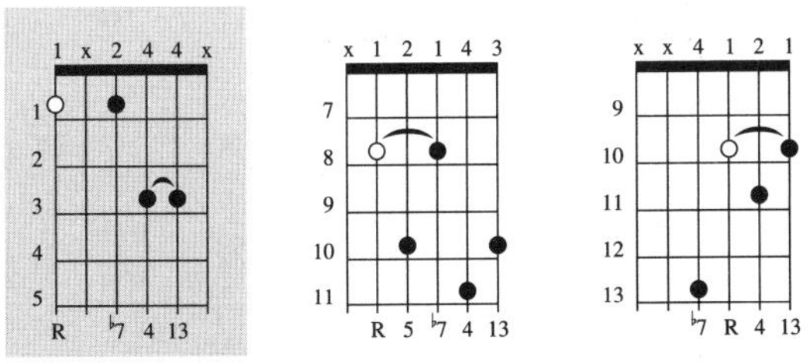

13sus4
1, 4, 5, ♭7, 13

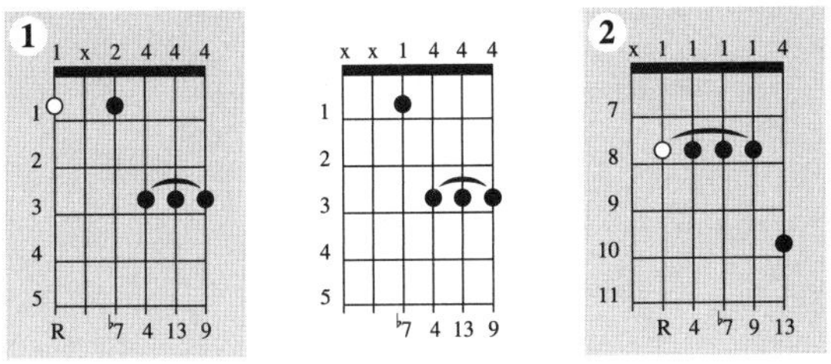

13add9sus4
1, 5, ♭7, 9, 13

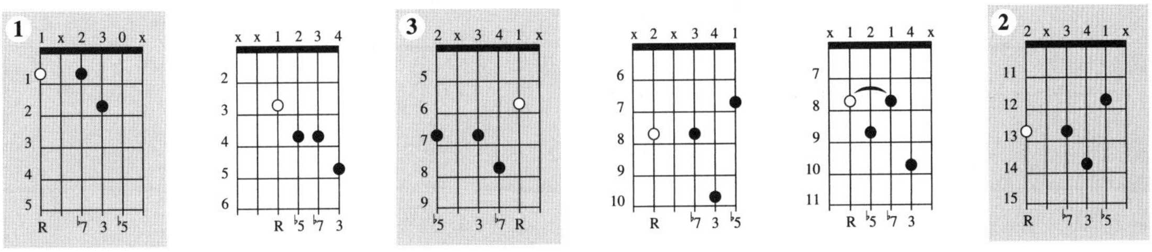

7♭5
1, 3, ♭5, ♭7

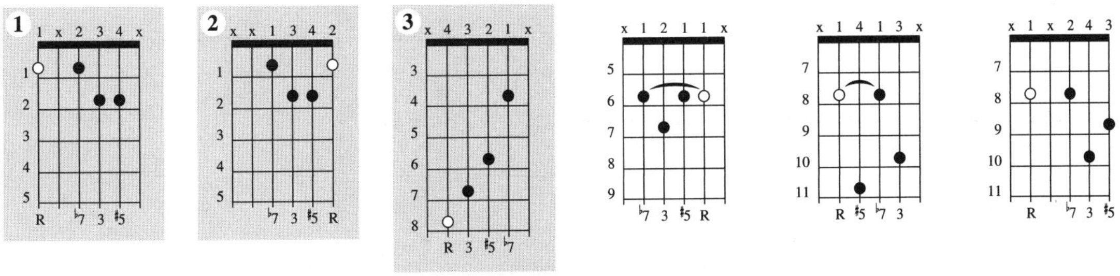

7♯5 (+7)
1, 3, ♯5, ♭7

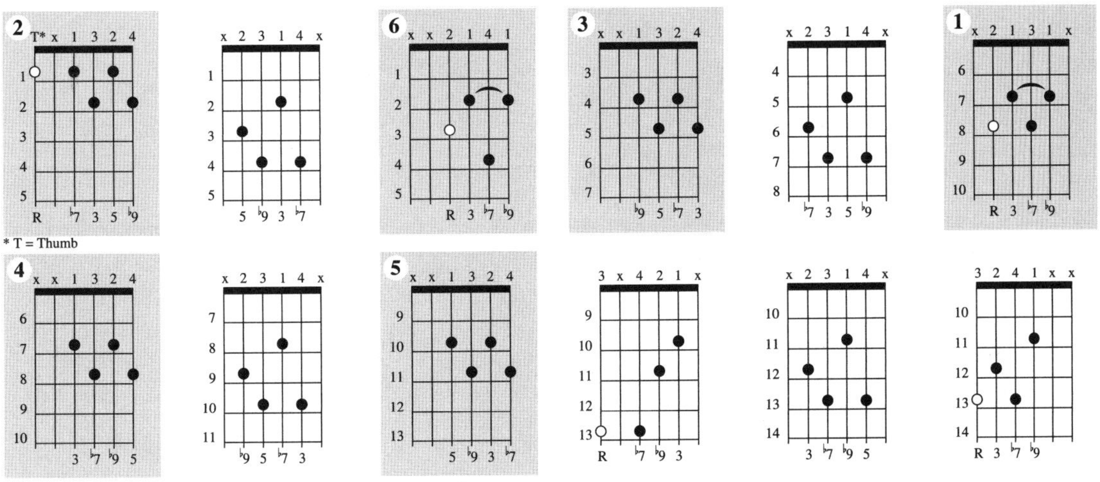

F

7♭9
1, 3, 5, ♭7, ♭9

* T = Thumb

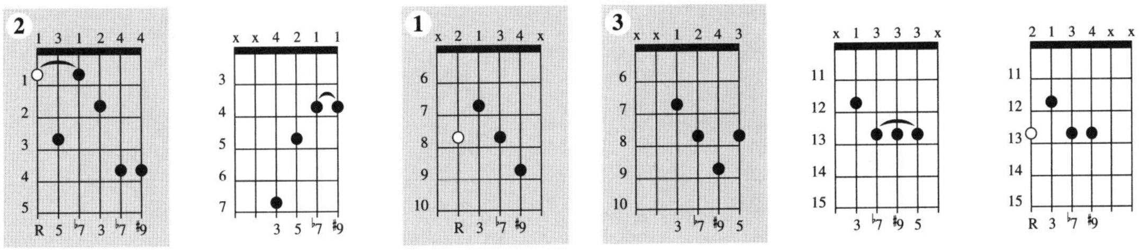

7♯9
1, 3, 5, ♭7, ♯9

F

7♭9♭5
1, 3, ♭5, ♭7, ♭9

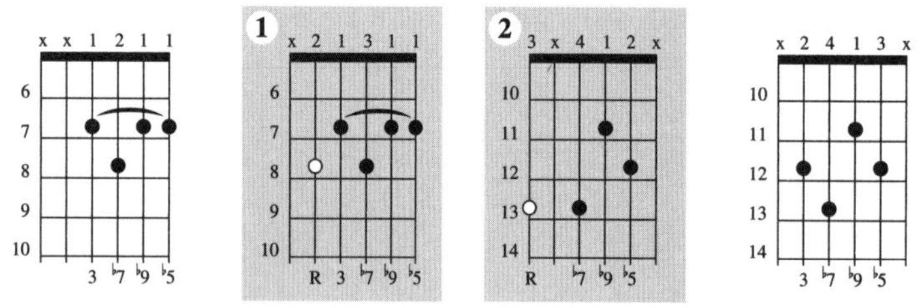

7♯9♭5
1, 3, ♭5, ♭7, ♯9

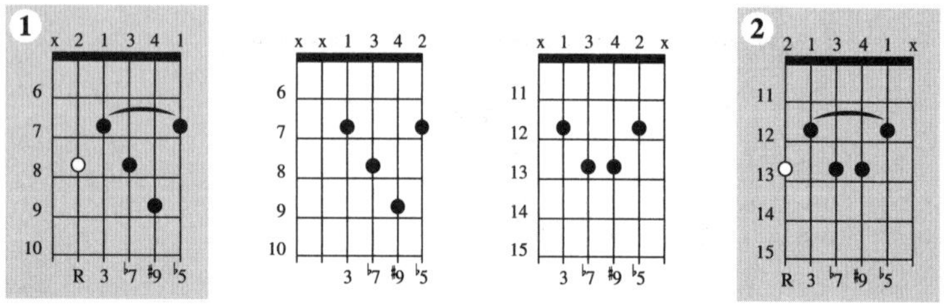

7♯5♭9 (+7♭9)
1, 3, ♯5, ♭7, ♭9

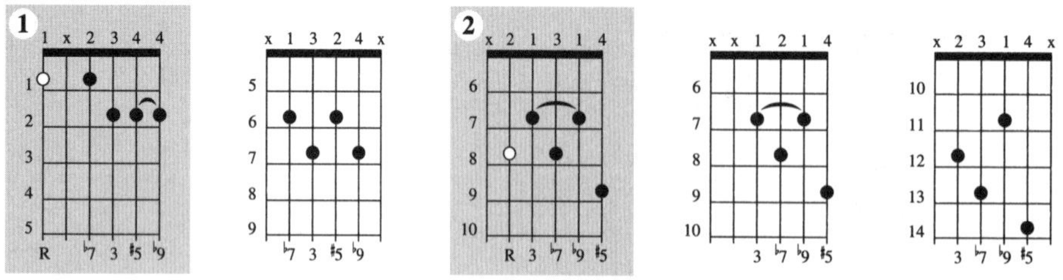

7♯5♯9
1, 3, ♯5, ♭7, ♯9

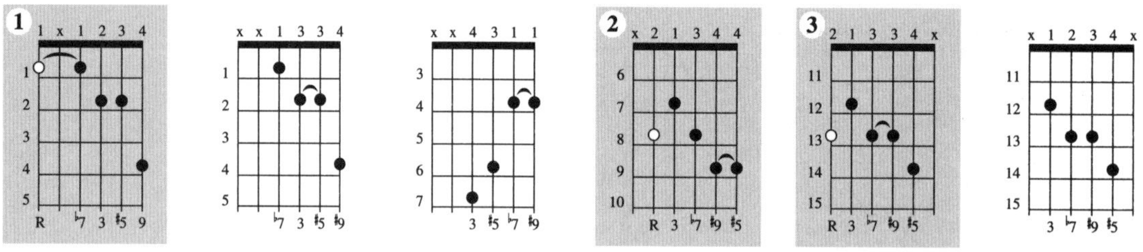

9♭5
1, 3, ♭5, ♭7, 9

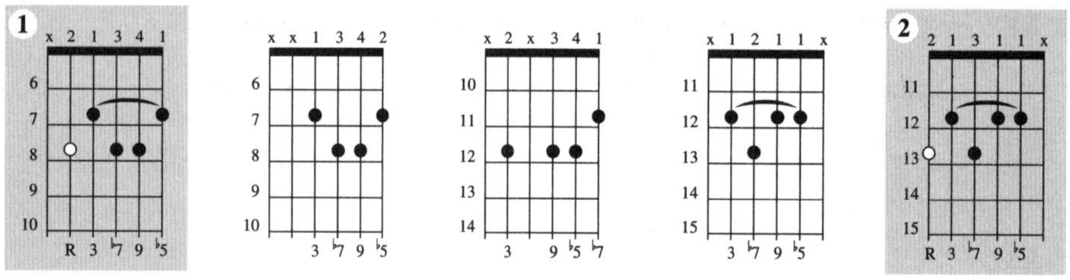

9♯5
1, 3, ♯5, ♭7, 9

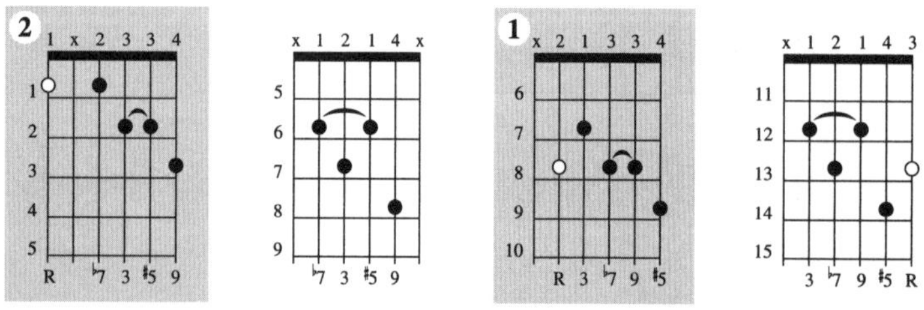

11♭5
1, 11, ♭5, ♭7

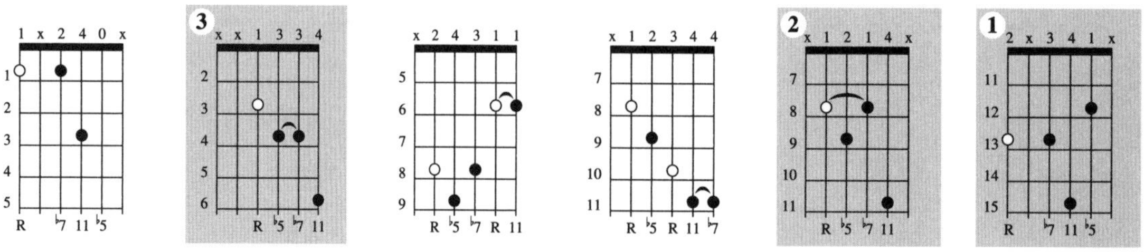

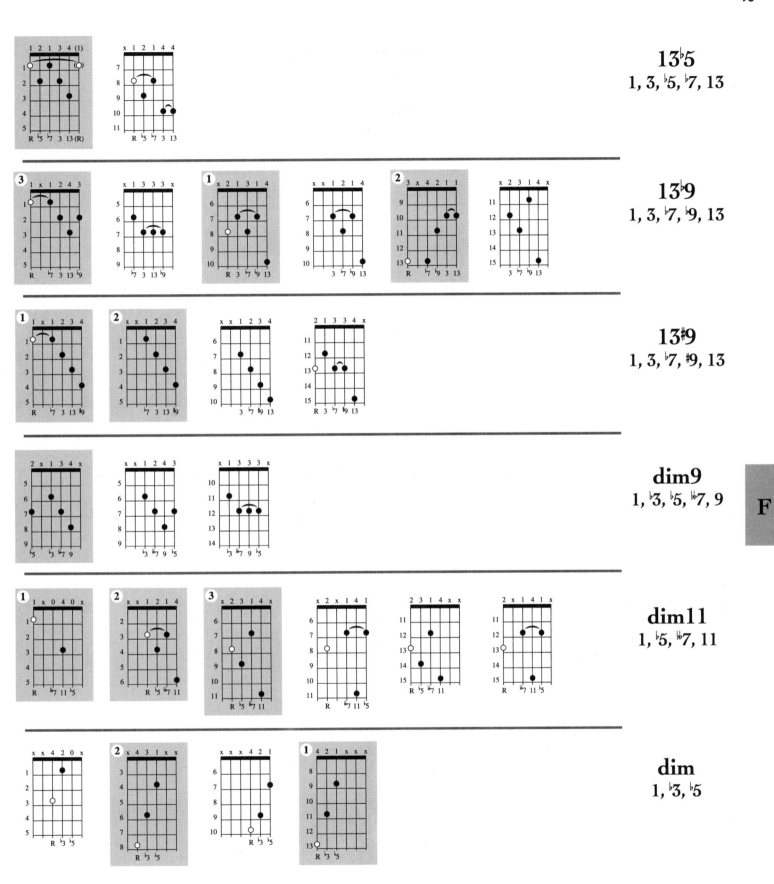

13♭5
1, 3, ♭5, ♭7, 13

13♭9
1, 3, ♭7, ♭9, 13

13♯9
1, 3, ♭7, ♯9, 13

dim9
1, ♭3, ♭5, ♭♭7, 9

dim11
1, ♭5, ♭♭7, 11

dim
1, ♭3, ♭5

F

dim7 (°7)
1, ♭3, ♭5, ♭♭7

F

Three-Note Voicings

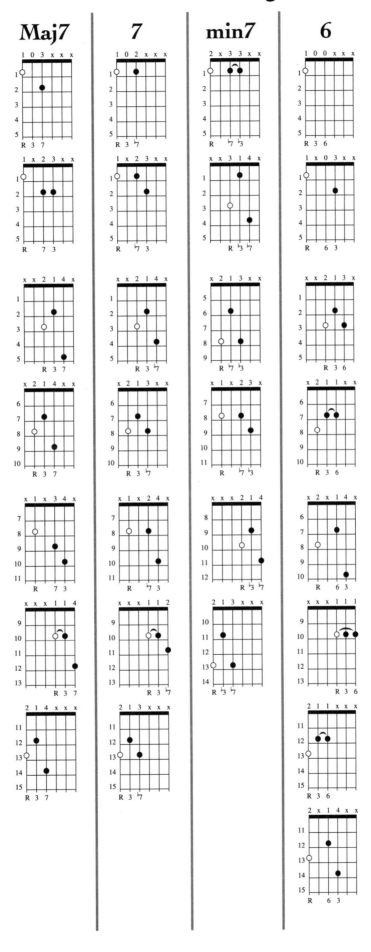

F

B♭/A♯

Maj
1, 3, 5

     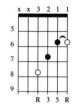

  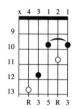

sus2
1, 2, 5

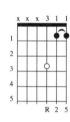  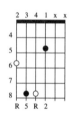  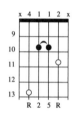

sus4
1, 4, 5

   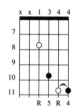

no 3rd
1, 5

 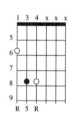 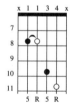

6
1, 3, 5, 6

  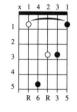  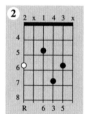 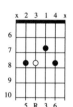

 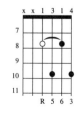 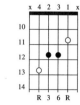

B♭
A♯

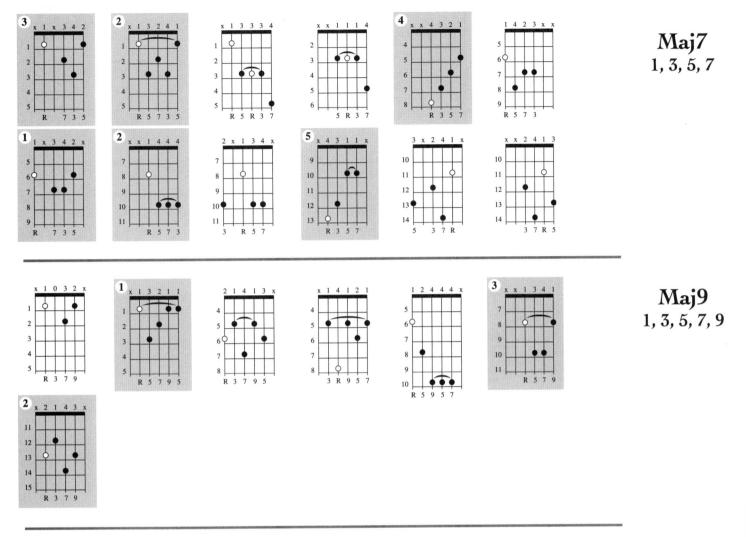

Maj7
1, 3, 5, 7

Maj9
1, 3, 5, 7, 9

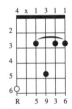

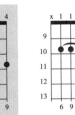

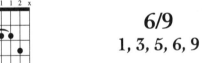

B♭
A♯

6/9
1, 3, 5, 6, 9

add9
1, 3, 5, 9

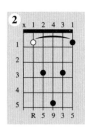 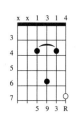   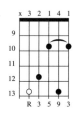

Maj11
1, 3, 5, 7, 11

  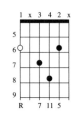 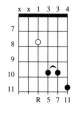 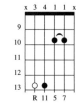

Maj13
1, 3, 5, 7, 13

  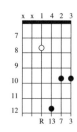 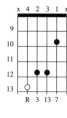

Maj13add9
1, 3, 5, 7, 9, 13

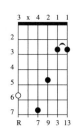   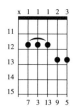

B♭
A♯

Maj13♯11
1, 3, 7, ♯11, 13

  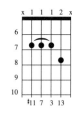 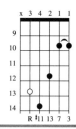

Maj7♯5
1, 3, ♯5, 7

   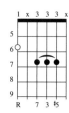 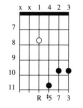 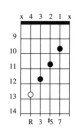

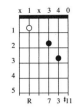

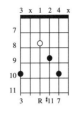

Maj7#11
1, 3, 7, #11

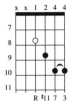
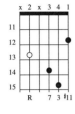

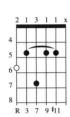
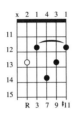

Maj9#11
1, 3, 7, 9, #11

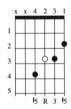
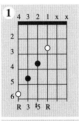

Augmented
(aug)
1, 3, #5

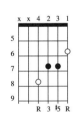

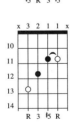

Bb
A#

min
1, ♭3, 5

min6
1, ♭3, 5, 6

min7
1, ♭3, 5, ♭7

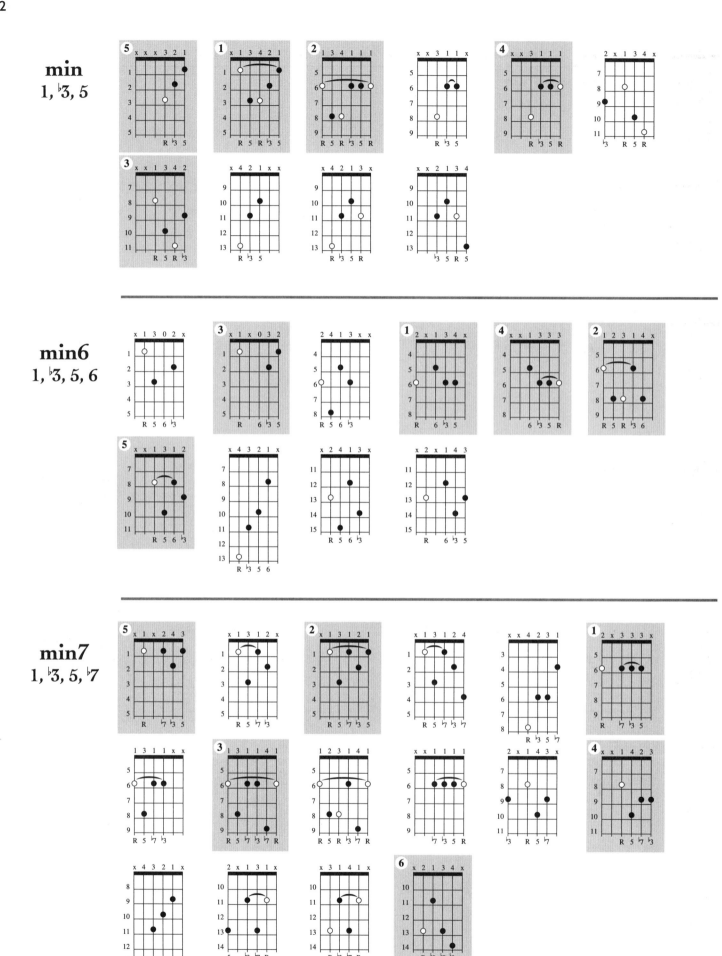

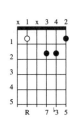 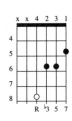   

minMaj7
1, ♭3, 5, 7

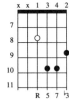 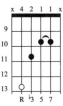

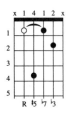    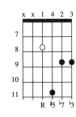

min7♯5
1, ♭3, ♯5, ♭7

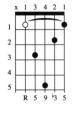 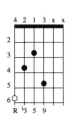 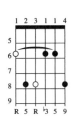   

minadd9
1, ♭3, 5, 9

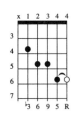 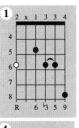    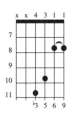

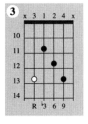 

min6/9
1, ♭3, 5, 6, 9

B♭
A♯

minadd9/11
1, ♭3, 5, 9, 11

min9
1, ♭3, 5, ♭7, 9

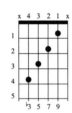

min9Maj7
1, ♭3, 5, 7, 9

min9add11
1, ♭3, 5, ♭7, 9, 11

min11
1, ♭3, 5, ♭7, 11

   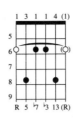

min13
1, ♭3, 5, ♭7, 13

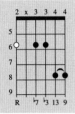 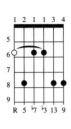 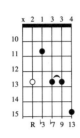

min13add9
1, ♭3, 5, ♭7, 9, 13

  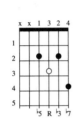 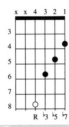  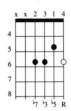

 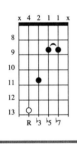  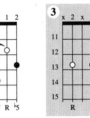

min7♭5
1, ♭3, ♭5, ♭7

   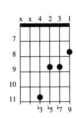 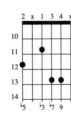 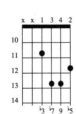

min9♭5
1, ♭3, ♭5, ♭7, 9

B♭
A♯

7
1, 3, 5, ♭7

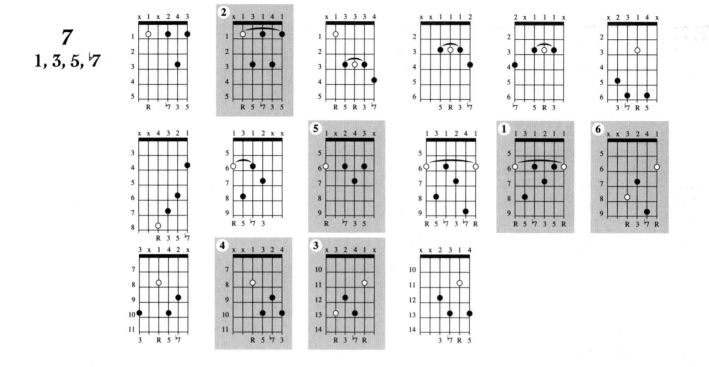

B♭
A♯

9
1, 3, 5, ♭7, 9

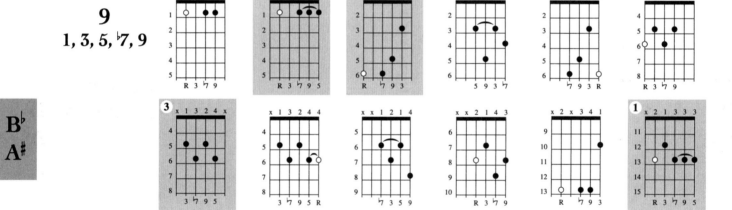

 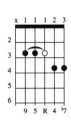 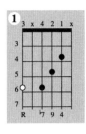 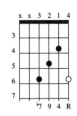 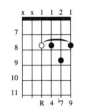 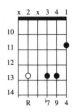

9sus4
1, 4, 5, ♭7, 9

 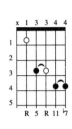 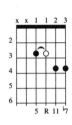   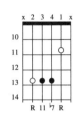

11(7sus4)
1, 5, ♭7, 11

 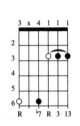   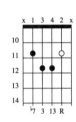 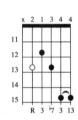

13
1, 3, 5, ♭7, 13

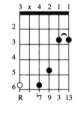  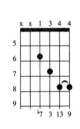 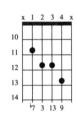 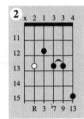

13add9
1, 3, 5, ♭7, 9, 13

B♭
A♯

13sus4
1, 4, 5, ♭7, 13

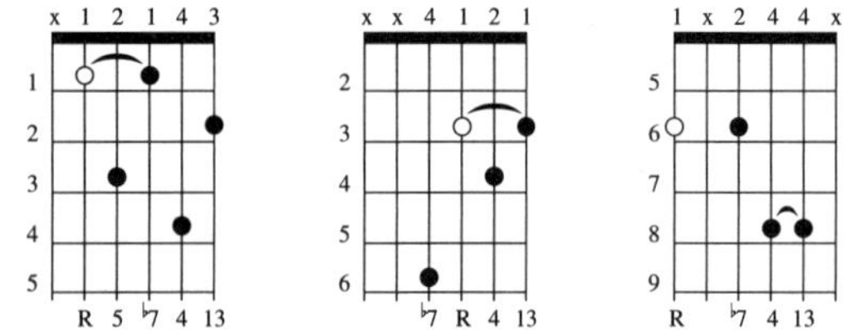

13add9sus4
1, 5, ♭7, 9, 13

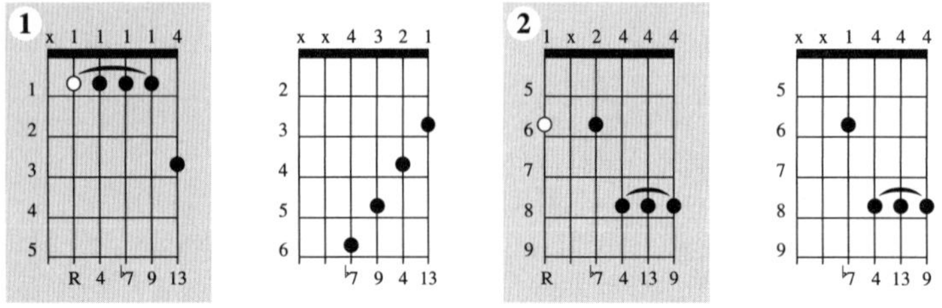

7♭5
1, 3, ♭5, ♭7

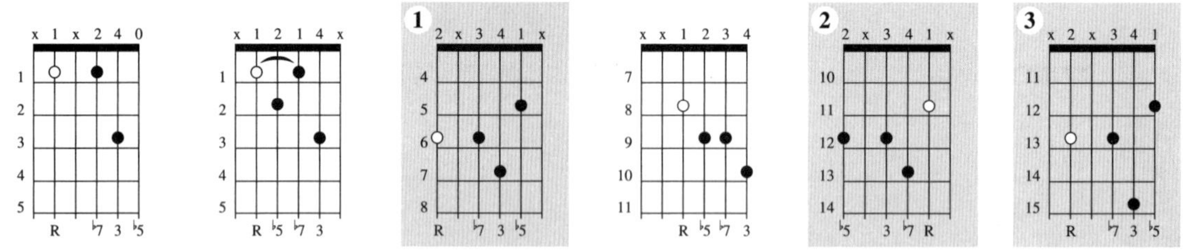

7♯5 (+7)
1, 3, ♯5, ♭7

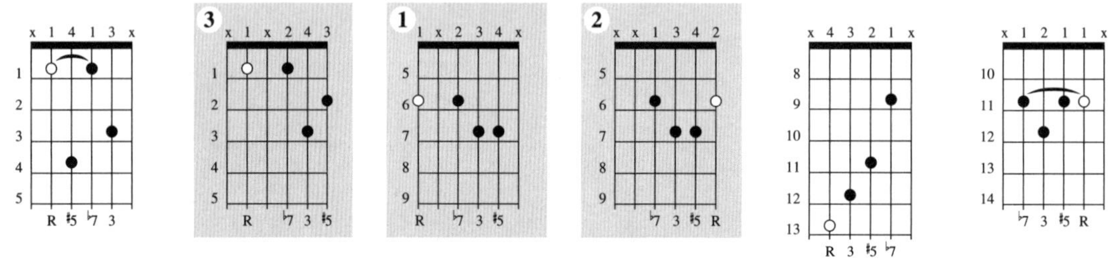

B♭
A♯

7♭9
1, 3, 5, ♭7, ♭9

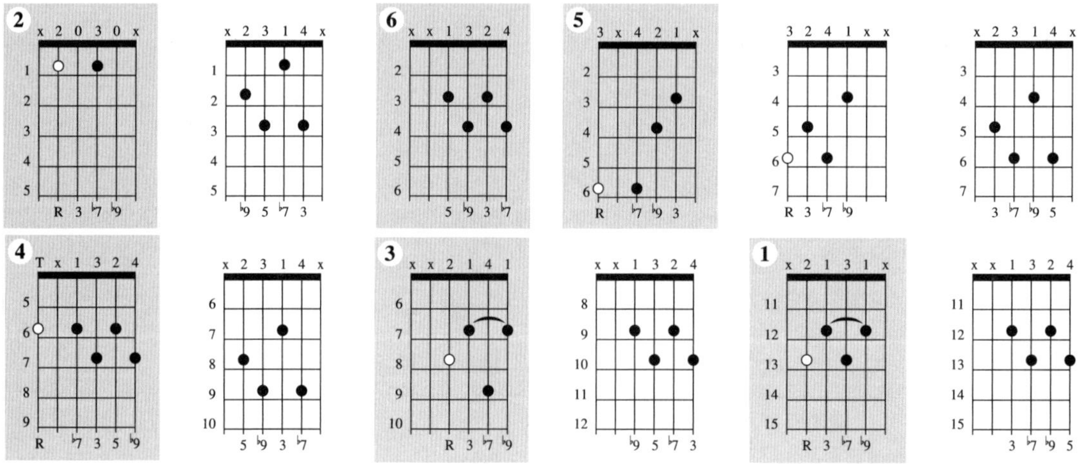

7♯9
1, 3, 5, ♭7, ♯9

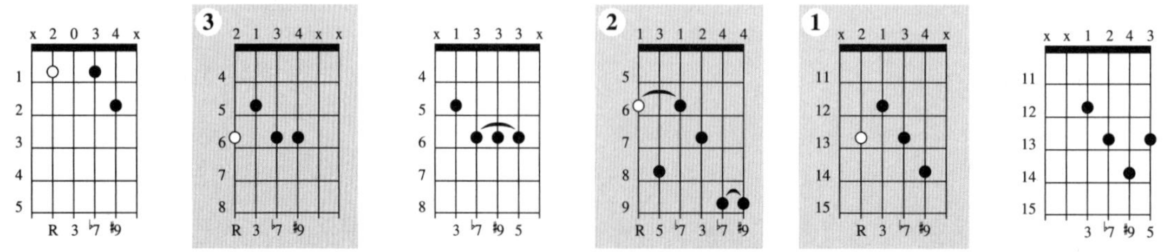

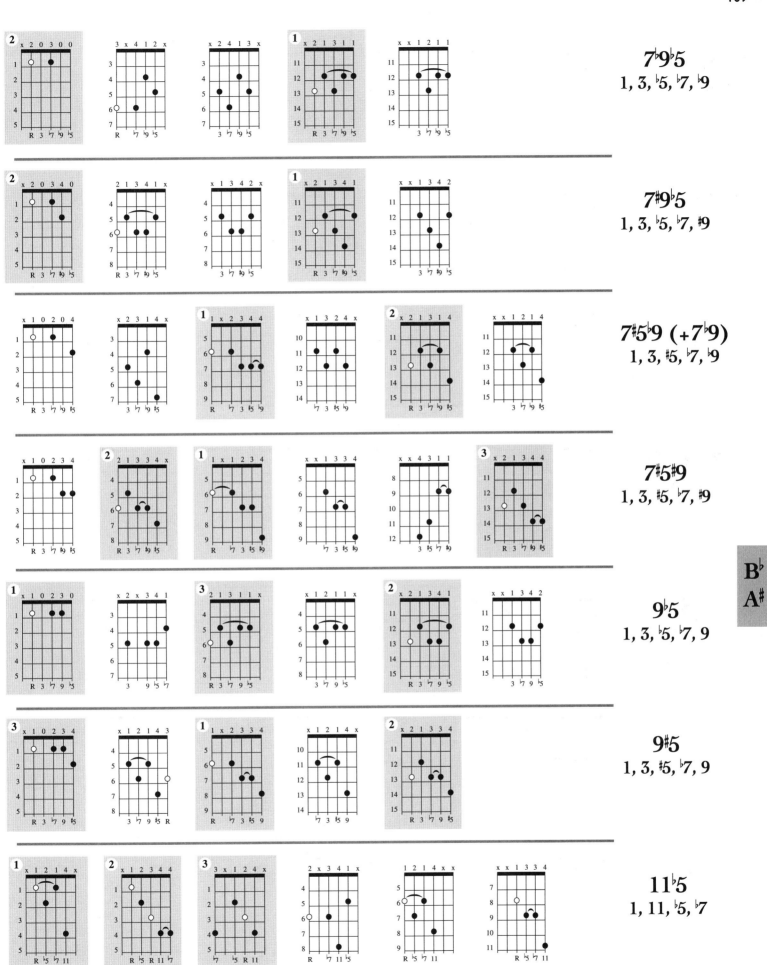

7♭9♭5
1, 3, ♭5, ♭7, ♭9

7♯9♭5
1, 3, ♭5, ♭7, ♯9

7♯5♭9 (+7♭9)
1, 3, ♯5, ♭7, ♭9

7♯5♯9
1, 3, ♯5, ♭7, ♯9

9♭5
1, 3, ♭5, ♭7, 9

9♯5
1, 3, ♯5, ♭7, 9

11♭5
1, 11, ♭5, ♭7

B♭
A♯

B♭
A♯

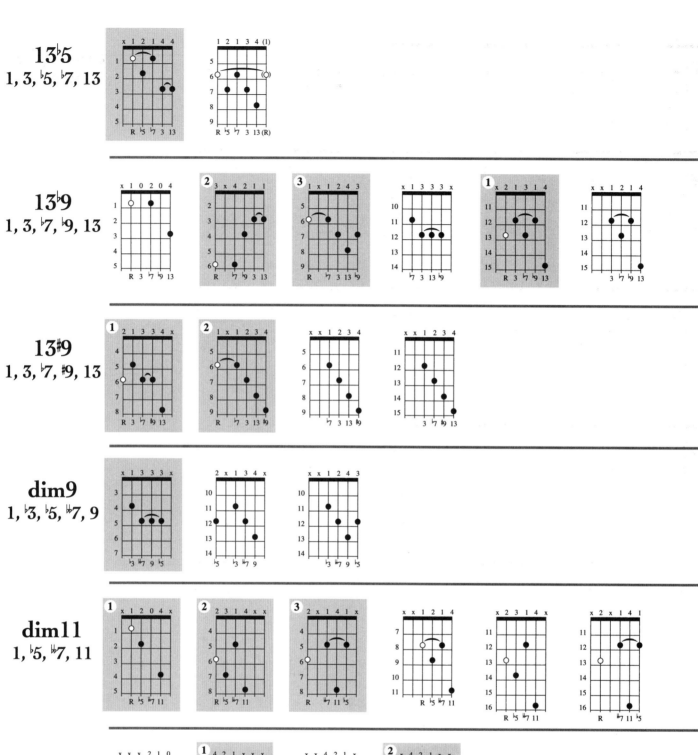

13♭5
1, 3, ♭5, ♭7, 13

13♭9
1, 3, ♭7, ♭9, 13

13♯9
1, 3, ♭7, ♯9, 13

dim9
1, ♭3, ♭5, ♭♭7, 9

dim11
1, ♭5, ♭♭7, 11

dim
1, ♭3, ♭5

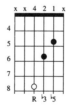

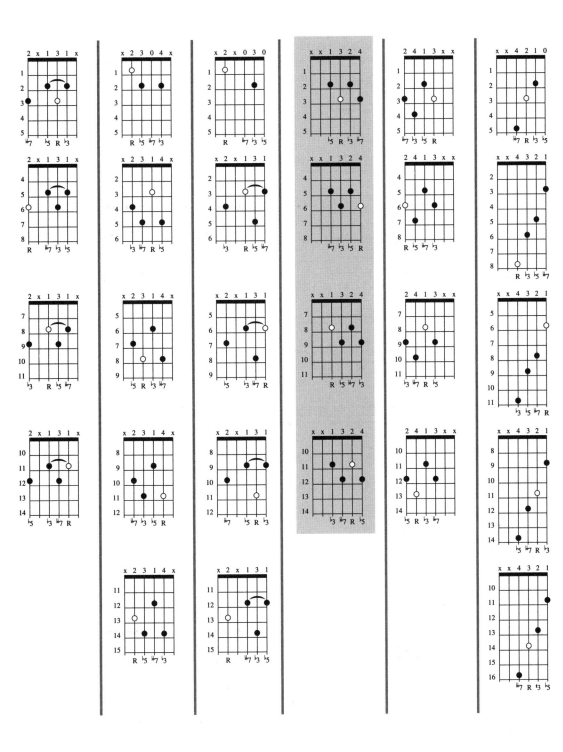

dim7 (°7)
1, ♭3, ♭5, ♭♭7

B♭
A#

Three-Note Voicings

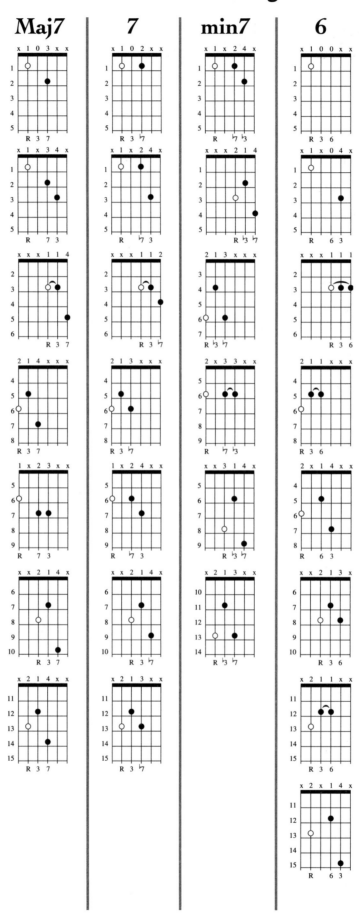

E♭/D#

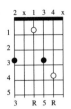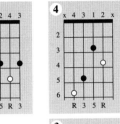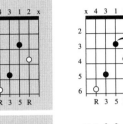

Maj
1, 3, 5

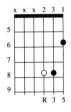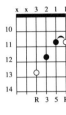

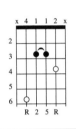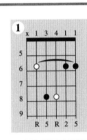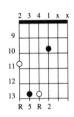

sus2
1, 2, 5

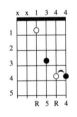

sus4
1, 4, 5

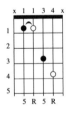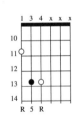

no 3rd
1, 5

E♭
D#

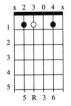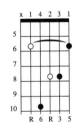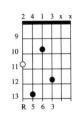

6
1, 3, 5, 6

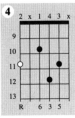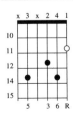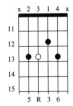

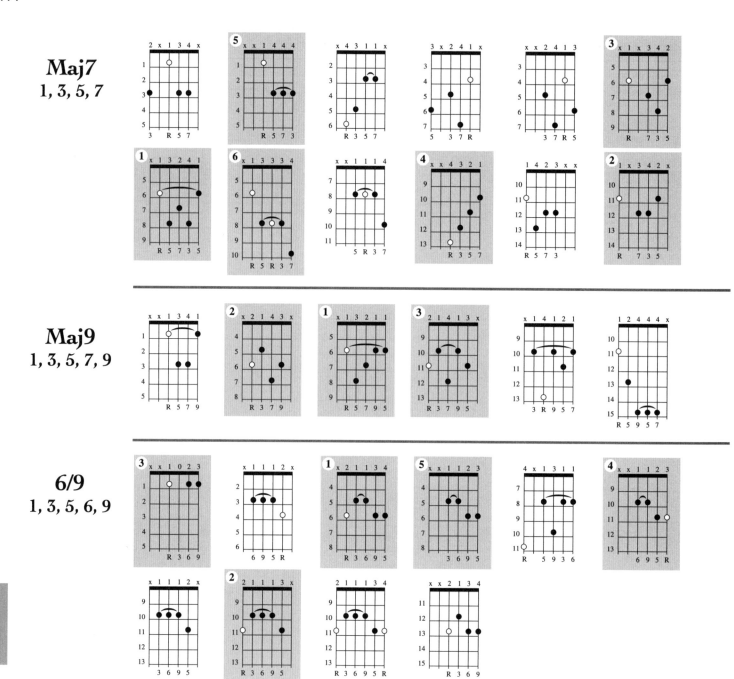

Maj7
1, 3, 5, 7

Maj9
1, 3, 5, 7, 9

6/9
1, 3, 5, 6, 9

E♭
D♯

add9
1, 3, 5, 9

Maj11
1, 3, 5, 7, 11

Maj13
1, 3, 5, 7, 13

Maj13add9
1, 3, 5, 7, 9, 13

Maj13♯11
1, 3, 7, ♯11, 13

Maj7♯5
1, 3, ♯5, 7

E♭
D♯

Maj7#11
1, 3, 7, #11

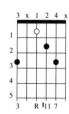 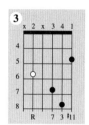 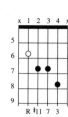 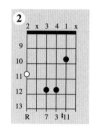 

Maj9#11
1, 3, 7, 9, #11

 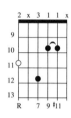 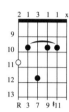

Augmented (aug)
1, 3, #5

 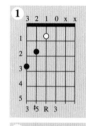  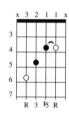

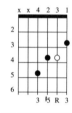  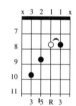 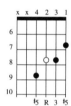

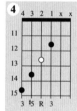 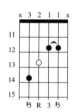 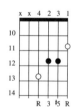

E♭
D#

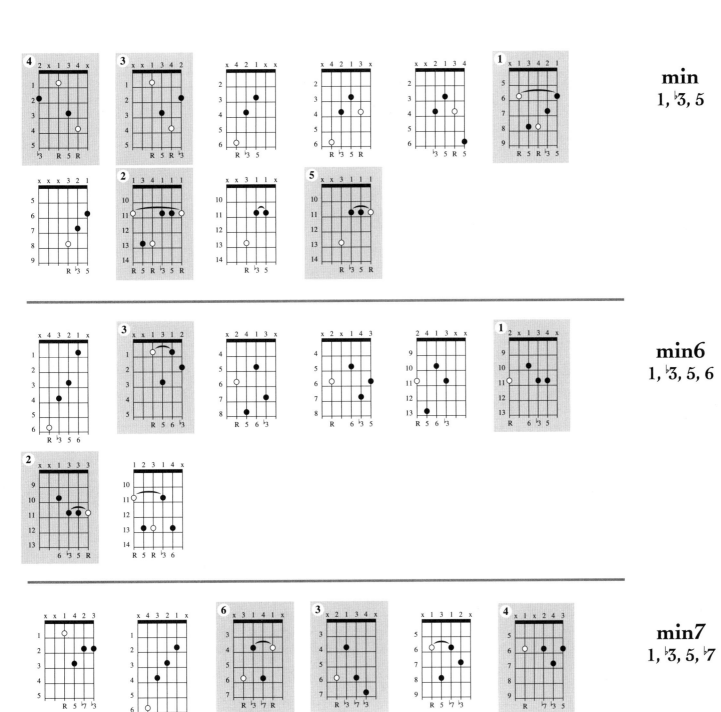

min
1, ♭3, 5

min6
1, ♭3, 5, 6

min7
1, ♭3, 5, ♭7

E♭
D♯

118

minMaj7
1, ♭3, 5, 7

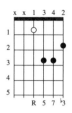  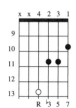

min7♯5
1, ♭3, ♯5, ♭7

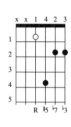  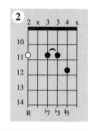 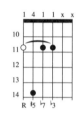

minadd9
1, ♭3, 5, 9

 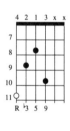  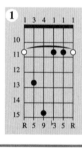 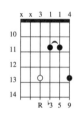 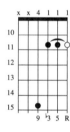

E♭ / D♯

min6/9
1, ♭3, 5, 6, 9

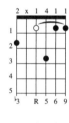 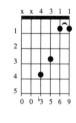   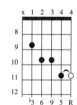 

minadd9/11
1, ♭3, 5, 9, 11

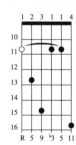

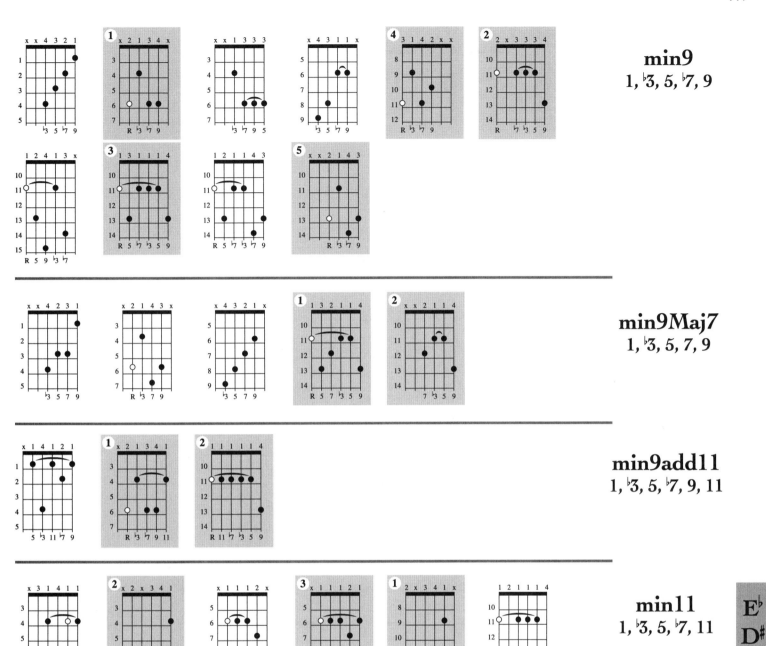

min9
1, ♭3, 5, ♭7, 9

min9Maj7
1, ♭3, 5, 7, 9

min9add11
1, ♭3, 5, ♭7, 9, 11

min11
1, ♭3, 5, ♭7, 11

E♭
D♯

min13
1, ♭3, 5, ♭7, 13

 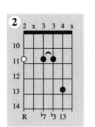 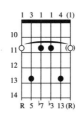 

min13add9
1, ♭3, 5, ♭7, 9, 13

 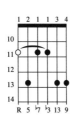 

min7♭5
1, ♭3, ♭5, ♭7

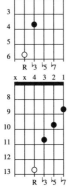  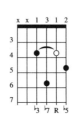   

 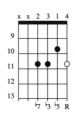

E♭
D♯

min9♭5
1, ♭3, ♭5, ♭7, 9

 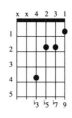  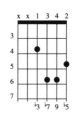 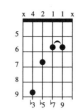 

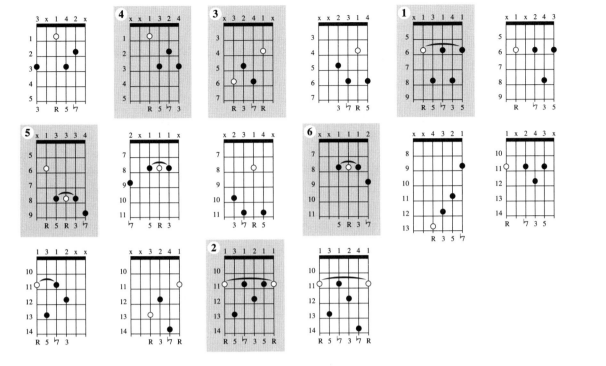

7
1, 3, 5, ♭7

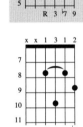
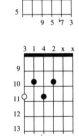

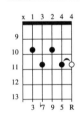

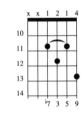
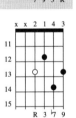

9
1, 3, 5, ♭7, 9

E♭
D#

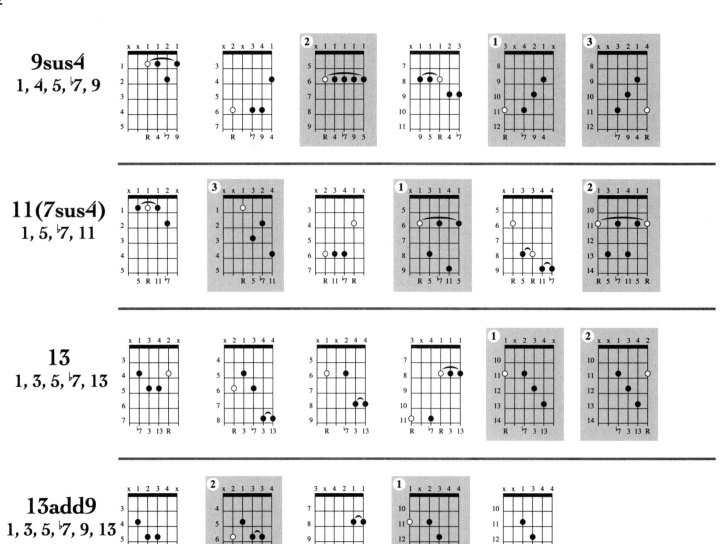

9sus4
1, 4, 5, ♭7, 9

11(7sus4)
1, 5, ♭7, 11

13
1, 3, 5, ♭7, 13

13add9
1, 3, 5, ♭7, 9, 13

E♭
D#

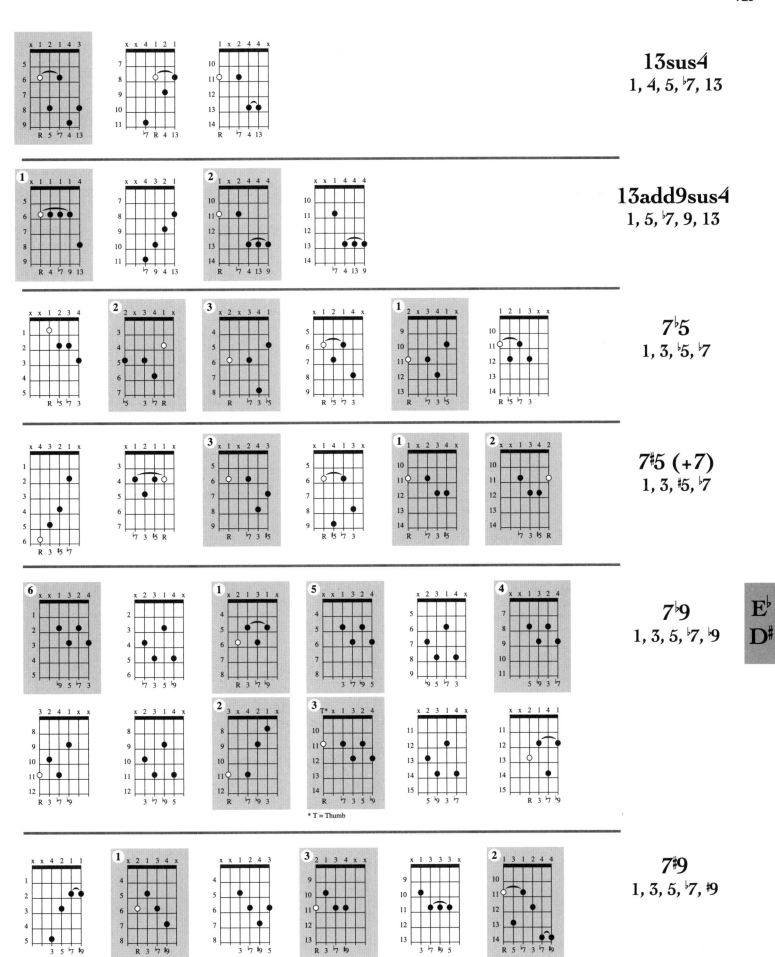

13sus4
1, 4, 5, ♭7, 13

13add9sus4
1, 5, ♭7, 9, 13

7♭5
1, 3, ♭5, ♭7

7♯5 (+7)
1, 3, ♯5, ♭7

7♭9
1, 3, 5, ♭7, ♭9

E♭
D♯

* T = Thumb

7♯9
1, 3, 5, ♭7, ♯9

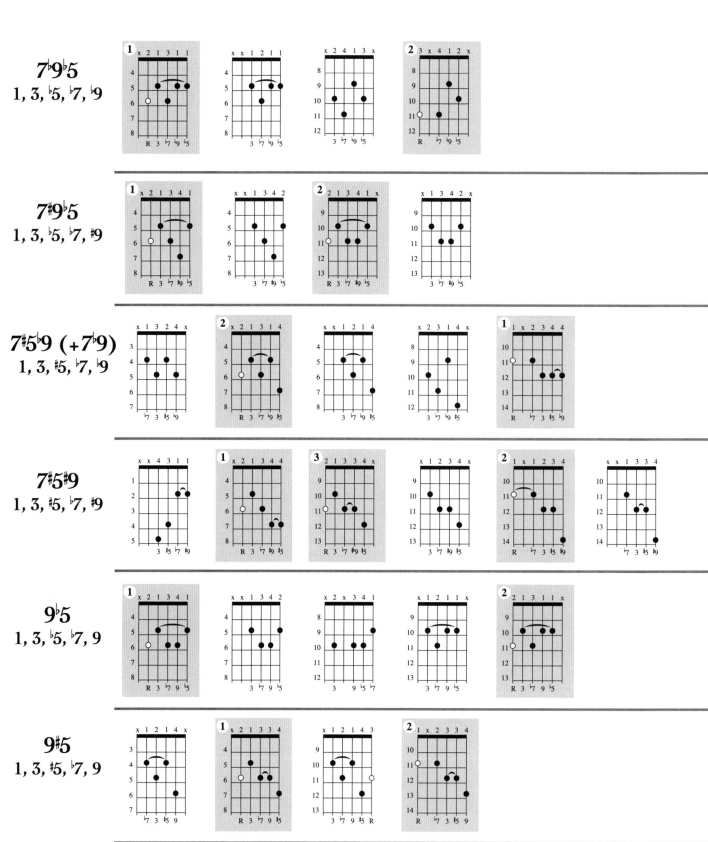

7♭9♭5
1, 3, ♭5, ♭7, ♭9

7♯9♭5
1, 3, ♭5, ♭7, ♯9

7♯5♭9 (+7♭9)
1, 3, ♯5, ♭7, ♭9

7♯5♯9
1, 3, ♯5, ♭7, ♯9

9♭5
1, 3, ♭5, ♭7, 9

9♯5
1, 3, ♯5, ♭7, 9

11♭5
1, 11, ♭5, ♭7

E♭
D♯

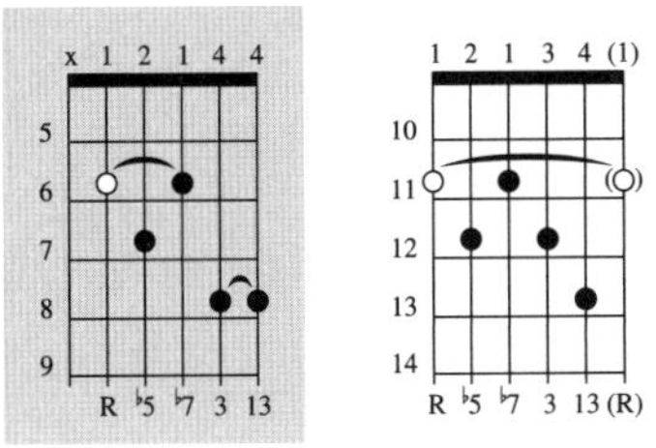

13♭5
1, 3, ♭5, ♭7, 13

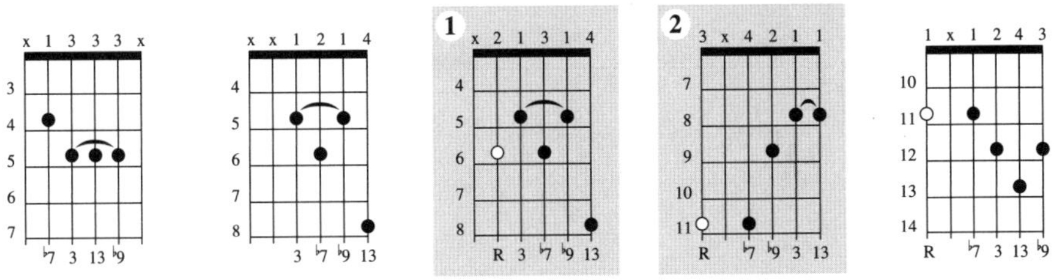

13♭9
1, 3, ♭7, ♭9, 13

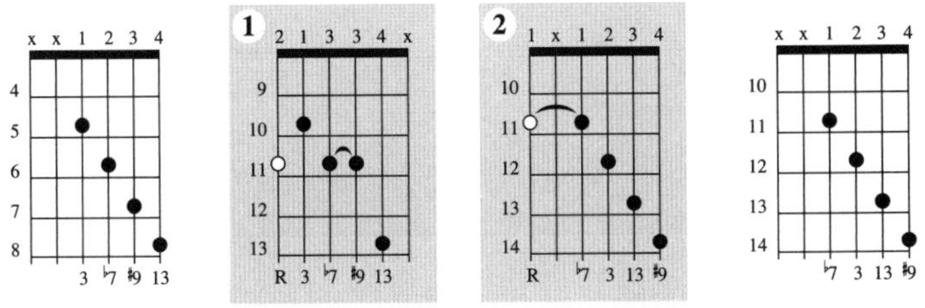

13#9
1, 3, ♭7, #9, 13

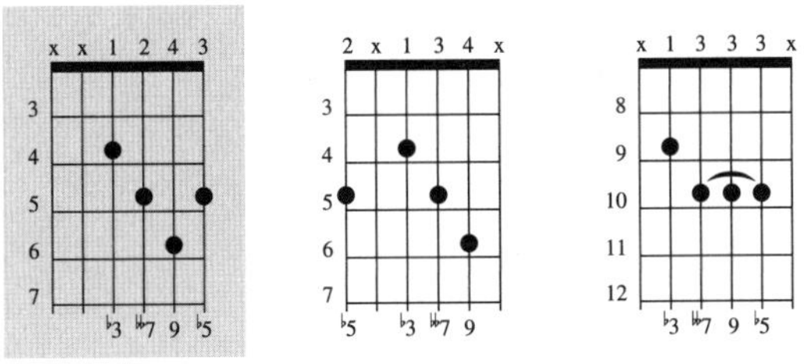

dim9
1, ♭3, ♭5, ♭♭7, 9

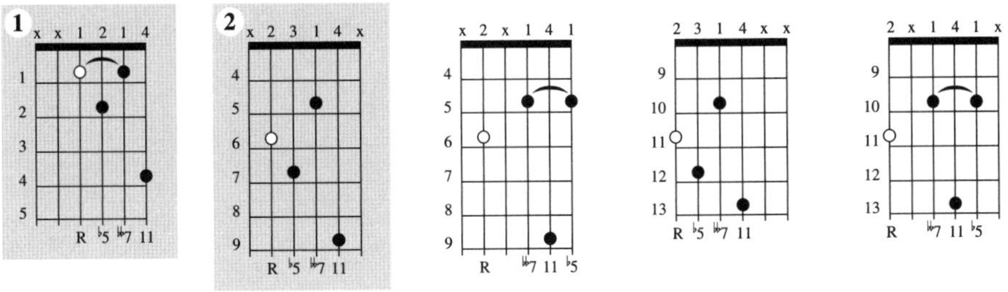

dim11
1, ♭5, ♭♭7, 11

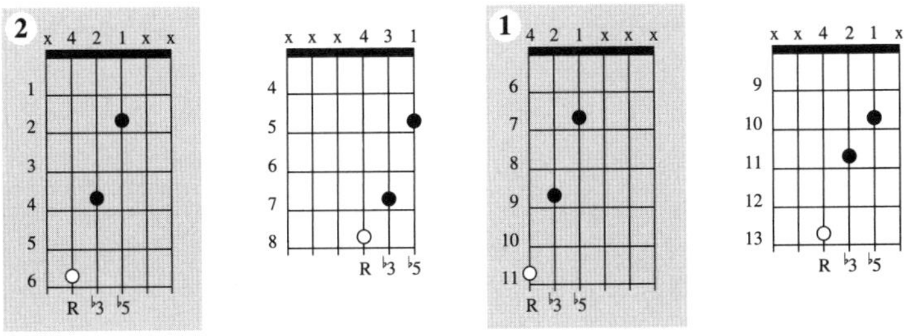

E♭
D#

dim
1, ♭3, ♭5

dim7 (°7)
1, ♭3, ♭5, ♭♭7

Three-Note Voicings

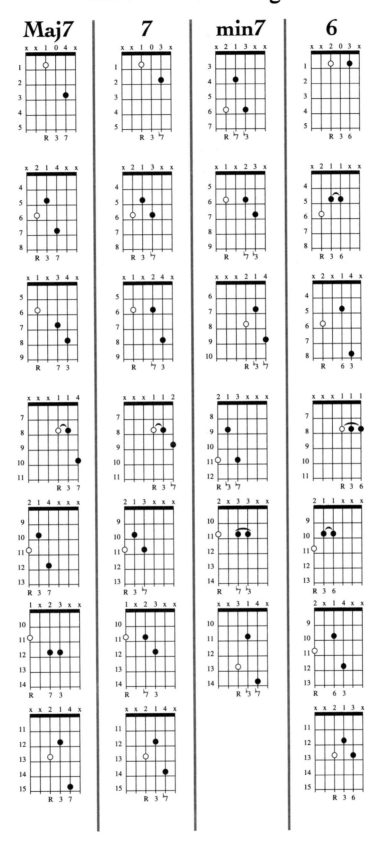

E♭
D♯

A♭/G♯

Maj
1, 3, 5

   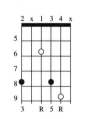  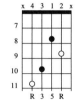

  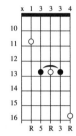 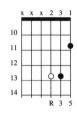

sus2
1, 2, 5

    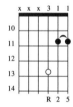

sus4
1, 4, 5

   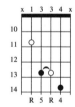

no 3rd
1, 5

 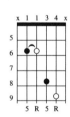 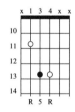

6
1, 3, 5, 6

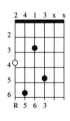  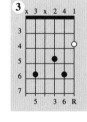   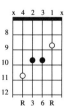

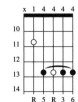 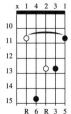

A♭
G♯

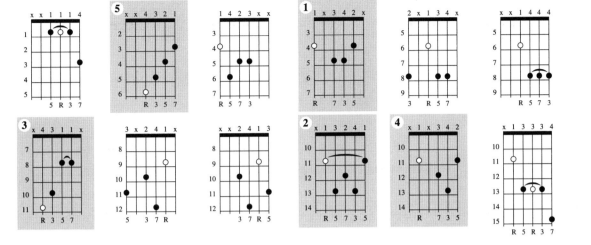

Maj7
1, 3, 5, 7

 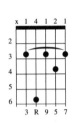 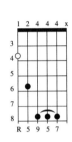 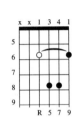 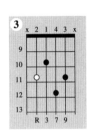 

Maj9
1, 3, 5, 7, 9

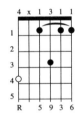   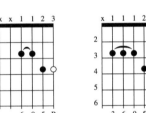 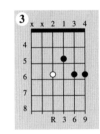

6/9
1, 3, 5, 6, 9

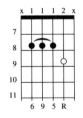  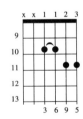

A♭
G♯

130

add9
1, 3, 5, 9

 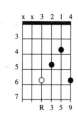 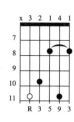 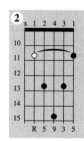

Maj11
1, 3, 5, 7, 11

 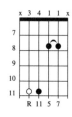 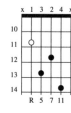 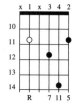

Maj13
1, 3, 5, 7, 13

 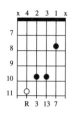 

Maj13add9
1, 3, 5, 7, 9, 13

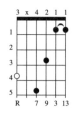   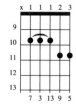

Maj13♯11
1, 3, 7, ♯11, 13

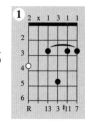  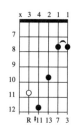 

A♭ G♯

Maj7♯5
1, 3, ♯5, 7

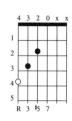  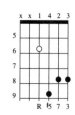  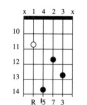 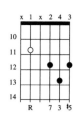

    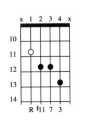 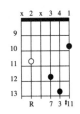

Maj7♯11
1, 3, 7, ♯11

 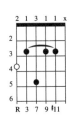 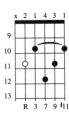

Maj9♯11
1, 3, 7, 9, ♯11

 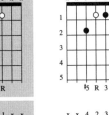 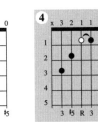

  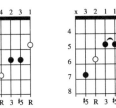

 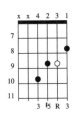 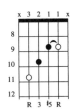 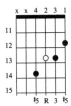

Augmented (aug)
1, 3, ♯5

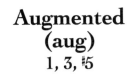
A♭
G♯

132

min
1, ♭3, 5

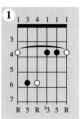 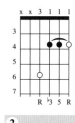 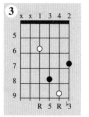 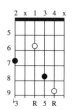 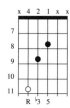 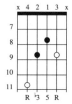

min6
1, ♭3, 5, 6

 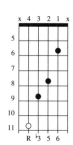 

min7
1, ♭3, 5, ♭7

A♭
G♯

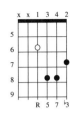
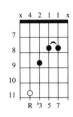

minMaj7
1, ♭3, 5, 7

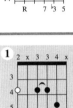

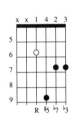
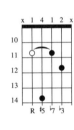

min7♯5
1, ♭3, ♯5, ♭7

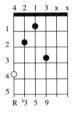

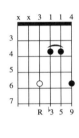

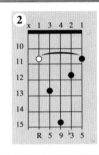

minadd9
1, ♭3, 5, 9

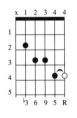

min6/9
1, ♭3, 5, 6, 9

A♭
G♯

minadd9/11
1, ♭3, 5, 9, 11

min9
1, ♭3, 5, ♭7, 9

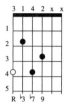   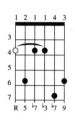  

 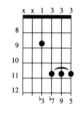 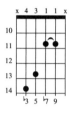

min9Maj7
1, ♭3, 5, 7, 9

  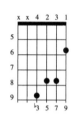 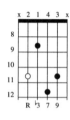 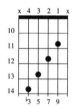

min9add11
1, ♭3, 5, ♭7, 9, 11

min11
1, ♭3, 5, ♭7, 11

A♭
G♯

 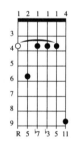    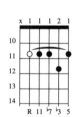

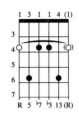   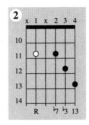

min13
1, ♭3, 5, ♭7, 13

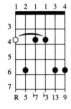  

min13add9
1, ♭3, 5, ♭7, 9, 13

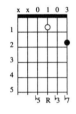 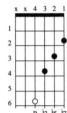  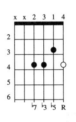  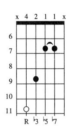

   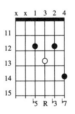

min7♭5
1, ♭3, ♭5, ♭7

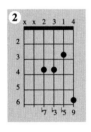  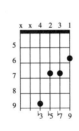 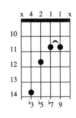 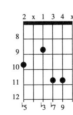 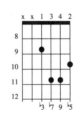

min9♭5
1, ♭3, ♭5, ♭7, 9

A♭
G♯

7
1, 3, 5, ♭7

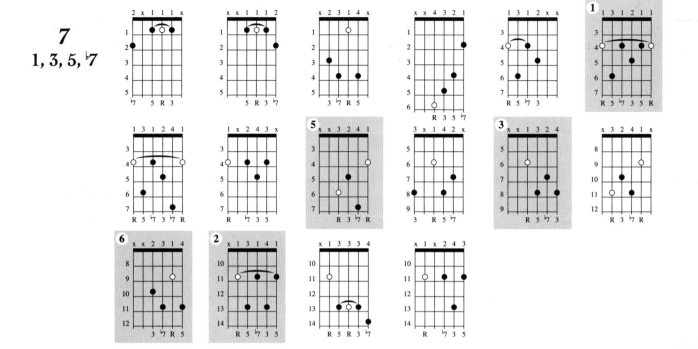

9
1, 3, 5, ♭7, 9

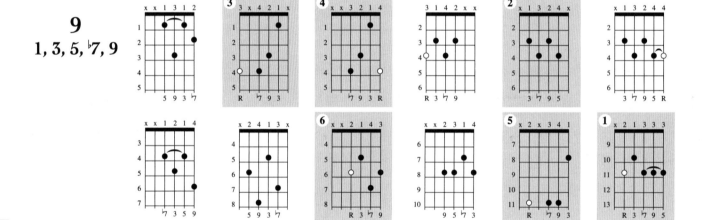

A♭
G♯

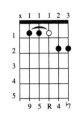   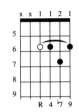 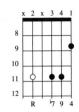 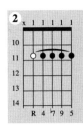

9sus4
1, 4, 5, ♭7, 9

 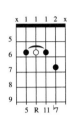  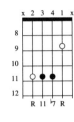  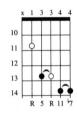

11(7sus4)
1, 5, ♭7, 11

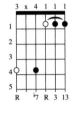   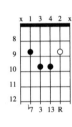 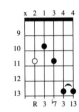 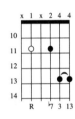

13
1, 3, 5, ♭7, 13

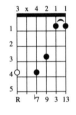   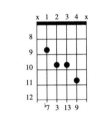 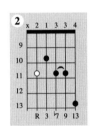

13add9
1, 3, 5, ♭7, 9, 13

A♭
G♯

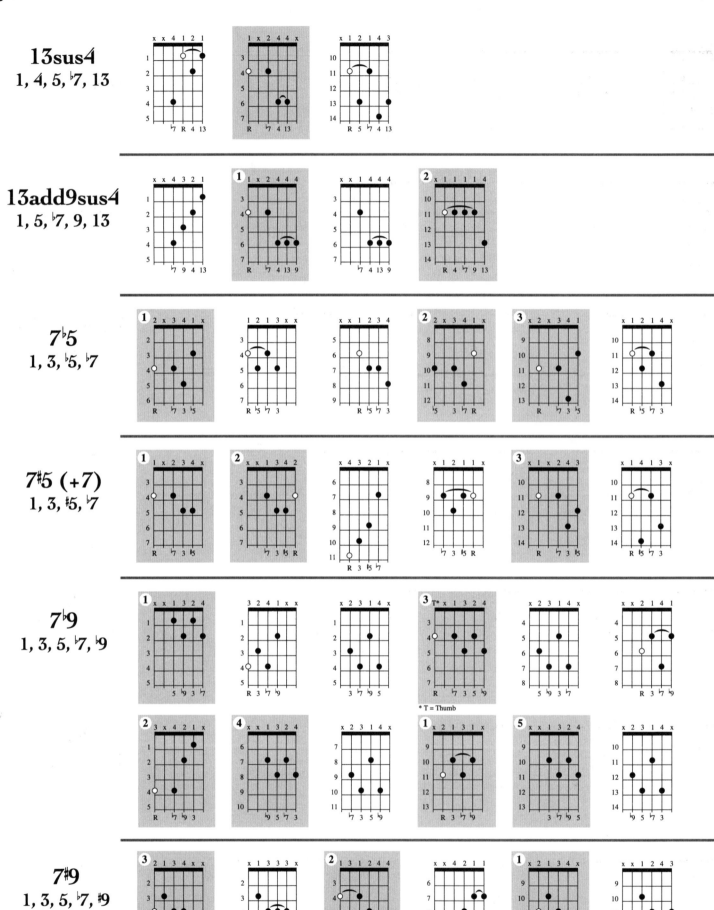

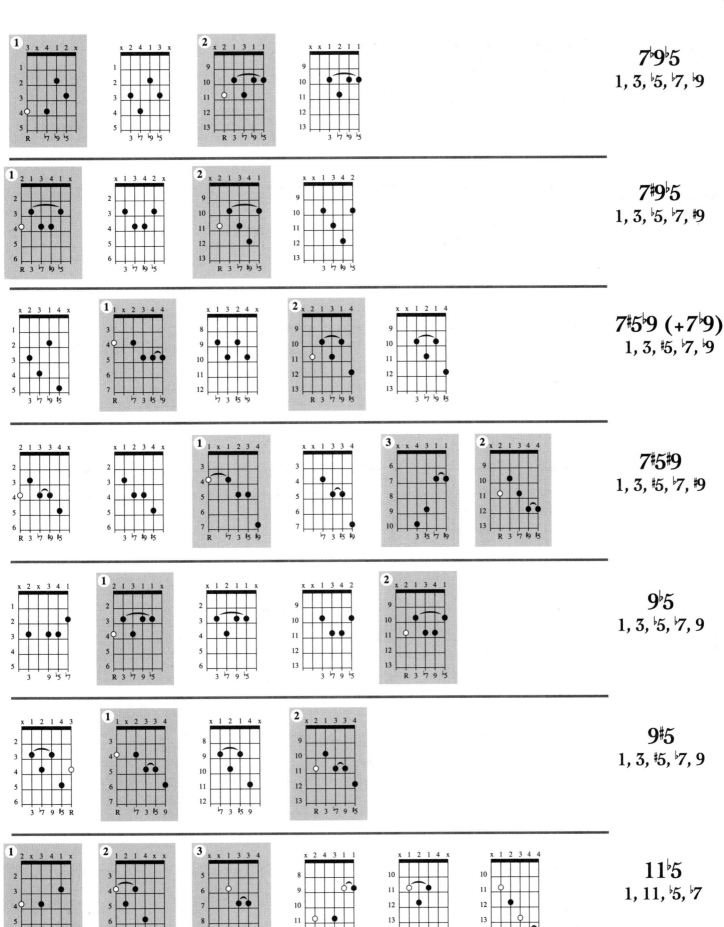

7♭9♭5
1, 3, ♭5, ♭7, ♭9

7♯9♭5
1, 3, ♭5, ♭7, ♯9

7♯5♭9 (+7♭9)
1, 3, ♯5, ♭7, ♭9

7♯5♯9
1, 3, ♯5, ♭7, ♯9

9♭5
1, 3, ♭5, ♭7, 9

9♯5
1, 3, ♯5, ♭7, 9

11♭5
1, 11, ♭5, ♭7

A♭
G♯

13♭5
1, 3, ♭5, ♭7, 13

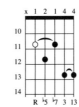

13♭9
1, 3, ♭7, ♭9, 13

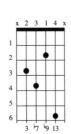

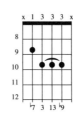
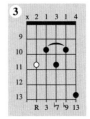
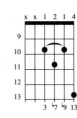

13♯9
1, 3, ♭7, ♯9, 13

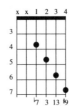
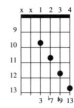

dim9
1, ♭3, ♭5, ♭♭7, 9

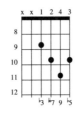
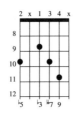

dim11
1, ♭5, ♭♭7, 11

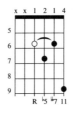
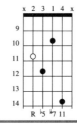
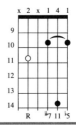

dim
1, ♭3, ♭5

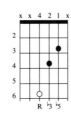

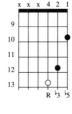

A♭
G♯

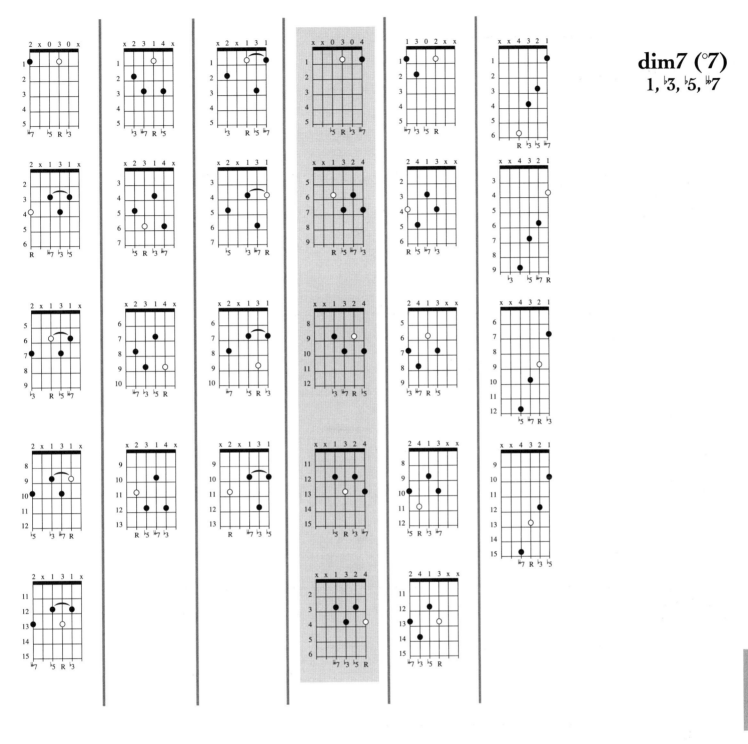

dim7 (°7)
1, ♭3, ♭5, ♭♭7

A♭
G#

Three-Note Voicings

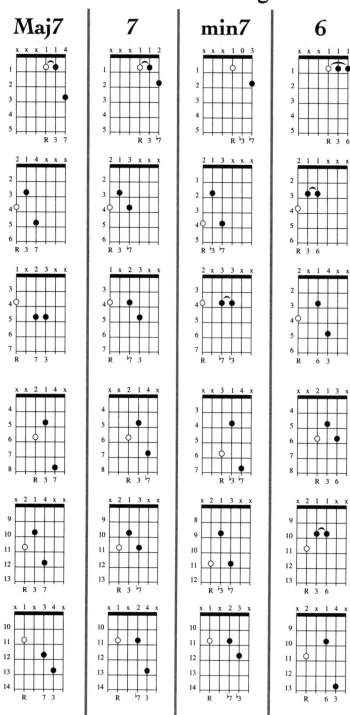

D♭/C♯

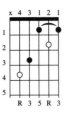

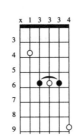
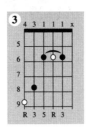

Maj
1, 3, 5

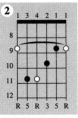
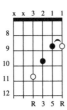
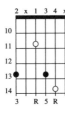

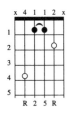

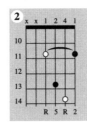

sus2
1, 2, 5

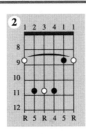
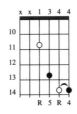

sus4
1, 4, 5

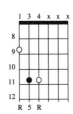
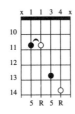

no 3rd
1, 5

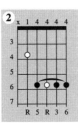
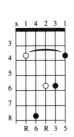

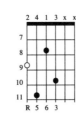

6
1, 3, 5, 6

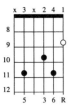
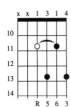

144

Maj7
1, 3, 5, 7

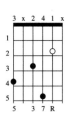

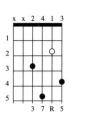

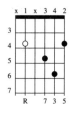
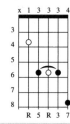

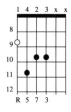

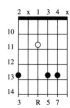

Maj9
1, 3, 5, 7, 9

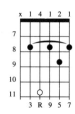
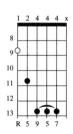
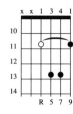

6/9
1, 3, 5, 6, 9

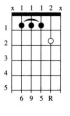

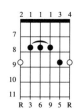

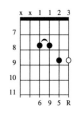

D♭
C♯

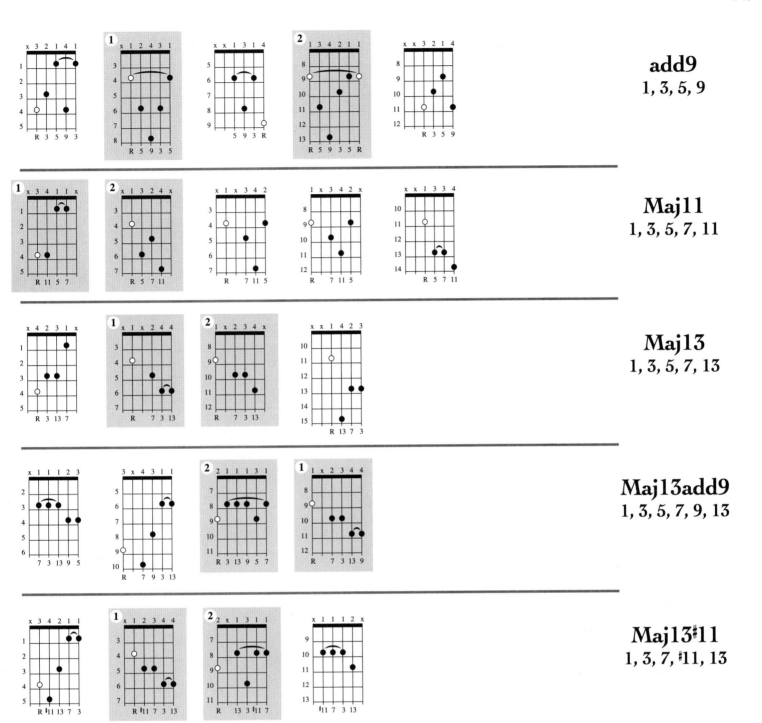

add9
1, 3, 5, 9

Maj11
1, 3, 5, 7, 11

Maj13
1, 3, 5, 7, 13

Maj13add9
1, 3, 5, 7, 9, 13

Maj13#11
1, 3, 7, #11, 13

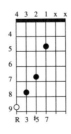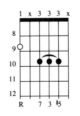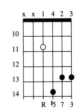

Maj7#5
1, 3, #5, 7

D♭
C#

Maj7#11
1, 3, 7, #11

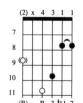
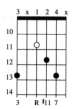
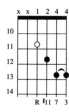

Maj9#11
1, 3, 7, 9, #11

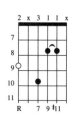
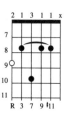

Augmented
(aug)
1, 3, #5

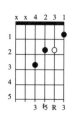

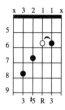
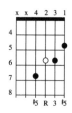

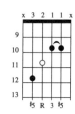
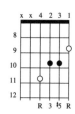

D♭
C♯

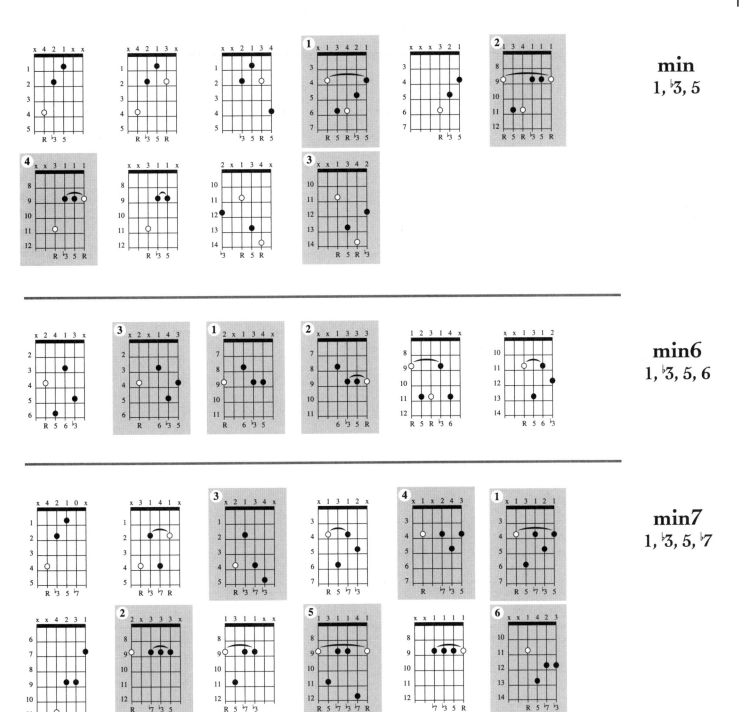

min
1, ♭3, 5

min6
1, ♭3, 5, 6

min7
1, ♭3, 5, ♭7

D♭
C♯

148

minMaj7
1, ♭3, 5, 7

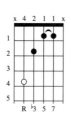  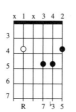 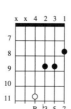  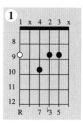

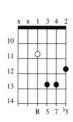

min7♯5
1, ♭3, ♯5, ♭7

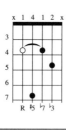  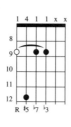  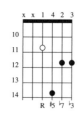

minadd9
1, ♭3, 5, 9

 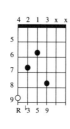  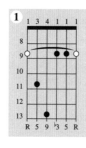 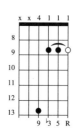 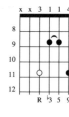

min6/9
1, ♭3, 5, 6, 9

 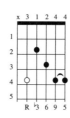 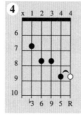   

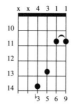

D♭
C♯

minadd9/11
1, ♭3, 5, 9, 11

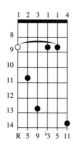

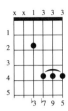
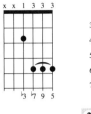
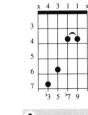
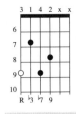
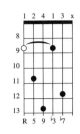

min9
1, ♭3, 5, ♭7, 9

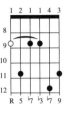
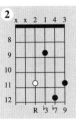

min9Maj7
1, ♭3, 5, 7, 9

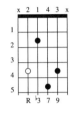
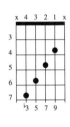

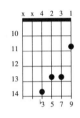

min9add11
1, ♭3, 5, ♭7, 9, 11

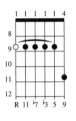
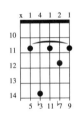

min11
1, ♭3, 5, ♭7, 11

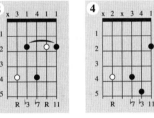

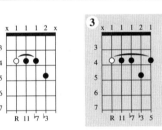

D♭
C#

150

min13
1, ♭3, 5, ♭7, 13

  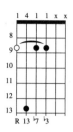 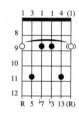

min13add9
1, ♭3, 5, ♭7, 9, 13

 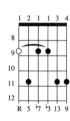 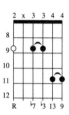

min7♭5
1, ♭3, ♭5, ♭7

 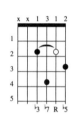   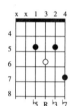 

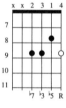  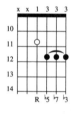

min9♭5
1, ♭3, ♭5, ♭7, 9

  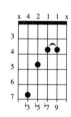   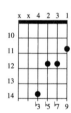

D♭
C♯

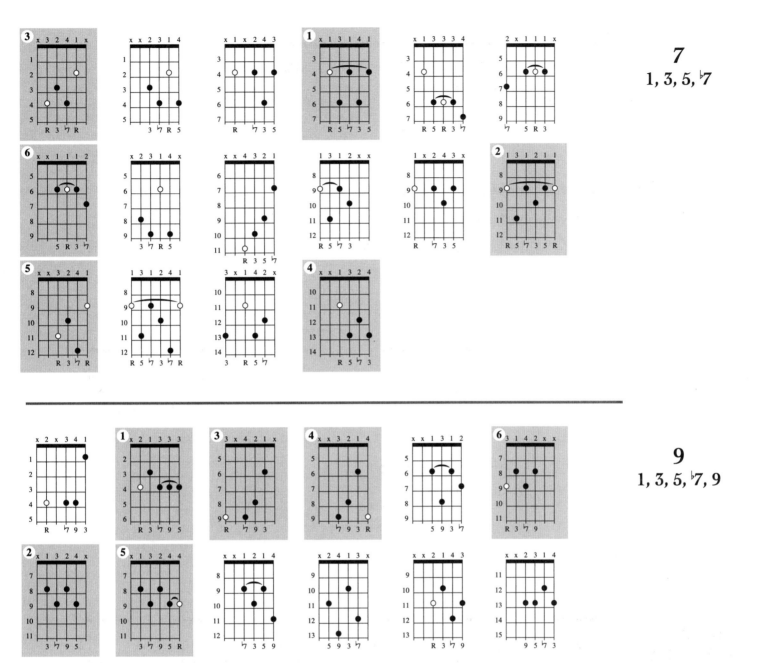

7
1, 3, 5, ♭7

9
1, 3, 5, ♭7, 9

D♭
C♯

9sus4
1, 4, 5, ♭7, 9

11(7sus4)
1, 5, ♭7, 11

13
1, 3, 5, ♭7, 13

13add9
1, 3, 5, ♭7, 9, 13

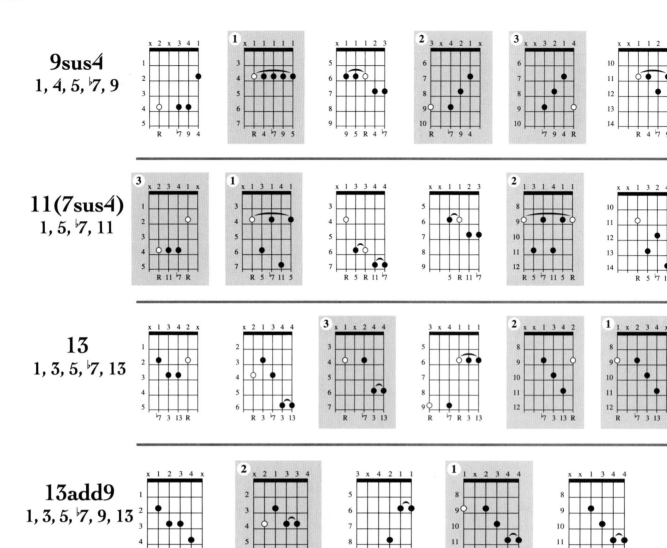

D♭
C#

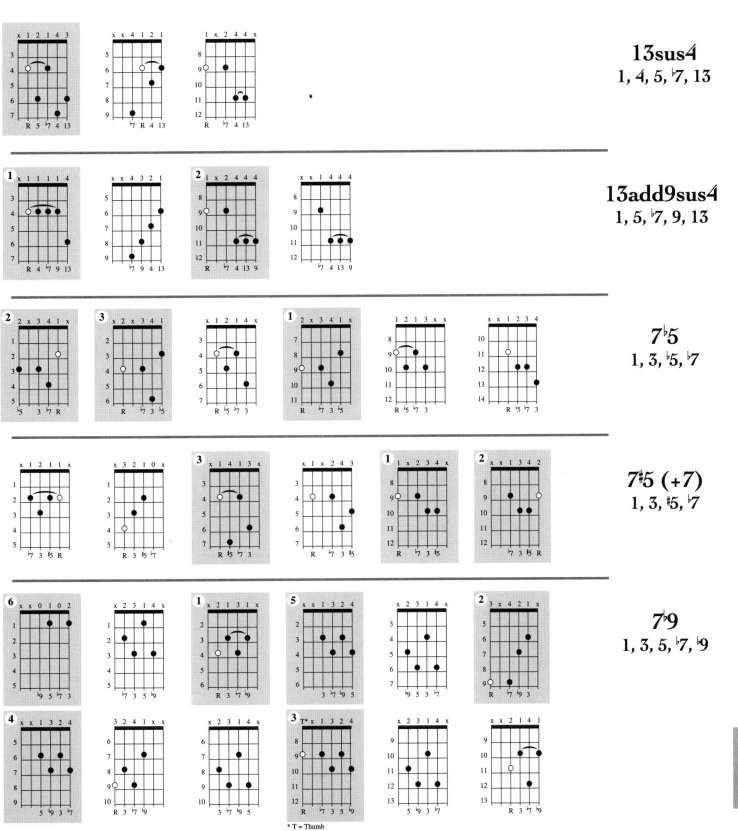

13sus4
1, 4, 5, ♭7, 13

13add9sus4
1, 5, ♭7, 9, 13

7♭5
1, 3, ♭5, ♭7

7♯5 (+7)
1, 3, ♯5, ♭7

7♭9
1, 3, 5, ♭7, ♭9

7♯9
1, 3, 5, ♭7, ♯9

* T = Thumb

D♭
C♯

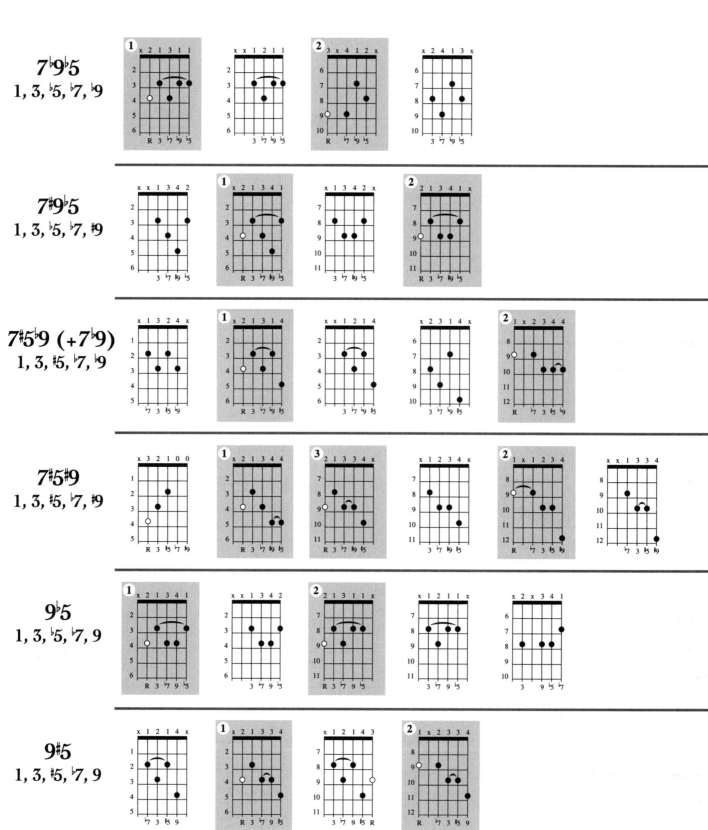

7♭9♭5
1, 3, ♭5, ♭7, ♭9

7♯9♭5
1, 3, ♭5, ♭7, ♯9

7♯5♭9 (+7♭9)
1, 3, ♯5, ♭7, ♭9

7♯5♯9
1, 3, ♯5, ♭7, ♯9

9♭5
1, 3, ♭5, ♭7, 9

9♯5
1, 3, ♯5, ♭7, 9

11♭5
1, 11, ♭5, ♭7

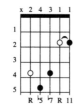

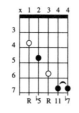
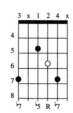

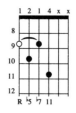

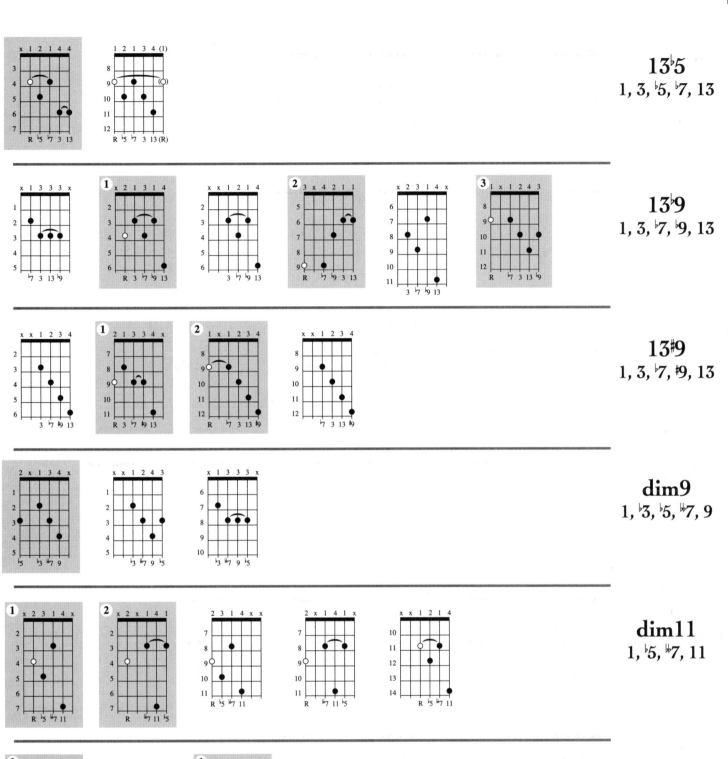

13♭5
1, 3, ♭5, ♭7, 13

13♭9
1, 3, ♭7, ♭9, 13

13♯9
1, 3, ♭7, ♯9, 13

dim9
1, ♭3, ♭5, ♭♭7, 9

dim11
1, ♭5, ♭♭7, 11

dim
1, ♭3, ♭5

D♭
C♯

dim7 (°7)
1, ♭3, ♭5, ♭♭7

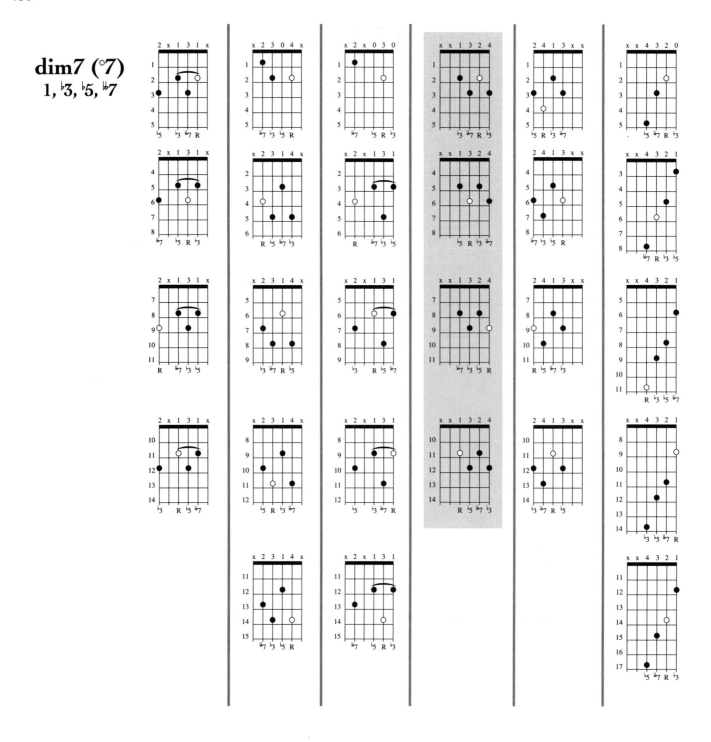

Three-Note Voicings

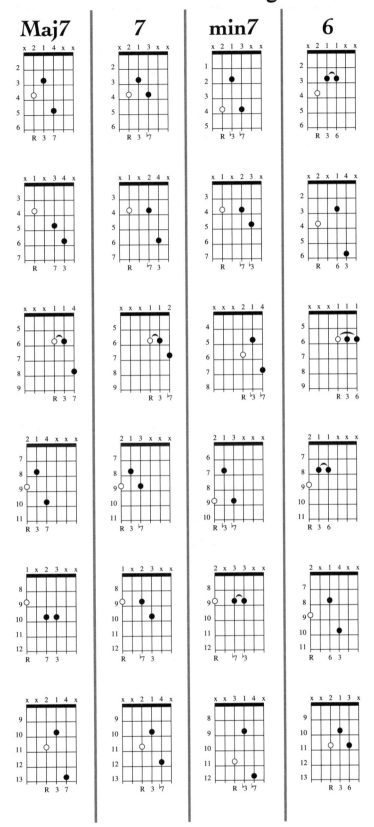

G♭/F♯

Maj
1, 3, 5

   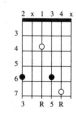  

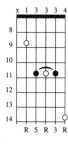 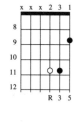 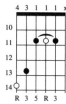

sus2
1, 2, 5

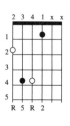    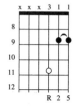

sus4
1, 4, 5

  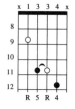 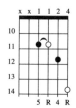

no 3rd
1,5

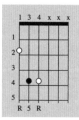 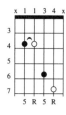 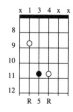

6
1, 3, 5, 6

 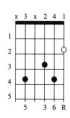 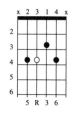   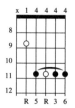

G♭ F♯

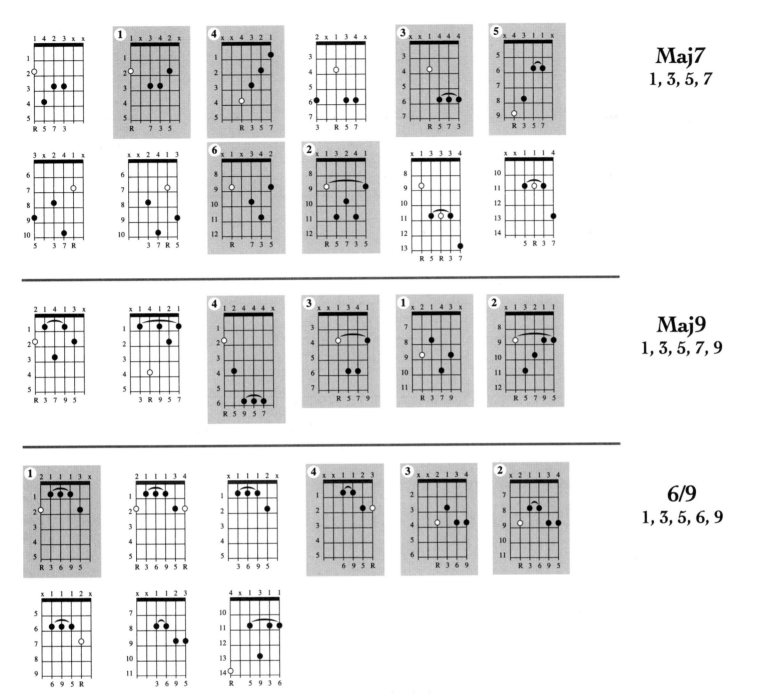

Maj7
1, 3, 5, 7

Maj9
1, 3, 5, 7, 9

6/9
1, 3, 5, 6, 9

G♭
F♯

add9
1, 3, 5, 9

 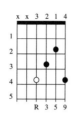 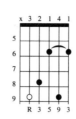  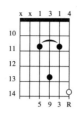

Maj11
1, 3, 5, 7, 11

  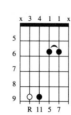 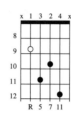 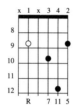

Maj13
1, 3, 5, 7, 13

 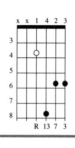 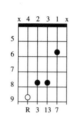 

Maj13add9
1, 3, 5, 7, 9, 13

  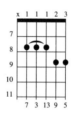 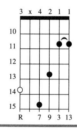

Maj13#11
1, 3, 7, #11, 13

 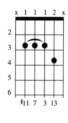 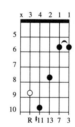 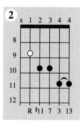

Maj7#5
1, 3, #5, 7

   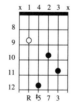 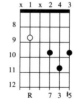 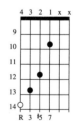

G♭
F#

  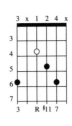 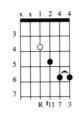 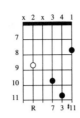 

Maj7♯11
1, 3, 7, ♯11

 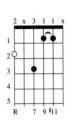 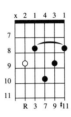

Maj9♯11
1, 3, 7, 9, ♯11

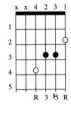  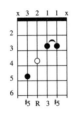

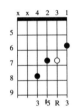  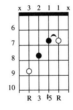

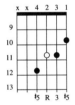 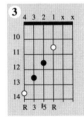 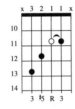

Augmented (aug)
1, 3, ♯5

G♭
F♯

min
1, ♭3, 5

min6
1, ♭3, 5, 6

min7
1, ♭3, 5, ♭7

G♭
F#

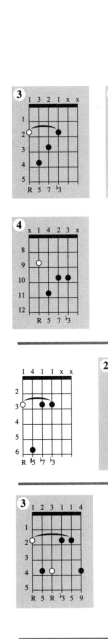
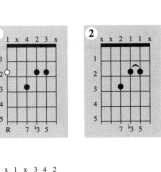
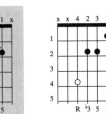
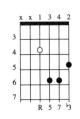
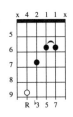

minMaj7
1, ♭3, 5, 7

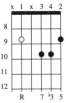

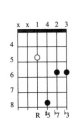
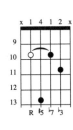

min7♯5
1, ♭3, ♯5, ♭7

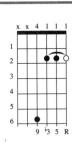
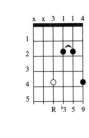

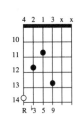

minadd9
1, ♭3, 5, 9

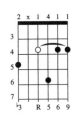

min6/9
1, ♭3, 5, 6, 9

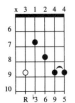

G♭
F♯

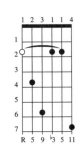

minadd9/11
1, ♭3, 5, 9, 11

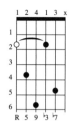

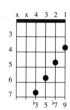

min9
1, ♭3, 5, ♭7, 9

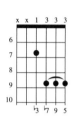

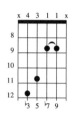

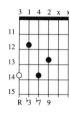

min9Maj7
1, ♭3, 5, 7, 9

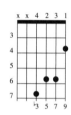

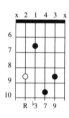

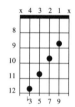

min9add11
1, ♭3, 5, ♭7, 9, 11

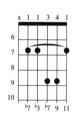

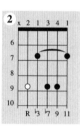

min11
1, ♭3, 5, ♭7, 11

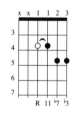

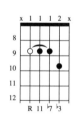

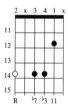

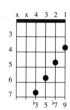

G♭
F♯

164

 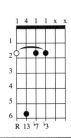 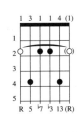 

min13
1, ♭3, 5, ♭7, 13

 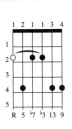 

min13add9
1, ♭3, 5, ♭7, 9, 13

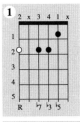 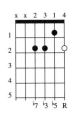 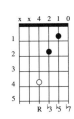 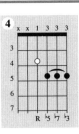 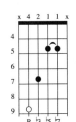 

min7♭5
1, ♭3, ♭5, ♭7

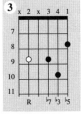 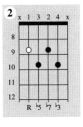 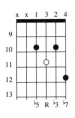

   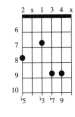 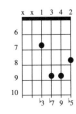 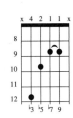

min9♭5
1, ♭3, ♭5, ♭7, 9

G♭
F♯

7
1, 3, 5, ♭7

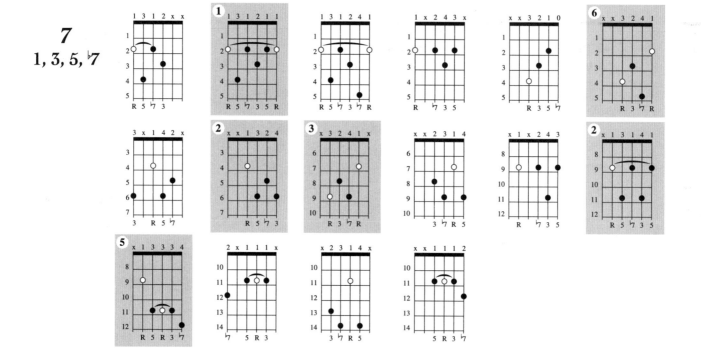

9
1, 3, 5, ♭7, 9

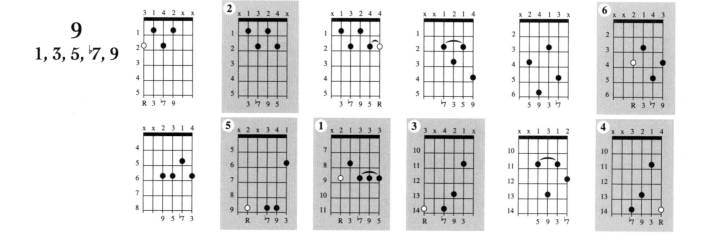

G♭
F#

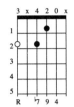 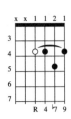   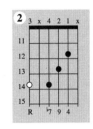 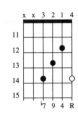

9sus4
1, 4, 5, ♭7, 9

 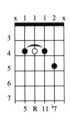  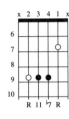  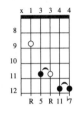

11(7sus4)
1, 5, ♭7, 11

   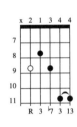 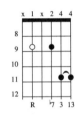 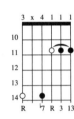

13
1, 3, 5, ♭7, 13

 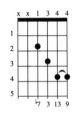 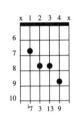  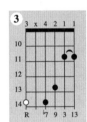

13add9
1, 3, 5, ♭7, 9, 13

G♭
F#

13sus4
1, 4, 5, ♭7, 13

 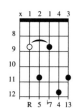 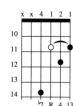

13add9sus4
1, 5, ♭7, 9, 13

  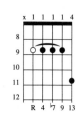 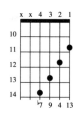

7♭5
1, 3, ♭5, ♭7

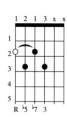 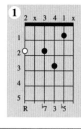    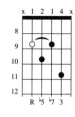

7♯5 (+7)
1, 3, ♯5, ♭7

 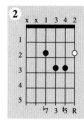  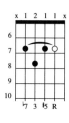 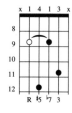 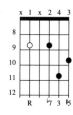

7♭9
1, 3, 5, ♭7, ♭9

 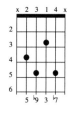   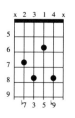 

* T = Thumb

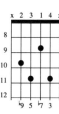  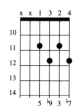 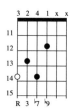 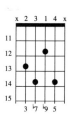

G♭
F♯

7♯9
1, 3, 5, ♭7, ♯9

 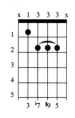  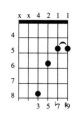  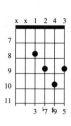

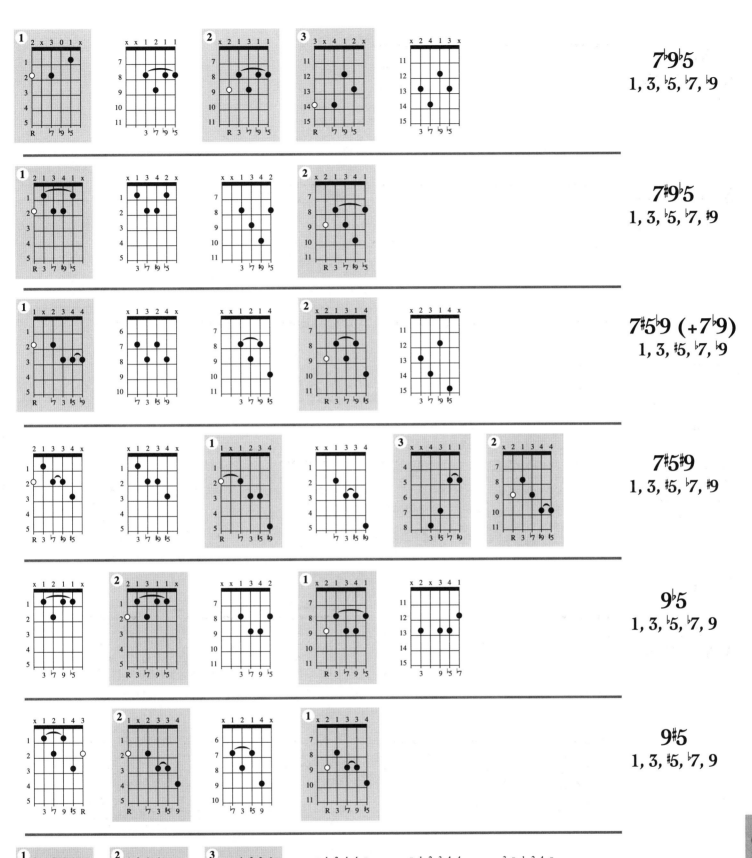

7♭9♭5
1, 3, ♭5, ♭7, ♭9

7#9♭5
1, 3, ♭5, ♭7, #9

7#5♭9 (+7♭9)
1, 3, #5, ♭7, ♭9

7#5#9
1, 3, #5, ♭7, #9

9♭5
1, 3, ♭5, ♭7, 9

9#5
1, 3, #5, ♭7, 9

11♭5
1, 11, ♭5, ♭7

G♭
F#

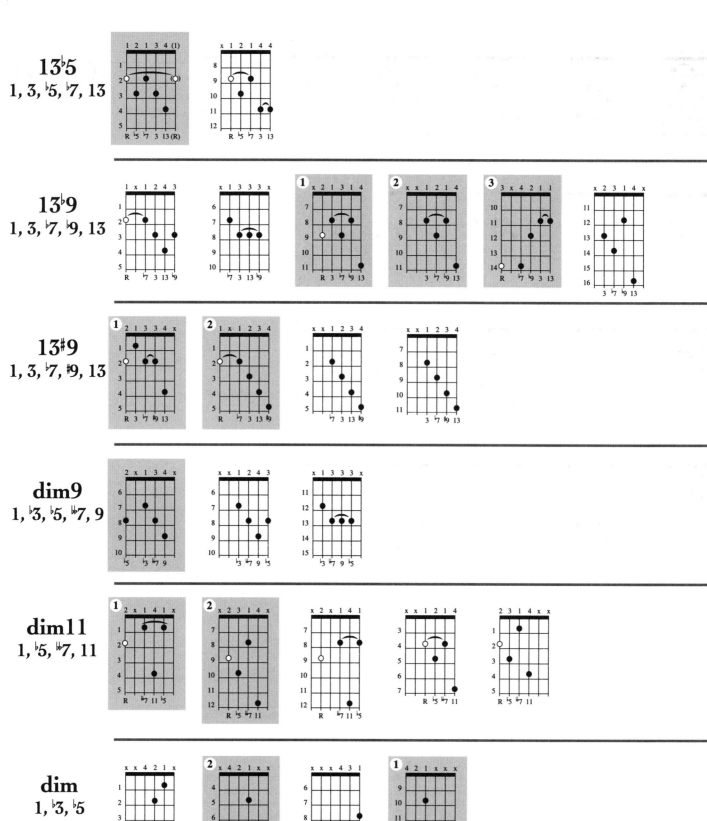

13♭5
1, 3, ♭5, ♭7, 13

13♭9
1, 3, ♭7, ♭9, 13

13♯9
1, 3, ♭7, ♯9, 13

dim9
1, ♭3, ♭5, ♭♭7, 9

dim11
1, ♭5, ♭♭7, 11

dim
1, ♭3, ♭5

G♭
F♯

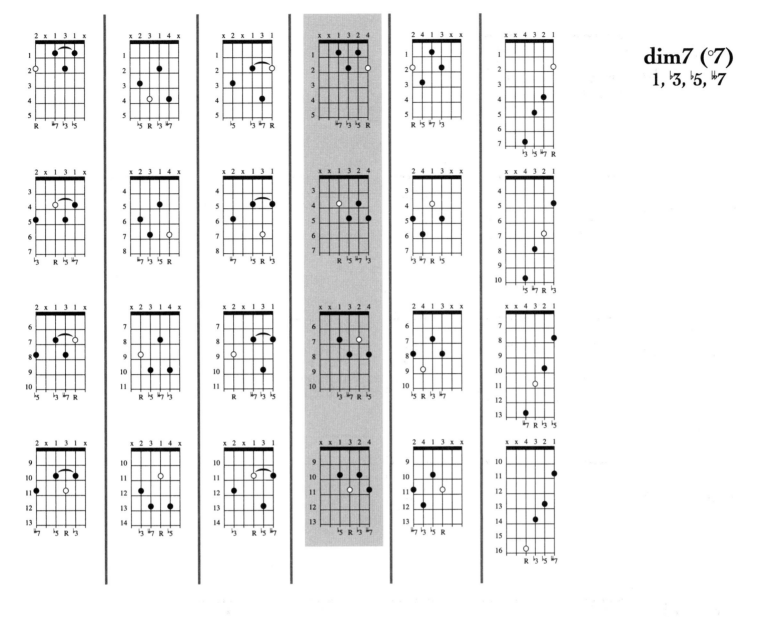

dim7 (°7)
1, ♭3, ♭5, ♭♭7

G♭
F#

Three-Note Voicings

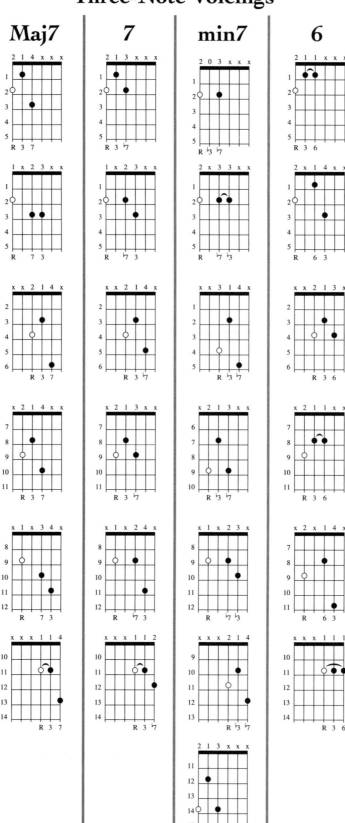

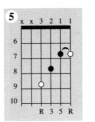

Maj
1, 3, 5

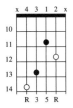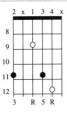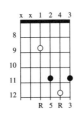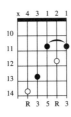

sus2
1, 2, 5

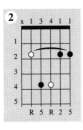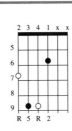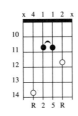

sus4
1, 4, 5

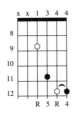

no 3rd
1, 5

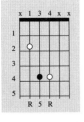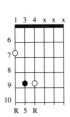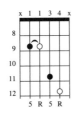

6
1, 3, 5, 6

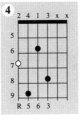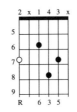
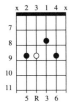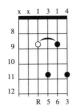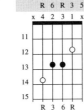

B

Maj7
1, 3, 5, 7

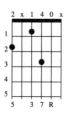 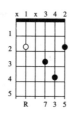  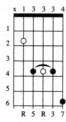 

 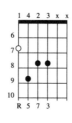  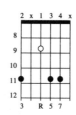  

Maj9
1, 3, 5, 7, 9

  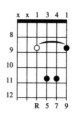 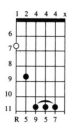 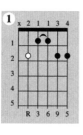 

6/9
1, 3, 5, 6, 9

   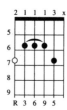 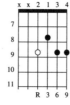

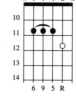

B

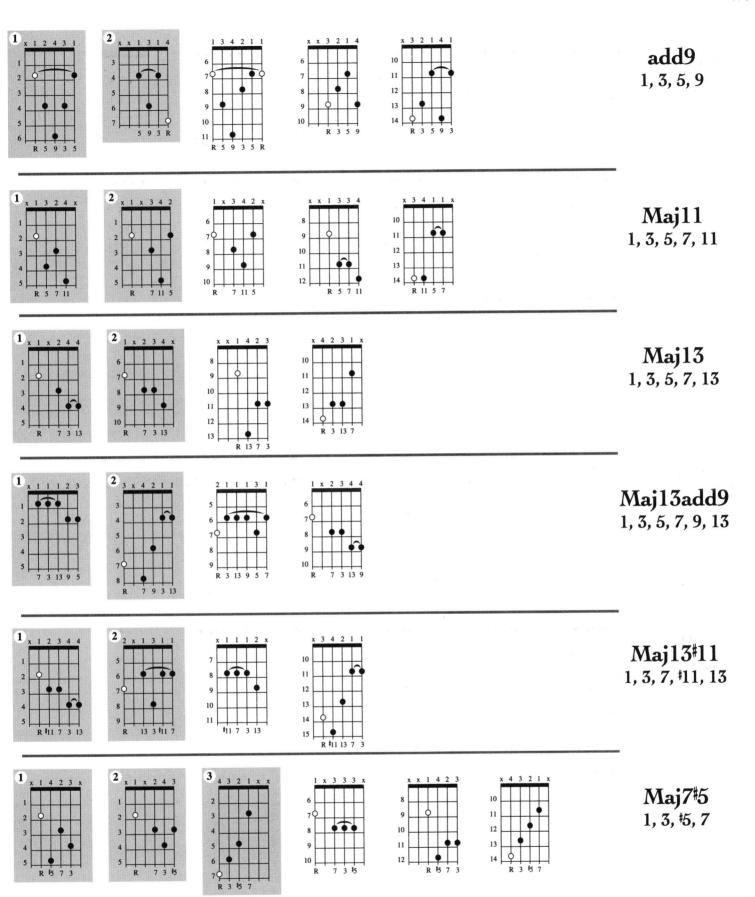

add9
1, 3, 5, 9

Maj11
1, 3, 5, 7, 11

Maj13
1, 3, 5, 7, 13

Maj13add9
1, 3, 5, 7, 9, 13

Maj13♯11
1, 3, 7, ♯11, 13

Maj7♯5
1, 3, ♯5, 7

B

Maj7♯11
1, 3, 7, ♯11

  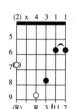 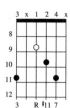 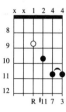

Maj9♯11
1, 3, 7, 9, ♯11

 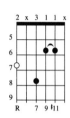 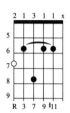

Augmented (aug)
1, 3, ♯5

  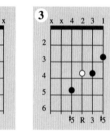 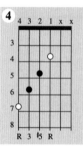

 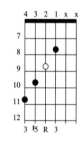 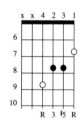 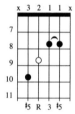

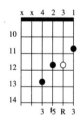 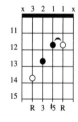 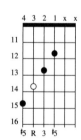

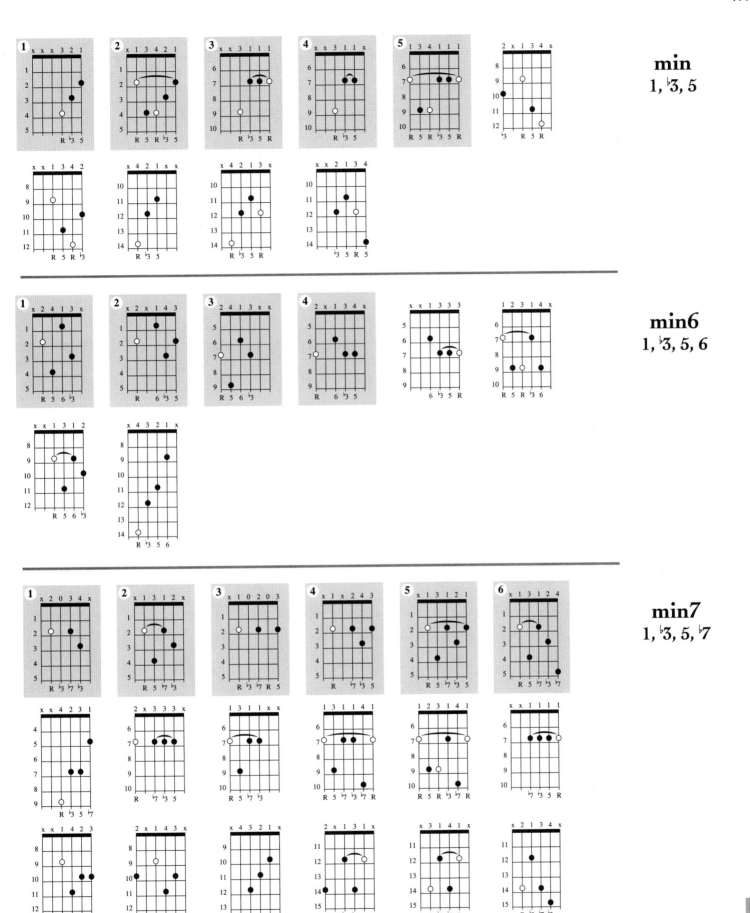

min
1, ♭3, 5

min6
1, ♭3, 5, 6

min7
1, ♭3, 5, ♭7

B

minMaj7
1, ♭3, 5, 7

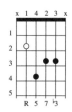 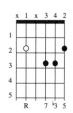    

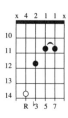

min7♯5
1, ♭3, ♯5, ♭7

  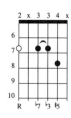 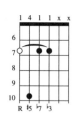 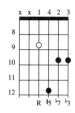

minadd9
1, ♭3, 5, 9

   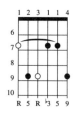 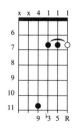 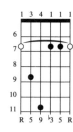

min6/9
1, ♭3, 5, 6, 9

  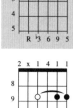  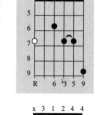 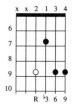

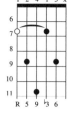 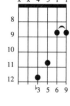 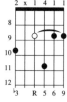 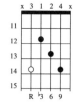

minadd9/11
1, ♭3, 5, 9, 11

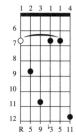

B

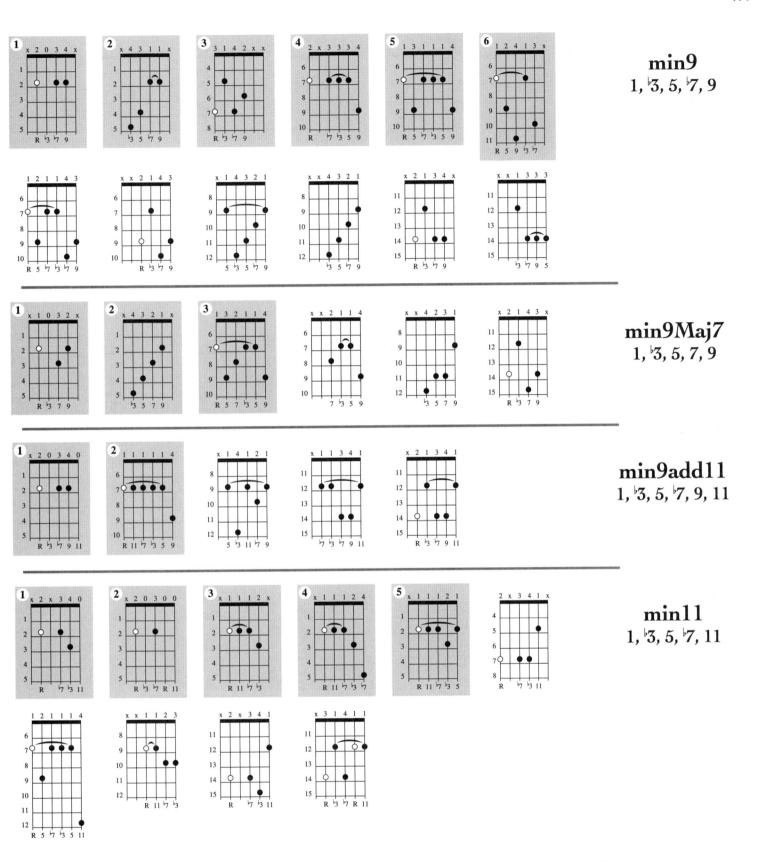

min9
1, ♭3, 5, ♭7, 9

min9Maj7
1, ♭3, 5, 7, 9

min9add11
1, ♭3, 5, ♭7, 9, 11

min11
1, ♭3, 5, ♭7, 11

B

min13
1, ♭3, 5, ♭7, 13

  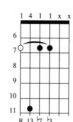 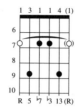

min13add9
1, ♭3, 5, ♭7, 9, 13

 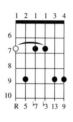 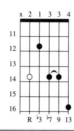

min7♭5
1, ♭3, ♭5, ♭7

     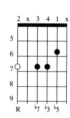

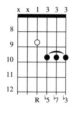 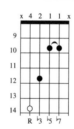 

min9♭5
1, ♭3, ♭5, ♭7, 9

    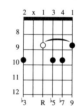 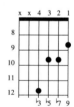

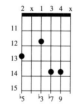 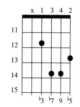

B

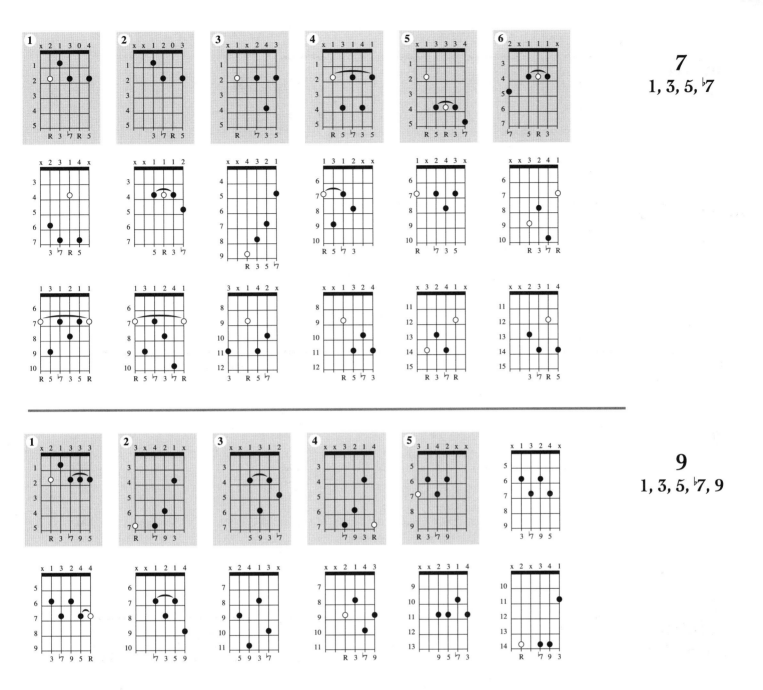

7
1, 3, 5, ♭7

9
1, 3, 5, ♭7, 9

B

9sus4
1, 4, 5, ♭7, 9

   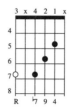 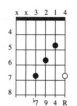 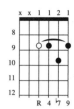

11(7sus4)
1, 5, ♭7, 11

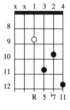 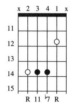

13
1, 3, 5, ♭7, 13

    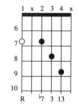 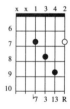

13add9
1, 3, 5, ♭7, 9, 13

  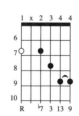 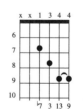 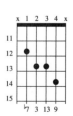

B

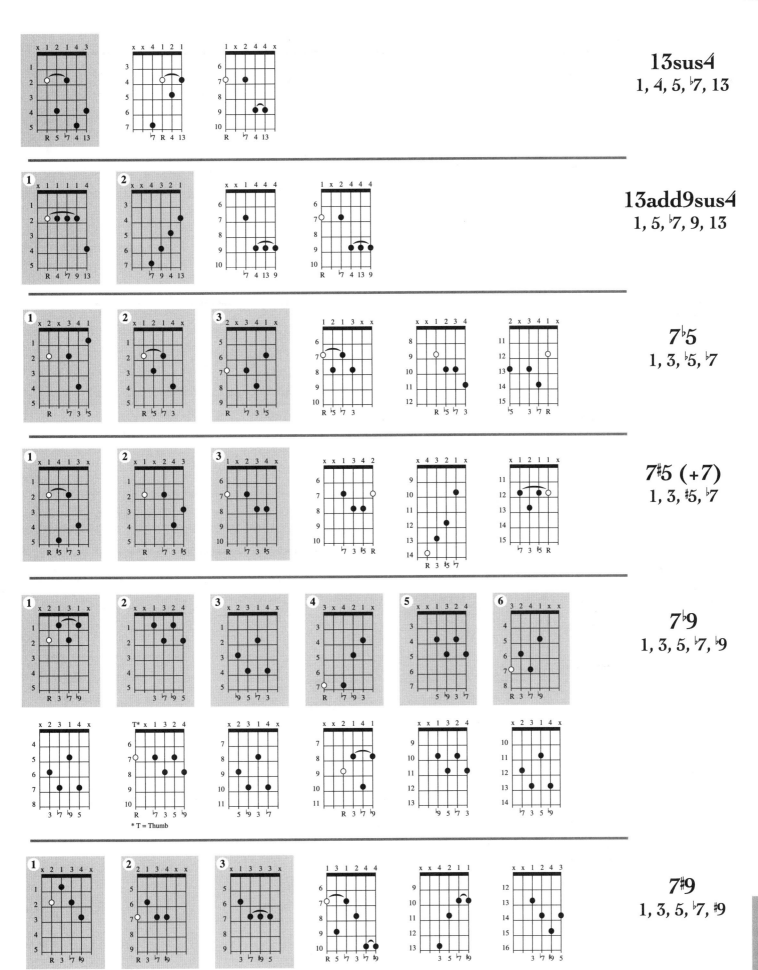

13sus4
1, 4, 5, ♭7, 13

13add9sus4
1, 5, ♭7, 9, 13

7♭5
1, 3, ♭5, ♭7

7♯5 (+7)
1, 3, ♯5, ♭7

7♭9
1, 3, 5, ♭7, ♭9

* T = Thumb

7♯9
1, 3, 5, ♭7, ♯9

B

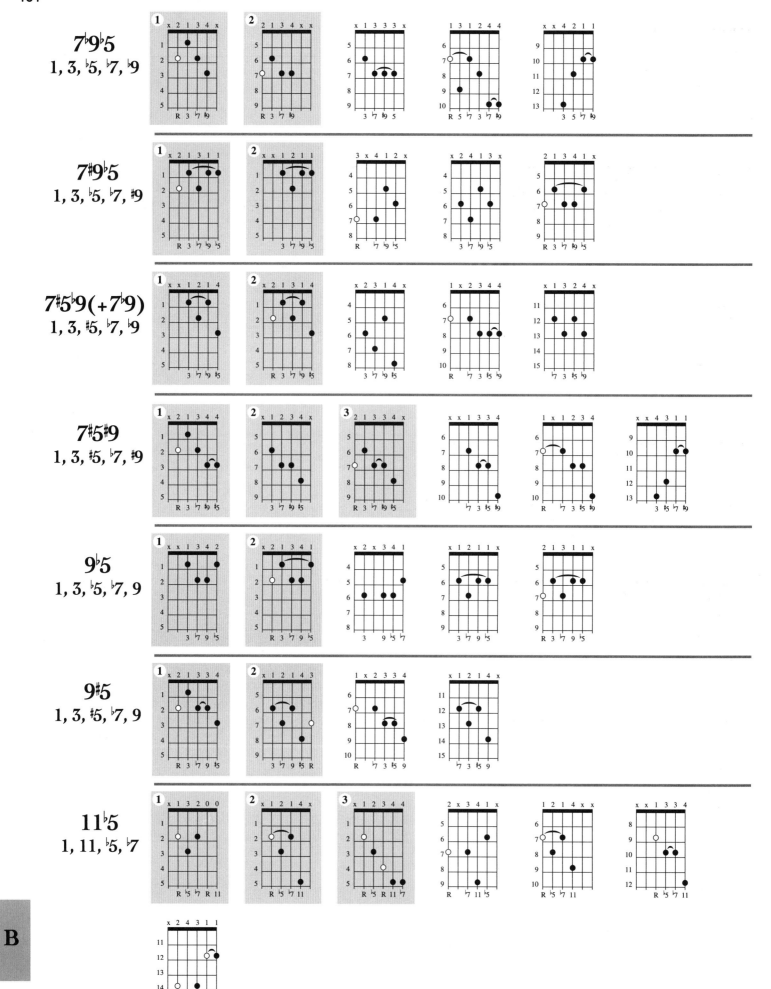

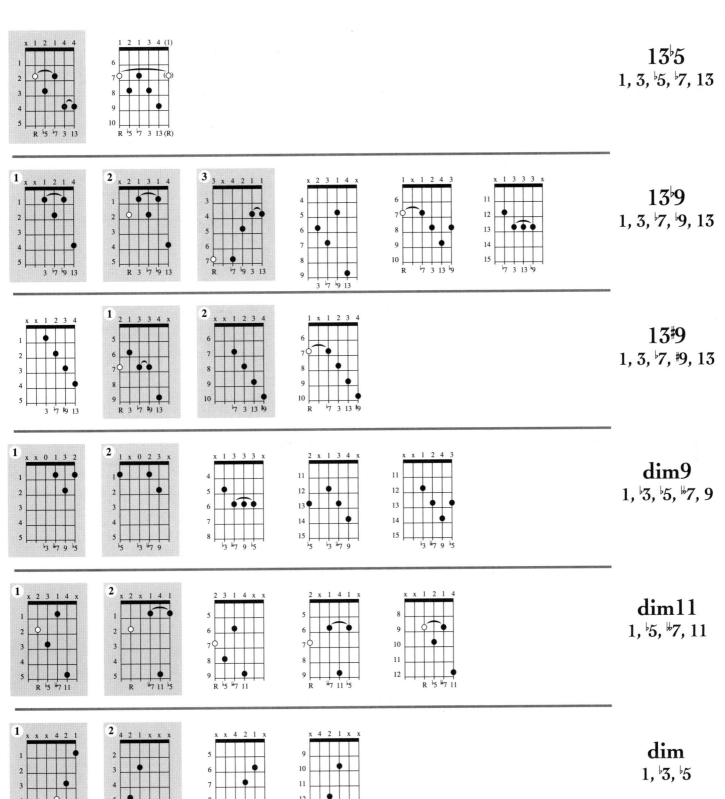

13♭5
1, 3, ♭5, ♭7, 13

13♭9
1, 3, ♭7, ♭9, 13

13#9
1, 3, ♭7, #9, 13

dim9
1, ♭3, ♭5, ♭♭7, 9

dim11
1, ♭5, ♭♭7, 11

dim
1, ♭3, ♭5

B

dim7 (°7)
1, ♭3, ♭5, ♭♭7

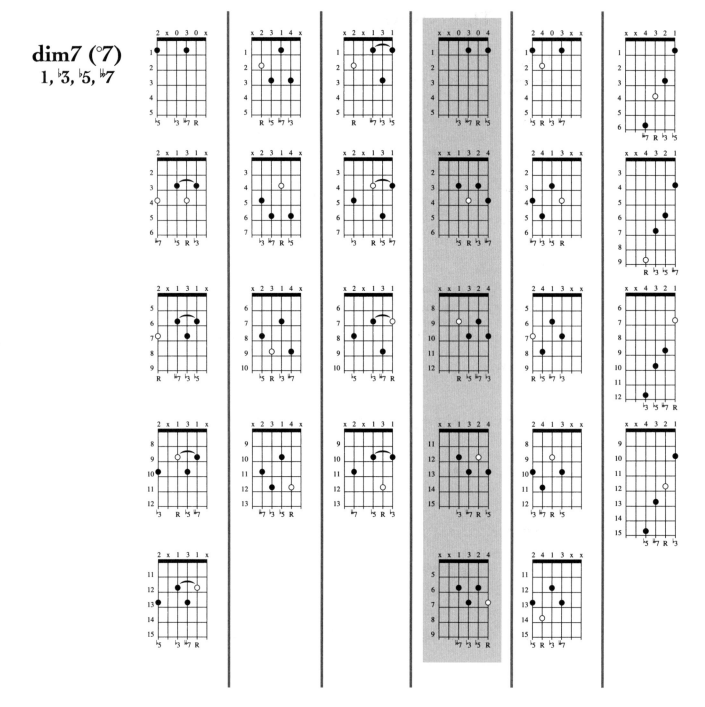

Three-Note Voicings

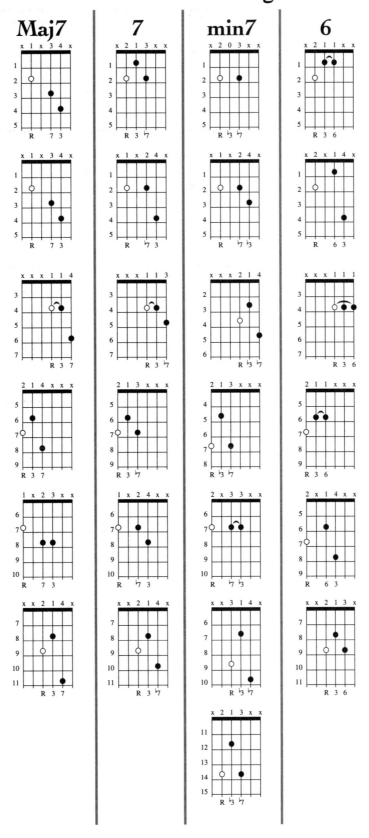

The Ultimate Guitar
SCALE BIBLE

Mark Dziuba

Contents

Contents—Scales Listed Alphabetically

SCALES LISTED BY TYPE

How to Use This Book

The *Ultimate Guitar Scale Bible* is a vast scale and chord/scale relationship reference tool. To get the most out of this book, a basic knowledge of music theory and improvisation will be helpful. All the scales in this book were chosen because of their usefulness in improvisational or compositional contexts. Use this book to supplement your existing scale knowledge and further your melodic and harmonic universe. Remember, these scales don't make the music. You do!

Each page includes:
- A brief description of the scale, including type, origin, construction and uses.
- A one-octave expression of the scale in standard music notation with tablature, always beginning with the note C as the root.
- An open position fingering with the note C as the root (the root is always shown as a black circle).
- A single-string fingering using the B (2nd) string with the note C as the root.
- Position fingerings in all twelve keys through the

circle of 4ths. In most cases, a large variety of different fingerings is offered in this section (rather than just the same fingering transposed around the fretboard). For an explanation of the circle of 4ths, see Appendix A on page 323.
- A two-note-per-string fingering, usually with an E root.
- A two-measure chord vamp over which to practice the scale (in standard notation with tablature and chord symbols).

The unique, two-measure vamps were created to help express the character of each scale. They were designed to be recorded or sequenced by you to use as backgrounds for exploration. Keep in mind that most of these vamps are based on the root of the scale described. All of the scales in this book may be superimposed over a variety of non-root based chord vamps. See page 325, "Diatonic Scale Superimposition."

I strongly suggest you read the appendices several times after paging through the book. They include important information on:
- Major scale construction and scale to "parallel major" comparison (used to determine the "flavor" of a scale).
- The circle of 4ths (the twelve keys)
- Definitions of important terms
- Scale and chord superimposition
- Practice techniques and suggestions
- Melodic harmony and how to create your own chord vamps

Each scale in this book can be classified into one of the following five types:

1. Harmonic System

    There are four harmonic systems (parent scales) used in Western music: major, harmonic minor, melodic minor (jazz minor) and harmonic major. Each one of these systems produces distinct modes that are derived by emphasizing different starting places within the scale. Each of these modes has its own unique tonality or sound.

2. Symmetric

    Symmetric scales are constructed from a repeating interval or set of intervals that equally divides the octave. These scales do not produce modes. A good example of this type of scale is the whole tone scale, constructed entirely of whole steps (for example, C-D-E-F#-G#-A#-C).

3. Hybrid

    Hybrid scales may contain elements of two or more common scales or may contain one or more "passing" or "chromatic" tones. For example, the *bebop dominant* scale (page 208) can be described as the *Mixolydian mode* (page 293, the 5th mode of the *major* scale, page 272) with a chromatic tone between the ♭7 and the root (C-D-E-F-G-A-B♭-B-C). In this book, hybrid also refers to any non-harmonic system or non-pentatonic variation.

4. Pentatonic

    Pentatonic usually refers to a five-note variation of the major scale and its relative minor. In this book, however, pentatonic scales include any five-note scale.

5. Exotic

    Any scale that is derived from a non-Western tradition. In this book, exotic scales are applied in a Western context. For example, *Kumoi* (page 249), a traditional Japanese scale, is applied in a minor/Major 9 harmonic context.

This book provides you with a wealth of musical scales or "flavors" but more importantly, it will help you learn ways of opening new creative pathways. Enjoy!

Aeolian (1 2 ♭3 4 5 ♭6 ♭7 8)

The *Aeolian mode* is the 6th mode of the major scale. It is commonly referred to as *natural minor*, the *relative minor scale* of the major scale. Diatonically, it works with ii, iii, or vi. In a modal context, Aeolian lends itself to a minor triad or the min7♭13 chord. The vamp at the bottom right corner of the page includes a minor triad and a min7♭13 chord.

Aeolian
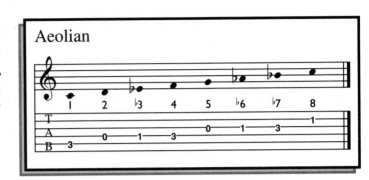

Open Position
C Aeolian

Single-String Fingering
C Aeolian
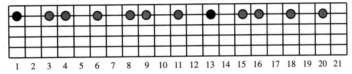

Position Fingerings Through the Circle of 4ths

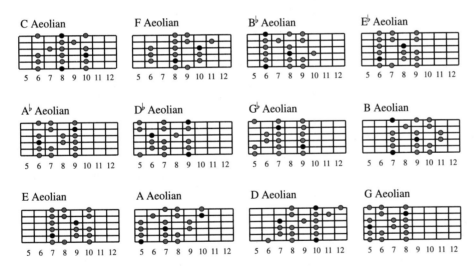

C Aeolian F Aeolian B♭ Aeolian E♭ Aeolian
A♭ Aeolian D♭ Aeolian G♭ Aeolian B Aeolian
E Aeolian A Aeolian D Aeolian G Aeolian

Two-Note-per-String Fingering

E Aeolian
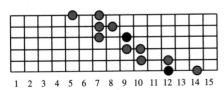

F Aeolian Vamp

Aeolian

Aeolian ♯11 (1 2 ♭3 ♯4 5 ♭6 ♭7 8)

The *Aeolian ♯11* scale is an interesting, seven-note hybrid scale that can be thought of as a combination of Lydian and Aeolian (the 4th and 6th modes of the major scale). Aeolian ♯11 contains elements of both. The vamp at the bottom right corner of the page accents all the key elements of Aeolian ♯11. Also try using Aeolian ♯11 within an altered dominant context (remember, ♭3 = ♯9).

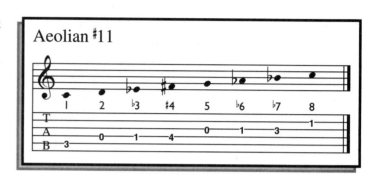

Aeolian ♯11

Open Position

C Aeolian ♯11

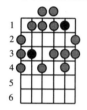

Single-String Fingering

C Aeolian ♯11

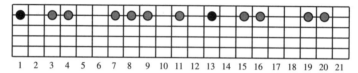

Position Fingerings Through the Circle of 4ths

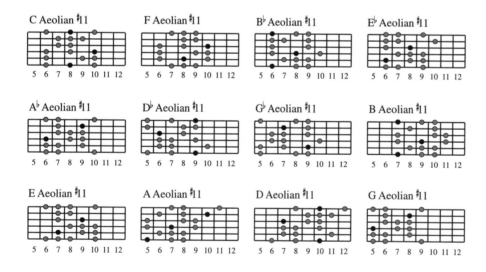

C Aeolian ♯11   F Aeolian ♯11   B♭ Aeolian ♯11   E♭ Aeolian ♯11

A♭ Aeolian ♯11   D♭ Aeolian ♯11   G♭ Aeolian ♯11   B Aeolian ♯11

E Aeolian ♯11   A Aeolian ♯11   D Aeolian ♯11   G Aeolian ♯11

Two-Note-Per-String Fingering

E Aeolian ♯11

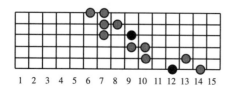

A Aeolian ♯11 Vamp

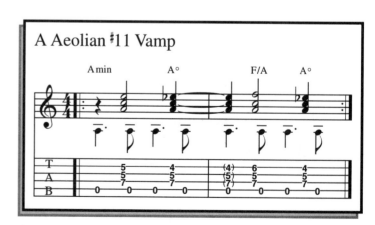

Aeolian Major (1 2 3 4 5 ♭6 ♭7 8)

The *Aeolian major* scale is the 5th mode of the *jazz minor* scale (page 247). It is also referred to as *Mixolydian* ♭6. Functionally, or modally, it can substitute for a dominant sus-type scale. It can also be used as an altered dominant sound. Aeolian major's altered dominant application is illustrated in the vamp at the bottom right corner of the page. The particular chords being emphasized are the 7♭13 and 7♯9.

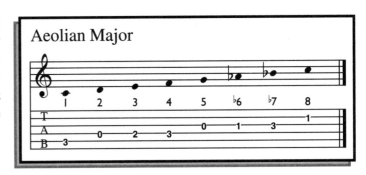

Aeolian Major

Open Position

C Aeolian Major

Single-String Fingering

C Aeolian Major

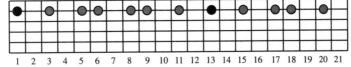

Position Fingerings Through the Circle of 4ths

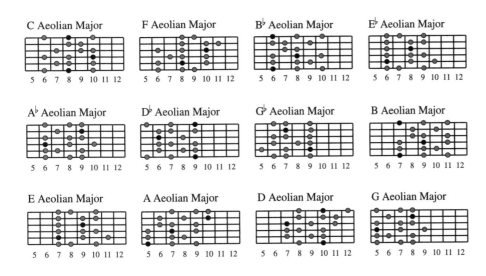

Two-Note-per-String Fingering

E Aeolian Major

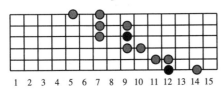

E Aeolian Major Vamp

Aeolian Major

Ake Bono (1 2 ♭3 5 ♭6 8)

Ake Bono is a traditional five-note Japanese scale. In a Western context, it can be thought of as a pentatonic version of the *Aeolian mode* (page 193, the 6th mode of the *major* scale, page 272). This scale works particularly well with a minor triad or a min7♭13 chord. The vamp at the bottom right corner of the page is the same as the one for Aeolian. Emphasize the scale's lowered 6th degree over the Fmin7♭13 chord in the first measure.

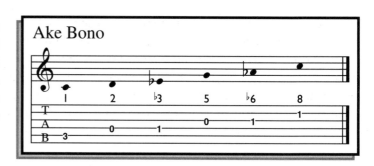

Ake Bono

Open Position

C Ake Bono

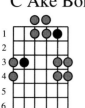

Single-String Fingering

C Ake Bono

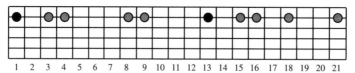

Ake Bono

Position Fingerings Through the Circle of 4ths

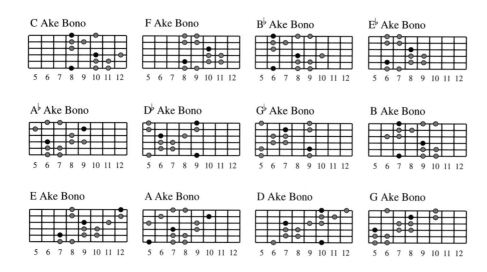

C Ake Bono F Ake Bono B♭ Ake Bono E♭ Ake Bono

A♭ Ake Bono D♭ Ake Bono G♭ Ake Bono B Ake Bono

E Ake Bono A Ake Bono D Ake Bono G Ake Bono

Two-Note-per-String Fingering

E Ake Bono

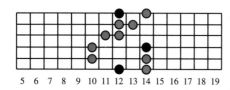

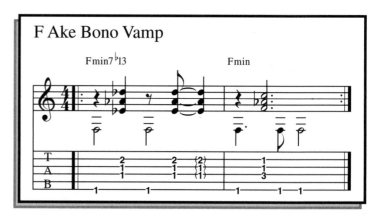

F Ake Bono Vamp

Fmin7♭13   Fmin

Altered Dominant (1 ♭2 ♭3 ♭4 ♭5 ♭6 ♭7 8)

The *altered dominant* scale is the 7th mode of the *jazz minor* scale (page 247). It is also known as the *Super Locrian mode, Locrian ♭4* and the *diminished whole tone* scale (scale degrees 1-5 form a *symmetrical diminished* scale (page 309) and scale degrees 4-1 form a *whole tone* scale (page 318). In a dominant 7 context, this scale contains the root, 3rd and ♭7 of the dominant chord and includes all of the available altered tensions: ♭9, ♯9, ♯11 and ♭13. The altered dominant scale is commonly used in functional harmony to give tension to the V7 chord. The vamp at the bottom right corner of the page uses a variety of altered dominant sounds to illustrate the effectiveness of this scale. This scale is a very important part of the jazz vocabulary. Keep in mind that you don't have to emphasize all of the altered tensions in this scale when soloing.

Altered Dominant

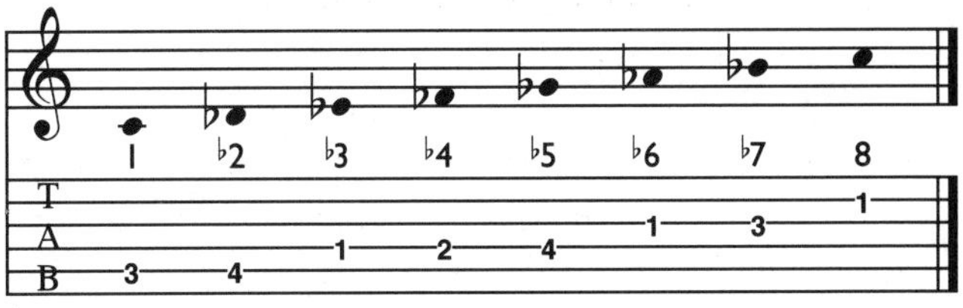

Open Position

C Altered Dominant

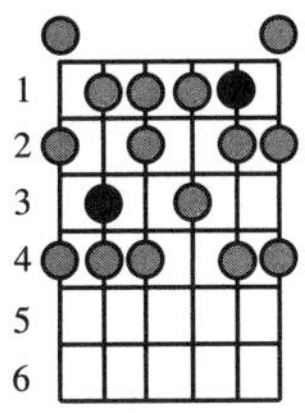

Single-String Fingering

C Altered Dominant

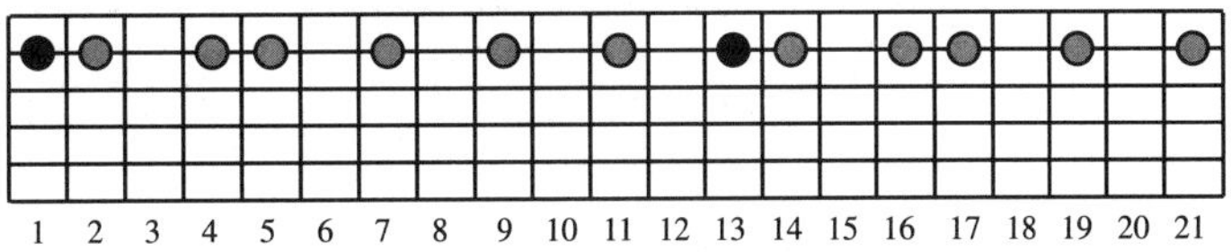

Position Fingerings Through the Circle of 4ths

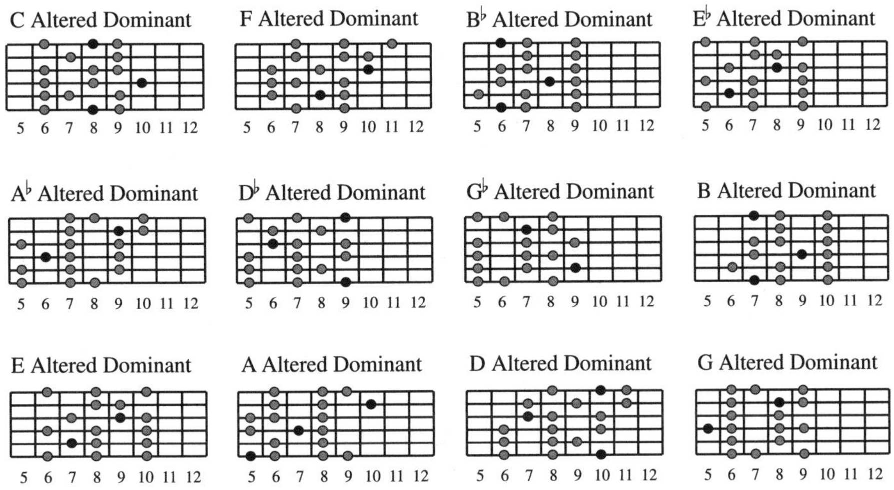

Two-Note-per-String Fingering

E Altered Dominant

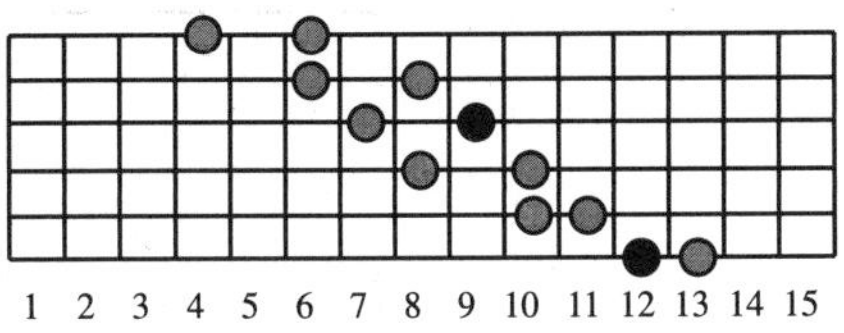

D Altered Dominant Vamp

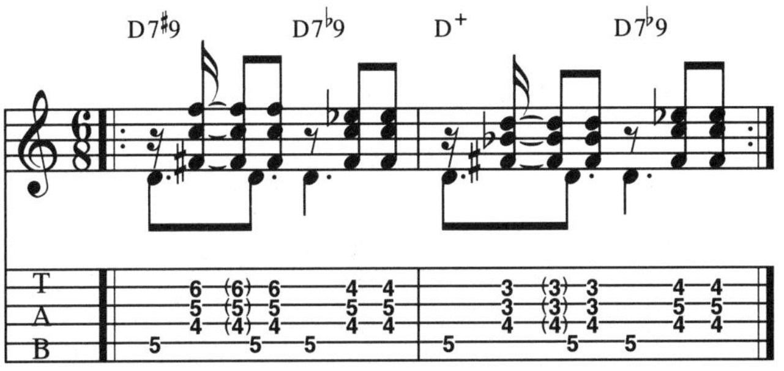

Altered Dominant ♭♭7 (1 ♭2 ♭3 ♭4 ♭5 ♭6 ♭♭7 8)

The *altered dominant* ♭♭7 scale (or *Locrian* ♭4♭♭7) is the 7th mode of the *harmonic minor* scale (page 239). This scale sounds dominant because it is an extension of the 5th mode of the harmonic minor (*Phrygian major*, page 299). It contains the major 3rd and all the altered tensions (♭9, ♯9, ♯11 and ♭13). Since the scale contains a diminished 7 chord, it makes an interesting substitute for the *symmetrical diminished* scale (page 309). The chords of the vamp at the bottom right corner of the page are built on 2 (B♭min, ii) and the root (A°7, I) of the scale. Altered dominant ♭♭7 can also be used over an altered dominant sound, even though the ♭7 is absent (the altered tensions make up for the ♭7's absence).

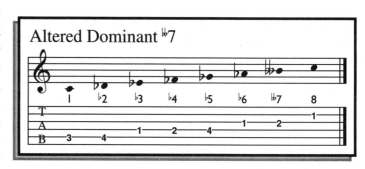

Altered Dominant ♭♭7

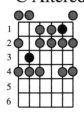

Altered Dominant ♭7

Open Position

C Altered Dominant♭♭7

Single-String Fingering

C Altered Dominant♭♭7

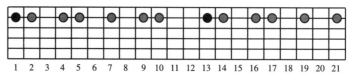

Position Fingerings Through the Circle of 4ths

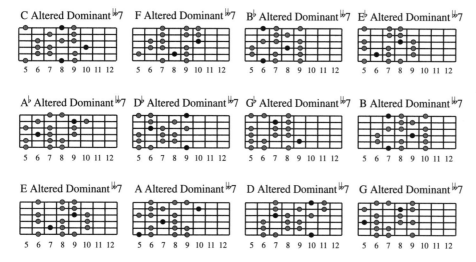

C Altered Dominant ♭♭7   F Altered Dominant ♭♭7   B♭ Altered Dominant ♭♭7   E♭ Altered Dominant ♭♭7

A♭ Altered Dominant ♭♭7   D♭ Altered Dominant ♭♭7   G♭ Altered Dominant ♭♭7   B Altered Dominant ♭♭7

E Altered Dominant ♭♭7   A Altered Dominant ♭♭7   D Altered Dominant ♭♭7   G Altered Dominant ♭♭7

Two-Note-per-String Fingering

E Altered Dominant ♭♭7

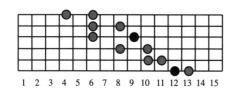

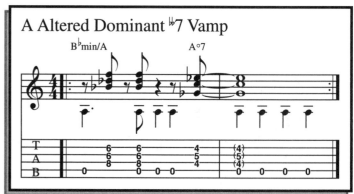

A Altered Dominant ♭7 Vamp

Augmented (1 #2 3 5 #5 7 8)

The *augmented scale* is a *symmetrical scale* (it is built from a repeating set of intervals) constructed by alternating augmented 2nds and half steps. It can be viewed as two augmented triads an augmented 2nd apart from each other. Normally, this scale is used over augmented chords. It can, however, be used with a major 7#5 chord. In the vamp at the bottom right corner of the page, the Maj7#5 sound is explored. The 2nd and 4th scale degrees tend to act like non-chord tones (*approach* or *leading tones*) that lead us to the 3 and the #5 of the Maj7#5 chord.

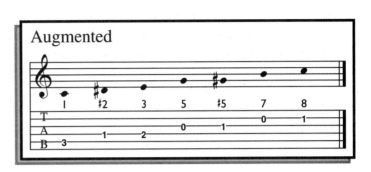

Augmented

Open Position
C Augmented

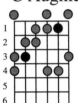

Single-String Fingering
C Augmented

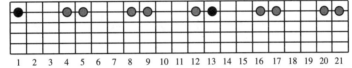

Position Fingerings Through the Circle of 4ths

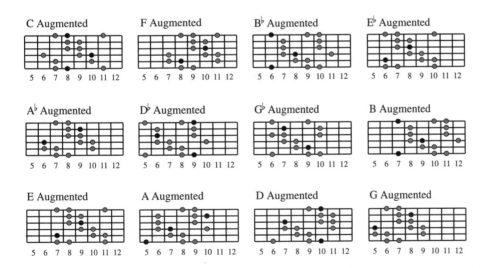

Two-Note-per-String Fingering

E Augmented

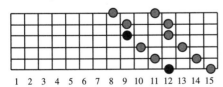

B♭ Augmented Vamp

Augmented

Augmented ♭9 (1 ♭2 ♭3 3 4 5 ♭6 6 7 8)

The *augmented ♭9* scale is a nine-note hybrid scale that produces augmented triads built on every scale degree. It contains nine augmented triads. Augmented ♭9 also resembles the *altered dominant* scale (page 197, the 7th mode of the *jazz minor* scale, page 247) in that it contains all the altered tensions except the ♭5 and does not include the ♭7. This scale is called augmented ♭9 to differentiate it from the *augmented 9* scale, page 201). Obviously, the augmented ♭9 can be applied to an augmented harmony, but it also works effectively in a min/Maj7 harmonic context. The vamp utilizes a V-I progression in melodic or harmonic minor (G7alt. to Cmin/Maj7). The augmented ♭9 scale contains pitches that work specifically for both chords.

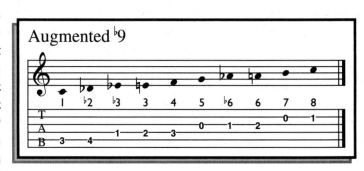

Augmented ♭9

Open Position

C Augmented ♭9

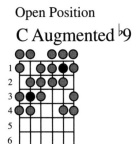

Single-String Fingering

C Augmented ♭9

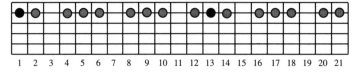

Position Fingerings Through the Circle of 4ths

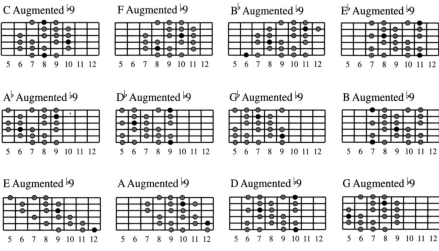

C Augmented ♭9 F Augmented ♭9 B♭ Augmented ♭9 E♭ Augmented ♭9

A♭ Augmented ♭9 D♭ Augmented ♭9 G♭ Augmented ♭9 B Augmented ♭9

E Augmented ♭9 A Augmented ♭9 D Augmented ♭9 G Augmented ♭9

Two-Note-per-String Fingering

E Augmented ♭9

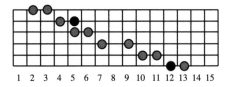

C Augmented ♭9 Vamp

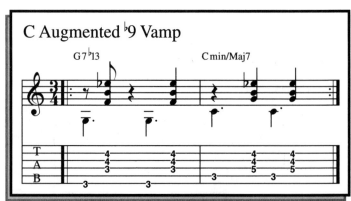

G7♭13   Cmin/Maj7

Augmented 9 (1 2 ♭3 3 ♯4 5 ♭6 ♭7 7 8)

The *augmented 9* scale is a nine-note hybrid scale. An augmented triad can be constructed on every scale degree. It contains nine augmented triads. The scale also resembles the *altered dominant* scale (page 197) in that it contains all of the altered tensions except the ♭9. Obviously, this scale can be applied to an augmented harmony, but it also works effectively in an altered dominant context. To emphasize the unaltered 9th and the altered possibilities of this scale, the vamp at the bottom right corner of the page utilizes a dom9♭5 without the 3rd.

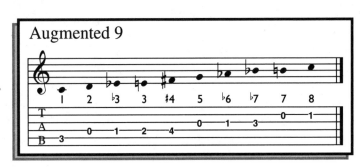
Augmented 9

Open position

C Augmented 9

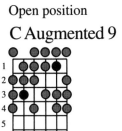

Single-String fingering

C Augmented 9

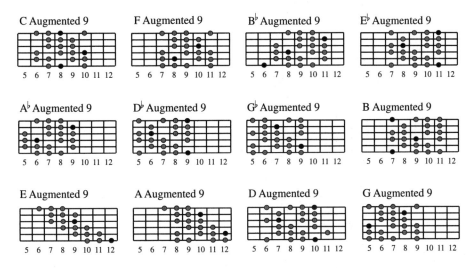

Position Fingerings Through the Circle of 4ths

C Augmented 9 | F Augmented 9 | B♭ Augmented 9 | E♭ Augmented 9

A♭ Augmented 9 | D♭ Augmented 9 | G♭ Augmented 9 | B Augmented 9

E Augmented 9 | A Augmented 9 | D Augmented 9 | G Augmented 9

Two Note-per-String Fingering

E Augmented 9

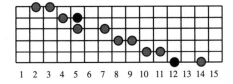

C Augmented 9 Vamp

C9♭5(no3)

Augmented Dominant (1 2 3 4 ♯5 6 ♭7 8)

The *augmented dominant* scale is a seven-note hybrid scale that resembles the *Mixolydian mode* (page 293, the 5th mode of the *major* scale, page 272) with an augmented 5th scale degree. The scale yields a dominant 7 chord with the ♯5 altered tension and can be applied to any altered dominant context. The vamp at the bottom right corner of the page shows how the augmented dominant scale, as specific as it may be, can be used successfully with a variety of altered dominant chord-types.

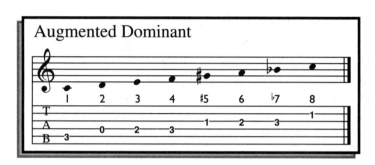

Augmented Dominant

Open Position

C Aug.Dom.

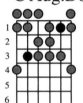

Single-String Fingering

C Aug.Dom.

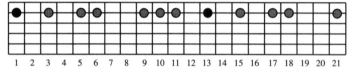

Position Fingerings Through the Circle of 4ths

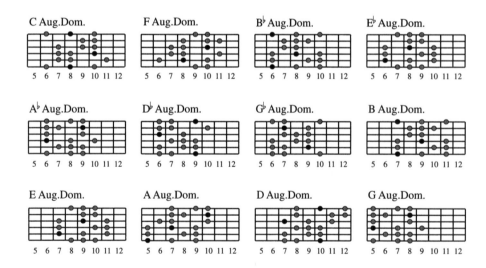

C Aug.Dom. F Aug.Dom. B♭ Aug.Dom. E♭ Aug.Dom.

A♭ Aug.Dom. D♭ Aug.Dom. G♭ Aug.Dom. B Aug.Dom.

E Aug.Dom. A Aug.Dom. D Aug.Dom. G Aug.Dom.

Two-Note-per-String Fingering

E Aug.Dom.

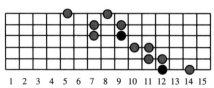

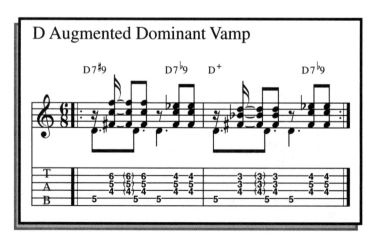

D Augmented Dominant Vamp

Augmented Dominant ♭9 (1 ♭2 3 4 ♯5 6 ♭7 8)

The *augmented dominant* ♭9 scale is a seven-note hybrid scale that contains an augmented dominant 7 chord with the ♭9 altered tension. It works specifically with the 7♭9 chord. Like the other hybrid altered dominant scales, it can be substituted for any altered dominant scale. The vamp at the bottom right corner of the page uses an augmented 7♭9 chord that reflects both of the alterations found in the scale (♯5 and ♭9).

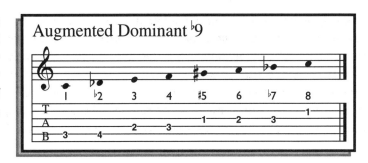

Augmented Dominant ♭9

Open Position

C Aug.Dom.♭9

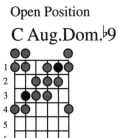

Single-String Fingering

C Aug.Dom.♭9

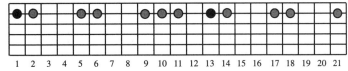

Position Fingerings Through the Circle of 4ths

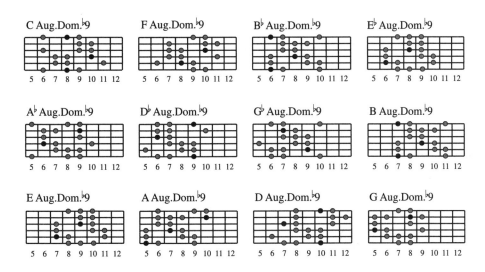

C Aug.Dom.♭9   F Aug.Dom.♭9   B♭ Aug.Dom.♭9   E♭ Aug.Dom.♭9

A♭ Aug.Dom.♭9   D♭ Aug.Dom.♭9   G♭ Aug.Dom.♭9   B Aug.Dom.♭9

E Aug.Dom.♭9   A Aug.Dom.♭9   D Aug.Dom.♭9   G Aug.Dom.♭9

Two-Note-per-String Fingering

E Aug.Dom.♭9

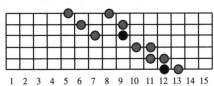

E Augmented Dominant ♭9 Vamp

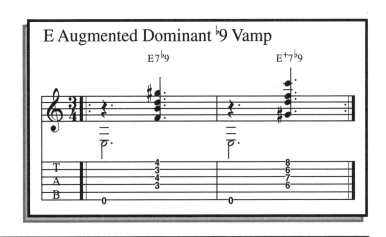

Augmented Dominant ♯9 (1 ♯2 3 4 ♯5 6 ♭7 8)

The *augmented dominant ♯9* scale is a seven-note hybrid scale that contains an augmented dominant 7 chord with the ♯9 altered tension. It works specifically with this chord. Like the other hybrid altered dominant scales, it can be substituted for any altered dominant situation. The vamp at the lower right corner of the page uses an augmented dom7♯9 chord that reflects both of the alterations found in the scale (♯5 and ♯9).

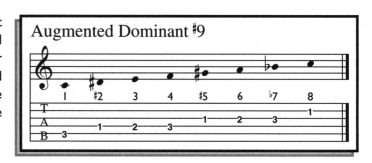

Augmented Dominant ♯9

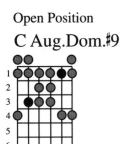

Open Position
C Aug.Dom.♯9

Single-String Fingering
C Aug.Dom.♯9

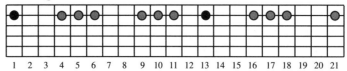

Position Fingerings Through the Circle of 4ths

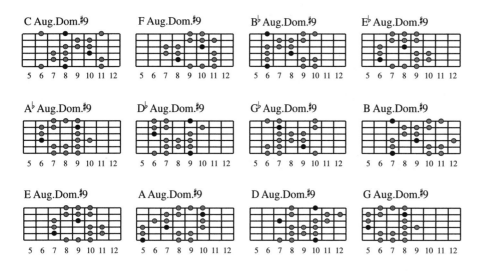

C Aug.Dom.♯9   F Aug.Dom.♯9   B♭ Aug.Dom.♯9   E♭ Aug.Dom.♯9

A♭ Aug.Dom.♯9   D♭ Aug.Dom.♯9   G♭ Aug.Dom.♯9   B Aug.Dom.♯9

E Aug.Dom.♯9   A Aug.Dom.♯9   D Aug.Dom.♯9   G Aug.Dom.♯9

Two-Note-per-String Fingering
E Aug.Dom.♯9

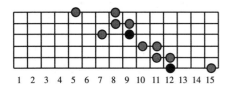

E Augmented Dominant ♯9 Vamp

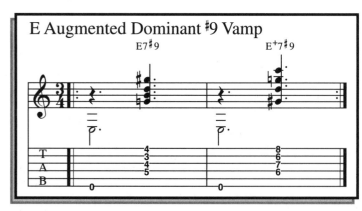

Augmented Minor/Major 7 (1 2 ♭3 4 ♯5 6 7 8)

The *augmented minor/major* scale is a seven-note hybrid scale that resembles the *jazz minor* (page 247) scale with a ♯5. It can also be thought as a variation of the *bebop melodic minor* (page 211) which has a chromatic passing tone between the 5th and 6th degrees. The ♯5 in this scale acts as a *chromatic approach tone* to the 6th scale degree. Augmented minor/major can be used within any minor/major 7 chord application. The harmony outlined in this vamp is the minor/major 9 chord (it is the same vamp as for melodic minor). The ♯5 of the scale should be used as a quick chromatic approach to the 6. Hanging on that pitch for too long results in a great deal of dissonance. Try substituting this scale for any minor/major 7 application.

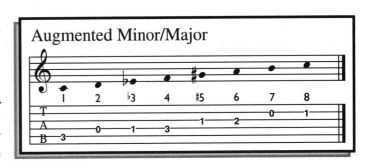

Augmented Minor/Major

Open Position

C AugMin/Maj7

Single-String Fingering

C AugMin/Maj7

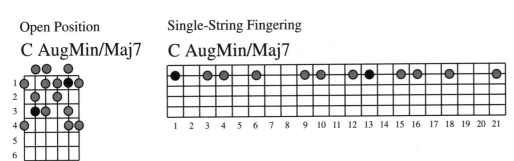

Position Fingerings Through the Circle of 4ths

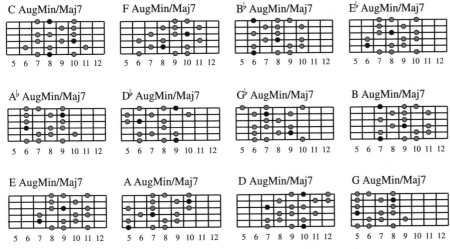

C AugMin/Maj7   F AugMin/Maj7   B♭ AugMin/Maj7   E♭ AugMin/Maj7

A♭ AugMin/Maj7   D♭ AugMin/Maj7   G♭ AugMin/Maj7   B AugMin/Maj7

E AugMin/Maj7   A AugMin/Maj7   D AugMin/Maj7   G AugMin/Maj7

Two-Note-per-String Fingering

E AugMin/Maj7

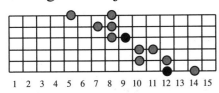

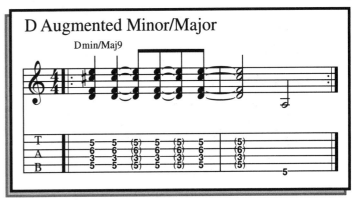

D Augmented Minor/Major

Dmin/Maj9

Augmented Minor/Major

Auxiliary Diminished, Whole/Half (1 2 ♭3 4 ♭5 ♭6 6 7 8)

The *auxiliary diminished* scale alternates between whole and half step intervals and contains eight tones. Each degree of the scale produces a diminished 7 chord which, because of the scale's symmetry, can substitute for each other. This whole-step/half-step scale is a perfect choice for playing over a diminished 7 chord. The half-step/whole-step version of this scale is known as the *symmetrical diminished* scale (page 309) and is usually used over an altered dominant 7 chord. The vamp at the bottom right corner of the page uses the diminished 7 chord to illustrate the auxiliary diminished sound.

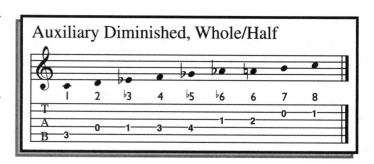

Auxiliary Diminished, Whole/Half

Open Position

C Dim. Whole/Half

Single-String Fingering

C Dim. Whole/Half

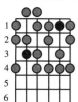
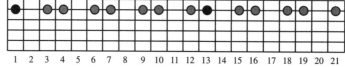

Position Fingerings Through the Circle of 4ths

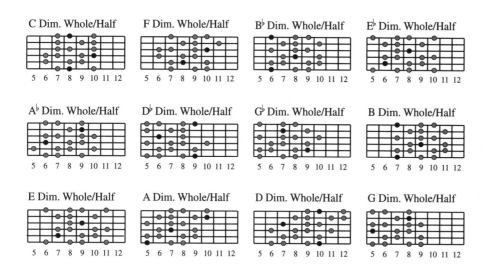

C Dim. Whole/Half   F Dim. Whole/Half   B♭ Dim. Whole/Half   E♭ Dim. Whole/Half

A♭ Dim. Whole/Half   D♭ Dim. Whole/Half   G♭ Dim. Whole/Half   B Dim. Whole/Half

E Dim. Whole/Half   A Dim. Whole/Half   D Dim. Whole/Half   G Dim. Whole/Half

Two-Note-per-String Fingering

E Dim. Whole/Half

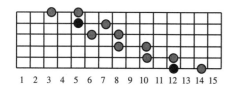

A Auxiliary Diminished, Whole/Half Vamp

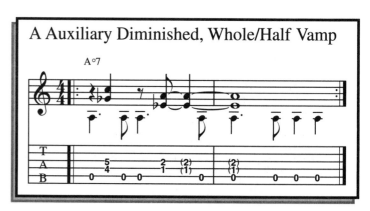

Banshiki-Cho (1 ♭3 4 ♯5 ♭7 8)

Banshiki-Cho is a traditional, five-note Japanese scale. In a Western context, it can be thought of as a pentatonic version of the *Dorian mode* (page 231, the 2nd mode of the *major* scale, page 272) with an added ♯5. This scale can be applied used over minor 7♯5 chord or in a natural minor harmonic context. The vamp at the bottom right corner of the page is the same as for the *Minor ♭6/11 Pentatonic* scale (page 284). Banshiki-Cho, however, emphasizes the ♭7, making it a perfect choice for this progression.

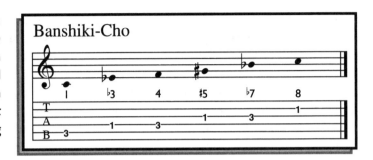

Banshiki-Cho

Open Position
C Banshiki-Cho

Single-String Fingering
C Banshiki-Cho

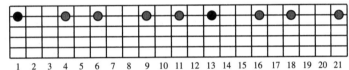

Position Fingerings Through the Circle of 4ths

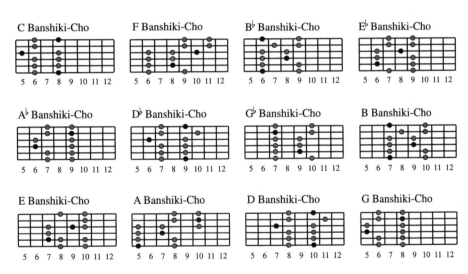

C Banshiki-Cho F Banshiki-Cho B♭ Banshiki-Cho E♭ Banshiki-Cho

A♭ Banshiki-Cho D♭ Banshiki-Cho G♭ Banshiki-Cho B Banshiki-Cho

E Banshiki-Cho A Banshiki-Cho D Banshiki-Cho G Banshiki-Cho

Two-Note-per-String Fingering

E Banshiki-Cho

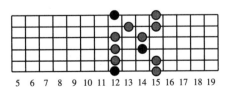

C Banshiki-Cho Vamp

Cmin7♯5   Cmin11

Banshiki-Cho

Bebop Dominant (1 2 3 4 5 6 ♭7 7 8)

The *bebop scales* are the traditional *Ionian* (*major,* page 272) *Dorian* (page 231) and *Mixolydian* (page 293) modes of the major and *jazz minor* (page 247) scales with an added chromatic passing tone. The *bebop dominant scale* is the Mixolydian mode (the 5th mode of the major scale) with a chromatic passing tone between the 7 and the root. This scale works well over dominant 7 chords and over I7 - IV7 progressions. In the vamp at the bottom right corner of the page, the I7 - IV7 progression provides a background for improvising with this scale. Also try using it over an unaltered, stationary dominant chord.

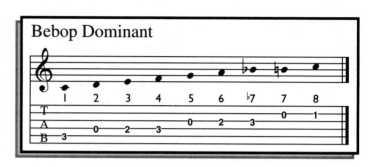

Bebop Dominant

Open Position

C Bebop Dominant

Single-String Fingering

C Bebop Dominant

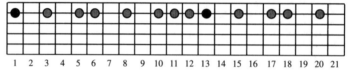

Position Fingerings Through the Circle of 4ths

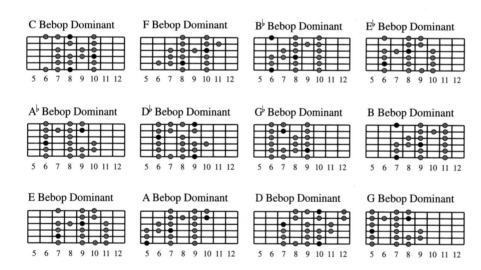

Two-Note-per-String Fingering

E Bebop Dominant

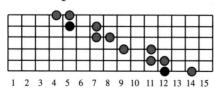

B♭ Bebop Dominant Vamp

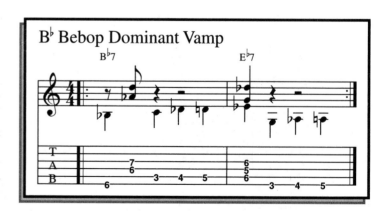

Bebop Dorian (1 2 ♭3 3 4 5 6 ♭7 8)

The *bebop Dorian* scale is the *Dorian mode* (page 231, the 2nd mode of the *major* scale, page 272) with a chromatic passing tone between the 3rd and the 4th degrees of the scale. This scale works well over stationary minor 7 chords or within a I - IV progression. In the vamp at the bottom right corner of the page, a stationary min7 chord provides the background for improvising with the bebop Dorian scale. Also try using it over a ii min7 - V7 progression.

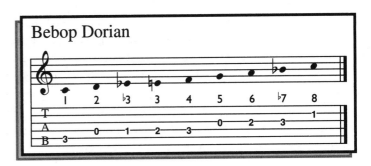

Bebop Dorian

Open Position
C Bebop Dorian

Single-String Fingering
C Bebop Dorian

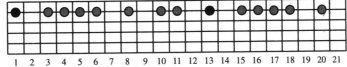

Position Fingerings Through the Circle of 4ths

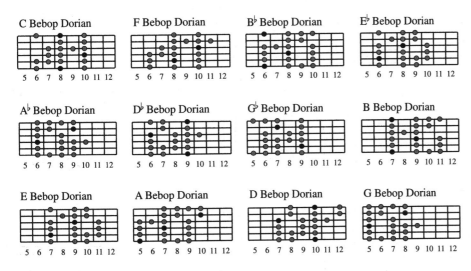

C Bebop Dorian · F Bebop Dorian · B♭ Bebop Dorian · E♭ Bebop Dorian
A♭ Bebop Dorian · D♭ Bebop Dorian · G♭ Bebop Dorian · B Bebop Dorian
E Bebop Dorian · A Bebop Dorian · D Bebop Dorian · G Bebop Dorian

Two-Note-per-String Fingering

E Bebop Dorian

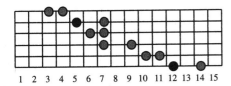

E Bebop Dorian Vamp
Emin7

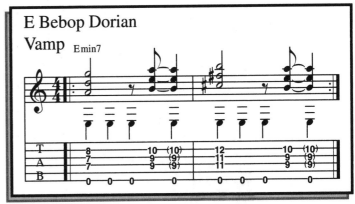

Bebop Major (1 2 3 4 ♯4 5 6 7 8)

The *bebop major* scale is the *Ionian mode* (page 272, 1st mode of the *major* scale) with a chromatic passing note between the 4th and the 5th degrees of the scale. This scale works well over major 7th and major 6th chords or a major triad. Like all the bebop scales, the chromatic passing tone adds a bit of tension to the situation which is quickly resolved. In the vamp at the bottom right corner of the page, a stationary Maj9 chord provides the background for improvising with the bebop major scale.

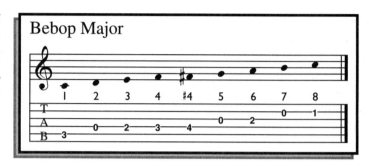

Bebop Major

Open Position

C Bebop Major

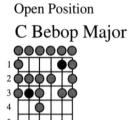

Single-String Fingering

C Bebop Major

Position Fingerings Through the Circle of 4ths

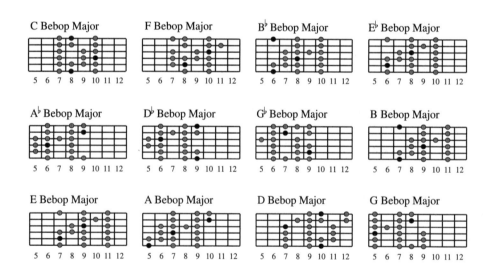

C Bebop Major

F Bebop Major

B♭ Bebop Major

E♭ Bebop Major

A♭ Bebop Major

D♭ Bebop Major

G♭ Bebop Major

B Bebop Major

E Bebop Major

A Bebop Major

D Bebop Major

G Bebop Major

Two-Note-per-String Fingering

E Bebop Major

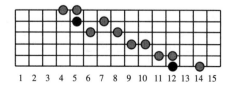

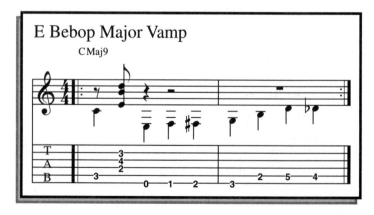

E Bebop Major Vamp

CMaj9

Bebop Melodic Minor (1 2 ♭3 4 ♯4 5 6 7 8)

The *bebop melodic minor* scale is the 1st mode of the *jazz minor* scale (page 247) with a chromatic passing tone between the 4th and the 5th degrees of the scale. This scale works well over a min/Maj7 (min△7) chord. In the vamp at the bottom right corner of the page, a stationary min/Maj9 chord provides the background for improvising with the bebop major scale.

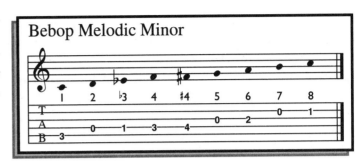

Bebop Melodic Minor

Open Position

C Bebop Melodic Minor

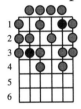

Single-String Fingering

C Bebop Melodic Minor

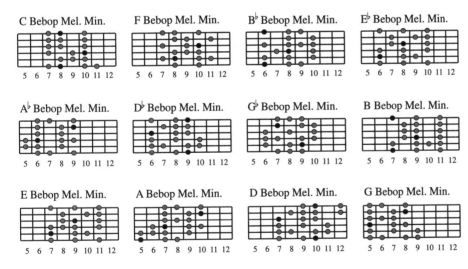

Position Fingerings Through the Circle of 4ths

C Bebop Mel. Min. F Bebop Mel. Min. B♭ Bebop Mel. Min. E♭ Bebop Mel. Min.

A♭ Bebop Mel. Min. D♭ Bebop Mel. Min. G♭ Bebop Mel. Min. B Bebop Mel. Min.

E Bebop Mel. Min. A Bebop Mel. Min. D Bebop Mel. Min. G Bebop Mel. Min.

Two-Note-per-String Fingering

E Bebop Mel. Min.

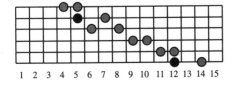

C Bebop Melodic Minor Vamp

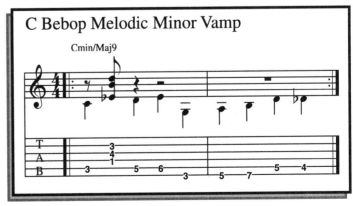

Bhairon (1 ♭2 3 4 5 ♭6 7 8)

Bhairon is a seven-note Indian *raga* (scale) which is also known as the *Persian* scale. In a Western context, it resembles *harmonic major* (page 238) with a ♭2 altered tension. Bhairon can also be applied in a *Phyrgian mode* (page 297, the 2nd mode of the *major* scale, page 272) context with the natural 7 scale degree acting as a leading tone. The vamp at the bottom right corner of the page illustrates using Bhairon as a Phrygian substitute. Try using it as an alternative to the various Phrygian-type scales (pages 297-302).

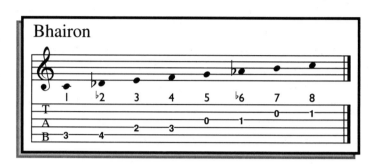

Bhairon

Open Position

C Bhairon

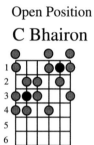

Single-String Fingering

C Bhairon

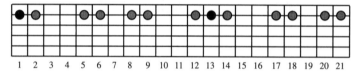

Position Fingerings Through the Circle of 4ths

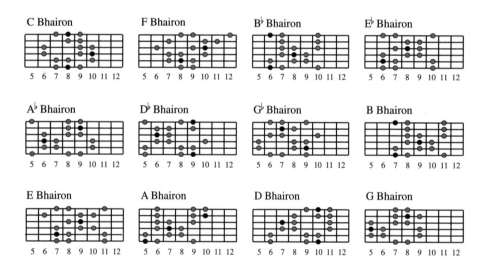

C Bhairon   F Bhairon   B♭ Bhairon   E♭ Bhairon

A♭ Bhairon   D♭ Bhairon   G♭ Bhairon   B Bhairon

E Bhairon   A Bhairon   D Bhairon   G Bhairon

Two-Note-per-String Fingering

E Bhairon

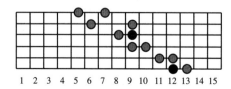

A Bhairon Vamp

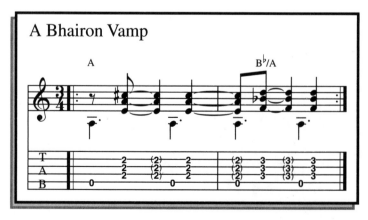

Buzurg (1 ♭2 3 4 ♯4 5 6 7 8)

Buzurg is an eight-note Arabian scale. It can be substituted for an *altered dominant* scale (page 197, the 7th mode of the *jazz minor* scale, page 247) or in a *minor pentatonic blues* context (see page 291). If the 5th scale degree is emphasized, Buzurg takes on an *altered dominant* sound (see page 197). With the focus on the 5th degree as the root, this scale could be interpreted as: 1-9-3-11-♭5-13-♭7-7-8. The natural 7th scale degree acts as a chromatic passing tone (as in the *bebop* scales, pages 208-211). The vamp at the bottom right corner of the page explores the altered dominant application of this scale.

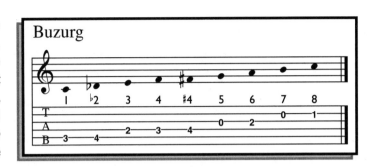

Buzurg

Open Position

C Buzurg

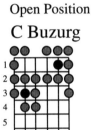

Single-String Fingering

C Buzurg

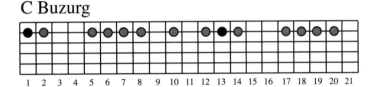

Position Fingerings Through the Circle of 4ths

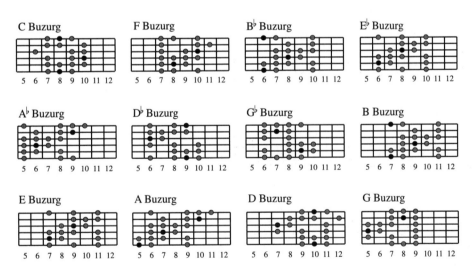

C Buzurg   F Buzurg   B♭ Buzurg   E♭ Buzurg

A♭ Buzurg   D♭ Buzurg   G♭ Buzurg   B Buzurg

E Buzurg   A Buzurg   D Buzurg   G Buzurg

Two-Note-per-String Fingering

E Buzurg

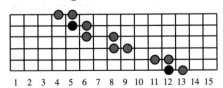

C Buzurg Vamp

G7♭5

Chromatic (1 ♭2 2 ♭3 3 4 ♯4 5 ♭6 6 ♭7 7 8)

The *chromatic* scale contains all twelve pitches of an octave arranged in consecutive half steps. Music that is said to contain *chromaticism* makes extensive use of the chromatic scale. The chromatic scale (or portions of it) can be applied in any circumstance. It is simply a matter of resolving the chromatic motion or activity to a stable, diatonic tonality. To play chromatically means to emphasize half-step activity. In the vamp at the bottom right corner of the page, the chord progression encourages chromaticism because of its half step motion. Try playing small portions of the scale over this vamp and learn to resolve to chord tones.

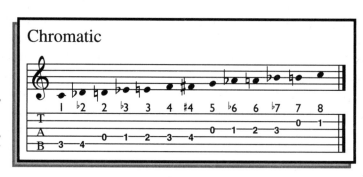

Chromatic

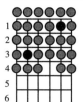

Open position

C Chromatic

Single-String Fingering

C Chromatic

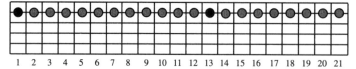

Position Fingerings Through the Circle of 4ths

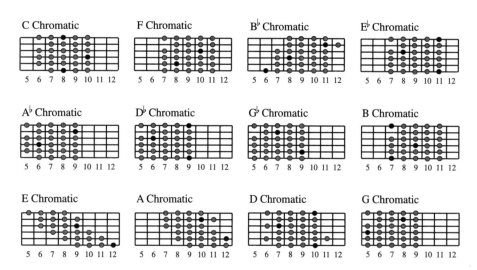

C Chromatic F Chromatic B♭ Chromatic E♭ Chromatic

A♭ Chromatic D♭ Chromatic G♭ Chromatic B Chromatic

E Chromatic A Chromatic D Chromatic G Chromatic

Two-Note-per-String Fingering

E Chromatic

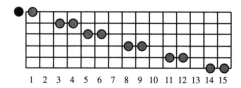

E Chromatic Vamp

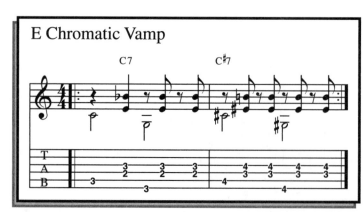

Chromatic Augmented (1 ♭2 2 3 4 #4 #5 6 ♭7 8)

The *chromatic augmented* scale is a nine-note scale that alternates between two half steps and one whole step (H-H-W-H-H-W and so on). You can create an augmented triad and a Maj7#5#11) chord from the root of this scale. As with the *semitone tritone* scales (pages 236, 311 and 317), the half steps in the chromatic augmented scale can be viewed as passing or leading tones to certain chord tones. The vamp at the bottom right corner of the page outlines some of the particular harmonies found in this scale.

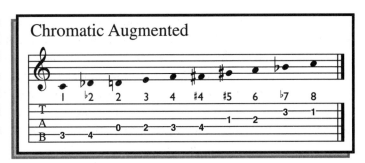

Chromatic Augmented

Open Position

C Chromatic Augmented

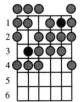

Single-String Fingering

C Chromatic Augmented

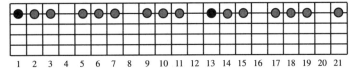

Position Fingerings Through the Circle of 4ths

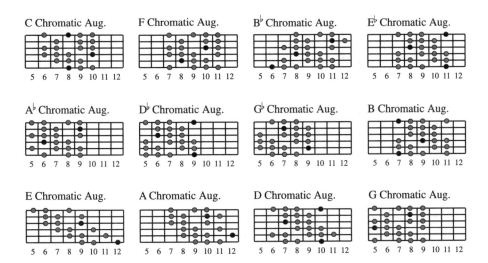

C Chromatic Aug.   F Chromatic Aug.   B♭ Chromatic Aug.   E♭ Chromatic Aug.

A♭ Chromatic Aug.   D♭ Chromatic Aug.   G♭ Chromatic Aug.   B Chromatic Aug.

E Chromatic Aug.   A Chromatic Aug.   D Chromatic Aug.   G Chromatic Aug.

Two-Note-per-String Fingering

E Chromatic Augmented

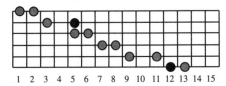

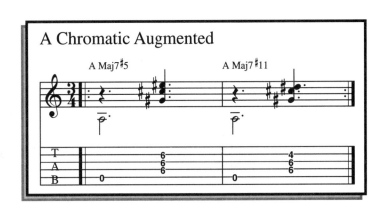

A Chromatic Augmented

A Maj7#5   A Maj7#11

Darbari (1 2 ♭3 4 5 ♭6 ♭7 7 8)

Darbari is as eight-note Indian *raga* (scale). In a Western context, it could be considered a bebop version of the *Aeolian mode* (page 193, the 6th mode of the *major* scale, page 272) because of the passing tone between ♭7 and 8. Darbari makes an interesting substitution for the Aeolian mode. The harmony outlined in the vamp at the bottom right corner of the page supports the Aeolian nature of this scale. The passing tone between ♭7 and 8 gives Darbari a jazz sound.

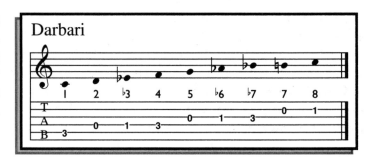

Darbari

Open Position
C Darbari

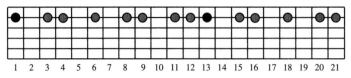

Single-String Fingering
C Darbari

Position Fingerings Through the Circle of 4ths

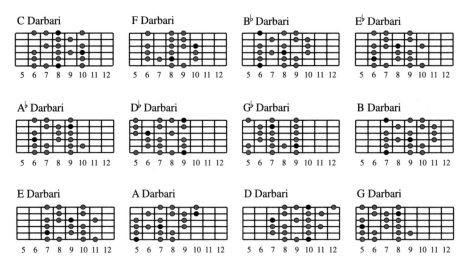

C Darbari | F Darbari | B♭ Darbari | E♭ Darbari
A♭ Darbari | D♭ Darbari | G♭ Darbari | B Darbari
E Darbari | A Darbari | D Darbari | G Darbari

Two-Note-per-String Fingering
E Darbari

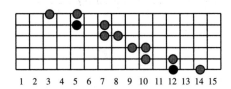

C Darbari Vamp

Darbari

Diminished Blues (1 ♭2 ♭3 3 ♯5 6 ♭7 8)

The *diminished blues* scale is a symmetrical scale that resembles the *symmetrical diminished* scale (page 309) except that it is divided by the interval of a major 3rd (H-W-H-major 3rd-H-H-W). It contains the dominant 7th chord accompanied by "blues-oriented" tensions, the ♭9 and ♯9. The vamp at the bottom right corner of the page is the same as the *Phrygian ♮6* scale vamp (page 300)—an altered dominant-type situation. Try altering between the two scale choices.

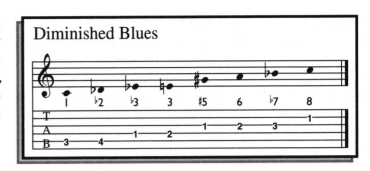

Diminished Blues

Open Position

C Dim. Blues

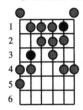

Single-String Fingering

C Dim. Blues

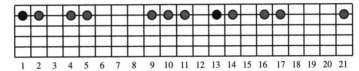

Position Fingerings Through the Circle of 4ths

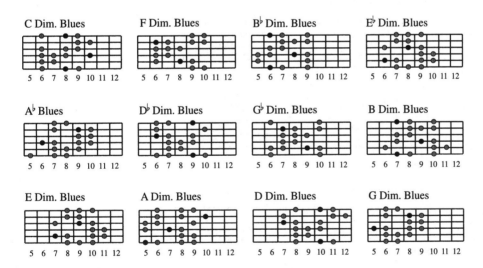

C Dim. Blues · F Dim. Blues · B♭ Dim. Blues · E♭ Dim. Blues

A♭ Blues · D♭ Dim. Blues · G♭ Dim. Blues · B Dim. Blues

E Dim. Blues · A Dim. Blues · D Dim. Blues · G Dim. Blues

Two-Note-per-String Fingering

E Dim. Blues

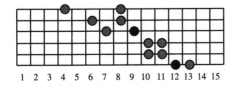

E Diminished Blues Vamp

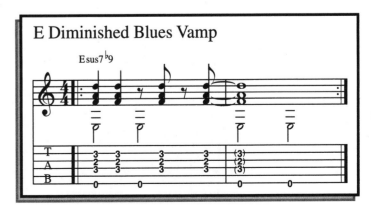

Diminished Blues

Diminished Tritonic (1 ♭3 4 ♭5 8)

The *diminished tritonic* scale is a four-note hybrid that can be considered a variation on the *tritonic scale* (page 314). A tritonic scale is built with three pitches arranged in ascending order from root to octave root. This form has a lowered 5th (♭5) and an added pitch, the ♭3. These two variations together with the root produce a diminished sound. This tritonic scale consists of: Root, ♭3, 4, ♭5 and an octave root, and is particularly useful for min7♭5 applications. Like triads, tritonic scales can be used as harmonic or non-harmonic sources for improvisation.

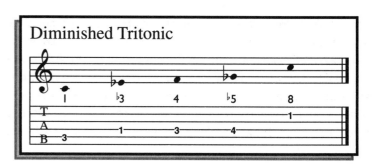

Diminished Tritonic

Open Position

C Dim. Tritonic

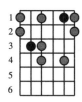

Single-String Fingering

C Dim. Tritonic

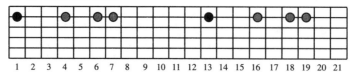

Position Fingerings Through the Circle of 4ths

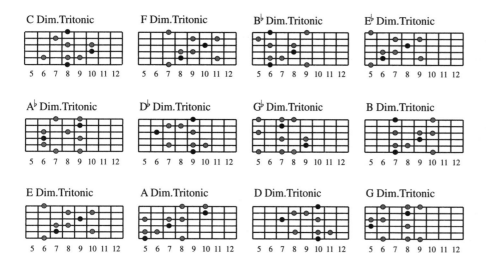

C Dim. Tritonic   F Dim. Tritonic   B♭ Dim. Tritonic   E♭ Dim. Tritonic

A♭ Dim. Tritonic   D♭ Dim. Tritonic   G♭ Dim. Tritonic   B Dim. Tritonic

E Dim. Tritonic   A Dim. Tritonic   D Dim. Tritonic   G Dim. Tritonic

Two-Note-per-String Fingering

E Dim. Tritonic

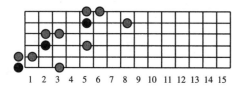

D Diminished Tritonic Vamp

Dmin7♭5

Dominant ♭5 (1 2 3 4 ♭5 6 ♭7 8)

The *Dominant ♭5* scale is a seven-note hybrid scale that closely resembles the *Mixolydian mode* (page 293, the 5th mode of the *major scale*, page 272) with an altered 5 (♭5). This scale works specifically with a 7♭5 chord. It can also be used in other altered dominant contexts. The vamp in the lower right corner of this page is the same as for the *Lydian ♭7* scale (page 257, the 4th mode of the *jazz minor* scale, page 247). Both choices work particularly well with the 7♭5 chord.

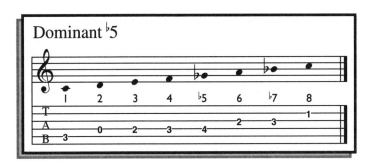

Dominant ♭5

Open Position

C Dominant ♭5

Single-String Fingering

C Dominant ♭5

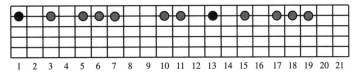

Position Fingerings Through the Circle of 4ths

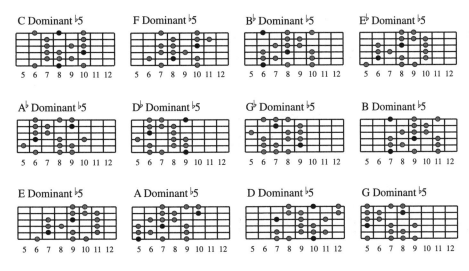

Two-Note-per-String Fingering

E Dominant ♭5

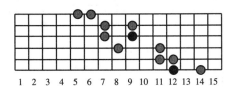

F Dominant ♭5 Vamp

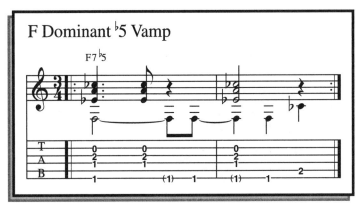

Dominant ♭5 ♭9 ♯9 (1 ♭2 ♭3 ♭4 ♭5 6 ♭7 8)

The *dominant ♭5♭9♯9* scale is a seven-note hybrid scale that can be applied specifically to a dominant 7th chord with ♭5, ♭9 and ♯9 altered tensions. It is very similar to the *altered dominant* scale (page 197, the 7th mode of the *jazz minor* scale, page 247), so it can also be applied to any altered dominant situation. The vamp at the bottom right corner of the page switches between two specific altered dominant chords that the scale addresses (A7♭5 and A7♭9♯9). Try using this scale over any altered dominant chord.

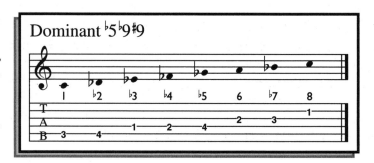

Dominant ♭5♭9♯9

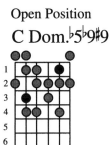

Open Position

C Dom.♭5♭9♯9

Single-String Fingering

C Dom.♭5♭9♯9

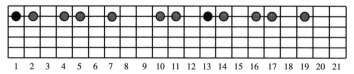

Position Fingerings Through the Circle of 4ths

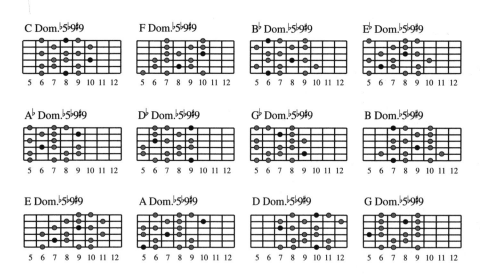

C Dom.♭5♭9♯9 F Dom.♭5♭9♯9 B♭ Dom.♭5♭9♯9 E♭ Dom.♭5♭9♯9

A♭ Dom.♭5♭9♯9 D♭ Dom.♭5♭9♯9 G♭ Dom.♭5♭9♯9 B Dom.♭5♭9♯9

E Dom.♭5♭9♯9 A Dom.♭5♭9♯9 D Dom.♭5♭9♯9 G Dom.♭5♭9♯9

Two-Note-per-String Fingering

E Dom.♭5♭9♯9

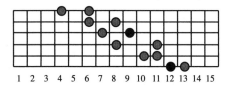

A Dominant ♭5♭9♯9 Vamp

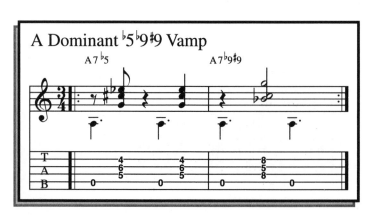

Dominant ♭9 ♯9 (1 ♭2 ♭3 ♭4 5 6 ♭7 8)

The *dominant* ♭9♯9 scale is a seven-note hybrid scale that can be applied specifically to a dominant 7 chord with the ♭9 and ♯9 altered tensions. It can also be applied to any *altered dominant* scale (page 197) situation. The vamp at the bottom right corner of the page alternates between a non-altered dominant and the specific altered dominant chord that the scale addresses—A7♭9♯9. Try using the dominant ♭9♯9 scale over any altered dominant chord.

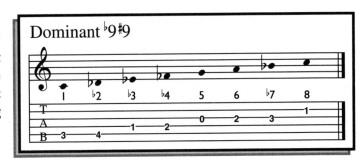

Dominant ♭9♯9

Open Position

C Dom.♭9♯9

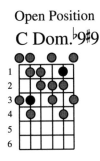

Single-String Fingering

C Dom.♭9♯9

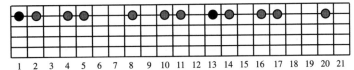

Position Fingerings Through the Circle of 4ths

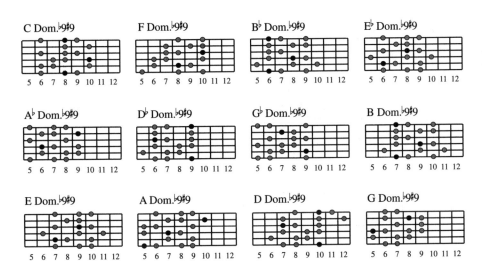

C Dom.♭9♯9 F Dom.♭9♯9 B♭ Dom.♭9♯9 E♭ Dom.♭9♯9

A♭ Dom.♭9♯9 D♭ Dom.♭9♯9 G♭ Dom.♭9♯9 B Dom.♭9♯9

E Dom.♭9♯9 A Dom.♭9♯9 D Dom.♭9♯9 G Dom.♭9♯9

Two-Note-per-String Fingering

E Dom.♭9♯9

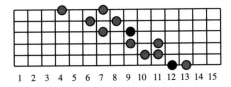

A Dominant ♭9♯9 Vamp

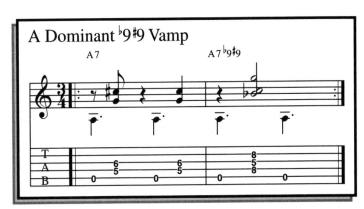

Dominant ♭9 #9 ♭13 (1 ♭2 ♭3 ♭4 5 ♭6 ♭7 8)

The *dominant ♭9#9♭13* scale is a seven-note hybrid scale that contains a dominant 7 chord (remember ♭4=3) with the ♭9,#9 and ♭13 (♭6) altered tensions. It is very similar to the *altered dominant* scale (page 197, the 7th mode of the *jazz minor* scale, page 247) except that it does not contain the #11 altered tension. It can, however, be used in any altered dominant situation, so the vamp at the bottom right corner of the page is the same as for the altered dominant. If a dominant 7 chord contains an altered tension, numerous altered dominant-type scales may be used, even if a particular tension is not in the harmony. The result will be tension where tension is required.

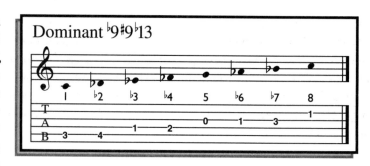

Dominant ♭9#9♭13

Open Position
C Dom.♭9#9♭13

Single-String Fingering
C Dom.♭9#9♭13

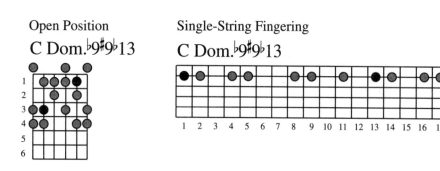

Position Fingerings Through the Circle of 4ths

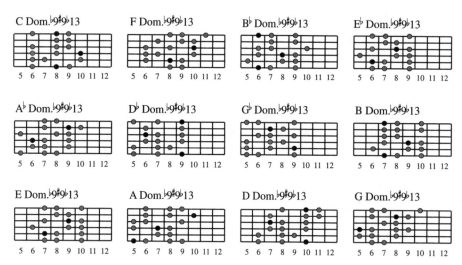

Two-Note-per-String Fingering
E Dom.♭9#9♭13

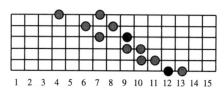

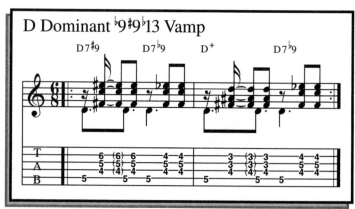

D Dominant ♭9#9♭13 Vamp

Dominant ♯9 (1 ♯2 3 4 5 6 ♭7 8)

The *dominant ♯9 scale* is a seven-note hybrid scale with a specific 7♯9 application. It can be thought as the *Mixolydian mode* (page 293, the 5th mode of the *major* scale, page 272) with an added ♯9 altered tension. This scale can be substituted for any altered dominant scale choice. The vamp is the same as for the *Four-Semitone Tritone* on page 236. It utilizes the 7♯9 chord to illustrate the scale's specific application.

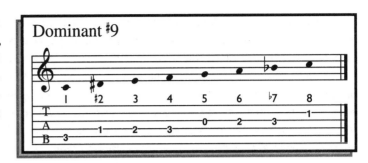

Dominant ♯9

Open Position

C Dominant ♯9

Single-String Fingering

C Dominant ♯9

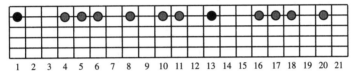

Position Fingerings Through the Circle of 4ths

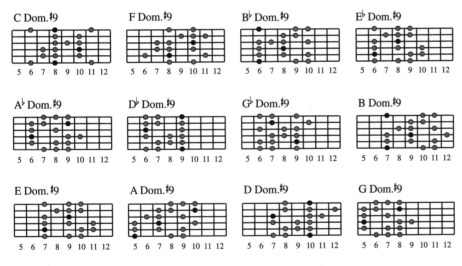

Two-Note-per-String Fingering

E Dominant ♯9

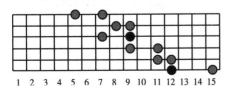

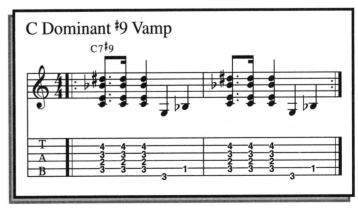

C Dominant ♯9 Vamp

Dominant ♭13 Pentatonic (1 3 5 ♭6 ♭7 8)

The *dominant ♭13 pentatonic* scale is five-note scale that works specifically with a 7♭13 chord. It can be considered a pentatonic version of the *Aeolian Major* scale (page 195, the 6th mode of the *jazz minor* scale, page 247). Along with its altered dominant application, dominant ♭13 pentatonic may also be used in a *Phrygian* context (pages 297-302). The vamp at the bottom right corner of the page uses the 7 ♭13 chord to illustrate this scale's specific application. Try substituting this scale in any altered dominant or Phrygian context.

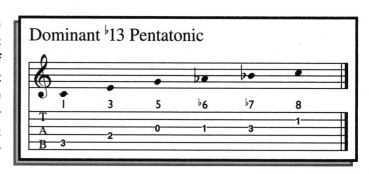
Dominant ♭13 Pentatonic

Open Position
C Dom.♭13 pent.

Single-String Fingering
C Dom.♭13 pent.

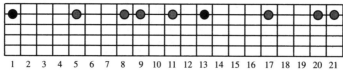

Position Fingerings Through the Circle of 4ths

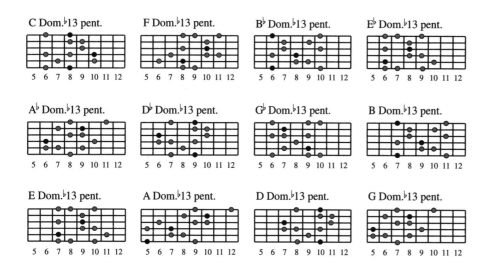

C Dom.♭13 pent.   F Dom.♭13 pent.   B♭ Dom.♭13 pent.   E♭ Dom.♭13 pent.

A♭ Dom.♭13 pent.   D♭ Dom.♭13 pent.   G♭ Dom.♭13 pent.   B Dom.♭13 pent.

E Dom.♭13 pent.   A Dom.♭13 pent.   D Dom.♭13 pent.   G Dom.♭13 pent.

Two-Note-per-String Fingering

E Dom.♭13 pent.

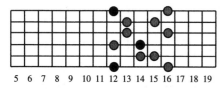

E Dominant ♭13 Pentatonic Vamp

Vertical side text: Dominant ♭13 Pentatonic

Dominant ♭9 ♯11 (1 ♭2 3 ♯4 5 6 ♭7 8)

The *dominant ♭9♯11* scale is a seven-note hybrid scale that contains a dominant 7 chord with the ♭9 and ♯11 altered tensions. It is very similar to the *altered dominant* scale (page 197, the 7th mode of the *jazz minor* scale, page 247), except that it does not contain the ♯9 or the ♭13 altered tensions. Like the other hybrid altered dominant scales, it can be substituted for any altered dominant scale application. The vamp at the bottom right corner of the page uses two altered dominant chord voicings that reflect both of the altered tensions found in the scale—the ♭9 and the ♯11.

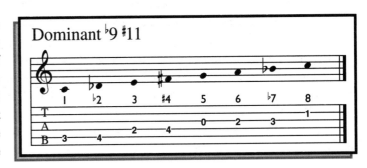

Dominant ♭9 ♯11

Open Position

C Dom.♭9♯11

Single-String Fingering

C Dom.♭9♯11

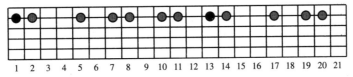

Position Fingerings Through the Circle of 4ths

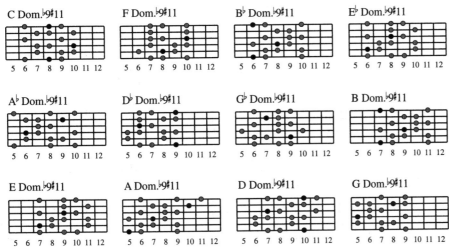

C Dom.♭9♯11 F Dom.♭9♯11 B♭ Dom.♭9♯11 E♭ Dom.♭9♯11

A♭ Dom.♭9♯11 D♭ Dom.♭9♯11 G♭ Dom.♭9♯11 B Dom.♭9♯11

E Dom.♭9♯11 A Dom.♭9♯11 D Dom.♭9♯11 G Dom.♭9♯11

Two-Note-per-String Fingering

E Dom.♭9♯11

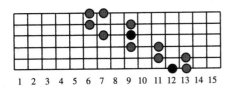

A Dominant ♭9 ♯11 Vamp

A7♭9♯11

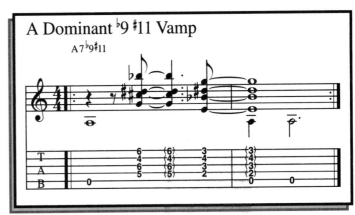

Dominant ♭9 ♯11 ♭13 (1 ♭2 3 ♯4 5 ♭6 ♭7 8)

The *dominant ♭9 ♯11 ♭13* scale is a seven-note hybrid scale that contains a dominant 7 chord with the ♭9, ♯11 and ♭13 altered tensions. It is very similar to the *altered dominant* scale (page 197, the 7th mode of the *jazz minor* scale, page 247) except that it does not contain the ♯9 altered tension. It can, however, be substituted in any altered dominant scale application. The vamp at the bottom right corner of this page uses three altered dominant chords that reflect each of the altered tensions found in the scale—the ♭9, ♯11 and ♭13.

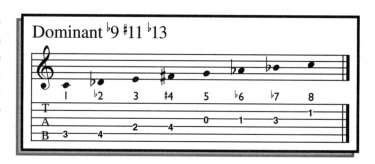

Dominant ♭9 ♯11 ♭13

Open Position

C Dom. ♭9♯11♭13

Single-String Fingering

C Dom. ♭9♯11♭13

Position Fingerings Through the Circle of 4ths

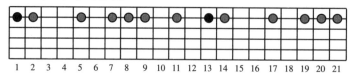

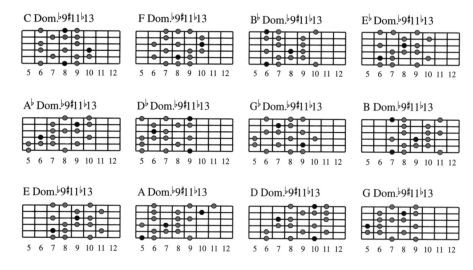

C Dom.♭9♯11♭13   F Dom.♭9♯11♭13   B♭ Dom.♭9♯11♭13   E♭ Dom.♭9♯11♭13

A♭ Dom.♭9♯11♭13   D♭ Dom.♭9♯11♭13   G♭ Dom.♭9♯11♭13   B Dom.♭9♯11♭13

E Dom.♭9♯11♭13   A Dom.♭9♯11♭13   D Dom.♭9♯11♭13   G Dom.♭9♯11♭13

Two-Note-per-String Fingering

E Dom.♭9♯11♭13

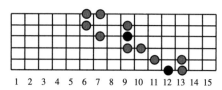

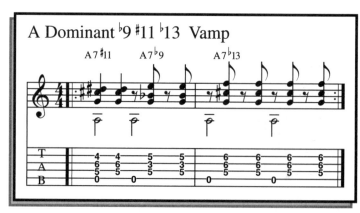

A Dominant ♭9 ♯11 ♭13 Vamp

A7♯11   A7♭9   A7♭13

Dominant sus4 ♭13 Pentatonic (1 2 4 ♭6 ♭7 8)

The *dominant sus4 ♭13 pentatonic* scale is a five-note scale that can be used over a dominant 7 chord with a suspended 4 and an added ♭13 altered tension (7sus♭13). It can be substituted for other 7sus♭13-type scales, including the *major ♭6 pentatonic* scale (page 275) and the *Aeolian Major* scale (page 195, the 5th mode of the *jazz minor* scale, page 247). The vamp uses two altered dominant suspended chords. Try using the dominant sus4 ♭13 pentatonic scale for *Phrygian* applications (pages 297-302) as well.

Dominant sus4 ♭13 Pentatonic

Open position

C Dom.sus4 ♭13 Pent.

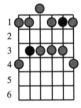

Single-string Fingering

C Dom.sus4 ♭13 Pent.

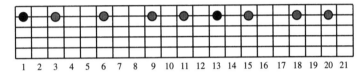

Position Fingerings Through the Circle of 4ths

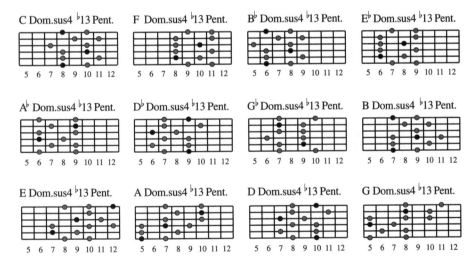

C Dom.sus4 ♭13 Pent.   F Dom.sus4 ♭13 Pent.   B♭ Dom.sus4 ♭13 Pent.   E♭ Dom.sus4 ♭13 Pent.

A♭ Dom.sus4 ♭13 Pent.   D♭ Dom.sus4 ♭13 Pent.   G♭ Dom.sus4 ♭13 Pent.   B Dom.sus4 ♭13 Pent.

E Dom.sus4 ♭13 Pent.   A Dom.sus4 ♭13 Pent.   D Dom.sus4 ♭13 Pent.   G Dom.sus4 ♭13 Pent.

Two-Note-per-String Fingering

E Dom.sus4 ♭13 Pent.

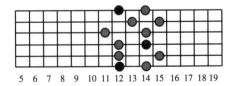

E Dominant sus4 ♭13 Pentatonic Vamp

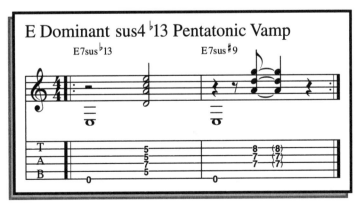

Dominant sus4 ♭13 Pentatonic

Dominant 9 Pentatonic (1 2 3 5 ♭7 8)

The *dominant 9 pentatonic* scale is a five-note scale which may be applied to a dominant 7 chord with an added 9. It can be considered a pentatonic version of the *Mixolydian mode* (page 293, the 5th mode of the *major* scale, page 272). The vamp at the bottom right corner of the page is the same as for the Mixolydian mode. Try altering between the two scale choices.

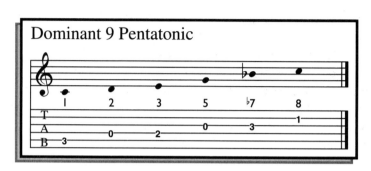

Dominant 9 Pentatonic

Open Position

C Dominant 9 Pentatonic

Single-String Fingering

C Dom. 9 Pent.

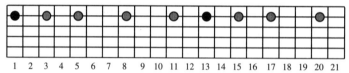

Position Fingerings Through the Circle of 4ths

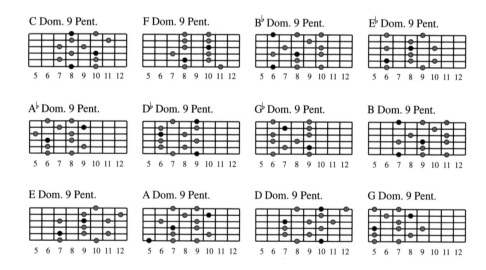

C Dom. 9 Pent.   F Dom. 9 Pent.   B♭ Dom. 9 Pent.   E♭ Dom. 9 Pent.

A♭ Dom. 9 Pent.   D♭ Dom. 9 Pent.   G♭ Dom. 9 Pent.   B Dom. 9 Pent.

E Dom. 9 Pent.   A Dom. 9 Pent.   D Dom. 9 Pent.   G Dom. 9 Pent.

Two-Note-per-String Fingering

E Dominant 9 Pentatonic

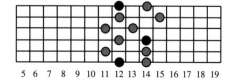

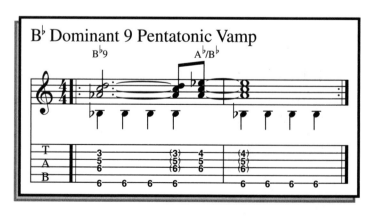

B♭ Dominant 9 Pentatonic Vamp

Dominant 13 (1 2 3 5 6 ♭7 8)

The *dominant 13* scale is a six-note hybrid scale with a specific dominant 13 chord or dominant 9/13 chord application. It can be considered a six-note version of the *Mixolydian mode* (page 293, the 5th mode of the *major* scale, page 272). The omission of the 4th scale degree gives this scale its specific emphasis on the 9 and 13 tensions. The harmony outlined in the vamp at the bottom right corner of the page is a dominant 7 chord with an added 13 tension. Use the dominant 13 scale to emphasize the essence of this type of harmony.

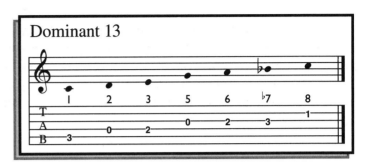

Dominant 13

Open Position

C Dominant 13

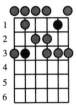

Single-String Fingering

C Dominant 13

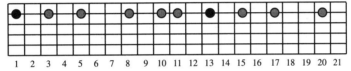

Position Fingerings Through the Circle of 4ths

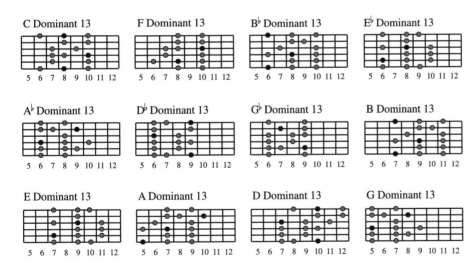

Two-Note-per-String Fingering

E Dominant 13

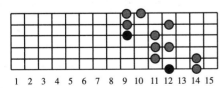

E Dominant 13 Vamp

Dominant 13 sus4 Pentatonic (1 2 4 6 ♭7 8)

The *dominant 13 sus4 pentatonic* scale is a five-note scale that can be played over a dominant 7 chord with a suspended 4 and an added 13 tension (13sus). It has a very specific application. It can be substituted for other unaltered dominant-type scales including: the *Mixolydian mode* (page 293, the 5th mode of the *major* scale, page 272) and the *dominant 9 pentatonic* scale (page 228). The vamp at the bottom right corner of the page is the same as for the Mixolydian mode. In the context of this progression, this scale emphasizes the 11 and 13 tensions.

Dominant 13 sus4 Pentatonic

Open position

C Dom. 13 sus4 Pent.

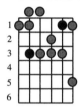

Single-String Fingering

C Dom. 13 sus4 Pent.

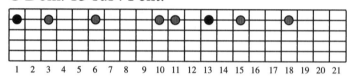

Position Fingerings Through the Circle of 4ths

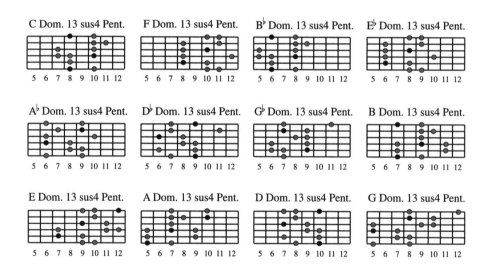

Two-Note-per-String Fingering

E Dom. 13 sus4 Pent.

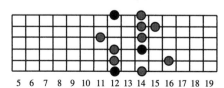

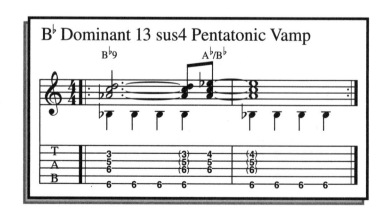
B♭ Dominant 13 sus4 Pentatonic Vamp

Dorian (1 2 ♭3 4 5 6 ♭7 8)

The *Dorian mode* is the 2nd mode of the major scale (page 272). The Dorian mode generates a min7 chord, which is very common, found in both functional and modal harmonic settings. Many players will superimpose the Dorian mode over other chords, for example: D Dorian over a G7 chord. This emphasizes desirable chord tensions or color tones of the G7. A good example of the use of Dorian can be found in the tune *So What* from Miles Davis' "Kind of Blue." The vamp at the bottom right corner of the page below illustrates Dorian over three minor-type chords. The Amin6 in the last measure emphasizes the very colorful 13 tension.

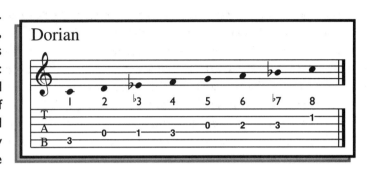

Dorian

Open Position

C Dorian

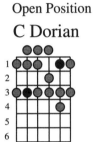

Single-String Fingering

C Dorian

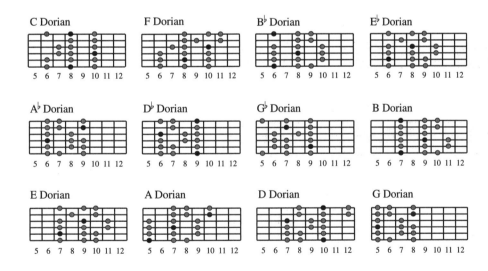

Position Fingerings Through the Circle of 4ths

C Dorian   F Dorian   B♭ Dorian   E♭ Dorian

A♭ Dorian   D♭ Dorian   G♭ Dorian   B Dorian

E Dorian   A Dorian   D Dorian   G Dorian

Two-Note-per-String Fingering

E Dorian

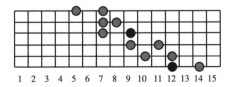

A Dorian Vamp

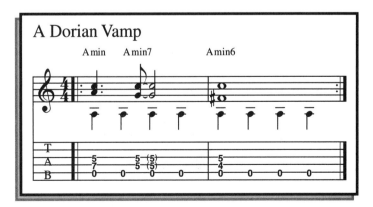

Dorian

Dorian ♯4 (1 2 ♭3 ♯4 5 6 ♭7 8)

The *Dorian ♯4* scale is the 4th mode of the *harmonic minor* scale (page 239). Dorian ♯4 is a rather specific sound. It can be used as a substitute for the *Dorian mode* (page 231), which produces a brighter sound, or the *Locrian mode* (page 251). If the 5 is omitted in the voicing, the sound is half diminished. The first measure of the vamp at the bottom right corner of the page demonstrates how Dorian ♯4 works within a minor context. The second measure utilizes the ♯4 in the voicing itself.

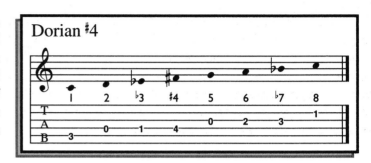

Dorian ♯4

Dorian ♯4

Open Position

C Dorian ♯4

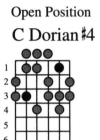

Single-String Fingering

C Dorian ♯4

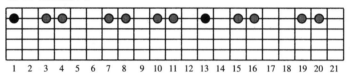

Position Fingerings Through the Circle of 4ths

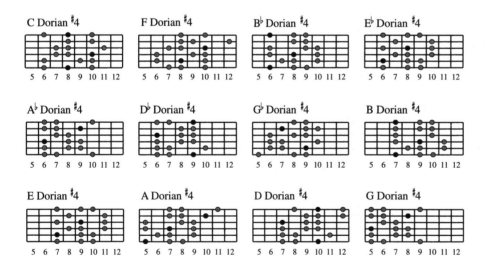

Two-Note-per-String Fingering

E Dorian ♯4

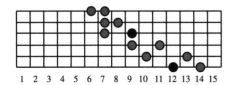

E Dorian ♯4 Vamp

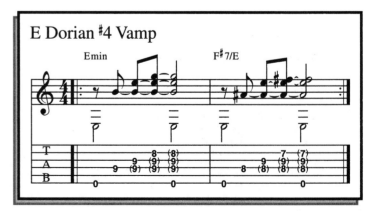

Dorian ♭5 (1 2 ♭3 4 ♭5 6 ♭7 8)

The *Dorian ♭5* scale is the 2nd mode of the *harmonic major* scale (page 238). The scale contains a min7♭5 chord, which makes it a good substitute for the various *Locrian* modes: *Locrian* (page 251), *Locrian* ♮2 (page 253) and *Locrian* ♮6 (page 254). The vamp at the bottom right corner of the page uses the min7♭5 chord to illustrate the specific application of Dorian ♭5. Use this scale as a substitute for the various Locrian-type sounds.

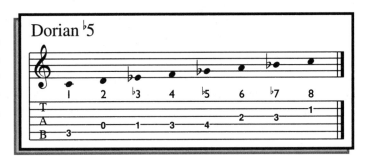

Dorian ♭5

Open Position

C Dorian ♭5

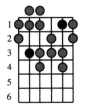

Single-String Fingering

C Dorian ♭5

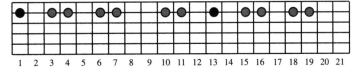

Position Fingerings Through the Circle of 4ths

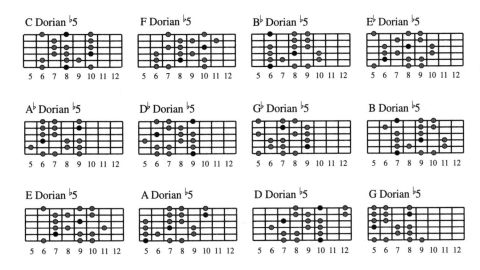

C Dorian ♭5
F Dorian ♭5
B♭ Dorian ♭5
E♭ Dorian ♭5
A♭ Dorian ♭5
D♭ Dorian ♭5
G♭ Dorian ♭5
B Dorian ♭5
E Dorian ♭5
A Dorian ♭5
D Dorian ♭5
G Dorian ♭5

Two-Note-per-String Fingering

E Dorian ♭5

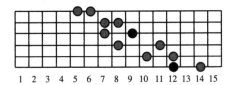

D Dorian ♭5 Vamp

Dorian Pentatonic (1 2 ♭3 5 ♭7 8)

The *Dorian pentatonic* scale is a five-note version of the *Dorian mode* (page 231, the 2nd mode of the *major* scale, page 272). It is also known as the *Pygmy* scale from Rwanda, Africa. The scale forms a min7 chord with an added 9, making it useful for any Dorian situation. The vamp at the bottom right corner of the page is the same as for the Dorian mode. The chords clearly emphasize the various flavors of the scale (min, min7 and min6).

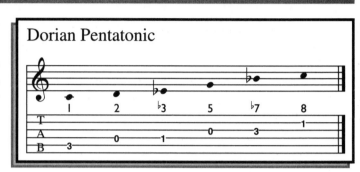
Dorian Pentatonic

Open Position

C Dorian Pent.

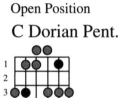

Single-String Fingering

C Dorian Pent.

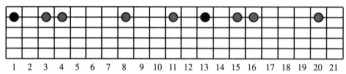

Position Fingerings Through the Circle of 4ths

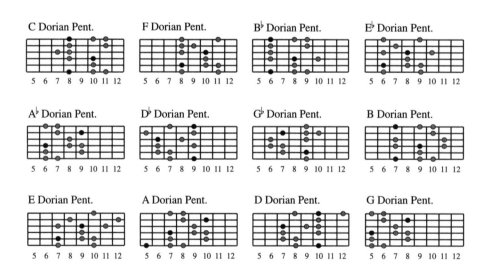

C Dorian Pent.

F Dorian Pent.

B♭ Dorian Pent.

E♭ Dorian Pent.

A♭ Dorian Pent.

D♭ Dorian Pent.

G♭ Dorian Pent.

B Dorian Pent.

E Dorian Pent.

A Dorian Pent.

D Dorian Pent.

G Dorian Pent.

Two-Note-per-String Fingering

E Dorian Pent.

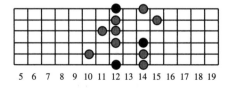

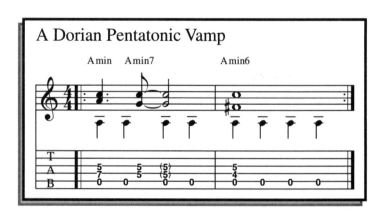
A Dorian Pentatonic Vamp

Egyptian (1 2 ♭3 ♯4 5 ♭6 7 8)

The *Egyptian* scale is an interesting seven-note hybrid that resembles the *harmonic minor* scale (page 239) with an added ♯11 altered tension. The name comes from its unique North African sound. This scale can be applied as a substitute for the *altered dominant* scale (page 197). The harmony outlined in the vamp at the bottom right corner of the page is an altered dominant 7 chord, A♭7♭5. Building the Egyptian scale starting on the 3rd of this chord produces the following chord/scale relationship: C=3rd of the chord, D=♭5, E♭=♯5, G♭=♭7, G=7 (which acts as a passing or leading tone, as in the bebop scales), A♭=root and B=♯9. In this context, the Egyptian scale provides important chord tones, altered tensions and passing tones.

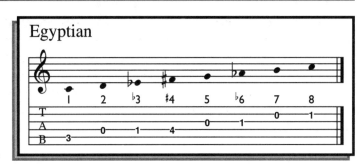

Egyptian

Open Position

C Egyptian

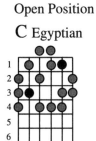

Single-String Fingering

C Egyptian

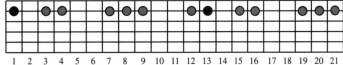

Position Fingerings Through the Circle of 4ths

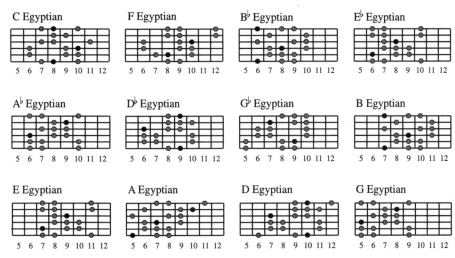

C Egyptian · F Egyptian · B♭ Egyptian · E♭ Egyptian

A♭ Egyptian · D♭ Egyptian · G♭ Egyptian · B Egyptian

E Egyptian · A Egyptian · D Egyptian · G Egyptian

Two-Note-per-String Fingering

E Egyptian

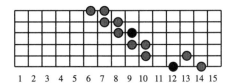

C Egyptian Vamp

A♭7♭5

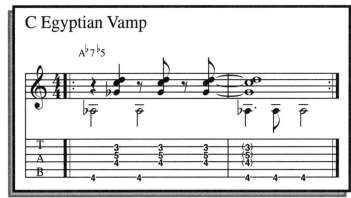

Four-Semitone Tritone (1 ♭2 2 ♭3 3 ♯4 5 ♭6 6 ♭7 8)

The *four-semitone tritone* scale is a eleven-note scale consisting of a pattern of four semitones (half steps) followed by a major 2nd interval (two half steps) that is repeated. It is a relatively new symmetrical scale that improvisers have been experimenting with recently. Depending on the application, the half steps in this scale could be viewed as passing or leading tones to certain chord tones. The chord built off the root of this scale is a dominant 7. Used in a dominant application, this scale provides the following natural and altered tensions: ♭9, 9, ♯9, ♯11, ♭13 and 13. The vamp at the bottom right corner of the page centers around the scale's altered dominant capacity.

Four-Semitone Tritone

Four Semitone Tritone

Open Position

C Four-Semitone Tritone

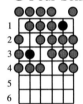

Single-String Fingering

C Four-Semitone Tritone

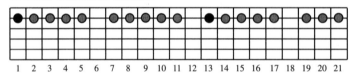

Position Fingerings Through the Circle of 4ths

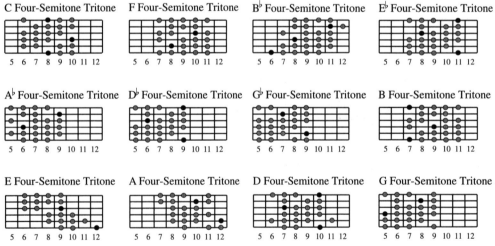

C Four-Semitone Tritone

F Four-Semitone Tritone

B♭ Four-Semitone Tritone

E♭ Four-Semitone Tritone

A♭ Four-Semitone Tritone

D♭ Four-Semitone Tritone

G♭ Four-Semitone Tritone

B Four-Semitone Tritone

E Four-Semitone Tritone

A Four-Semitone Tritone

D Four-Semitone Tritone

G Four-Semitone Tritone

Two-Note-per-String Fingering

E Four-Semitone Tritone

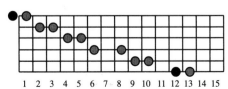

C Four-Semitone Tritone Vamp

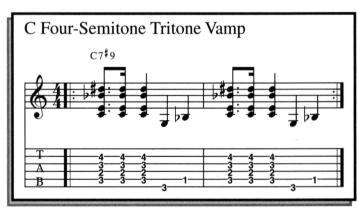

Goonkali (1 ♭2 4 5 ♭6 8)

Goonkali is a traditional five-note Indian *raga* (scale). In a Western context, Goonkali translates into a *sus4♭9♭13 pentatonic* scale, which makes it an excellent substitution for any *Phrygian* (pages 297-302) or altered dominant-type choice. Goonkali emphasizes the 4th degree, giving it a suspended quality, and includes the ♭9 and ♭13 altered tensions found in many dominant 7 applications. The vamp at the bottom right corner of the page is the same as for Phrygian (page 297). It emphasizes both Phrygian and sus4 altered uses.

Goonkali

Open Position

C Goonkali

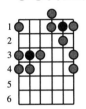

Single-String Fingering

C Goonkali

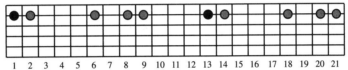

Position Fingerings Through the Circle of 4ths

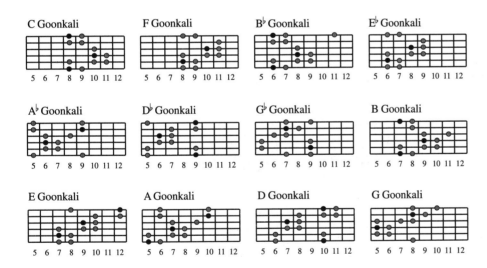

C Goonkali   F Goonkali   B♭ Goonkali   E♭ Goonkali

A♭ Goonkali   D♭ Goonkali   G♭ Goonkali   B Goonkali

E Goonkali   A Goonkali   D Goonkali   G Goonkali

Two-Note-per-String Fingering

E Goonkali

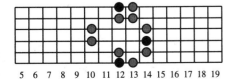

A Goonkali Vamp

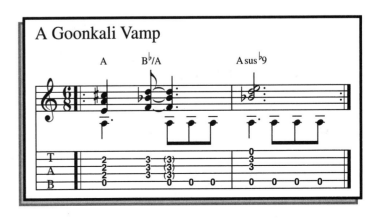

Goonkali

Harmonic Major (1 2 3 4 5 ♭6 7 8)

The *harmonic major* scale is constructed by the following sequence of whole (W) and half (H) steps: W-W-H-W-H-W+H (augmented 2nd)-H. Like the *harmonic minor* scale (page 239), the augmented 2nd interval (♭6-7) gives this scale its characteristic sound. The harmonic major scale provides seven interesting modes that are found in a variety of contexts. They are: 1st mode=*Harmonic Major 9* (Ionian ♭6), 2nd mode=*Dorian ♭5*, 3rd mode=*Phrygian ♭4*, 4th mode=*Lydian ♭3*, 5th mode=*Mixolydian ♭9*, 6th mode=*Lydian Augmented #2* and 7th mode=*Locrian ♭♭7*. These modes may be thought of as "exotic" or altered versions of their unaltered counterparts. In the vamp at the bottom right corner of the page, harmonic major is superimposed over a chord with a different root. G Harmonic Major over the chord B/C produces a B Altered Dominant sound (G=♭13, A=♭7, B=root, C=♭9, D=#9, E♭=3 and F#=5).

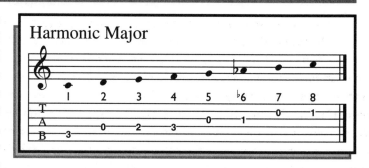

Harmonic Major

Open Position **C Harmonic Maj.**

Single-String Fingering **C Harmonic Major**

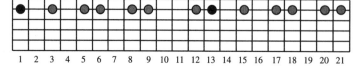

Position Fingerings Through the Circle of 4ths

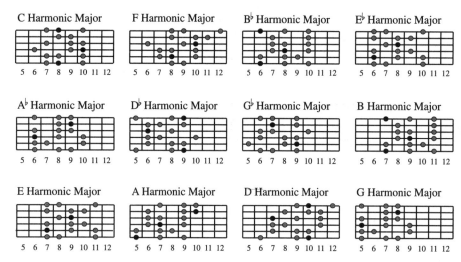

C Harmonic Major   F Harmonic Major   B♭ Harmonic Major   E♭ Harmonic Major

A♭ Harmonic Major   D♭ Harmonic Major   G♭ Harmonic Major   B Harmonic Major

E Harmonic Major   A Harmonic Major   D Harmonic Major   G Harmonic Major

Two-Note-per-String Fingering

E Harmonic Major

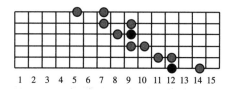

G Harmonic Major Vamp

Harmonic Minor (1 2 ♭3 4 5 ♭6 7 8)

The *harmonic minor* scale is constructed by the following sequence of whole (W) and half (H) steps: W-H-W-W-H-W+H (augmented 2nd)-H. The augmented 2nd (♭6-7) gives this scale its characteristic sound. The harmonic minor scale also produces seven interesting modes that can be useful in a variety of contexts. They are: 1st mode=*harmonic minor* (Aeolian ♮7), 2nd mode=*Locrian ♮6* (page 254), 3rd mode=*Ionian augmented* (page 244), 4th mode=*Dorian #4* (page 232), 5th mode=*Phrygian major* (page 299), 6th mode=*Lydian #9* (page 258) and 7th mode=*altered dominant ♭♭7* (page 198). Because of its leading tone, the harmonic minor scale works well over a ii-V progression (iimin7♭5-V7alt.). The vamp below illustrates this scale's use within a minor ii-V progression. The leading tone (raised 7th degree) is actually 3 of the V7 chord, which makes this scale a great choice for this progression.

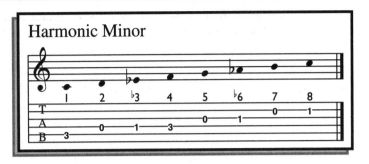

Harmonic Minor

Open Position
C Harmonic Minor

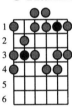

Single-String Fingering
C Harmonic Minor

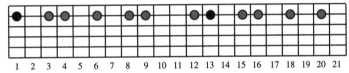

Position Fingerings Through the Circle of 4ths

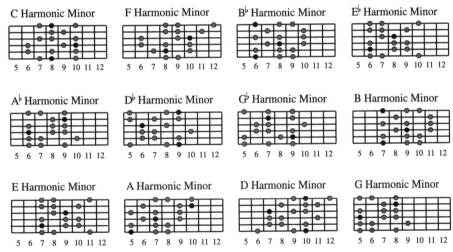

C Harmonic Minor   F Harmonic Minor   B♭ Harmonic Minor   E♭ Harmonic Minor

A♭ Harmonic Minor   D♭ Harmonic Minor   G♭ Harmonic Minor   B Harmonic Minor

E Harmonic Minor   A Harmonic Minor   D Harmonic Minor   G Harmonic Minor

Two-Note-per-String Fingering

E Harmonic Minor

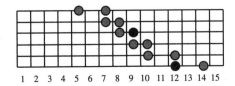

C Harmonic Minor Vamp

Harmonic Minor ♭5 (1 2 ♭3 4 ♭5 ♭6 7 8)

The *harmonic minor* ♭5 scale is a seven-note hybrid scale that resembles a *harmonic minor* scale (page 239) with a ♭5. It can be superimposed in an altered dominant context. The harmony outlined in the vamp at the bottom right corner of the page is quite specific to the scale. The chord E♭/E was formed by spelling a major triad built on the 7th degree of the E Harmonic Minor ♭5 scale (D♯-G-B♭ = E♭-G-B♭). The bass line contains pitches from the scale. The end result is a dissonant, altered dominant sound. With the 2nd scale degree, F♯ as the root, this chord could be construed as F♯13♭9 (E♭/D♯=13, G=♭9, B♭/A♯=3rd, E=♭7).

Harmonic Minor ♭5

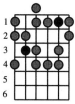

Open Position

C Harm. Min.♭5

Single-String Fingering

C Harm. Min.♭5

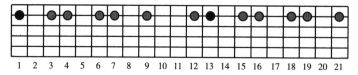

Position Fingerings Through the Circle of 4ths

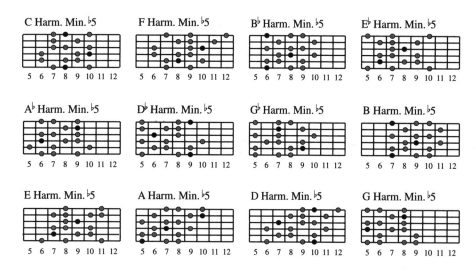

C Harm. Min. ♭5	F Harm. Min. ♭5	B♭ Harm. Min. ♭5	E♭ Harm. Min. ♭5
A♭ Harm. Min. ♭5	D♭ Harm. Min. ♭5	G♭ Harm. Min. ♭5	B Harm. Min. ♭5
E Harm. Min. ♭5	A Harm. Min. ♭5	D Harm. Min. ♭5	G Harm. Min. ♭5

Two-Note-per-String Fingering

E Harm. Min.♭5

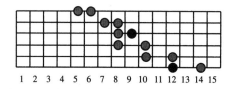

E Harmonic Minor ♭5 Vamp

Harmonic Sus4 (1 2 4 5 ♭6 7 8)

The *harmonic sus4* scale is a six-note hybrid scale that resembles the *harmonic minor* scale (page 239) with the ♭3rd scale degree omitted. The harmonic sus4 scale can be construed as a suspended 4th version of the harmonic minor scale, and so it can be applied to harmonic minor situations. It can also be viewed as a substitute for the *altered dominant* scale (page 197). The scale degrees are: 1, 2, sus4 (11), 5, ♭13, 7 (which acts as a leading tone to the root), 8. The vamp at the bottom right illustrates the scale's altered dominant application. The harmony outlined reflects the special tones of the scale (sus4 and ♭13). Try using this scale in any altered dominant context.

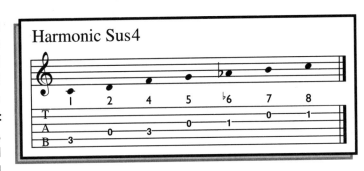

Harmonic Sus4

Open Position
C Harm. Sus4

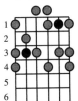

Single-String Fingering
C Harm. Sus4

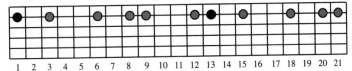

Position Fingerings Through the Circle of 4ths

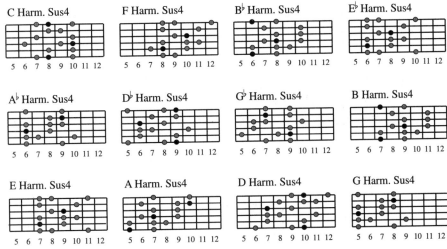

Two-Note-per-String Fingering

E Harm. Sus4

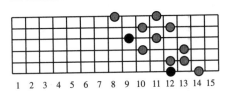

G Harmonic Sus4 Vamp

Hungarian Major (1 2 ♭3 4 ♭5 ♭6 ♭♭7 8)

The *Hungarian major* scale is an interesting seven-note scale that can be applied in various *Locrian* (pages 251-254) or min7♭5 contexts. It contains both the ♭6 and natural 6 (♭♭7) scale degrees, which makes it a particularly colorful choice. The vamp at the bottom right of the page is the same as for the *Locrian* ♭2 scale (page 253, the 6th mode of the *jazz minor* scale, page 247). Experiment with the two types of 6th scale degrees.

Hungarian Major

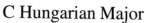

Open Position

C Hungarian Maj.
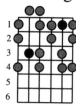

Single-String Fingering

C Hungarian Major
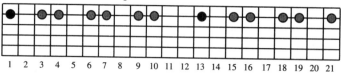

Position Fingerings Through the Circle of 4ths

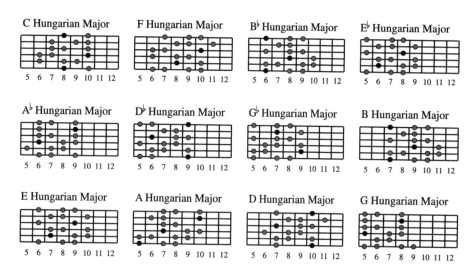

C Hungarian Major • F Hungarian Major • B♭ Hungarian Major • E♭ Hungarian Major

A♭ Hungarian Major • D♭ Hungarian Major • G♭ Hungarian Major • B Hungarian Major

E Hungarian Major • A Hungarian Major • D Hungarian Major • G Hungarian Major

Two-Note-per-String Fingering

E Hungarian Major
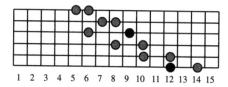

A Hungarian Major Vamp

Dmin/A · Amin7♭5 · Dmin/A · Amin7♭5

Ionian ♭5 (1 2 3 4 ♭5 6 7 8)

The *Ionian ♭5* scale is a hybrid scale that resembles the *Ionian mode* (page 272, the 1st mode of the *major* scale) with a flatted 5th degree. Ionian ♭5 is similar in applications to the *Lydian augmented* scale (page 260, 3rd mode of the *jazz minor* scale, page 247). It can be used with a Maj7♭5 or Maj7♯11. Within these applications, consider the 4th scale degree a passing tone to the ♭5. The vamp at the bottom right corner of the page uses the Maj7♭5 sound to explore the ionian ♭5 scale.

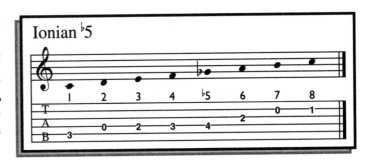

Ionian ♭5

Open Position

C Ionian ♭5

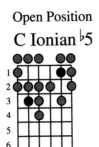

Single-String Fingering

C Ionian ♭5

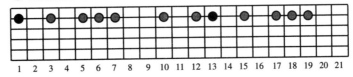

Position Fingerings Through the Circle of 4ths

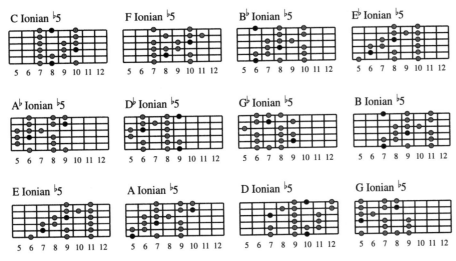

C Ionian ♭5   F Ionian ♭5   B♭ Ionian ♭5   E♭ Ionian ♭5

A♭ Ionian ♭5   D♭ Ionian ♭5   G♭ Ionian ♭5   B Ionian ♭5

E Ionian ♭5   A Ionian ♭5   D Ionian ♭5   G Ionian ♭5

Two-Note-per-String Fingering

E Ionian ♭5

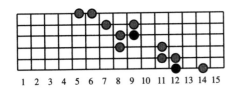

E♭ Ionian ♭5 Vamp

E♭Maj7♭5

Ionian Augmented (1 2 3 4 ♯5 6 7 8)

The *Ionian augmented* scale is the 3rd mode of the *harmonic minor* scale (page 239). It can be substituted for the *Lydian augmented* scale (page 260) resulting in a softer, less harsh sound. Its functional and modal usage is similar to Lydian augmented. The two chords in the vamp below emphasize the ♯5 (AMaj7♯5) and the natural 11 (B°/A) scale degrees. Remember to avoid the natural 11 in Maj7th voicings (the 11 right next to the 3 produces an unwanted minor 2nd dissonance).

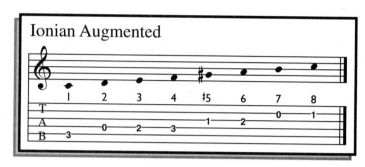
Ionian Augmented

Open Position

C Ionian Augmented

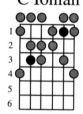

Single-String Fingering

C Ionian Augmented

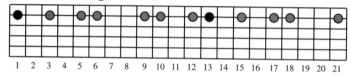

Position Fingerings Through the Circle of 4ths

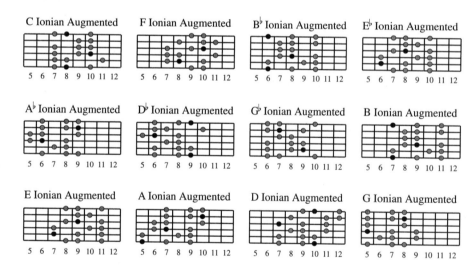

Two-Note-per-String Fingering

E Ionian Augmented

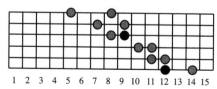

A Ionian Augmented Vamp

Iraq (1 ♭2 ♭3 4 ♭5 ♭6 ♭7 7 8)

Iraq is an eight-note Arabian scale. In a Western context, Iraq can be viewed as a bebop version of the *Locrian mode* (page 251, the 7th mode of the *major* scale, page 272). Remember that the bebop-type scales add passing tones. The passing tone in this scale acts as the leading tone to the root. The vamp at the bottom right is the same as for the Locrian mode. Iraq makes an excellent alternative in any Locrian context. The passing tone imparts a jazz quality to the scale.

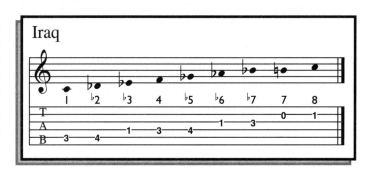

Iraq

Open Position

C Iraq

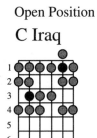

Single-String Fingering

C Iraq

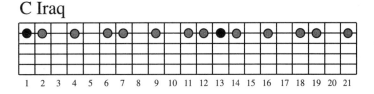

Position Fingerings Through the Circle of 4ths

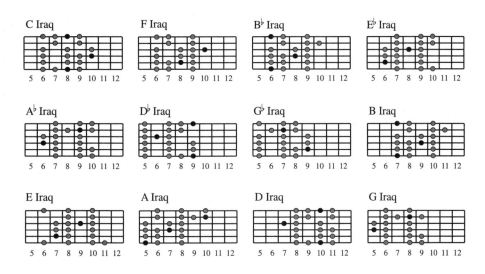

C Iraq   F Iraq   B♭ Iraq   E♭ Iraq

A♭ Iraq   D♭ Iraq   G♭ Iraq   B Iraq

E Iraq   A Iraq   D Iraq   G Iraq

Two-Note-per-String Fingering

E Iraq

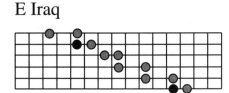

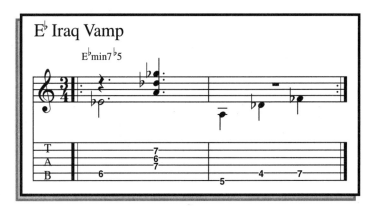

E♭ Iraq Vamp

E♭min7♭5

Iwato (1 ♭2 4 ♭5 ♭7 8)

Iwato is a traditional five-note Japanese scale. In a Western context, Iwato translates into a *dominant sus ♭5 ♭9 pentatonic* scale, which may be applied to an altered dominant sound. Iwato emphasizes the 4th degree, giving it a suspended quality. Even though the 3 is not in the scale, the presence of the ♭7, with the ♭5 and ♭9 altered tensions, makes Iwato a good altered dominant pentatonic choice. The vamp at the bottom right illustrates how Iwato can be used in an altered dominant context. Both chords emphasize the important aspects of this scale: the 4, ♭5, ♭7 and ♭9.

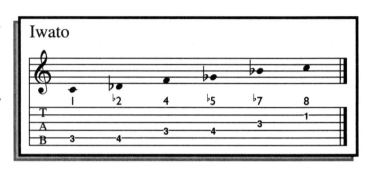

Iwato

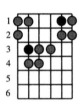
Iwato

Open Position
C Iwato

Single-String Fingering
C Iwato

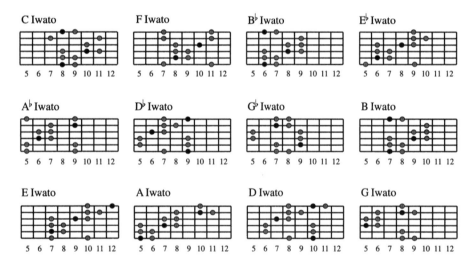

Position Fingerings Through the Circle of 4ths

C Iwato   F Iwato   B♭ Iwato   E♭ Iwato

A♭ Iwato   D♭ Iwato   G♭ Iwato   B Iwato

E Iwato   A Iwato   D Iwato   G Iwato

Two-Note-per-String Fingering

E Iwato

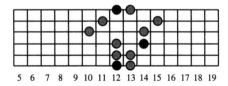

A Iwato Vamp

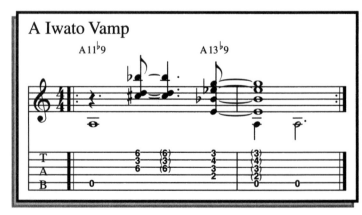

Jazz Minor/Melodic Minor (1 2 ♭3 4 5 6 7 8)

The *jazz minor* (or *melodic minor*, ascending*) is constructed by the following sequence of whole (W) and half (H) steps: W, H, W, W, W, W, H. The jazz minor scale produces seven interesting modes found in a variety of contexts. They are: 1st mode=jazz minor (*Ionian* ♭3), 2nd mode=*Phrygian* ♮6, 3rd mode=*Lydian Augmented*, 4th mode=*Lydian* ♭7, 5th mode=*Aeolian major*, 6th mode=*Locrian* ♮2 and 7th mode=*altered dominant*. As you can see, the names of these modes are variations on the names of the *major* (page 272) scale modes. Three of these modes are altered dominant-oriented (Lydian dominant, Aeolian major and altered dominant) and work well over dominant 7 chords containing altered tensions (♭9, ♯9, ♭5, ♭13). The vamp below demonstrates how jazz minor can be used in a min/Maj9 chord context.

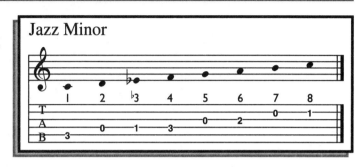

Jazz Minor

Open Position

C Jazz Minor

Single-String Fingering

C Jazz Minor

* In a classical context, the *melodic minor* scale ascends just as shown here for the jazz minor, but it descends differently, as a *natural minor* (*Aeolian*) scale (page 193).

Position Fingerings Through the Circle of 4ths

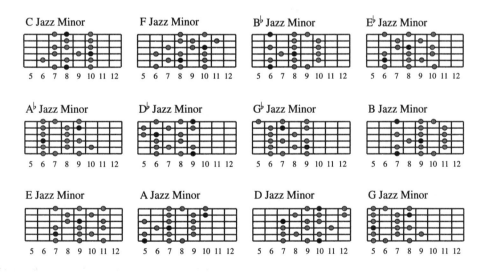

C Jazz Minor   F Jazz Minor   B♭ Jazz Minor   E♭ Jazz Minor

A♭ Jazz Minor   D♭ Jazz Minor   G♭ Jazz Minor   B Jazz Minor

E Jazz Minor   A Jazz Minor   D Jazz Minor   G Jazz Minor

Two-Note-per-String Fingering

E Jazz Minor

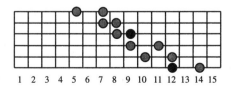

D Jazz Minor Vamp

Dmin/Maj9

Kokin-Choshi (1 ♭2 4 5 ♭7 8)

Kokin-Choshi is a traditional five-note Japanese scale. In a Western context, Kokin-Choshi translates into a *dominant sus♭9 pentatonic* scale, which may be applied to a *Phrygian* (pages 297-302) or altered dominant (page 197) sound. It works particularly well with a 7sus♭9 chord. The vamp at the bottom right corner of the page is the same as for the Phrygian (page 297).

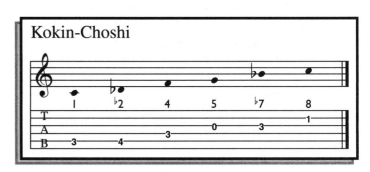

Kokin-Choshi

Open Position
C Kokin-Choshi

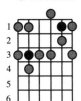

Single-String Fingering
C Kokin-Choshi

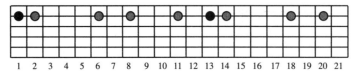

Position Fingerings Through the Circle of 4ths

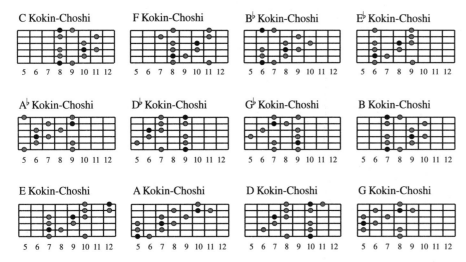

Two-Note-per-String Fingering

E Kokin-Choshi

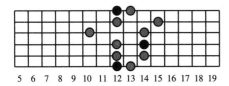

E Kokin-Choshi Vamp

Kumoi (1 2 ♭3 5 6 8)

Kumoi is a traditional five-note Japanese scale. In a Western context, Kumoi translates into a *minor 6 pentatonic* scale, which may be used to play over min6 or a min/Maj7 sounds. The vamp at the bottom right corner of the page is the same as for the *jazz minor* scale (page 247). Try alternating between the two choices.

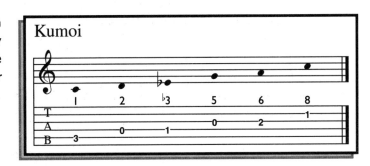

Kumoi

Open Position

C Kumoi

Single-String Fingering

C Kumoi

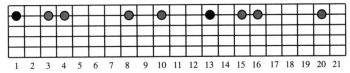

Position Fingerings Through the Circle of 4ths

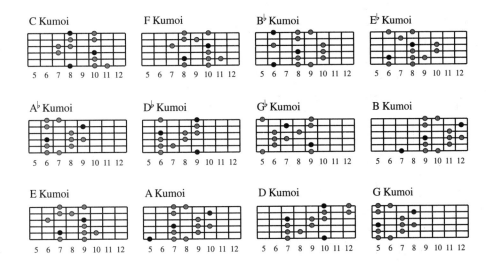

Two-Note-per-String Fingering

E Kumoi

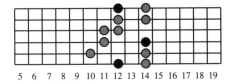

D Kumoi Vamp

Dmin/Maj9

250

Leading-Tone Blues (1 ♯4 6 ♭7 7 8)

The *leading-tone blues* scale is an interesting five-note scale that resembles a pentatonic version of the *Lydian* ♭7 scale (page 257, the 4th mode of the *jazz minor* scale, page 247) with an added passing tone (the leading tone, a major 7 above the root) between ♭7 and 8. There is a strong emphasis on the ♯4 and the ♭7, which gives the scale a distinctive 7♯11 application. The vamp at the bottom right corner of the page is the same as for Lydian ♭7. The passing tone between the ♭7 and 8 helps provide a stronger resolution to the root. Try substituting the this scale for any 7♯11 or in any *minor pentatonic blues* (page 291) context.

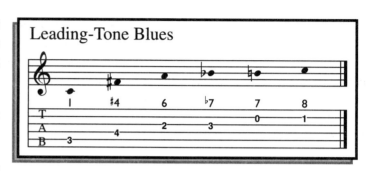

Leading-Tone Blues

Leading-Tone Blues

Open Position

C Leading-Tone Blues

Single-String Fingering

C Leading-Tone Blues

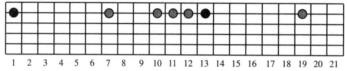

Position Fingerings Through the Circle of 4ths

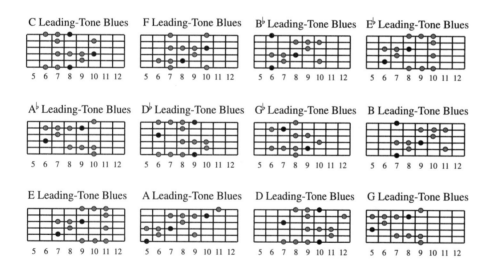

C Leading-Tone Blues   F Leading-Tone Blues   B♭ Leading-Tone Blues   E♭ Leading-Tone Blues

A♭ Leading-Tone Blues   D♭ Leading-Tone Blues   G♭ Leading-Tone Blues   B Leading-Tone Blues

E Leading-Tone Blues   A Leading-Tone Blues   D Leading-Tone Blues   G Leading-Tone Blues

Two-Note-per-String Fingering

E Leading-Tone Blues

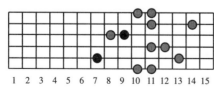

F Leading-Tone Blues Vamp

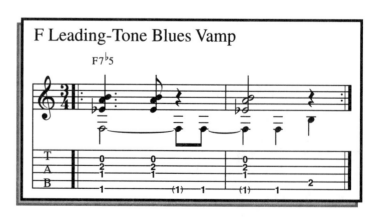

Locrian (1 ♭2 ♭3 4 ♭5 ♭6 ♭7 8)

The *Locrian mode* is the 7th mode of the *major* scale (page 272). It is interpreted as a min7♭5 (half-diminished) sound. Locrian is the diatonic chord scale for the vii chord in a major key, but *Locrian* ♮2 (page 253) is a better choice for the ii chord in a minor key (also a min7♭5). Both will work in the context of ii7♭5-V-I progression. The vamp at the bottom right corner of the page uses the min7♭5 chord to illustrate the use of the Locrian mode. The original bebop musicians seemed to prefer Locrian in a min7♭5 context.

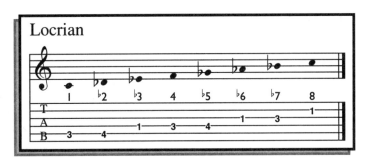

Locrian

Open Position

C Locrian

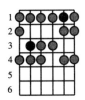

Single-String Fingering

C Locrian

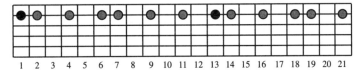

Position Fingerings Through the Circle of 4ths

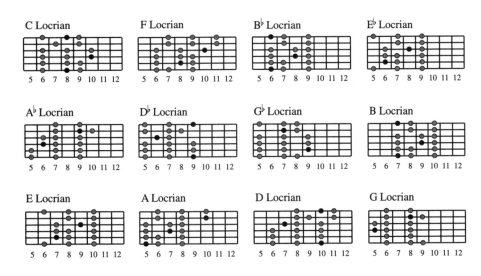

Two-Note-per-String Fingering

E Locrian

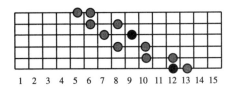

E♭ Locrian Vamp

E♭min7♭5

Locrian

Locrian ♭♭7 (1 ♭2 ♭3 4 ♭5 ♭6 ♭♭7 8)

The *Locrian* ♭♭7 scale is the 7th mode of the *harmonic major* scale (page 238). This scale is a variation on the *Locrian* mode (page 251, the 7th mode of the *major* scale, page 272) and can be used as a substitute for the various Locrian modes (Locrian, *Locrian* ♮2, page 253 and *Locrian* ♮6, page 254). The absence of a "real" 7th scale degree, in combination with the augmented 2nd interval from ♭♭7 to 1, makes this Locrian variation particularly melodic. The vamp at the bottom right corner of the page captures the Locrian ♭♭7 sound by using the min7♭5 and accenting the scale's ♭♭7 (A) found in the F+/E chord.

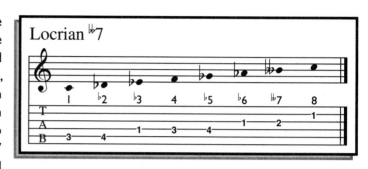

Locrian ♭♭7

Open Position

C Locrian ♭♭7

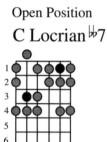

Single-String Fingering

C Locrian ♭♭7

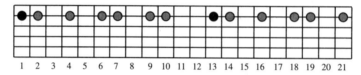

Position Fingerings Through the Circle of 4ths

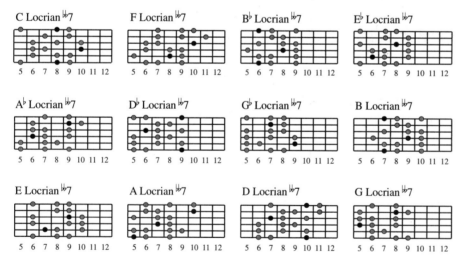

C Locrian ♭♭7   F Locrian ♭♭7   B♭ Locrian ♭♭7   E♭ Locrian ♭♭7

A♭ Locrian ♭♭7   D♭ Locrian ♭♭7   G♭ Locrian ♭♭7   B Locrian ♭♭7

E Locrian ♭♭7   A Locrian ♭♭7   D Locrian ♭♭7   G Locrian ♭♭7

Two-Note-per-String Fingering

E Locrian ♭♭7

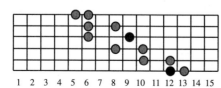

E Locrian ♭♭7 Vamp

Emin7♭5   F+/E   Emin7♭5   F+/E

Locrian ♮2 (1 2 ♭3 4 ♭5 ♭6 ♭7 8)

The *Locrian ♮2 scale* is the 6th mode of the *jazz minor* scale (page 247). The natural 9 (2) gives this mode a bit more stability as compared to the *Locrian mode* (page 251), which has a ♭2 degree. Locrian ♮2 can be used with any min7♭5 chord in a functional progression. This particular variation on the Locrian mode is popular among jazz musicians. The vamp at the bottom right corner of the page uses all the pitches in the scale except the natural 2. If you emphasize the 2, you'll really hear the special quality of that pitch. Try substituting this scale for any Locrian application.

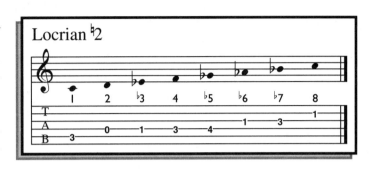

Locrian ♮2

Open Position
C Locrian ♮2

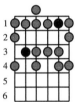

Single-String Fingering
C Locrian ♮2

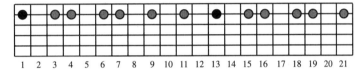

Position Fingerings Through the Circle of 4ths

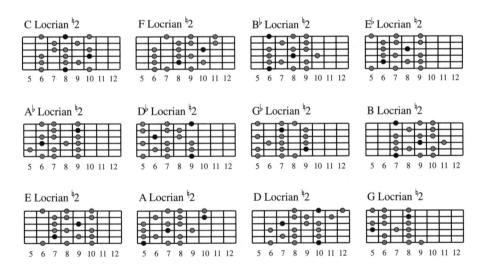

Two-Note-per-String Fingering

E Locrian ♮2

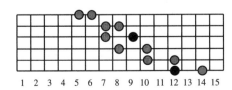

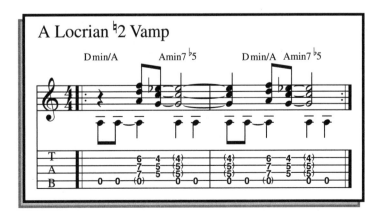

A Locrian ♮2 Vamp

Locrian ♮6 (1 ♭2 ♭3 4 ♭5 6 ♭7 8)

The *Locrian ♮6* scale is the 2nd mode of the *harmonic minor* scale (page 239). Locrian ♮6 produces a min7♭5 (half diminished) chord with a natural 13th tension. This scale is not as common as the other Locrian choices, but it will work as a substitute. The vamp in E at the bottom right corner of the page illustrates Locrian ♮6's min7♭5 application but also includes a chord (F+/E) that is specific to this scale because it includes the natural ♮6, C#.

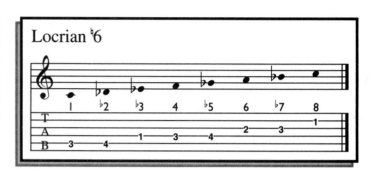

Locrian ♮6

Open Position
C Locrian ♮6

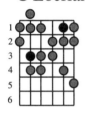

Single-String Fingering
C Locrian ♮6

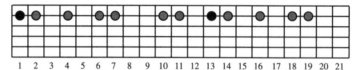

Position Fingerings Through the Circle of 4ths

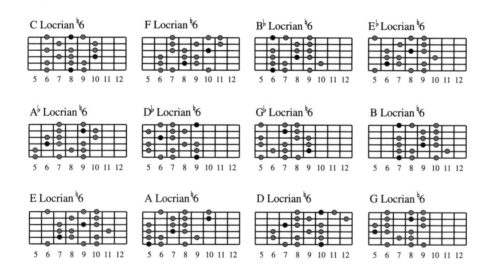

C Locrian ♮6 · F Locrian ♮6 · B♭ Locrian ♮6 · E♭ Locrian ♮6
A♭ Locrian ♮6 · D♭ Locrian ♮6 · G♭ Locrian ♮6 · B Locrian ♮6
E Locrian ♮6 · A Locrian ♮6 · D Locrian ♮6 · G Locrian ♮6

Two-Note-per-String Fingering

E Locrian ♮6

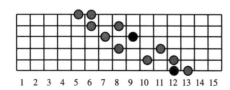

E Locrian ♮6 Vamp

Lydian (1 2 3 ♯4 5 6 7 8)

The *Lydian mode* is the 4th mode of the *major* scale (*Ionian mode*, page 272). The ♯4 of the scale provides a colorful alternative to the Maj7/Ionian sound. Modally, the ♯4 is usually voiced in the upper structure of the chord as a ♯11. The sound of the Lydian mode is tense, aggressive and expansive. The vamp at the bottom right corner of the page expresses the essence of the Lydian sound by emphasizing the 3, 7 and ♯11 of the chord. Try centering around these pitches when improvising with this scale.

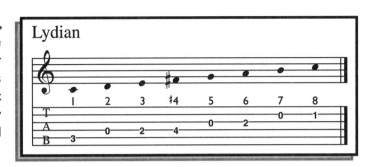

Lydian

Open Position

C Lydian

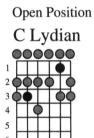

Single-String Fingering

C Lydian

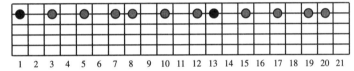

Position Fingerings Through the Circle of 4ths

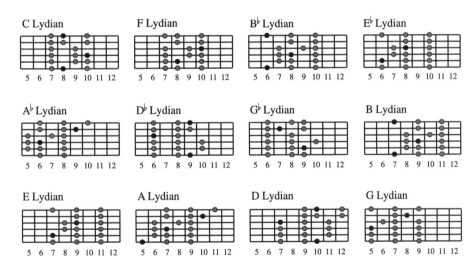

C Lydian   F Lydian   B♭ Lydian   E♭ Lydian

A♭ Lydian   D♭ Lydian   G♭ Lydian   B Lydian

E Lydian   A Lydian   D Lydian   G Lydian

Two-Note-per-String Fingering

E Lydian

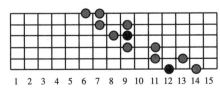

G Lydian Vamp

GMaj7♯11

Lydian

Lydian ♭3 (1 2 ♭3 ♯4 5 6 7 8)

The Lydian ♭3 scale is the 4th mode of the *harmonic major* scale (page 238). This scale is a variation on the *Lydian mode* (page 255) of the *major* scale (page 272) and it works well over a min6/9 chord in either a functional or modal harmonic situation. The ♯4 acts as a chromatic passing tone to 5. The vamp in A at the bottom right corner of the page utilizes the min6/9 chord (second measure) and a *Phrygian*-type voicing (page 297) built on the 7th scale degree (G♯ or A♭) in measure one (A♭/A).

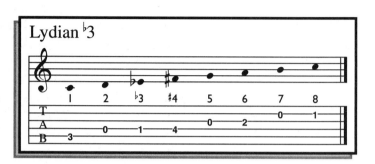

Lydian ♭3

Open Position

C Lydian ♭3

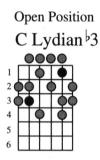

Single-String Fingering

C Lydian ♭3

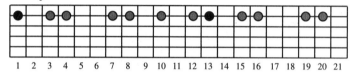

Position Fingerings Through the Circle of 4ths

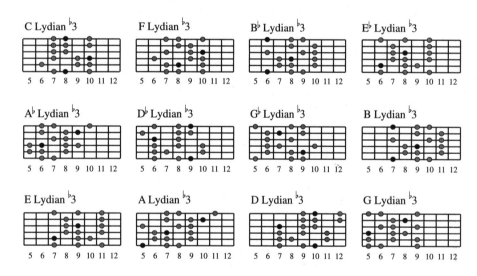

C Lydian ♭3 · F Lydian ♭3 · B♭ Lydian ♭3 · E♭ Lydian ♭3 · A♭ Lydian ♭3 · D♭ Lydian ♭3 · G♭ Lydian ♭3 · B Lydian ♭3 · E Lydian ♭3 · A Lydian ♭3 · D Lydian ♭3 · G Lydian ♭3

Two-Note-per-String Fingering

E Lydian ♭3

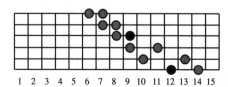

A Lydian ♭3 Vamp

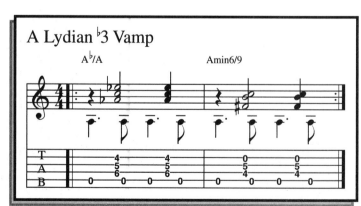

Lydian ♭7 (1 2 3 #4 5 6 ♭7)

The *Lydian* ♭7 scale is the 4th mode of the *jazz minor* scale (page 247). It is often referred to as *Lydian dominant* and is often used over a tritone substitution (♭II7-I) context. The vamp in F at the bottom right corner of the page below illustrates the Lydian ♭7 scale with a 7♭5♭13 chord. This scale can be used as a substitute for any altered dominant situation.

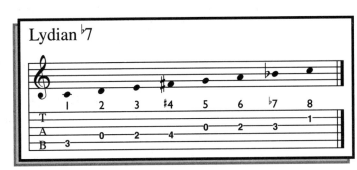

Lydian ♭7

Open Position
C Lydian ♭7

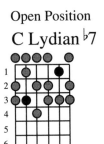

Single-String Fingering
C Lydian ♭7

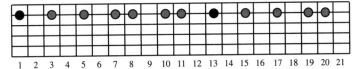

Position Fingerings Through the Circle of 4ths

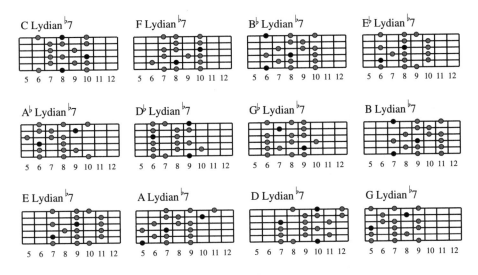

C Lydian ♭7 F Lydian ♭7 B♭ Lydian ♭7 E♭ Lydian ♭7

A♭ Lydian ♭7 D♭ Lydian ♭7 G♭ Lydian ♭7 B Lydian ♭7

E Lydian ♭7 A Lydian ♭7 D Lydian ♭7 G Lydian ♭7

Two-Note-per-String Fingering

E Lydian ♭7

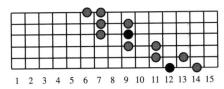

F Lydian ♭7 Vamp

F7 ♭5♭13

Lydian #9 (1 #2 3 #4 5 6 7 8)

The *Lydian #9* scale is the 6th mode of the *harmonic minor* scale (page 239). It can used as a substitute for the *Lydian mode* (page 255) to produce a brighter sound. The #2 (#9) acts as a chromatic passing tone to the 3rd degree. Lydian #9 also works well over a VII/I voicing (for example, A♭/A). In measure one of the vamp in A at the bottom right corner of the page, make sure to use the #9 as a passing tone. In measure two, however, the #9 should be stressed as an important chord tone.

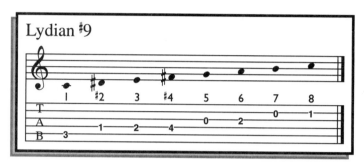

Lydian #9

Lydian #9

Open Position

C Lydian #9

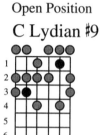

Single-String Fingering

C Lydian #9

Position Fingerings Through the Circle of 4ths

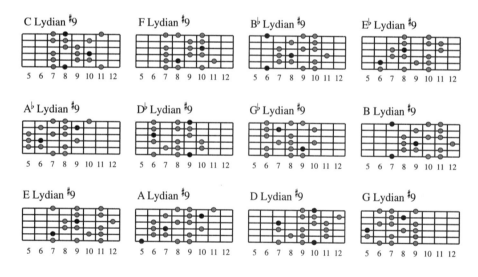

C Lydian #9

F Lydian #9

B♭ Lydian #9

E♭ Lydian #9

A♭ Lydian #9

D♭ Lydian #9

G♭ Lydian #9

B Lydian #9

E Lydian #9

A Lydian #9

D Lydian #9

G Lydian #9

Two-Note-per-String Fingering

E Lydian #9

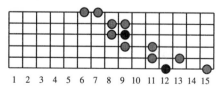

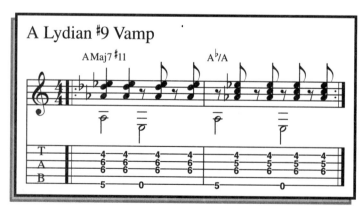

A Lydian #9 Vamp

AMaj7 #11   A♭/A

Lydian 6/9 Pentatonic (1 2 ♯4 5 6 8)

The *Lydian 6/9 pentatonic* scale is a five-note that works well with *major* (page 272) and *Lydian* (page 255) sounds. It can be thought of as a pentatonic version of the *Lydian mode* (the 4th mode of the major scale). Along with the ♯4 (♯11), this scale emphasizes the 9 and 13 tensions, making it a very colorful pentatonic choice. The vamp at the bottom right corner of the page is the same as for the *major 6 diminished* scale (page 276). It includes one Maj6 chord. The tensions emphasized in this scale add color to this very stable tonality. Try substituting this scale for Lydian or major 6 diminished.

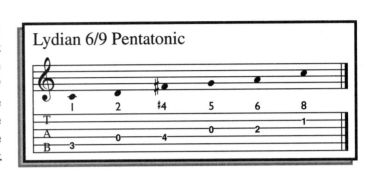

Lydian 6/9 Pentatonic

Open Position

C Lydian 6/9 Pent.

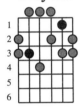

Single-String Fingering

C Lydian 6/9 Pent.

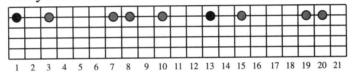

Position Fingerings Through the Circle of 4ths

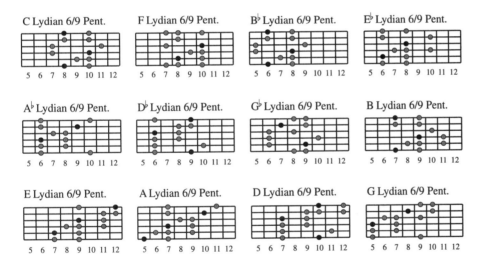

Two-Note-per-String Fingering

E Lydian 6/9 Pent.

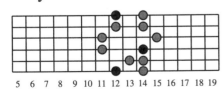

A Lydian 6/9 Pentatonic Vamp

Lydian 6/9 Pentatonic

Lydian Augmented (1 2 3 ♯4 ♯5 6 7 8)

The *Lydian augmented* scale is the 3rd mode of the *jazz minor* scale (page 247). It is commonly found in contemporary jazz harmony. Functionally, Lydian augmented may be used for the Maj7 or Maj7♯11 sound. It also works well with a dominant 7 chord voiced with the 7th in the bass. In the vamp at the bottom right corner of the page, both of these applications are explored with G+Maj7 and A7 (with the 7 in the bass). Also try using the Lydian augmented scale for augmented (♯5) situations.

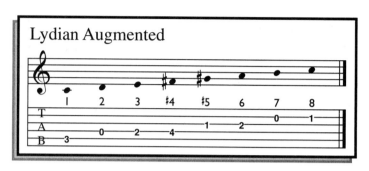

Lydian Augmented

Open Position

C Lydian Augmented

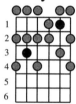

Single-String Fingering

C Lydian Augmented

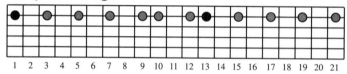

Position Fingerings Through the Circle of 4ths

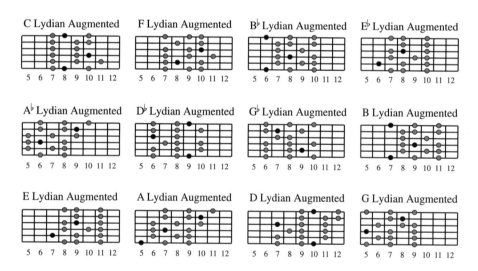

Two-Note-per-String Fingering

E Lydian Augmented

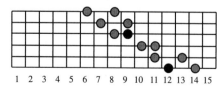

G Lydian Augmented Vamp

Lydian Augmented ♯2 (1 ♯2 3 ♯4 ♯5 6 7 8)

The *Lydian augmented* ♯2 scale, another version of the *Lydian mode* (page 255), is the 6th mode of the *harmonic major* scale (page 238). However, the raised 2nd scale degree renders this scale unusable in a normal Lydian context. In the vamp at the bottom right corner of the page, this scale is being used in an altered dominant context: B7♭9 voiced with the ♭9 (C) in the bass. This is a rather specific context.

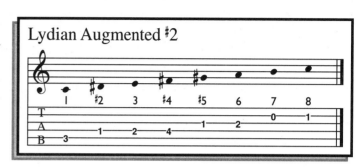

Lydian Augmented ♯2

Open Position

C Lydian Augmented ♯2

Single-String Fingering

C Lydian Augmented ♯2

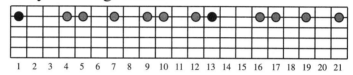

Position Fingerings Through the Circle of 4ths

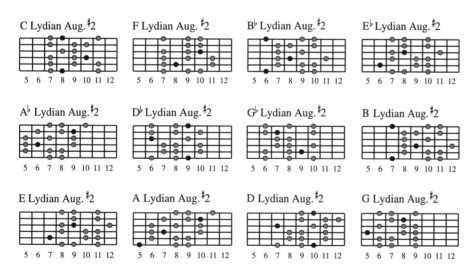

Two-Note-per-String Fingering

E Lydian Augmented ♯2

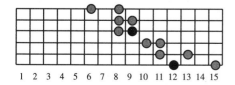

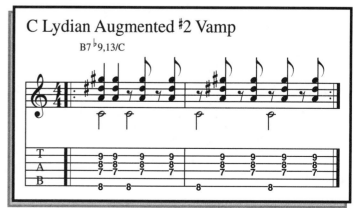

C Lydian Augmented ♯2 Vamp

B7♭9,13/C

Lydian Augmented ♭3 (1 2 ♭3 ♯4 ♯5 6 7 8)

The *Lydian augmented* ♭3 scale is a hybrid scale that contains six augmented 2nds (scale degrees: 1-♯2 or ♭3, ♯2-♯4, ♯4-♯5, ♯5-7, 6-8 and 7-2). The 7 chord built from the root spells a min/Maj7aug♯11. The vamp at the bottom right corner of the page illustrates two favorite Lydian augmented ♭3 applications: a major triad with a ♭2 in the bass and a min6/9 chord.

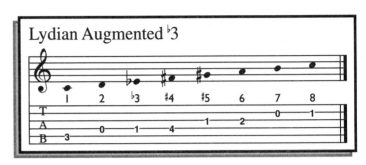
Lydian Augmented ♭3

Open Position
C Lydian Augmented ♭3

Single-String Fingering
C Lydian Augmented ♭3

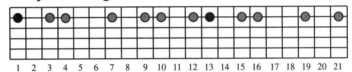

Position Fingerings Through the Circle of 4ths

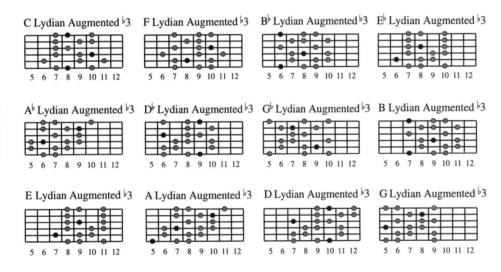

C Lydian Augmented ♭3   F Lydian Augmented ♭3   B♭ Lydian Augmented ♭3   E♭ Lydian Augmented ♭3

A♭ Lydian Augmented ♭3   D♭ Lydian Augmented ♭3   G♭ Lydian Augmented ♭3   B Lydian Augmented ♭3

E Lydian Augmented ♭3   A Lydian Augmented ♭3   D Lydian Augmented ♭3   G Lydian Augmented ♭3

Two-Note-per-String Fingering
E Lydian Augmented ♭3

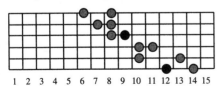

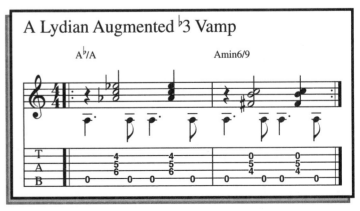

A Lydian Augmented ♭3 Vamp

Lydian Augmented Pentatonic (1 2 ♯4 ♯5 6 8)

The *Lydian augmented pentatonic* scale is a five-note scale that works specifically with *Lydian* (page 255) or Maj7aug♯11 sounds. It can be viewed as a pentatonic version of the *Lydian augmented* scale (page 260, the 3rd mode of the *jazz minor* scale, page 247). The vamp at the bottom right corner of the page explores the ♯5 and ♯11 qualities of the scale by using the following 7 chords: B/G (G+Maj7) and A7/G (A7 with the 7th in the bass). Try using this scale over augmented triads as well.

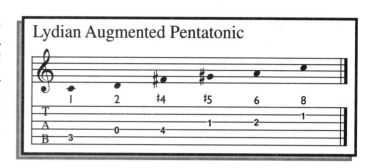

Open Position
C Lydian Aug. Pent.

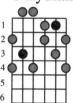

Single-String Fingering
C Lydian Aug. Pent.

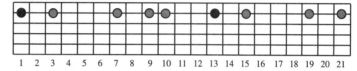

Position Fingerings Through the Circle of 4ths

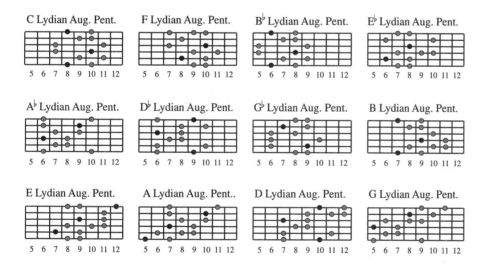

C Lydian Aug. Pent. F Lydian Aug. Pent. B♭ Lydian Aug. Pent. E♭ Lydian Aug. Pent.

A♭ Lydian Aug. Pent. D♭ Lydian Aug. Pent. G♭ Lydian Aug. Pent. B Lydian Aug. Pent.

E Lydian Aug. Pent. A Lydian Aug. Pent.. D Lydian Aug. Pent. G Lydian Aug. Pent.

Two-Note-per-String Fingering
E Lydian Aug. Pent.

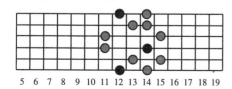

G Lydian Augmented Pentatonic Vamp

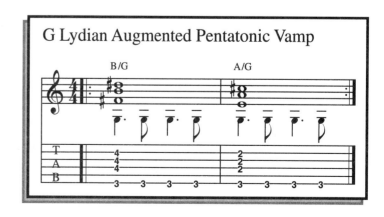

Lydian Diminished (1 2 ♭3 ♯4 5 6 7 8)

The *Lydian diminished* scale is the same scale as the *Lydian ♭3* scale (page 256). Its application, however, is quite different. It is called Lydian diminished because the scale contains a diminished 7 chord (built on the root) and a Major 7♯11 Lydian chord (built on the 3rd degree). The vamp at the bottom right corner of the page provides a diminished chord situation for the use of this scale.

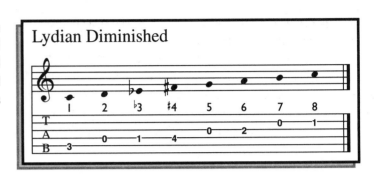

Lydian Diminished

Open Position

C Lydian Diminished

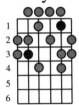

Single-String Fingering

C Lydian Diminished

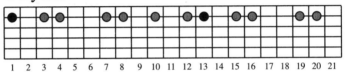

Position Fingerings Through the Circle of 4ths

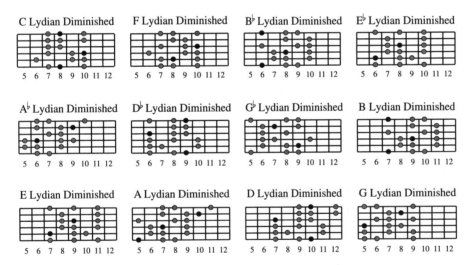

C Lydian Diminished

F Lydian Diminished

B♭ Lydian Diminished

E♭ Lydian Diminished

A♭ Lydian Diminished

D♭ Lydian Diminished

G♭ Lydian Diminished

B Lydian Diminished

E Lydian Diminished

A Lydian Diminished

D Lydian Diminished

G Lydian Diminished

Two-Note-per-String Fingering

E Lydian Diminished

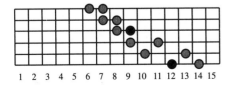

C Lydian Diminished Vamp

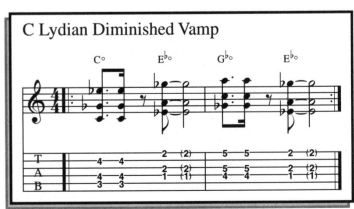

Lydian Dominant 13 Pentatonic (1 3 #4 6 ♭7 8)

The *Lydian dominant 13 pentatonic* scale is a five-note scale that can be thought of as a pentatonic version of the *Lydian* ♭7 (page 257, the 4th mode of the *jazz minor* scale, page 247). This scale differs from other Lydian ♭7 pentatonic types by emphasizing the 3rd scale degree, which makes this version the most obvious Lydian dominant choice. The vamp at the bottom right corner of the page below clearly outlines the dominant 13#11 harmony and how this specific scale is applied.

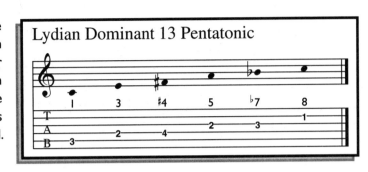

Lydian Dominant 13 Pentatonic

Open Position

C Lydian Dom.13 Pent.

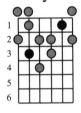

Single-String Fingering

C Lydian Dom.13 Pent.

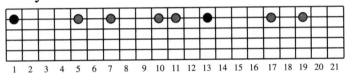

Position Fingerings Through the Circle of 4ths

C Lydian Dom.13 Pent.   F Lydian Dom.13 Pent.   B♭ Lydian Dom.13 Pent.   E♭ Lydian Dom.13 Pent.

A♭ Lydian Dom.13 Pent.   D♭ Lydian Dom.13 Pent.   G♭ Lydian Dom.13 Pent.   B Lydian Dom.13 Pent.

E Lydian Dom.13 Pent.   A Lydian Dom.13 Pent.   D Lydian Dom.13 Pent.   G Lydian Dom.13 Pent.

Two-Note-per-String Fingering

E Lydian Dom.13 Pent.

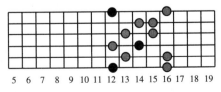

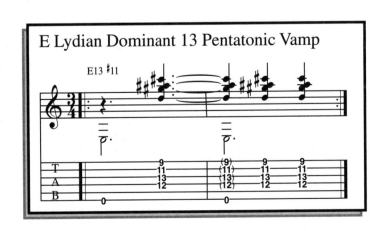

E Lydian Dominant 13 Pentatonic Vamp

Lydian Dominant 9 Pentatonic (1 2 #4 6 ♭7 8)

The *Lydian dominant 9 pentatonic* scale is a five-note scale that works well with Lydian dominant (7♭5) tonalities. It can be thought of as a pentatonic version of the Lydian ♭7 scale (page 257, the 4th mode of the *jazz minor* scale, page 247). Even considering the absence of the 3rd degree, this scale clearly defines the Lydian dominant sound. The vamp at the bottom right corner of the page is the same for Lydian ♭7. The harmony is 7♭5 (♭5 can be viewed as the #4—the Lydian altered tension). This pentatonic version is a poignant substitute for Lydian ♭7.

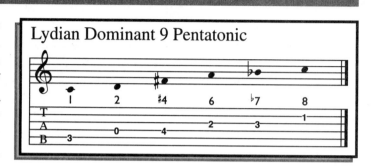

Lydian Dominant 9 Pentatonic

Open Position

C Lydian Dom.9 Pent.

Single-String Fingering

C Lydian Dom.9 Pent.

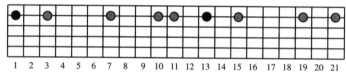

Position Fingerings Through the Circle of 4ths

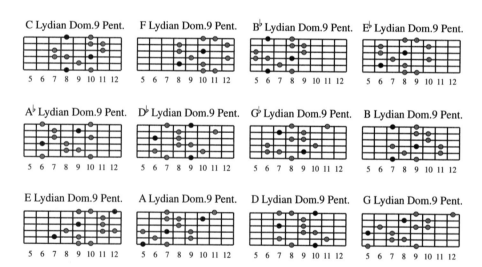

Two-Note-per-String Fingering

E Lydian Dom.9 Pent.

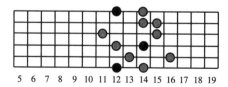

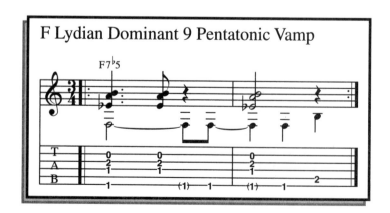

F Lydian Dominant 9 Pentatonic Vamp

Lydian Harmonic Major ♯9 (1 ♯2 3 ♯4 5 ♭6 7 8)

The *Lydian harmonic major* ♯9 is an interesting, seven-note hybrid scale that contains elements from various scales. It can be described as a *harmonic major* scale (page 238) with Lydian characteristics (♯4 and ♯9). This scale can be applied to the specific harmony that the scale produces. It can also be used in a superimposed altered dominant context. The first measure of the vamp at the bottom right corner of the page was derived from the diatonic harmony of the scale (C/E♭ and E♭+). The second measure uses an altered dominant sound (C7♯9). This scale contains the leading tone, which can be used as a chromatic passing tone to the tonic (as in some of the bebop scales).

Lydian Harmonic Major ♯9

Open Position
C Lydian Harm.Maj.♯9

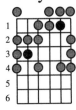

Single-String Fingering
C Lydian Harm.Maj.♯9

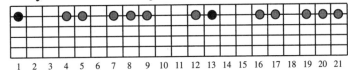

Position Fingerings Through the Circle of 4ths

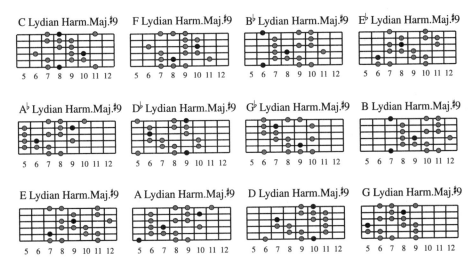

Two-Note-per-String Fingering
E Lydian Harm.Maj.♯9

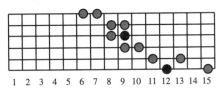

C Lydian Harmonic Major ♯9 Vamp

Lydian Harmonic Major (1 2 3 ♯4 5 ♭6 7 8)

The *Lydian harmonic major* scale is a seven-note hybrid scale that can be considered a Lydian (♯4) version of the *harmonic major* scale (page 238). Since the ♯4 (♯11) is an acceptable tension on the major 7 chord (the harmony based on the root of the harmonic major), Lydian harmonic major can work in the same contexts as harmonic major. The vamp at the bottom right corner of the page is the same as for the harmonic major scale. It is a superimposed context. The harmony (B/C) defines the essence of the C Lydian Harmonic Major.

Lydian Harmonic Major

Open Position

C Lydian Harm. Maj.

Single-String Fingering

C Lydian Harm. Maj.

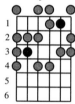

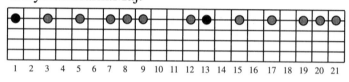

Position Fingerings Through the Circle of 4ths

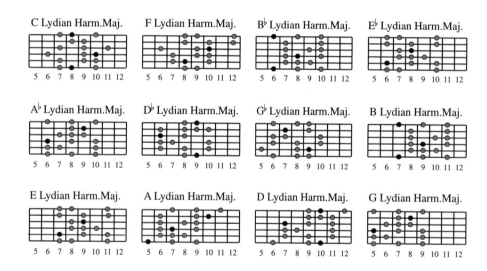

C Lydian Harm. Maj.   F Lydian Harm. Maj.   B♭ Lydian Harm. Maj.   E♭ Lydian Harm. Maj.

A♭ Lydian Harm. Maj.   D♭ Lydian Harm. Maj.   G♭ Lydian Harm. Maj.   B Lydian Harm. Maj.

E Lydian Harm. Maj.   A Lydian Harm. Maj.   D Lydian Harm. Maj.   G Lydian Harm. Maj.

Two-Note-per-String Fingering

E Lydian Harm. Maj.

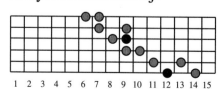

G Lydian Harmonic Major Vamp

Lydian Pentatonic (1 3 ♯4 5 7 8)

The *Lydian pentatonic* scale is a five-note scale that can be thought of as a pentatonic version of the *Lydian mode* (page 255, the 4th mode of the *major* scale, page 272). It is also known as the traditional Japanese scale, *Shimo-Chidori*. The Lydian pentatonic scale differs from other Lydian pentatonic types by emphasizing the 3rd scale degree, which makes this version the most obvious Lydian choice. The vamp at the bottom right corner of the page is the same as for the Lydian mode. This scale clearly outlines the Maj7♯11 harmony in the progression.

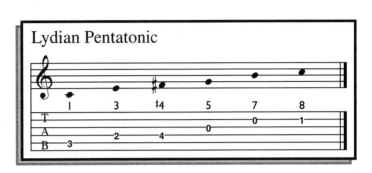

Lydian Pentatonic

Open Position

C Lydian Pent.

Single-String Fingering

C Lydian Pent.

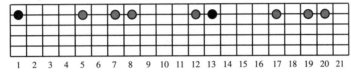

Position Fingerings Through the Circle of 4ths

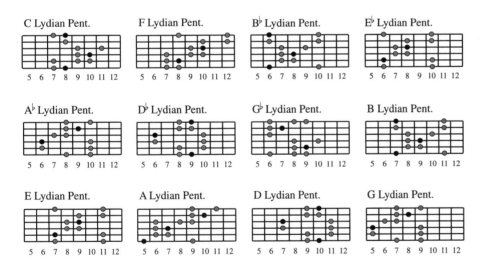

C Lydian Pent. F Lydian Pent. B♭ Lydian Pent. E♭ Lydian Pent.

A♭ Lydian Pent. D♭ Lydian Pent. G♭ Lydian Pent. B Lydian Pent.

E Lydian Pent. A Lydian Pent. D Lydian Pent. G Lydian Pent.

Two-Note-per-String Fingering

E Lydian Pent.

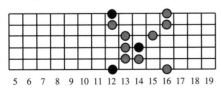

G Lydian Pentatonic Vamp

GMaj7♯11

Lydian Sus2 Pentatonic (1 2 #4 6 7 8)

The *Lydian sus2 pentatonic* scale is a five-note scale that works specifically with a Maj7sus2#11 sound. It can be thought of as another pentatonic version of the *Lydian mode* (page 255, the 4th mode of the *major* scale, page 272). The emphasis on the 2nd scale degree (or the 9) is what makes this a scale with such a highly specific application. The vamp at the lower right corner of the page uses the specific harmony generated by this scale (Maj7sus2#11). This scale can also be used for any Lydian (or major) context.

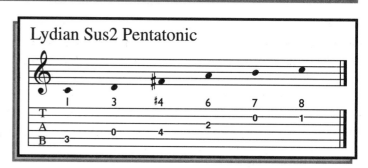

Lydian Sus2 Pentatonic

Open position

C Lydian sus2 pent.

Single string fingering

C Lydian sus2 pent.

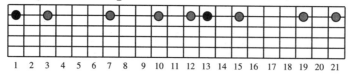

Position Fingerings Through the Circle of 4ths

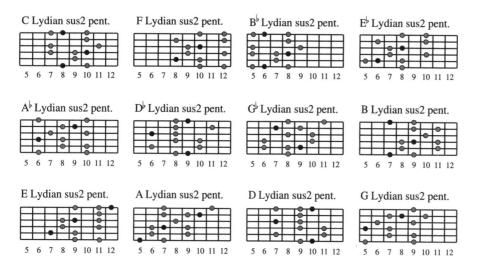

C Lydian sus2 pent.   F Lydian sus2 pent.   B♭ Lydian sus2 pent.   E♭ Lydian sus2 pent.

A♭ Lydian sus2 pent.   D♭ Lydian sus2 pent.   G♭ Lydian sus2 pent.   B Lydian sus2 pent.

E Lydian sus2 pent.   A Lydian sus2 pent.   D Lydian sus2 pent.   G Lydian sus2 pent.

Two-Note-per-String Fingering

E Lydian sus2 pent.

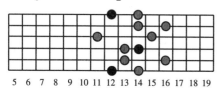

E Lydian Sus2 Pentatonic Vamp

EMaj7sus2#11

Lydiphrygian ♮6 (1 ♭2 ♭3 ♯4 5 6 ♭7 8)

The *Lydiphrygian* scale is an interesting seven-note hybrid scale that can viewed as a combination of the *Lydian* mode (page 255, the 4th mode of the *major* scale, page 272) and the *Phrygian ♮6* scale shown on page 300 (the 2nd mode of the *jazz minor* scale, page 247). The scale contains elements of both. It can also be seen as an altered dominant-type scale without the 3rd scale degree (the ♭3 is now a ♯9). The vamp at the bottom right corner of the page outlines a harmonic context that emphasizes elements of this scale. The accidentals in each chord voicing reflect the notes as they appear in the scale. Try using Lydiphrygian in an altered dominant context as well.

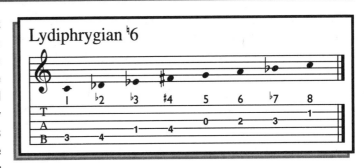

Lydiphrygian ♮6

Open Position

C Lydiphrygian ♮6

Single-String Fingering

C Lydiphrygian ♮6

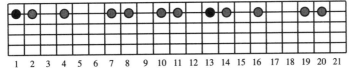

Position Fingerings Through the Circle of 4ths

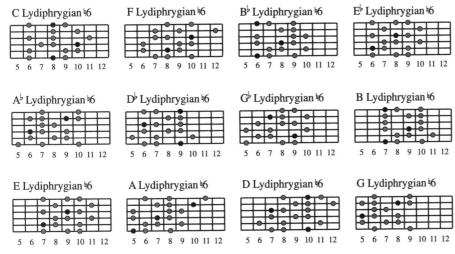

C Lydiphrygian ♮6   F Lydiphrygian ♮6   B♭ Lydiphrygian ♮6   E♭ Lydiphrygian ♮6

A♭ Lydiphrygian ♮6   D♭ Lydiphrygian ♮6   G♭ Lydiphrygian ♮6   B Lydiphrygian ♮6

E Lydiphrygian ♮6   A Lydiphrygian ♮6   D Lydiphrygian ♮6   G Lydiphrygian ♮6

Two-Note-per-String Fingering

E Lydiphrygian ♮6

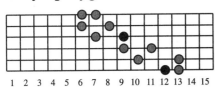

A Lydiphrygian ♮6 Vamp

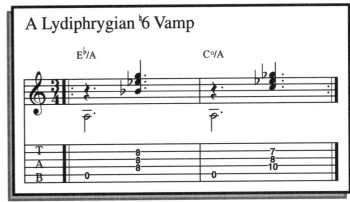

Major (Ionian) (1 2 3 4 5 6 7 8)

The *major* scale and its harmonic system has been the foundation of Western music for over five hundred years. It is constructed with the following sequence of whole (W) and half (H) steps: W, W, H, W, W, W, H. The major scale generates seven modes: 1st mode=Ionian, 2nd mode=*Dorian* (page 231), 3rd mode=*Phrygian* (page 297), 4th mode=*Lydian* (page 255), 5th mode=*Mixolydian* (page 293), 6th mode=*Aeolian* (page 193) and the 7th mode=*Locrian* (page 251). All seven modes and their corresponding chords are used in functional, modal and many other harmonic contexts. For functional

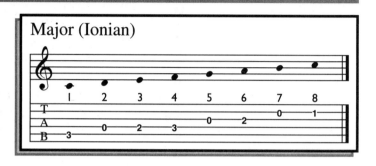

harmony, the 4th degree is an unwanted dissonance which is avoided. The 4 can resolve to the 3 or be raised up a half step to the ♯4. In the vamp at the bottom right corner of the page, the 4th scale degree has been avoided within the chord structures. Remember to use the 4th degree as a passing tone.

Open Position

C Major

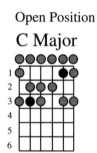

Single-String Fingering

C Major

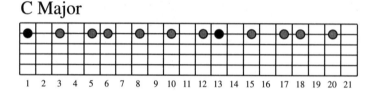

Position Fingerings Through the Circle of 4ths

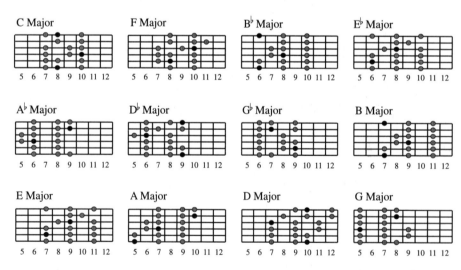

Two-Note-per-String Fingering

E Major

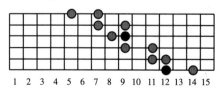

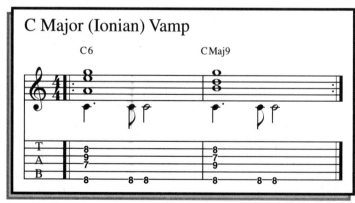

Major ♭2 ♭6 Pentatonic (1 ♭2 3 4 ♭6 8)

The *major ♭2 ♭6 pentatonic* is a five-note scale. It can be thought of as a pentatonic version of the *Phrygian major* scale (page 299, the 5th mode of the harmonic minor scale). This scale will work in the same contexts as the Phrygian major mode, so the vamp at the bottom right corner of the page is the same as for that scale. The scale works well in an altered dominant context as illustrated in measure two. Try substituting the major ♭2 ♭6 pentatonic scale for other altered dominant choices.

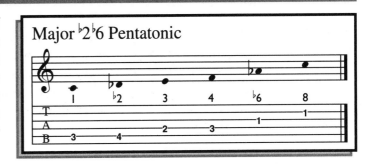

Major ♭2 ♭6 Pentatonic

Open Position

C Maj.♭2♭6 Pent.

Single-String Fingering

C Maj.♭2♭6 Pent.

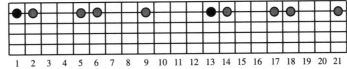

Position Fingerings Through the Circle of 4ths

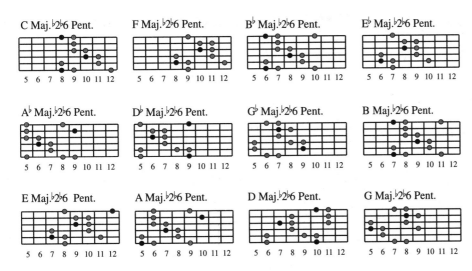

C Maj.♭2♭6 Pent. F Maj.♭2♭6 Pent. B♭ Maj.♭2♭6 Pent. E♭ Maj.♭2♭6 Pent.

A♭ Maj.♭2♭6 Pent. D♭ Maj.♭2♭6 Pent. G♭ Maj.♭2♭6 Pent. B Maj.♭2♭6 Pent.

E Maj.♭2♭6 Pent. A Maj.♭2♭6 Pent. D Maj.♭2♭6 Pent. G Maj.♭2♭6 Pent.

Two-Note-per-String Fingering

E Major ♭2♭6 Pentatonic

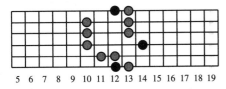

G Major ♭2♭6 Pentatonic Vamp

Major ♭2 ♭6 Pentatonic

Major ♭2 Pentatonic (1 ♭2 3 5 6 8)

The *major ♭2 pentatonic* scale is a five-note hybrid scale which is most commonly applied to a dominant 7 chord with a ♭9. It substitutes well for many of the altered dominant scale choices and can be considered a pentatonic version of the *Mixolydian ♭9* scale (page 294). The vamp at the bottom right corner of the page is the same as the Mixolydian ♭9 vamp. Try alternating between the two choices.

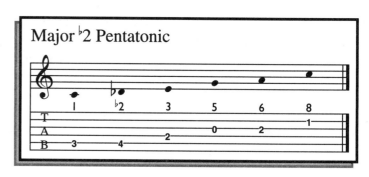
Major ♭2 Pentatonic

Major ♭2 Pentatonic (side tab)

Open Position
C Major ♭2 Pentatonic
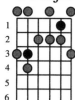

Single-String Fingering
C Major ♭2 Pentatonic
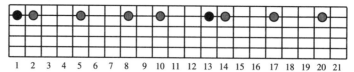

Position Fingerings Through the Circle of 4ths

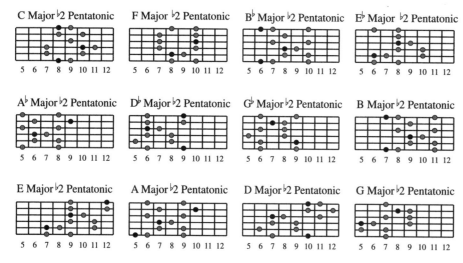

C Major ♭2 Pentatonic · F Major ♭2 Pentatonic · B♭ Major ♭2 Pentatonic · E♭ Major ♭2 Pentatonic

A♭ Major ♭2 Pentatonic · D♭ Major ♭2 Pentatonic · G♭ Major ♭2 Pentatonic · B Major ♭2 Pentatonic

E Major ♭2 Pentatonic · A Major ♭2 Pentatonic · D Major ♭2 Pentatonic · G Major ♭2 Pentatonic

Two-Note-per-String Fingering
E Major ♭2 Pentatonic
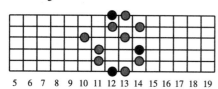

A Major ♭2 Pentatonic Vamp
A 13♭9

Major ♭6 Pentatonic (1 2 3 5 ♭6 8)

The *major ♭6 pentatonic* scale is a five-note scale that can be thought of as pentatonic version of the *Aeolian major* scale (page 195, the 5th mode of the *jazz minor* scale, page 247). Like the Aeolian major, the major ♭6 pentatonic can be used in an altered dominant context (the scale contains the ♭13 altered tension). The vamp at the bottom right corner of the page is the same as for Aeolian major. The sound is an altered dominant with an emphasis on the ♭13 altered tension.

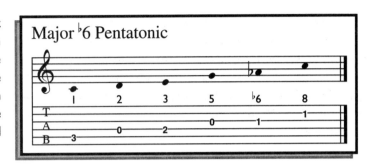

Major ♭6 Pentatonic

Open Position

C Major ♭6 Pentatonic

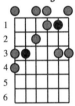

Single-String Fingering

C Major ♭6 Pentatonic

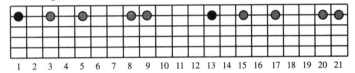

Position Fingerings Through the Circle of 4ths

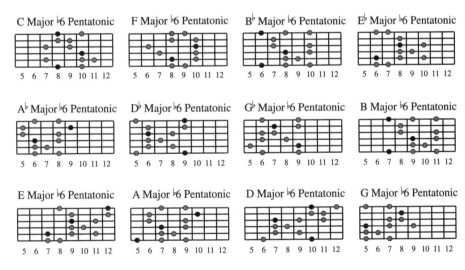

Two-Note-per-String Fingering

E Major ♭6 Pentatonic

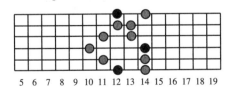

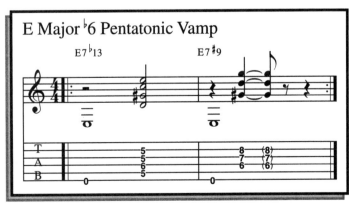

E Major ♭6 Pentatonic Vamp

Major ♭6 Pentatonic

Major 6 Diminished (1 2 3 4 5 ♭6 6 7 8)

The *major 6 diminished* scale is basically a Maj6 chord scale with an added chromatic tone between the 5th and 6th degrees. The addition of this ♭6 produces a diminished 7 chord built on the 2nd scale degree (D-F-A♭-C♭). Superimposing this diminished 7 chord over the sound of a Maj6 creates some added tension. To play over the vamp in A at the bottom right corner of the page, try using the diminished 7 chord built on the 2nd scale degree (B).

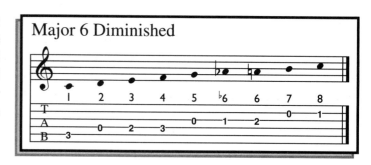

Major 6 Diminished

Open Position

C Maj.6 Diminished

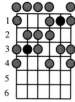

Single-String Fingering

C Maj.6 Diminished

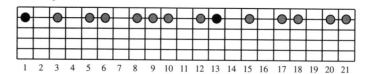

Position Fingerings Through the Circle of 4ths

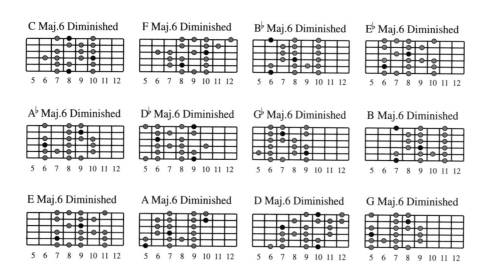

C Maj.6 Diminished   F Maj.6 Diminished   B♭ Maj.6 Diminished   E♭ Maj.6 Diminished

A♭ Maj.6 Diminished   D♭ Maj.6 Diminished   G♭ Maj.6 Diminished   B Maj.6 Diminished

E Maj.6 Diminished   A Maj.6 Diminished   D Maj.6 Diminished   G Maj.6 Diminished

Two-Note-per-String Fingering

E Maj.6 Diminished

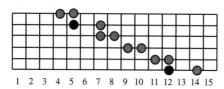

A Major 6 Diminished Vamp

Major 7 Augmented Pentatonic (1 2 3 ♯5 7 8)

The *major 7 augmented pentatonic* is a five-note scale that can be thought of as pentatonic version of the *Ionian augmented* scale (page 244, the 3rd mode of the *harmonic minor* scale, page 239). Like Ionian augmented, this scale can be used in a Maj7♯5 harmonic context (the scale contains the ♯5 altered tension). The vamp in A at the bottom right corner of the page is the same as for Ionian augmented. The sound is Maj7♯5 and ii°/I (B°/A) with emphasis on the ♯5 altered tension.

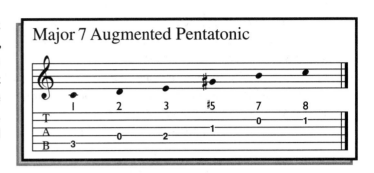

Major 7 Augmented Pentatonic

Open Position
C Maj7 aug. Pent.

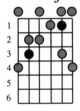

Single-String Fingering
C Maj7 aug. Pent.

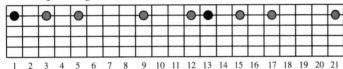

Position Fingerings Through the Circle of 4ths

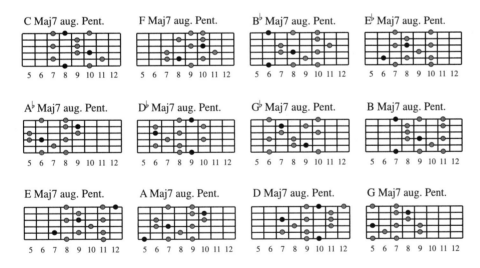

Two-Note-per-String Fingering
E Maj7 aug. Pent.

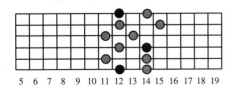

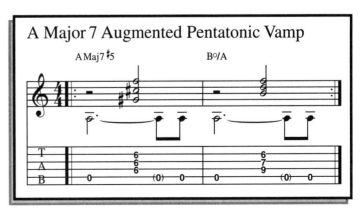

A Major 7 Augmented Pentatonic Vamp

Major 13 Pentatonic (1 3 5 6 7 8)

The *major 13 pentatonic* scale is a five-note scale that can be considered another pentatonic version of the *major* scale (page 272). It differs from the *major pentatonic* scale (page 280) by emphasizing the 6th (13th) scale degree, making it a good choice within the specific harmonic context of a Maj7add13. The harmonic progression used in the vamp in G at the bottom right corner of the page is an Asus/G (essentially a Gsus9/13) alternating with a GMaj13 chord. The vamp clearly emphasizes the 13. Try substituting this scale for any major pentatonic application.

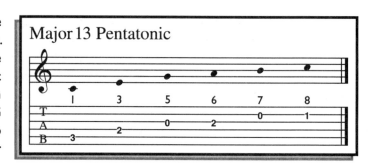

Major 13 Pentatonic

Open Position

C Maj13 Pent.

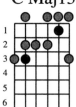

Single-String Fingering

C Maj13 Pent.

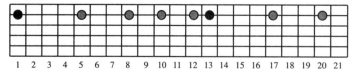

Position Fingerings Through the Circle of 4ths

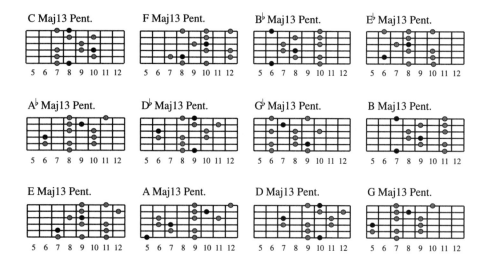

C Maj13 Pent.   F Maj13 Pent.   B♭ Maj13 Pent.   E♭ Maj13 Pent.

A♭ Maj13 Pent.   D♭ Maj13 Pent.   G♭ Maj13 Pent.   B Maj13 Pent.

E Maj13 Pent.   A Maj13 Pent.   D Maj13 Pent.   G Maj13 Pent.

Two-Note-per-String Fingering

E Maj13 Pent.

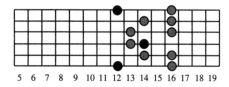

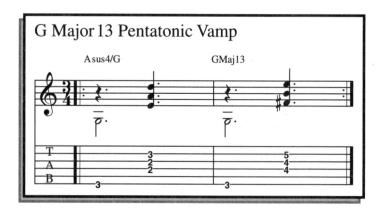

G Major 13 Pentatonic Vamp

Major 13 sus4 Pentatonic (1 2 4 6 7 8)

The *major 13 sus4 pentatonic* scale is a five-note scale which may be used in a major context. When playing over a major 7 chord, care should be taken with the 4th (11th) degree because it creates unwanted tension (the interval between the 3rd and the 4th degree is a minor 2nd, a sound generally avoided on a Maj7). The vamp at the bottom right corner of the page has two chords that include major 13 sus4 pentatonic's inherent tensions: the 9, 11 and the 13.

Major 13 sus4 Pentatonic

Open Position

C Maj. 13 sus4 Pent.

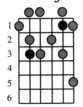

Single-String Fingering

C Maj. 13 sus4 Pent.

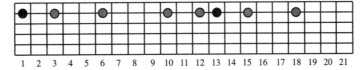

Position Fingerings Through the Circle of 4ths

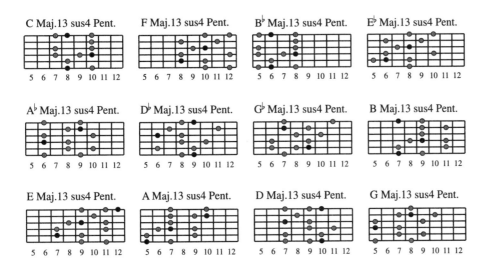

Two-Note-per-String Fingering

E Maj. 13 sus4 Pent.

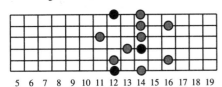

A Major 13 sus4 Pentatonic Vamp

Major Pentatonic (1 2 3 5 6 8)

The *major pentatonic* scale is a five-note scale that does not contain a tritone or half step. This gives the scale a neutral, non-dissonant quality that lends it a natural, melodic quality. If the tonic (1st degree) of the scale is stressed, it suggests a major sound. If the 5 is stressed, it suggests the relative minor (see *minor pentatonic*, page 290). The major pentatonic scale is formed by joining consecutive 5ths. For example, starting from C: C-G-D-A-E. Structured in alphabetical order, this becomes 1-2-3-5-6 of a *major* scale (page 272): C-D-E-G-A. The vamp at the bottom right corner of the page illustrates the major pentatonic sound through the use of simple triads and their inversions, which gives it a "gospel" quality.

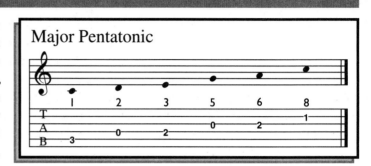

Major Pentatonic

Open Position

C Major Pentatonic

Single-String Fingering

C Major Pentatonic

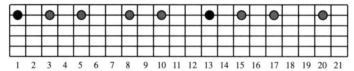

Position Fingerings Through the Circle of 4ths

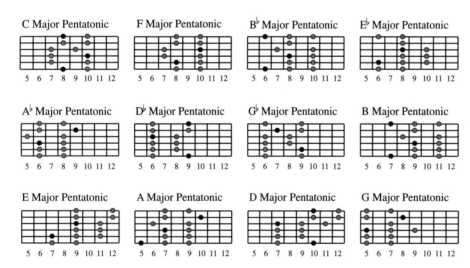

Two-Note-per-String Fingering

E Major Pentatonic

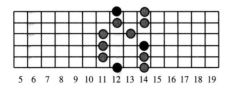

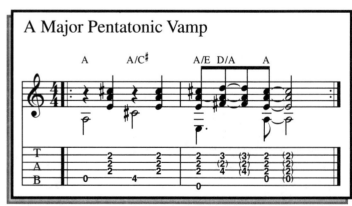

A Major Pentatonic Vamp

Major Pentatonic Blues (1 2 ♭3 3 5 6 8)

The *major pentatonic blues* scale is a six-note scale that is a variation on the *major pentatonic* scale (page 280). It includes the ♭3 degree, (often called a *blue note*) which moves to the natural 3rd producing the characteristic "blues" sound. This scale works particularly well in a *Mixolydian* context (page 293, the 5th mode of the *major* scale, page 272), where the natural 3 is emphasized. The vamp at the bottom right corner of the page is the same as for the Mixolydian mode. Be sure to resolve the ♭3 up to the natural 3.

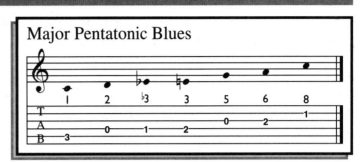

Major Pentatonic Blues

Open Position
C Maj. Pent. Blues

Single-String Fingering
C Maj. Pent. Blues

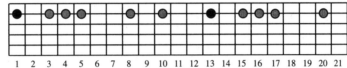

Position Fingerings Through the Circle of 4ths

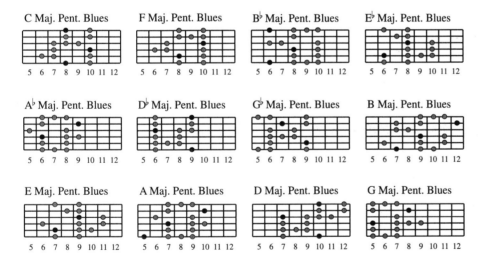

C Maj. Pent. Blues   F Maj. Pent. Blues   B♭ Maj. Pent. Blues   E♭ Maj. Pent. Blues

A♭ Maj. Pent. Blues   D♭ Maj. Pent. Blues   G♭ Maj. Pent. Blues   B Maj. Pent. Blues

E Maj. Pent. Blues   A Maj. Pent. Blues   D Maj. Pent. Blues   G Maj. Pent. Blues

Two-Note-per-String Fingering

E Maj. Pent. Blues

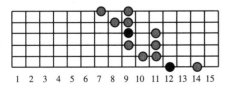

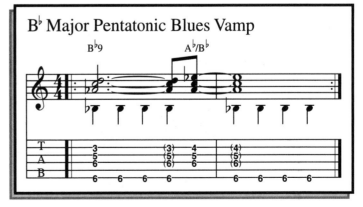

B♭ Major Pentatonic Blues Vamp

Major Pentatonic Blues

Marwa (1 ♭2 3 ♯4 6 7 8)

Marwa is a six-note Indian *raga* (scale). In a Western context, it resembles the Lydian mode (page 255, the 4th mode of the *major* scale, page 272) with a ♭9 altered tension and the 5th scale degree omitted. When used in a superimposed context, Marwa can substitute for any of the minor blues-oriented scales. If the ♯4 is emphasized, Marwa takes on a rather minor bluesy sound. With the focus on the ♯4 as the root, the scale could be interpreted as: 1-♭3-4-♭5-♭7-8 (the same formula as the *minor pentatonic blues* scale, page 291). The vamp at the bottom right corner of the page explores this superimposed blues sound.

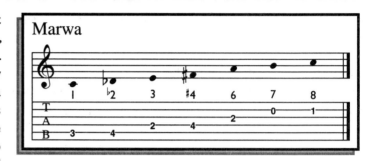

Marwa

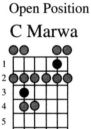

Open Position

C Marwa

Single-String Fingering

C Marwa

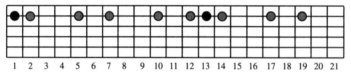

Position Fingerings Through the Circle of 4ths

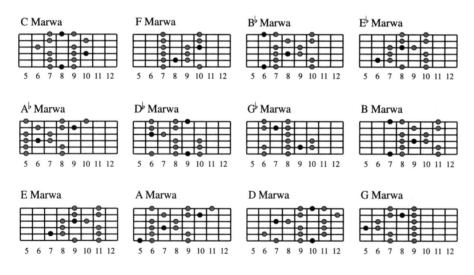

C Marwa   F Marwa   B♭ Marwa   E♭ Marwa

A♭ Marwa   D♭ Marwa   G♭ Marwa   B Marwa

E Marwa   A Marwa   D Marwa   G Marwa

Two-Note-per-String Fingering

E Marwa

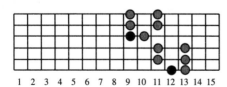

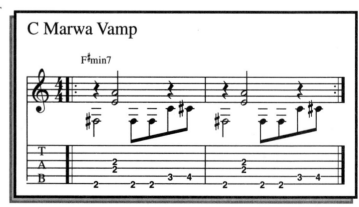

C Marwa Vamp

Min/Maj 11 Pentatonic (1 ♭3 4 5 7 8)

The *min/Maj 11 pentatonic* scale is a five-note scale that can be considered a pentatonic version of the *jazz minor* (page 247) or *harmonic minor* (page 239) scales. It can be used in min/Maj7 contexts. In the case of playing over min/Maj7 chords, the natural 4th (11th) scale degree is an acceptable tension. (This scale degree is avoided when playing over Maj7 chords; the combination of the 3rd and 4th degrees produces a minor 2nd interval, which is not acceptable in most cases.) The vamp at the bottom right corner of the page uses a min/Maj9 chord to demonstrate the effectiveness of this interesting pentatonic scale. Use it as a substitute for jazz or harmonic minor.

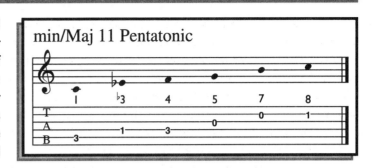

min/Maj 11 Pentatonic

Open Position

C min/Maj 11 Pent.

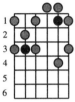

Single-String Fingering

C min/Maj 11 Pent.

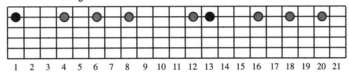

Position Fingerings Through the Circle of 4ths

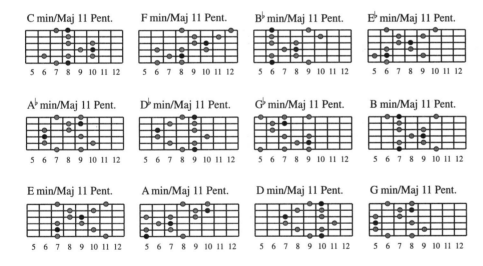

C min/Maj 11 Pent.

F min/Maj 11 Pent.

B♭ min/Maj 11 Pent.

E♭ min/Maj 11 Pent.

A♭ min/Maj 11 Pent.

D♭ min/Maj 11 Pent.

G♭ min/Maj 11 Pent.

B min/Maj 11 Pent.

E min/Maj 11 Pent.

A min/Maj 11 Pent.

D min/Maj 11 Pent.

G min/Maj 11 Pent.

Two-Note-per-String Fingering

E min/Maj 11 Pent.

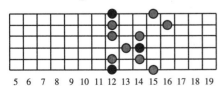

D min/Maj 11 Pentatonic Vamp

D min/Maj9

min/Maj 11 Pentatonic

Minor ♭6/11 Pentatonic (1 ♭3 4 5 ♭6 8)

The *minor ♭6/11 pentatonic* scale is a five-note scale that can be applied to specific minor contexts that include the ♭6 scale degree. Therefore, this scale can be thought of as a pentatonic version of the *Aeolian mode* (page 193, the 6th mode of the *major* scale, page 272), *harmonic minor* (page 239) or the *Phrygian mode* (page 297, the 2nd mode of the major scale). The vamp at the bottom right corner of the page emphasizes the ♭6 (♭13) and 11 by using min7 chords that include those tensions. Try substituting this scale for the Aeolian, harmonic minor and Phrygian scales.

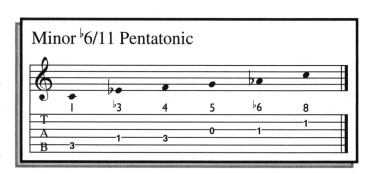

Minor ♭6/11 Pentatonic

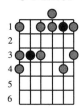

Open Position

C Minor ♭6/11 Pent.

Single-String Fingering

C Minor ♭6/11 Pent.

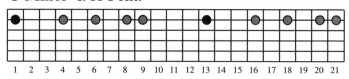

Position Fingerings Through the Circle of 4ths

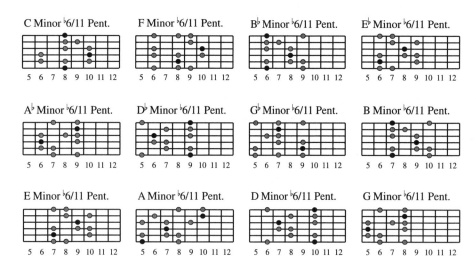

C Minor ♭6/11 Pent.   F Minor ♭6/11 Pent.   B♭ Minor ♭6/11 Pent.   E♭ Minor ♭6/11 Pent.

A♭ Minor ♭6/11 Pent.   D♭ Minor ♭6/11 Pent.   G♭ Minor ♭6/11 Pent.   B Minor ♭6/11 Pent.

E Minor ♭6/11 Pent.   A Minor ♭6/11 Pent.   D Minor ♭6/11 Pent.   G Minor ♭6/11 Pent.

Two-Note-per-String Fingering

E Minor ♭6/11 Pent.

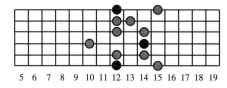

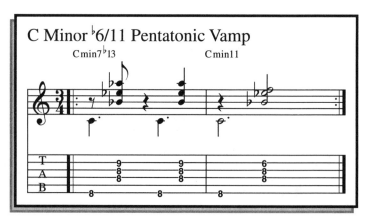

C Minor ♭6/11 Pentatonic Vamp

Cmin7♭13   Cmin11

Minor 3rd/Minor 2nd (1 #2 3 5 #5 7 8)

The *minor 3rd/minor 2nd* scale is a symmetric scale composed of alternating minor 3rd and minor 2nd intervals. The scale produces augmented triads built on each scale degree, which makes it an ideal augmented sound resource. This vamp at the bottom right corner of the page is the same as the vamp for *Lydian augmented* (page 260). Try alternating between both scale choices.

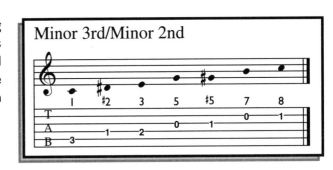

Minor 3rd/Minor 2nd

Open Position

C min3rd/min2nd

Single-String Fingering

C min3rd/min2nd

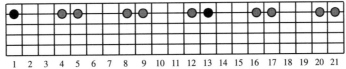

Position Fingerings Through the Circle of 4ths

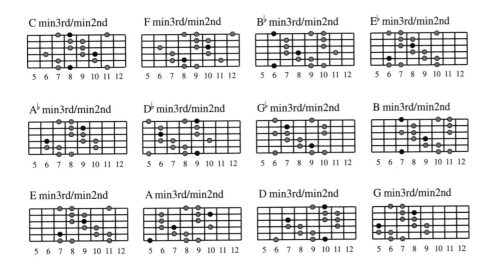

C min3rd/min2nd

F min3rd/min2nd

B♭ min3rd/min2nd

E♭ min3rd/min2nd

A♭ min3rd/min2nd

D♭ min3rd/min2nd

G♭ min3rd/min2nd

B min3rd/min2nd

E min3rd/min2nd

A min3rd/min2nd

D min3rd/min2nd

G min3rd/min2nd

Two-Note-per-String Fingering

E min3rd/min2nd

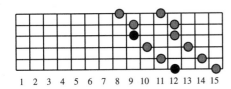

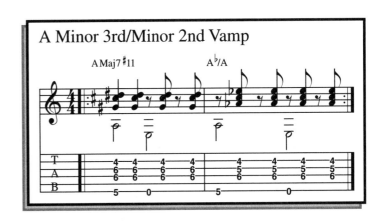

A Minor 3rd/Minor 2nd Vamp

Minor 3rd/Minor 2nd

Minor 6 Diminished (1 2 ♭3 4 5 ♭6 6 7 8)

The *minor 6 diminished* scale is basically a nine-note min6 chord scale with an added chromatic tone between the 5th and 6th degrees. The addition of this ♭6 creates a diminished 7 chord starting on the 2nd scale degree: 2-4-♭6-7. In C, that's D-F-A♭-B or C♯°. In A, that's B-D-F-A♭. Use this chord over the sound of the Amin6 outlined in the vamp in A at the bottom right corner of the page. The result will be some interesting added tension.

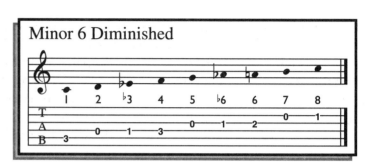

Minor 6 Diminished

Open Position
C Minor 6 Diminished

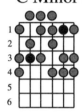

Single-String Fingering
C Minor 6 Diminished

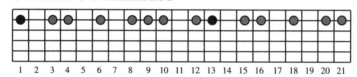

Position Fingerings Through the Circle of 4ths

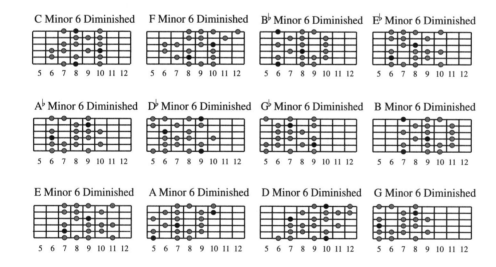

Two-Note-per-String Fingering
E Minor 6 Diminished

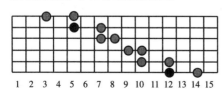

A Minor 6 Diminished Vamp

Amin6

Minor 6 ♭9 Pentatonic (1 ♭2 ♭3 4 6 8)

The *minor 6♭9* pentatonic scale is a five-note scale which can be applied in a *Phrygian* context (page 297) such as over the 7sus13♭9 chord. It also substitutes well for many of the Phrygian- or altered dominant-type scales. It can be considered a pentatonic version of the Phrygian mode. The vamp at the bottom right corner of the page is the same as for *Phrygian ♮6* (page 300). Even though this scale has a lowered ♭6 (♭13), it also works well over the E7sus♭9 chord. Try alternating between the different Phrygian choices.

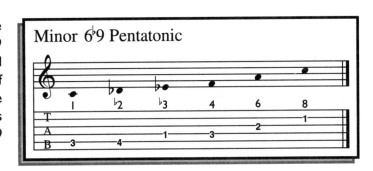

Minor 6♭9 Pentatonic

Open Position

C Minor 6♭9 Pentatonic

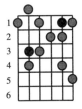

Single-String Fingering

C Minor 6♭9 Pentatonic

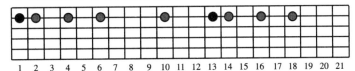

Position Fingerings Through the Circle of 4ths

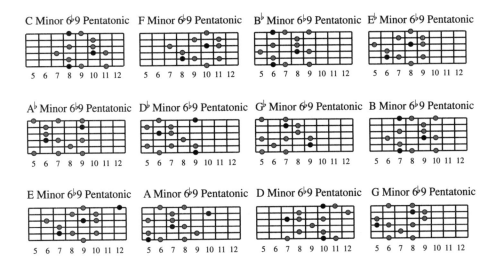

C Minor 6♭9 Pentatonic F Minor 6♭9 Pentatonic B♭ Minor 6♭9 Pentatonic E♭ Minor 6♭9 Pentatonic

A♭ Minor 6♭9 Pentatonic D♭ Minor 6♭9 Pentatonic G♭ Minor 6♭9 Pentatonic B Minor 6♭9 Pentatonic

E Minor 6♭9 Pentatonic A Minor 6♭9 Pentatonic D Minor 6♭9 Pentatonic G Minor 6♭9 Pentatonic

Two-Note-per-String Fingering

E Minor 6♭9 Pentatonic

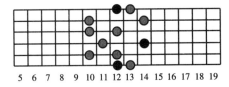

E Minor 6♭9 Pentatonic Vamp

Esus7♭9

Minor 7♭5 Pentatonic (1 ♭3 4 ♭5 ♭7 8)

The *minor 7♭5 pentatonic* scale is a five-note scale which may be applied to the min7♭5 chord. It substitutes well for any of the Locrian-type scales (pages 251-254) and can be considered a pentatonic version of the *Dorian♭5* scale (page 233). The vamp at the bottom right corner of the page is the same as for the Dorian♭5. Try alternating between the two choices.

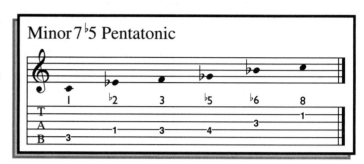

Minor 7♭5 Pentatonic

Minor7♭5 Pentatonic *(side tab)*

Open Position

C Minor7♭5 Pentatonic

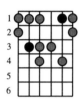

Single-String Fingering

C Minor7♭5 Pentatonic

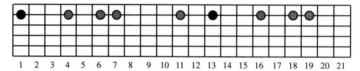

Position Fingerings Through the Circle of 4ths

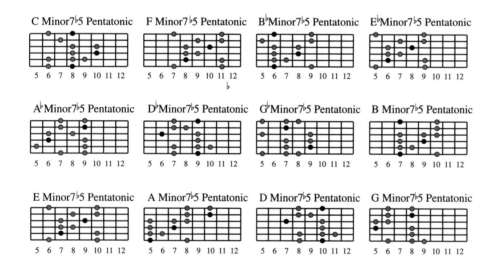

C Minor7♭5 Pentatonic   F Minor7♭5 Pentatonic   B♭Minor7♭5 Pentatonic   E♭Minor7♭5 Pentatonic

A♭Minor7♭5 Pentatonic   D♭Minor7♭5 Pentatonic   G♭Minor7♭5 Pentatonic   B Minor7♭5 Pentatonic

E Minor7♭5 Pentatonic   A Minor7♭5 Pentatonic   D Minor7♭5 Pentatonic   G Minor7♭5 Pentatonic

Two-Note-per-String Fingering

E Minor7♭5 Pentatonic

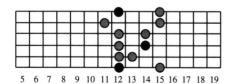

D Minor7♭5 Pentatonic Vamp

Dmin7♭5

Minor 13 Pentatonic (1 ♭3 5 ♭6 ♭7 8)

The *minor 13 pentatonic* scale is a five-note scale that works specifically with min7 (*Dorian mode*, page 231, the 2nd mode of the *major* scale, page 272) harmonies. Minor 13 pentatonic can be considered another pentatonic version of the Dorian mode. It differs from the *Dorian pentatonic* scale (page 234) by emphasizing perhaps the most distinctive characteristic of the Dorian sound, the natural 6 (13). The vamp at the bottom right corner of the page is the same as for the Dorian mode. It clearly outlines the Dorian application by progressing from a simple minor triad to the min7 and finally a min6 chord, which emphasizes the 13 tension.

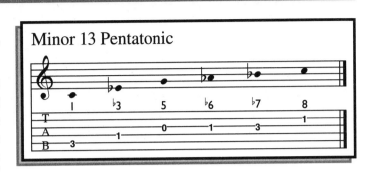

Minor 13 Pentatonic

Open Position
C Minor13 Pent.
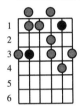

Single-String Fingering
C Minor13 Pent.
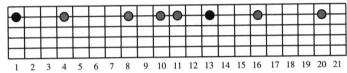

Position Fingerings Through the Circle of 4ths

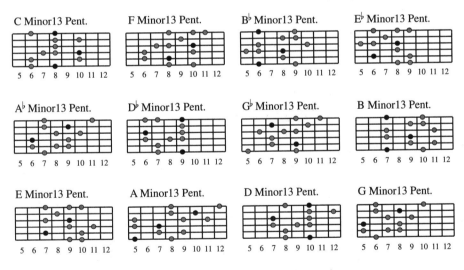

Two-Note-per-String Fingering
E Minor13 Pent.
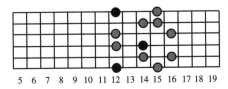

A Minor 13 Pentatonic Vamp

Minor Pentatonic (1 ♭3 4 5 ♭7 8)

The *minor pentatonic* scale is the relative minor of the *major pentatonic* scale (page 280). It is built on the 5th degree of the major pentatonic scale (a major 6th above the root) and produces the whole step (W) half step (H) structure of W+H-W-W-W+H-W. This scale works particularly well in a blues context and is the basis for the "blues scale" (*minor pentatonic blues*, page 291). Much of the music of West Africa is based on this very pure, melodic scale. In the vamp at the bottom right corner of the page, a min7 chord is used to provide the background for this very popular scale. Think B.B. King, *The Thrill is Gone*.

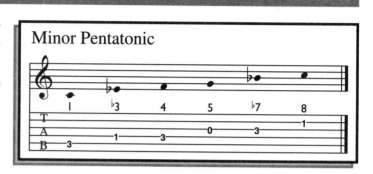

Minor Pentatonic

Open Position

C Minor Pent.

Single-String Fingering

C Minor Pent.

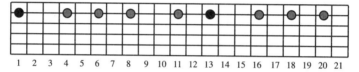

Position Fingerings Through the Circle of 4ths

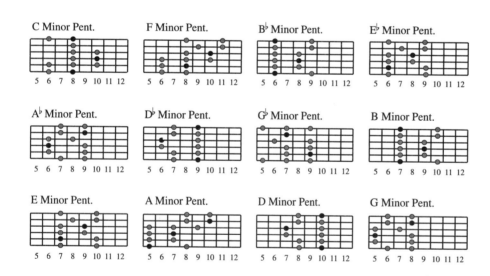

Two-Note-per-String Fingering

E Minor Pent.

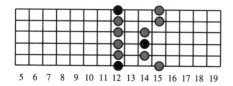

A Minor Pentatonic Vamp

Minor Pentatonic Blues (1 ♭3 4 ♯4 5 ♭7 8)

The *minor pentatonic blues scale* is very popular among guitarists. It is a variation on the *minor pentatonic scale* (page 290). This scale contains the ♯4 (or ♭5), which moves to the 5. The ♯4 alteration, along with the ♭7, are at the heart of this scale's blues sound. The minor pentatonic blues scale can be applied within a major or minor blues context. The vamp at the bottom right corner of the page illustrates that even though the scale does not include the major 3rd, it will work over a dominant 7 chord.

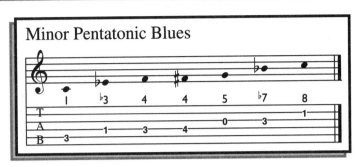

Minor Pentatonic Blues

Open Position

C Minor Pent. Blues

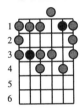

Single-String Fingering

C Minor Pent. Blues

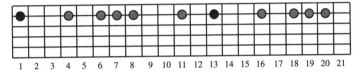

Position Fingerings Through the Circle of 4ths

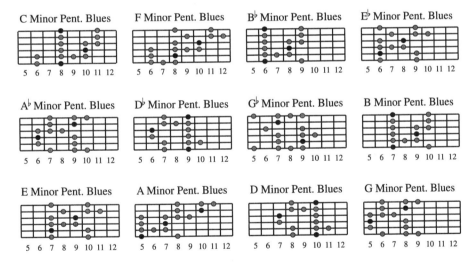

Two-Note-per-String Fingering

E Minor Pent. Blues

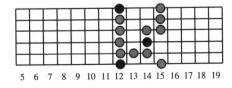

B♭ Minor Pentatonic Blues Vamp

Minor Pentatonic Blues

Minor/Major #11 Pentatonic (1 ♭3 #4 5 7 8)

The *minor/major #11 pentatonic* scale is a five-note scale that can be thought of as a pentatonic version of the *Lydian ♭3* scale (page 256, the 4th mode of the *harmonic major* scale, page 238). This scale is a variation on the *Lydian pentatonic* scale (page 269) and works well over a min/Maj7#11 chord in a functional or modal situation. The vamp at the bottom right corner of the page is the same as for Lydian ♭3. Pentatonic versions of larger scales often carry a bit more weight because of their concentrated nature. Minor/major #11 pentatonic emphasizes the ♭3, #11 and 7, which together clearly define the harmony.

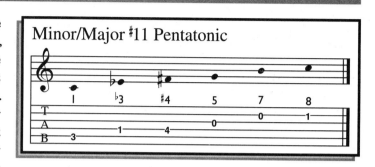

Minor/Major #11 Pentatonic

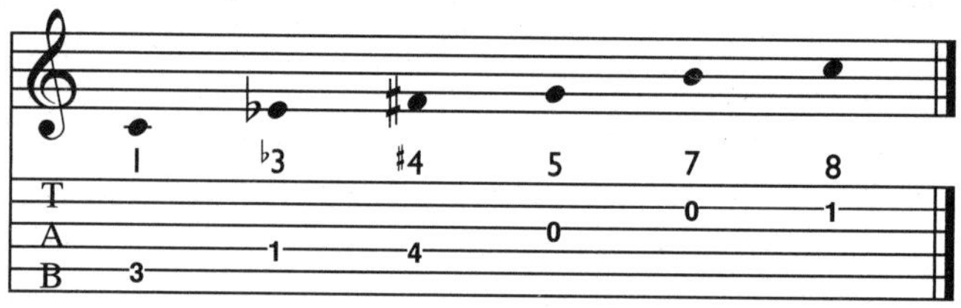

Open Position

C min/Maj #11 Pent.

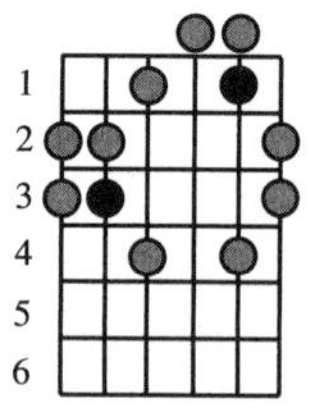

Single-String Fingering

C min/Maj #11 Pent.

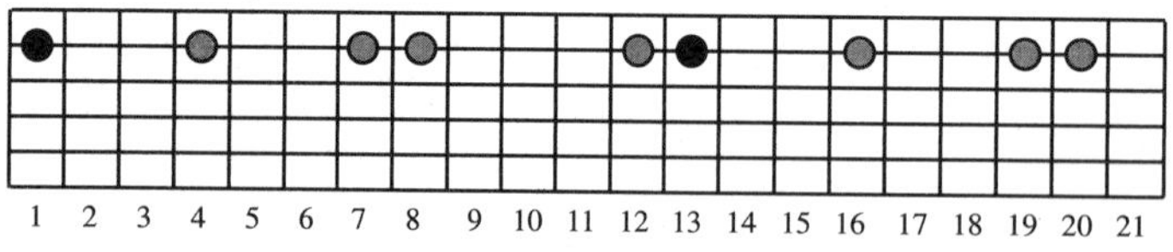

Position Fingerings Through the Circle of 4ths

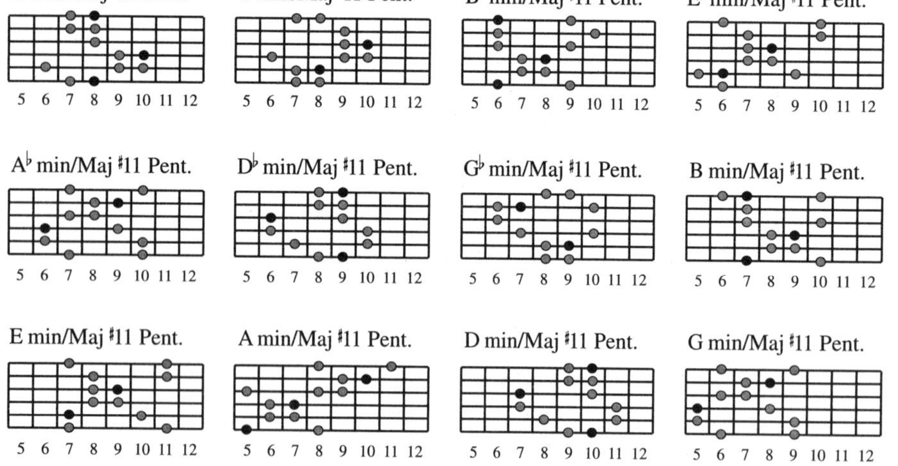

Two-Note-per-String Fingering

E min/Maj #11 Pent.

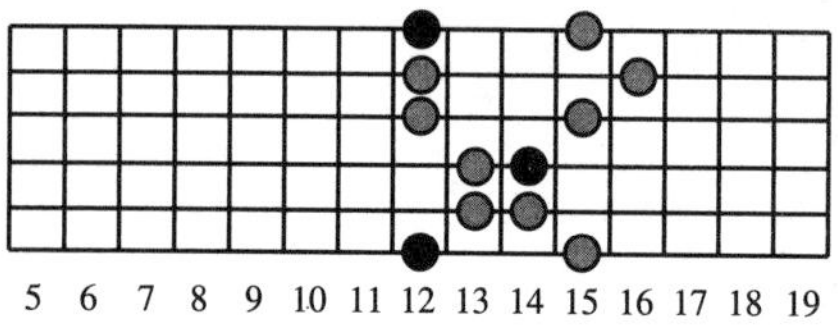

A Minor/Major #11 Pentatonic Vamp

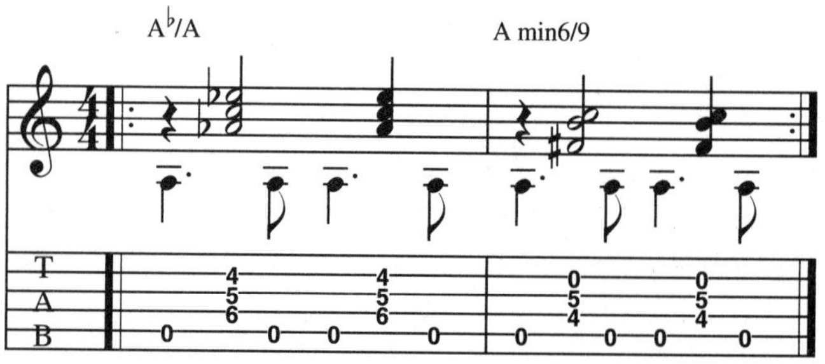

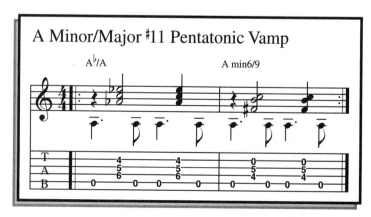

Mixolydian (1 2 3 4 5 6 ♭7 8)

The *Mixolydian mode* is the 5th mode of the *major* scale (page 272). The ♭7 scale degree gives this mode an unaltered dominant character. Stressing the 3rd scale degree gives a stable, functional dominant quality. Stressing the 4th scale degree creates a suspended quality more typical of a modal context. Check out Herbie Hancock's *Maiden Voyage*. In the vamp at the bottom right corner of the page, the dominant sound is expressed with the dominant 9 chord. The suspended or dominant 11 sound is illustrated in the second measure (A♭/B♭). Try using Mixolydian in your blues playing where the minor pentatonic is usually applied.

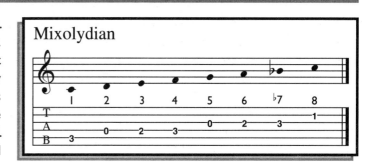

Mixolydian

Open Position

C Mixolydian

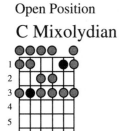

Single-String Fingering

C Mixolydian

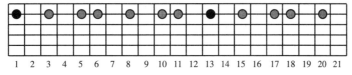

Position Fingerings Through the Circle of 4ths

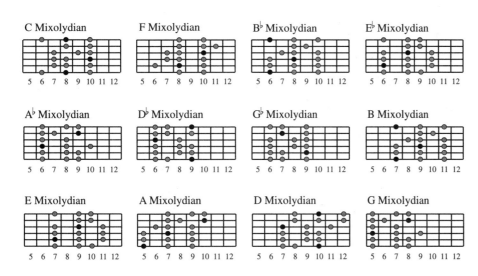

Two-Note-per-String Fingering

E Mixolydian

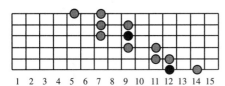

B♭ Mixolydian Vamp

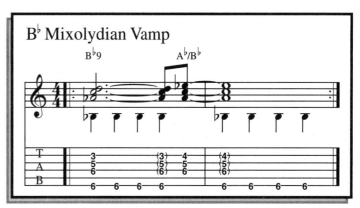

Mixolydian

Mixolydian ♭9 (1 ♭2 3 4 5 6 ♭7 8)

The *Mixolydian* ♭*9* scale is the 5th mode of the *harmonic major* scale (page 238). Mixolydian ♭9 is dominant in function. This scale works specifically with a dominant 13♭9 chord. It can be used as a substitute for any altered dominant-type scale. The vamp in A at the bottom right corner of the page illustrates the specific altered dominant use of Mixolydian ♭9. You can use any variation of a dominant chord containing the ♭9 as a substitute for the A13♭9.

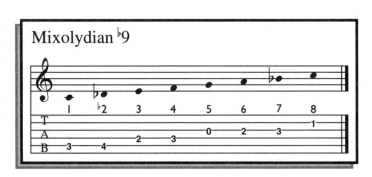

Mixolydian ♭9

Open Position

C Mixolydian ♭9

Single-String Fingering

C Mixolydian ♭9

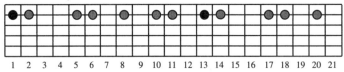

Position Fingerings Through the Circle of 4ths

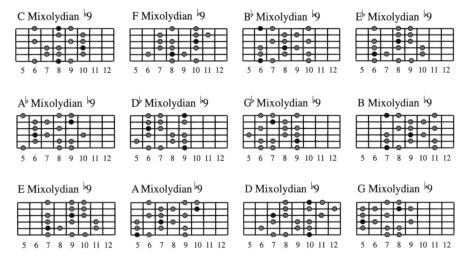

C Mixolydian ♭9   F Mixolydian ♭9   B♭ Mixolydian ♭9   E♭ Mixolydian ♭9

A♭ Mixolydian ♭9   D♭ Mixolydian ♭9   G♭ Mixolydian ♭9   B Mixolydian ♭9

E Mixolydian ♭9   A Mixolydian ♭9   D Mixolydian ♭9   G Mixolydian ♭9

Two-Note-per-String Fingering

E Mixolydian ♭9

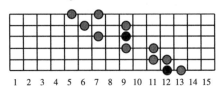

A Mixolydian ♭9 Vamp

A 13♭9

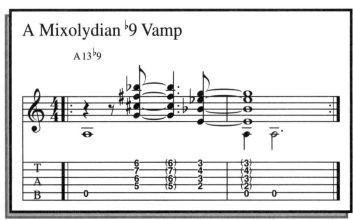

Noh (1 2 4 5 ♯5 6 7 8)

Noh is a traditional seven-note Japanese scale. In a Western context it can be viewed as a variation on the Ionian augmented scale (page 244, the 3rd mode of the harmonic minor scale, page 239). Noh contains no 3 and includes a natural 5. Together, the 5 and the ♯5 create a passing tone situation to 6. Like the Ionian augmented scale, Noh can be used within a Maj7♯5 context. Care should be taken with 4 since it creates tension against 3.

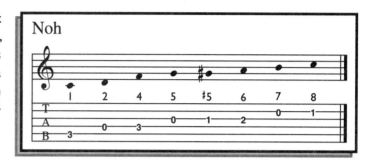

Open Position

C Noh

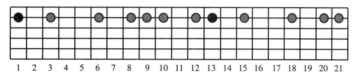

Single-String Fingering

C Noh

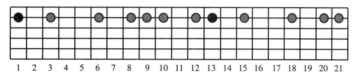

Position Fingerings Through the Circle of 4ths

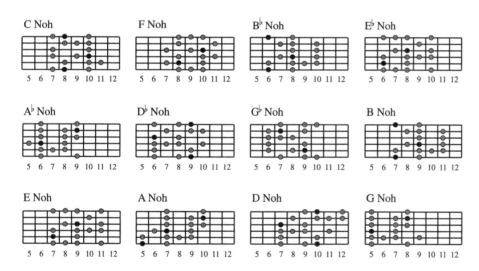

Two-Note-per-String Fingering

E Noh

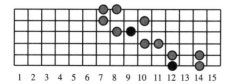

A Noh Vamp

Pelog (1 ♭2 ♭3 5 ♭6 8)

Pelog is a traditional Javanese five-note scale which can be also be applied in a *Phrygian* context (page 297). It can be considered a pentatonic version of the Phrygian scale and can substitute for many of the Phrygian or altered dominant scale choices. Pelog differs from other Phrygian pentatonic scales by the inclusion of the 5th scale degree instead of the 4th, which gives the sound a more stable or "tonic" feeling. The vamp at the bottom right corner of the page is the same as for Phrygian. It explores the use of Pelog over ♭II/I (in this case, the B♭/A chord) and a sus4♭9 chord. Try alternating between Pelog and the other Phrygian choices.

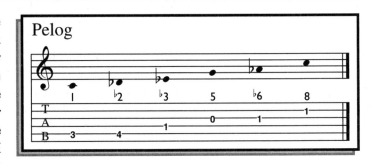

Pelog

(page 297)

Pelog

Open Position

C Pelog

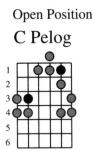

Single-String Fingering

C Pelog

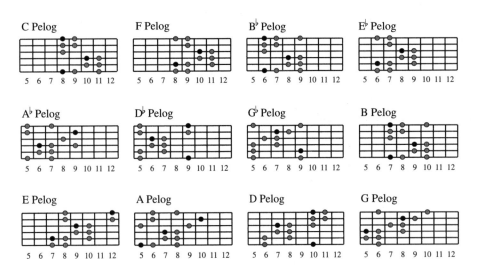

Position Fingerings Through the Circle of 4ths

C Pelog   F Pelog   B♭ Pelog   E♭ Pelog

A♭ Pelog   D♭ Pelog   G♭ Pelog   B Pelog

E Pelog   A Pelog   D Pelog   G Pelog

Two-Note-per-String Fingering

E Pelog

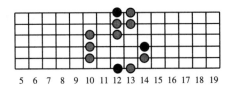

A Pelog Vamp

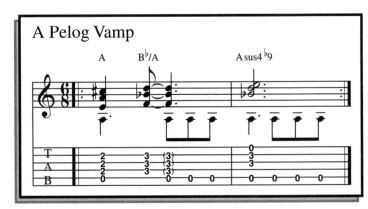

Phrygian (1 ♭2 ♭3 4 5 ♭6 ♭7 8)

The *Phrygian mode* is the 3rd mode of the *major* scale (page 272). Because of the ♭2, the Phrygian sound is often associated with Spanish themes. Keep in mind that the root position diatonic 7 chord produced from this scale does *not* reflect the Phrygian sound. Functionally, Phrygian is interpreted as ♭II/I or as a dominant 7sus♭9. The vamp at the bottom right corner of the page illustrates both the Spanish and altered dominant sounds of Phrygian.

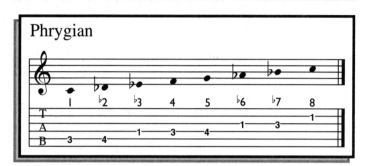

Phrygian

Open Position

C Phrygian

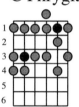

Single-String Fingering

C Phrygian

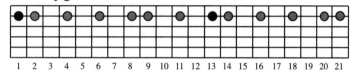

Position Fingerings Through the Circle of 4ths

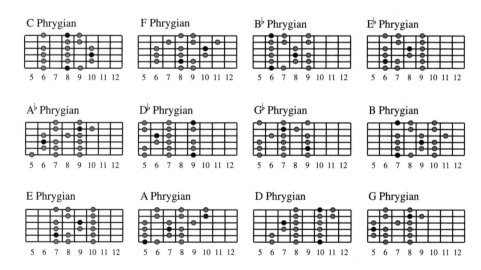

C Phrygian · F Phrygian · B♭ Phrygian · E♭ Phrygian
A♭ Phrygian · D♭ Phrygian · G♭ Phrygian · B Phrygian
E Phrygian · A Phrygian · D Phrygian · G Phrygian

Two-Note-per-String Fingering

E Phrygian

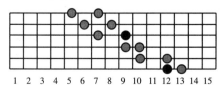

A Phrygian Vamp

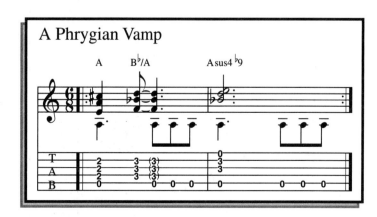

Phrygian

Phrygian ♭4 (1 ♭2 ♭3 ♭4 5 ♭6 ♭7 8)

The *Phrygian ♭4* scale is the 3rd mode of the *harmonic major* scale (page 238). This scale can be thought of as an altered dominant rather than Phrygian scale. The scales contains a dominant 7 chord with the following altered tensions: ♭9, #9 and ♭13. The inclusion of a 7#9 in the vamp at the bottom right corner of the page illustrates the altered dominant application of the Phrygian ♭4 scale. The other altered tensions in the scale provide plenty of color.

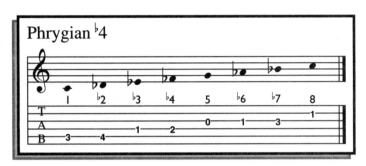
Phrygian ♭4

Open Position
C Phrygian ♭4

Single-String Fingering
C Phrygian ♭4

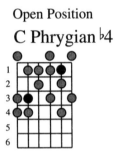
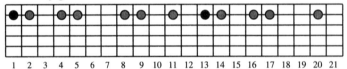

Position Fingerings Through the Circle of 4ths

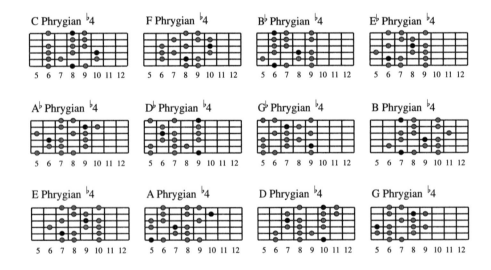

C Phrygian ♭4   F Phrygian ♭4   B♭ Phrygian ♭4   E♭ Phrygian ♭4

A♭ Phrygian ♭4   D♭ Phrygian ♭4   G♭ Phrygian ♭4   B Phrygian ♭4

E Phrygian ♭4   A Phrygian ♭4   D Phrygian ♭4   G Phrygian ♭4

Two-Note-per-String Fingering

E Phrygian ♭4

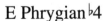
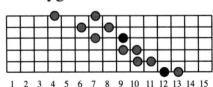

E Phrygian ♭4 Vamp

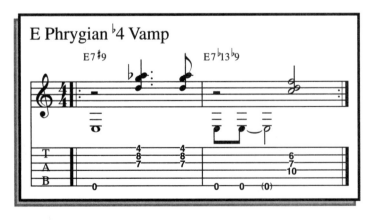

Phrygian ♭4

Phrygian Major (1 ♭2 3 4 5 ♭6 ♭7 8)

The *Phrygian major* scale is the 5th mode of the *harmonic minor* scale (page 239). It is the dominant scale of the harmonic minor system. This is the sound heard in the Jewish folk song, *Hava Nagilah*. Functionally, Phrygian major works over altered dominant harmonies. The vamp at the bottom right corner of the page demonstrates the use of this scale over both a Phrygian sound (A♭/G) and an altered dominant sound (G7♭13).

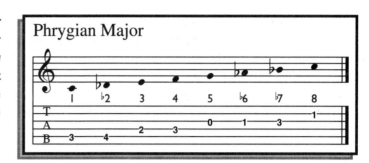

Phrygian Major

Open Position

C Phrygian Major

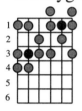

Single-String Fingering

C Phrygian Major

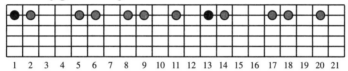

Position Fingerings Through the Circle of 4ths

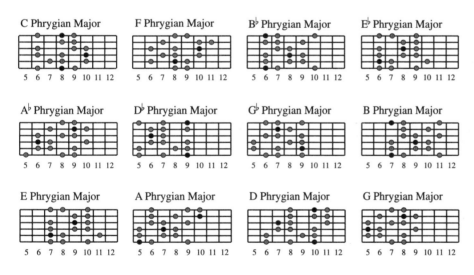

C Phrygian Major

F Phrygian Major

B♭ Phrygian Major

E♭ Phrygian Major

A♭ Phrygian Major

D♭ Phrygian Major

G♭ Phrygian Major

B Phrygian Major

E Phrygian Major

A Phrygian Major

D Phrygian Major

G Phrygian Major

Two-Note-per-String Fingering

E Phrygian Major

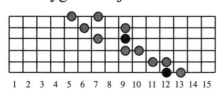

G Phrygian Major Vamp

Phrygian Major

Phrygian ♮6 (1 ♭2 ♭3 4 5 6 ♭7 8)

The *Phrygian ♮6* scale is the 2nd mode of the *jazz minor* scale (page 247). It is used primarily in modal contexts. It can be interpreted as a sus4 ♭9 13 chord scale and may be substituted for any altered dominant sound. The vamp at the bottom right corner of the page includes a sus4 7♭9 to illustrate the effectiveness of this scale. Try using Phrygian ♮6 over any altered dominant chord.

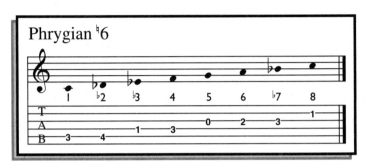

Open Position

C Phrygian ♮6

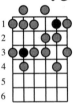

Single-String Fingering

C Phrygian ♮6

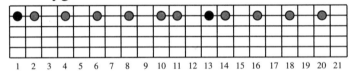

Position Fingerings Through the Circle of 4ths

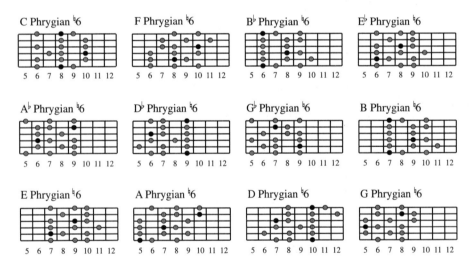

Two-Note-per-String Fingering

E Phrygian ♮6

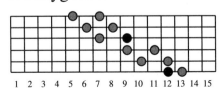

E Phrygian ♮6 Vamp

Phrygian Pentatonic (1 ♭2 4 6 ♭7 8)

The *Phrygian pentatonic* scale is a five-note scale most commonly applied over a Phrygian sound such as the 7sus4 13♭9 chord. It substitutes well for many of the Phrygian- or altered dominant-type scales and can be considered a pentatonic version of the *Phrygian mode* (page 297). This vamp is the same as the Phrygian scale vamp. Try alternating between the two choices.

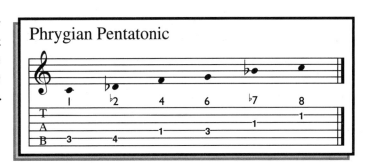
Phrygian Pentatonic

Open Position

C Phrygian Pentatonic

Single-String Fingering

C Phrygian Pentatonic

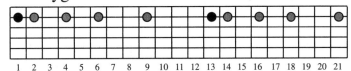

Position Fingerings Through the Circle of 4ths

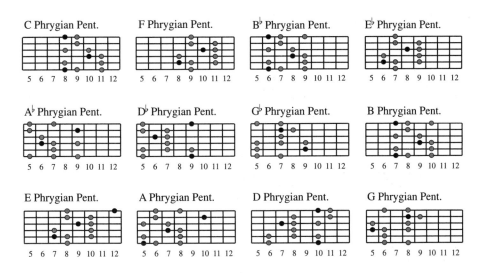

C Phrygian Pent.   F Phrygian Pent.   B♭ Phrygian Pent.   E♭ Phrygian Pent.

A♭ Phrygian Pent.   D♭ Phrygian Pent.   G♭ Phrygian Pent.   B Phrygian Pent.

E Phrygian Pent.   A Phrygian Pent.   D Phrygian Pent.   G Phrygian Pent.

Two-Note-per-String Fingering

E Phrygian Pentatonic

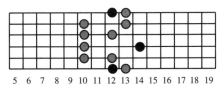

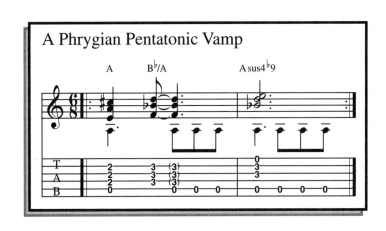
A Phrygian Pentatonic Vamp

Phrygian Pentatonic

Phrygilydian (1 ♭2 ♭3 #4 5 ♭6 ♭7 8)

The *Phrygilydian* scale is an interesting seven-note hybrid scale that can viewed as a combination of *Phrygian* and *Lydian* (pages 297 and 255 respectively, the 3rd and 4th modes of the *major* scale, page 272). The scale contains elements of both. It can also be seen as an altered dominant-type scale without the 3rd scale degree (the ♭3 is now a #9). The vamp in C at the bottom right corner of the page outlines a rather odd harmonic context, B♭Maj7sus4♭5/A. It is an interesting sound that can also be construed as an altered dominant chord (A7♭9#11 with the 3rd omitted).

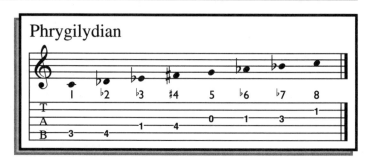

Phrygilydian

Phrygilydian

Open Position
C Phrygilydian

Single-String Fingering
C Phrygilydian

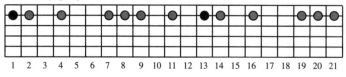

Position Fingerings Through the Circle of 4ths

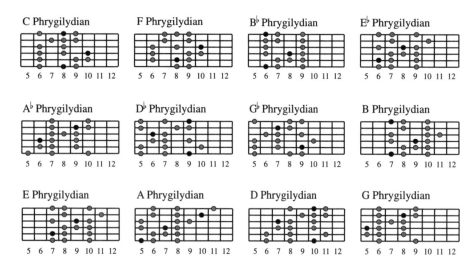

C Phrygilydian F Phrygilydian B♭ Phrygilydian E♭ Phrygilydian

A♭ Phrygilydian D♭ Phrygilydian G♭ Phrygilydian B Phrygilydian

E Phrygilydian A Phrygilydian D Phrygilydian G Phrygilydian

Two-Note-per-String Fingering
E Phrygilydian

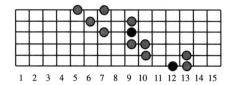

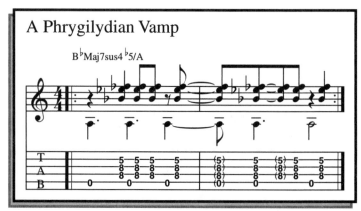

A Phrygilydian Vamp

B♭Maj7sus4♭5/A

Purvi (1 ♭2 3 ♯4 5 ♭6 7 8)

Purvi is a six-note Indian *raga* (scale). When used in a superimposed context, Purvi can substitute for any of the minor/Major oriented scales such as the *jazz minor* scale (page 247). If the ♯4 is emphasized, Purvi takes on a min/Maj7 sound. With the focus on the 2nd degree as the root, the scale could be reinterpreted as: 1-♭3-4-♯4-5-♭7-7-8. The ♯4 and ♭7 scale degrees act as passing tones and help to color the scale. The vamp at the bottom right corner of the page explores this superimposed min/Maj7 sound. Use the C Purvi scale over the D♭ harmony. Try using Purvi as a substitute for the jazz minor scale over stationary min/Maj7 chords.

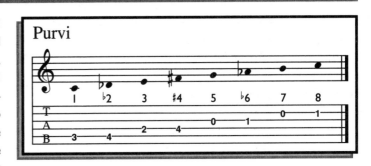

Purvi

Open Position

C Purvi

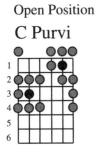

Single-String Fingering

C Purvi

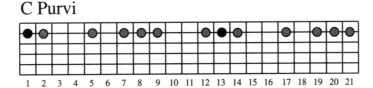

Position Fingerings Through the Circle of 4ths

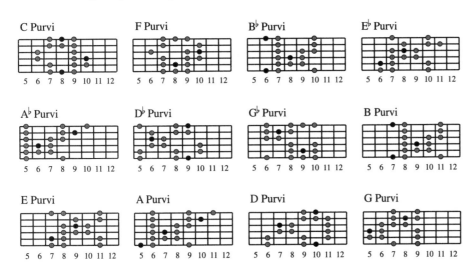

Two-Note-per-String Fingering

E Purvi

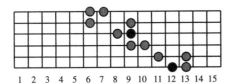

C Purvi Vamp

Purvi

Sho (1 2 ♭3 4 5 6 8)

Sho is a traditional six-note Japanese scale. In a Western context, Sho is a perfect chord scale for the min6 chord. It can also be applied to *Dorian* (page 231) or *jazz minor* (page 247) contexts. The vamp at the bottom right corner of the page includes the min6 chord. Try substituting Sho for other min6-type scales including: Dorian, *minor 6 diminished* (page 286) and *Kumoi* (page 249).

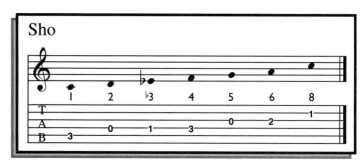

Sho

Open position

C Sho

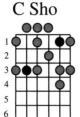

Single-String Fingering

C Sho

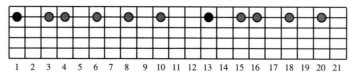

Position Fingerings Through the Circle of 4ths

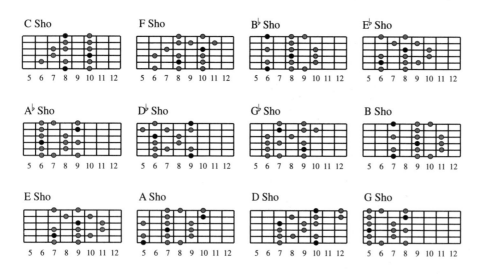

Two-Note-per-String Fingering

E Sho

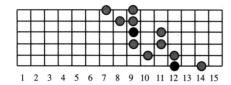

A Sho Vamp

Sho (#2) (1 ♭2 ♭3 ♭4 ♭5 ♭7 8)

Sho #2 is a traditional six-note Japanese scale. It is a variation on the Sho scale (page 304) but differs in pitch and harmonic quality. In a Western context, it resembles the *altered dominant* scale (page 197, the 7th mode of the *jazz minor* scale, page 247) but does not include the 6th scale degree. Sho #2 can be applied in altered dominant situations. Viewed as an altered dominant application, this scale contains the following altered tensions: ♭9, #9 and #11. The ♭4 is interpreted as a 3. The chords outlined in the vamp at the bottom right corner of the page are all altered dominant variations.

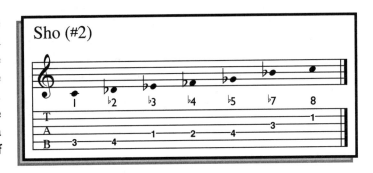

Open Position
C Sho (#2)
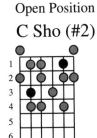

Single-String Fingering
C Sho (#2)
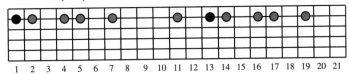

Position Fingerings Through the Circle of 4ths

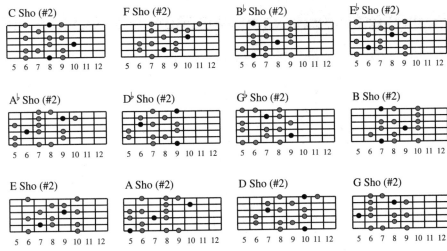

Two-Note-per-String Fingering
E Sho (#2)
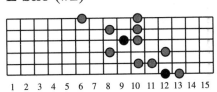

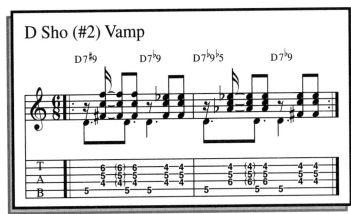

Sus4 ♭13 Pentatonic (1 2 4 5 ♭6 8)

The *sus4 ♭13 pentatonic* scale is a five-note scale that can be thought of as pentatonic version of either the *Aeolian major* scale (page 195, the 5th mode of the *jazz minor* scale, page 247) or the *harmonic major* scale (page 238). It is also very similar to the *major ♭6 pentatonic* scale (page 275) but emphasizes the 4th scale degree instead of the 3rd. This gives it a true sus4 application. The scale also contains the ♭13 altered tension, which makes it an excellent choice for Phrygian or altered dominant (7 sus♭13) situations. The vamp at the bottom right corner of the page explores the suspended and altered dominant side of this scale. Emphasis is placed on the ♭13 altered tension and the suspended 4th. Sus4 ♭13 pentatonic is a good substitution for any the *Phrygian* (page 297) or *altered dominant* (page 197) scale.

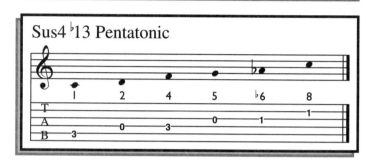

Sus4 ♭13 Pentatonic

Open Position

C sus4 ♭13 pent.

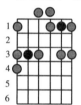

Single-String Fingering

C sus4 ♭13 pent.

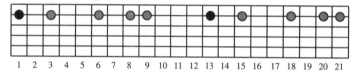

Position Fingerings Through the Circle of 4ths

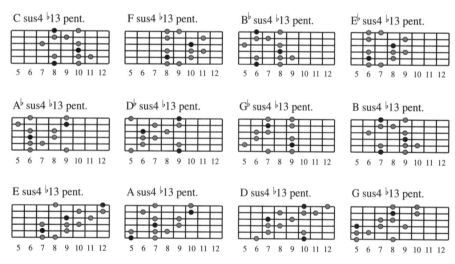

C sus4 ♭13 pent.   F sus4 ♭13 pent.   B♭ sus4 ♭13 pent.   E♭ sus4 ♭13 pent.

A♭ sus4 ♭13 pent.   D♭ sus4 ♭13 pent.   G♭ sus4 ♭13 pent.   B sus4 ♭13 pent.

E sus4 ♭13 pent.   A sus4 ♭13 pent.   D sus4 ♭13 pent.   G sus4 ♭13 pent.

Two-Note-per-String Fingering

E sus4 ♭13 pent.

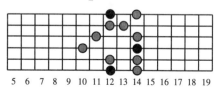

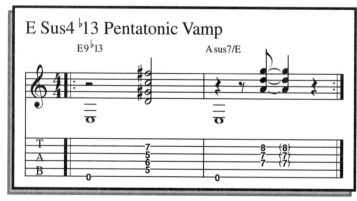

E Sus4 ♭13 Pentatonic Vamp

Sus4 Pentatonic (1 2 4 5 6 8)

The *sus4 pentatonic* scale is a five-note scale that closely resembles the *major pentatonic* scale (page 280) except that this version emphasizes the 4th scale degree instead of the 3rd. Since this scale contains no 7, it is usually applied over a suspended triad or 6 chord context. The vamp at the bottom right corner of the page is the same as for the *tritonic* scale (page 314). Both the sus4 pentatonic and tritonic scales can be applied to suspended 4th situations. Dsus4 is used in the progression to accommodate the D Sus4 Pentatonic scale.

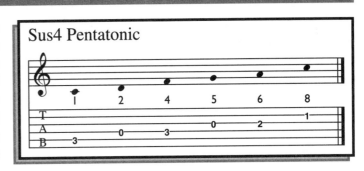

Sus4 Pentatonic

Open Position

C sus4 Pent.

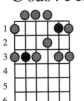

Single-String Fingering

C sus4 Pent.

Position Fingerings Through the Circle of 4ths

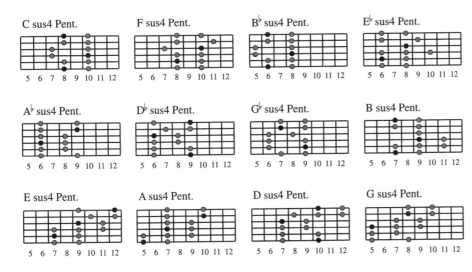

Two-Note-per-String Fingering

E sus4 Pent.

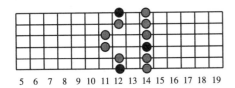

D Sus4 Pentatonic Vamp

Sus4 Pentatonic

Sus4 ♭9 ♭5 Pentatonic (1 ♭2 4 ♭5 6 8)

The *sus4 ♭9 ♭5 pentatonic* scale is a five-note scale. It can be thought of as a pentatonic version of the *Locrian ♮6* scale (page 254, the 2nd mode of the *harmonic minor* scale, page 239). Sus4 ♭9 ♭5 pentatonic works in the same contexts as Locrian ♮6. The vamp at the bottom right corner of the page is the same as for Locrian Nat. 6. The scale works well over a min7♭5 chord or ♭II+/I. Try substituting the sus4 ♭9 ♭5 pentatonic for other Locrian-type scale choices.

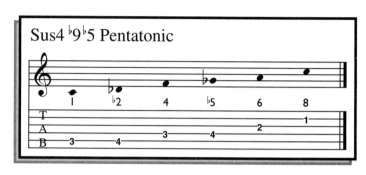

Sus4 ♭9♭5 Pentatonic

Open Position
C sus4 ♭9♭5 Pent.

Single-String Fingering
C sus4 ♭9♭5 Pent.

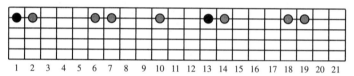

Position Fingerings Through the Circle of 4ths

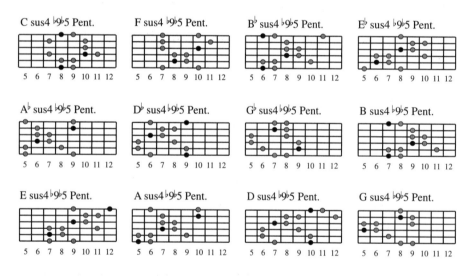

Two-Note-per-String Fingering
E sus4 ♭9♭5 Pent.

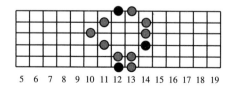

E Sus4 ♭9♭5 Pentatonic Vamp

Symmetrical Diminished, Half/Whole (1 ♭2 ♭3 ♭4 ♭5 5 6 ♭7 8)

The *symmetrical diminished* is an eight-tone scale that alternates between half-step and whole-step intervals. Each degree of the scale produces a diminished 7 chord, which because of the scale's symmetry, can substitute for each other. This half-step/whole-step scale can be viewed as an altered dominant scale choice (1, ♭9, #9, 3, ♭5, 5, 6, ♭7). The whole-step/half-step version of this scale is often called the *auxiliary diminished* scale (page 206) and is usually used over a diminished 7 chord. The vamp at the bottom right corner of the page demonstrates the altered dominant side of the symmetrical diminished scale, including #9, ♭9 and ♭5 dominant chords.

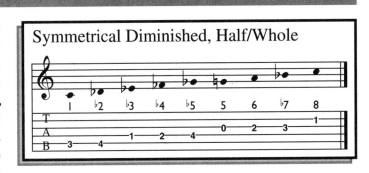

Symmetrical Diminished, Half/Whole

Open Position

C Dim. Half/Whole

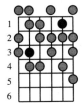

Single-String Fingering

C Dim. Half/Whole

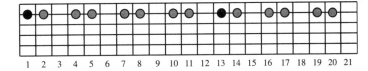

Position Fingerings Through the Circle of 4ths

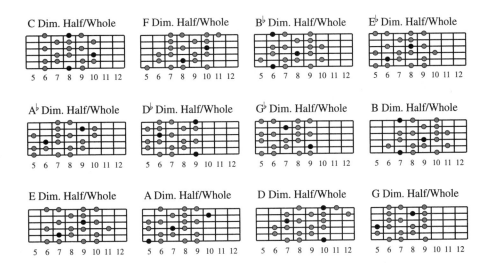

Two-Note-per-String Fingering

E Dim. Half/Whole

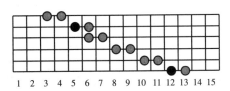

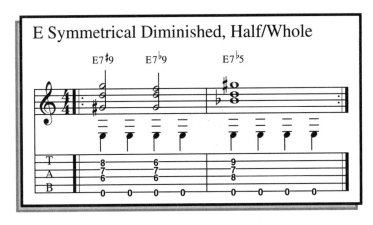

E Symmetrical Diminished, Half/Whole

Tetratonic (1 4 ♭5 7 8)

The *tetratonic scale* is a four-note scale that produces the following symmetrical arrangement of pitches: perfect 4th, minor 2nd, perfect 4th, minor 2nd (scale degrees: 1-4-♭5-7-8). It is derived from the *auxiliary diminished* scale (page 206) starting on the root or the *symmetrical diminished* (page 309) scale starting on the 2nd scale degree and can be applied in similar circumstances. The vamp at the bottom right corner of the page is the same as for the symmetrical diminished scale. Try alternating between the two choices.

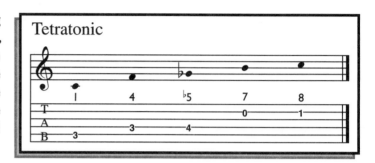

Tetratonic

Open Position

C Tetratonic

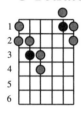

Single-String Fingering

C Tetratonic

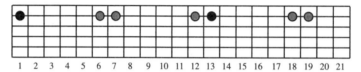

Position Fingerings Through the Circle of 4ths

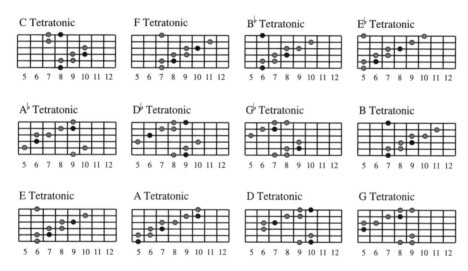

C Tetratonic   F Tetratonic   B♭ Tetratonic   E♭ Tetratonic

A♭ Tetratonic   D♭ Tetratonic   G♭ Tetratonic   B Tetratonic

E Tetratonic   A Tetratonic   D Tetratonic   G Tetratonic

Two-Note-per-String Fingering

E Tetratonic

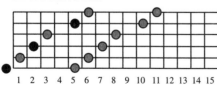

E Tetratonic Vamp

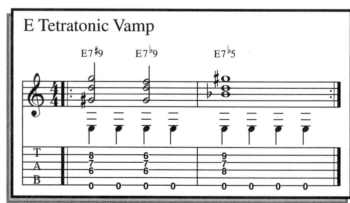

Three-Semitone Tritone (1 ♭2 2 ♭3 ♭5 5 ♭6 6 8)

The *three-semitone tritone* scale is an eight-note scale with a pattern of three half steps followed by a minor 3rd interval that is repeated. It is a relatively new symmetrical scale that improvisers have been experimenting with recently. Depending on the application, the half steps in this scale could be viewed as passing or leading tones to certain chord tones. In the vamp at the bottom right corner of the page, the scale defines the important chord tones within the progression (♭3, ♭5 of the Amin7♭5 and the 3rd, 5th and ♭7 of the B7/A).

Three-Semitone Tritone

Open Position

C Three-Semitone Tritone

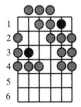

Single-String Fingering

C Three-Semitone Tritone

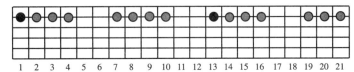

Position Fingerings Through the Circle of 4ths

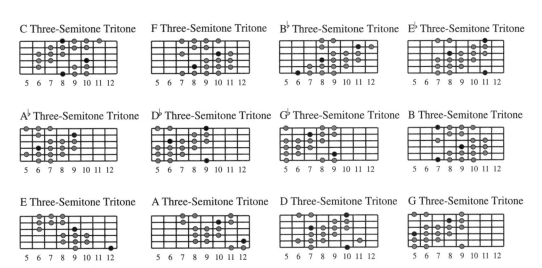

Two-Note-per-String Fingering

E Three-Semitone Tritone

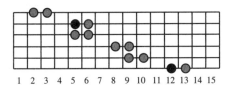

A Three-Semitone Tritone Vamp

Todi (1 ♭2 ♭3 ♯4 5 ♭6 7 8)

Todi is a seven-note Indian *raga* (scale). When used in a superimposed context, Todi can be substituted for the *altered dominant* scale (page 197, the 7th mode of the *jazz minor* scale, page 247) or in *minor pentatonic blues* (page 291) contexts. If the ♭6 scale degree is emphasized, Todi takes on a dominant sound. With the focus on ♭6 as the root, this scale could be reinterpreted as: 1-♯9-3-11-5-♭7-7-8. The natural 7th scale degree acts as a passing tone to the root (as in the *bebop* scales, pages 208-211). The vamp at the bottom right corner of the page explores this superimposed dominant 7 application. Use the C Todi scale to play over the A♭ harmony.

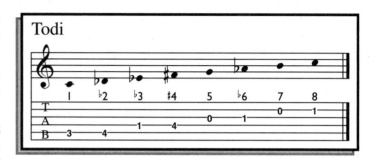

Todi

Open Position
C Todi

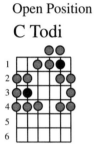

Single-String Fingering
C Todi

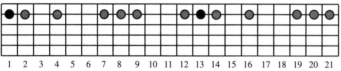

Position Fingerings Through the Circle of 4ths

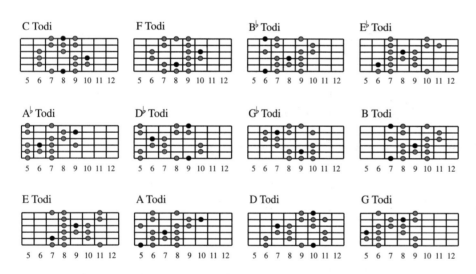

Two-Note-per-String Fingering

E Todi

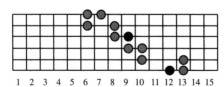

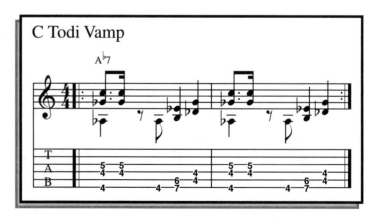

C Todi Vamp

Tritone (1 ♭2 3 ♯4 5 ♭7 8)

The *tritone* scale is part of the diminished harmonic system. It is a symmetrical scale that combines two augmented triads together a *tritone* (an augmented 4th, a distance of three whole steps) apart. The tritone scale forms a dominant 7♭9♯11 chord (1-♭9-3-♯11-5-♭7). The E7♭9♯11 in the vamp at the bottom right corner of the page is the specific harmony that this scale works over. Try using the tritone scale for any altered dominant application.

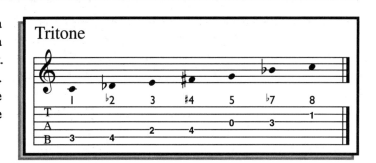

Tritone

Open Position
C Tritone
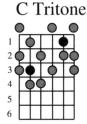

Single-String Fingering
C Tritone
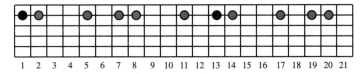

Position Fingerings Through the Circle of 4ths
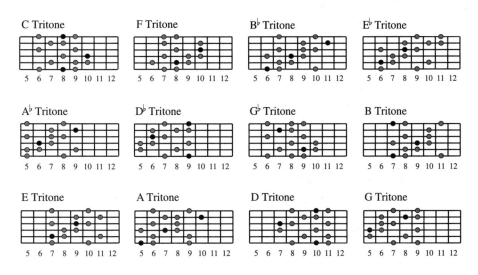

Two-Note-per-String Fingering
E Tritone
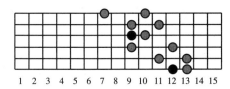

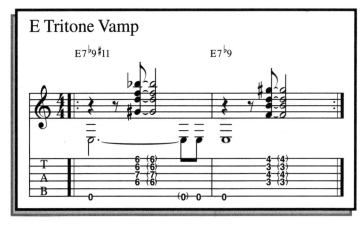

E Tritone Vamp

Tritonic (1 4 5 8)

A *tritonic* scale is built of three pitches arranged in ascending order from root to octave. Forms not considered tritonic include traditional triads and their inversions or any form comprised of pitches that would be impractical for use in performance. The tritonic scale presented here consists of a root, 4, 5 and octave (8) and is particularly useful for sus4 applications. Like triads, tritonic scales can be used as harmonic or non-harmonic sources for improvisation. The vamp at the bottom right corner of the page uses the suspended 4 sound to illustrate the use of this scale based on the root of the chord. The limited number of scale degrees makes the tritonic scale an excellent scale for superimposition applications.

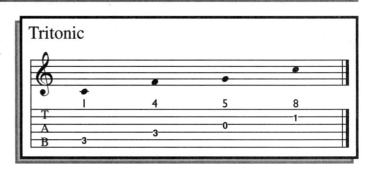

Tritonic

Open Position
C Tritonic

Single-String Fingering
C Tritonic

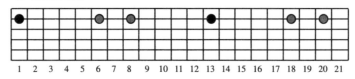

Position Fingerings Through the Circle of 4ths

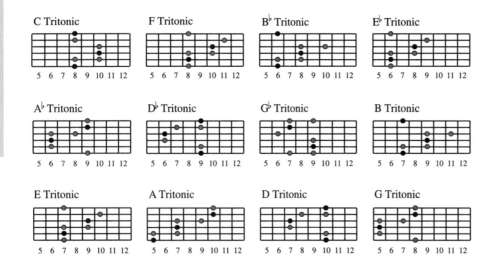

C Tritonic   F Tritonic   B♭ Tritonic   E♭ Tritonic

A♭ Tritonic   D♭ Tritonic   G♭ Tritonic   B Tritonic

E Tritonic   A Tritonic   D Tritonic   G Tritonic

Two-Note-per-String Fingering
E Tritonic

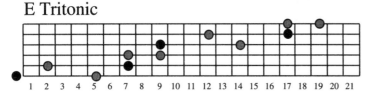

D Tritonic Vamp

Dsus4

Tritonic 1st Inversion (1 2 5 8)

The *tritonic 1st inversion* scale is the 1st inversion of the *tritonic* scale (page 314). The inversion process is the same as for any chord. This scale starts on the 2nd degree of the tritonic scale—the 1st inversion of C-F-G-C is F-G-C-F. On its own, the formula is 1-2-5-8. This scale works well with a triad with an added 9 (or sus2 chord) and no 3, as demonstrated in the vamp at the bottom right corner of the page.

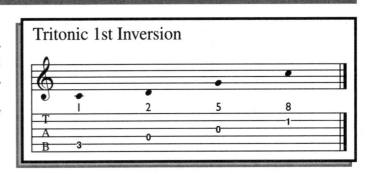

Tritonic 1st Inversion

Open Position

C Tritonic 1st Inversion

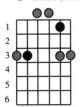

Single-String Fingering

C Tritonic 1st Inversion

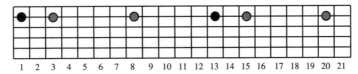

Position Fingerings Through the Circle of 4ths

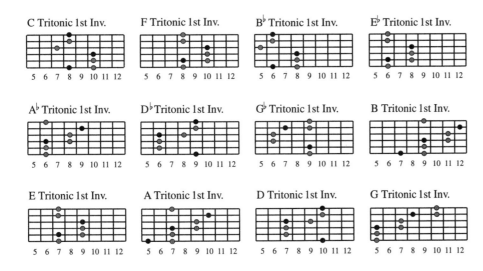

C Tritonic 1st Inv.   F Tritonic 1st Inv.   B♭ Tritonic 1st Inv.   E♭ Tritonic 1st Inv.

A♭ Tritonic 1st Inv.   D♭ Tritonic 1st Inv.   G♭ Tritonic 1st Inv.   B Tritonic 1st Inv.

E Tritonic 1st Inv.   A Tritonic 1st Inv.   D Tritonic 1st Inv.   G Tritonic 1st Inv.

Two-Note-per-String Fingering

E Tritonic 1st Inversion

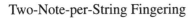
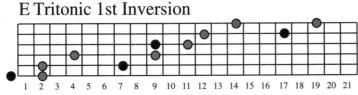

G Tritonic 1st Inversion Vamp

G(add9)no3

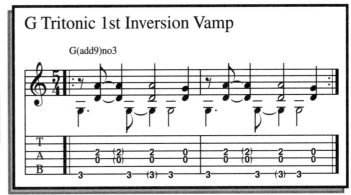

Tritonic 2nd Inversion (1 4 ♭7 8)

The *tritonic 2nd inversion* scale is the 2nd inversion of the *tritonic* scale (page 314). The inversion process is the same as for any chord. This scale starts on the 3rd degree of the tritonic scale. The 2nd inversion of C-F-G-C is G-C-F-G. On its own, the formula is 1-4-♭7-8. This scale works well with a dominant 7 or a dominant 7 sus4 chord. The vamp at the bottom right corner of the page is the same as for the *Mixolydian mode* (page 293). Try alternating between the two choices. The challenge of the tritonic scales is to be able to cover the entire fretboard (check out the two-note-per-string fingering for each).

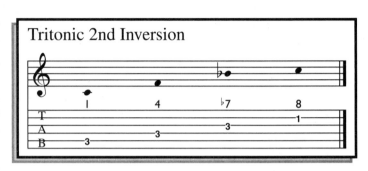

Tritonic 2nd Inversion

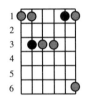

Open Position

C Tritonic 2nd Inversion

Single-String Fingering

C Tritonic 2nd Inversion

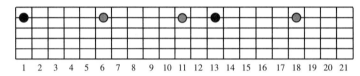

Position Fingerings Through the Circle of 4ths

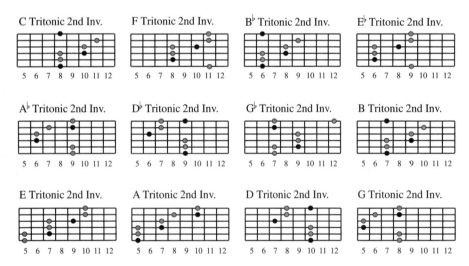

C Tritonic 2nd Inv. F Tritonic 2nd Inv. B♭ Tritonic 2nd Inv. E♭ Tritonic 2nd Inv.

A♭ Tritonic 2nd Inv. D♭ Tritonic 2nd Inv. G♭ Tritonic 2nd Inv. B Tritonic 2nd Inv.

E Tritonic 2nd Inv. A Tritonic 2nd Inv. D Tritonic 2nd Inv. G Tritonic 2nd Inv.

Two-Note-per-String Fingering

E Tritonic 2nd Inversion

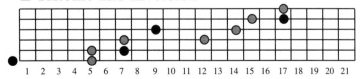

B♭ Tritonic 2nd Inversion Vamp

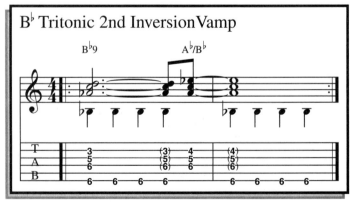

Two-Semitone Tritone (1 ♭2 2 ♯4 5 ♭6 8)

The *two-semitone tritone* scale is a six-note scale with a pattern of two half steps followed by a major 3rd that is repeated. It is a relatively new symmetrical scale that improvisers have been experimenting with recently. This scale could have an altered dominant or diatonic application. In the vamp at the bottom right corner of the page, the scale is used in a diatonic chord progression from the *jazz minor* scale (page 247). This scale substitutes for any of the modes of the jazz minor scale.

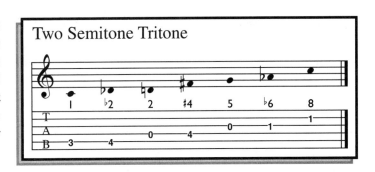

Two Semitone Tritone

Open Position

C Two-Semitone Tritone

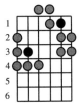

Single-String Fingering

C Two-Semitone Tritone

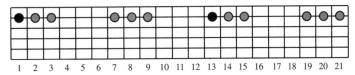

Position Fingerings Through the Circle of 4ths

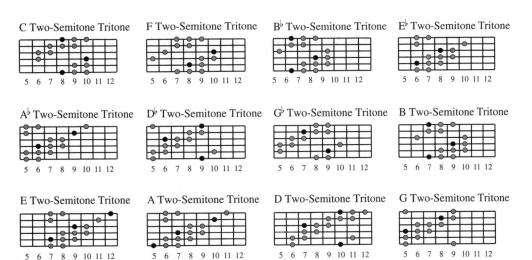

Two-Note-per-String Fingering

E Two-Semitone Tritone

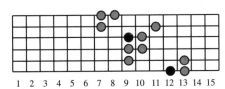

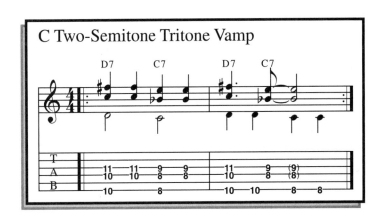

C Two-Semitone Tritone Vamp

Whole Tone (1 2 3 ♯4 ♯5 ♯6 8)

The *whole tone* scale is a six-tone scale comprised of whole step intervals. This scale contains two augmented triads a whole step apart. In whole-tone scale harmony, there is no change in tonality regardless of which scale degree is functioning as root. The diatonic 7 chord of the whole tone scale is dominant 7 augmented (with the ♭9 and the sharp ♯11). The vamp at the bottom right corner of the page demonstrates the altered dominant character of the whole tone scale (highlighting the ♯5/♭13) and the ♯4/♭5).

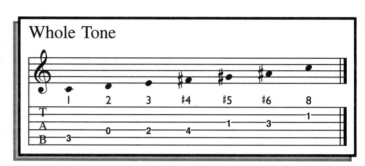

Whole Tone

Open Position
C Whole Tone

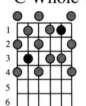

Single-String Fingering
C Whole Tone

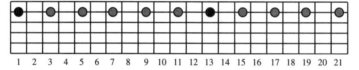

Position Fingerings Through the Circle of 4ths

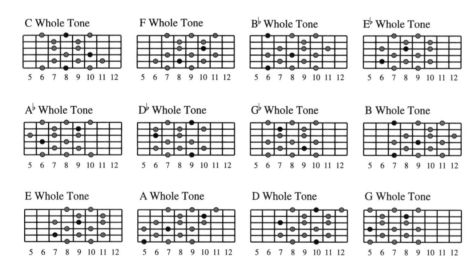

C Whole Tone   F Whole Tone   B♭ Whole Tone   E♭ Whole Tone

A♭ Whole Tone   D♭ Whole Tone   G♭ Whole Tone   B Whole Tone

E Whole Tone   A Whole Tone   D Whole Tone   G Whole Tone

Two-Note-per-String Fingering
E Whole Tone

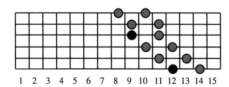

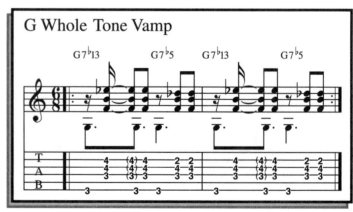

G Whole Tone Vamp

Whole Tone Chromatic (1 2 3 4 ♭5 ♭6 ♭7 7 8)

The *whole tone chromatic* scale is an eight-note symmetrical scale that alternates between pairs of whole and half steps: W-W-H-H-W-W-H-H. It can be interpreted as an altered dominant chord scale with a leading tone (natural 7, one half step below 8). It also works well with 7♭5 and/or 7♭13 chords. The vamp at the bottom right corner of the page is centered around an altered dominant sound. The whole tone chromatic scale works well in any altered dominant situation.

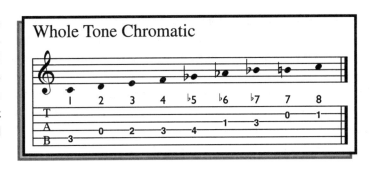

Whole Tone Chromatic

Open Position

C Whole Tone Chromatic

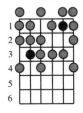

Single string fingering

C Whole Tone Chromatic

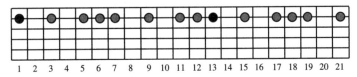

Position Fingerings Through the Circle of 4ths

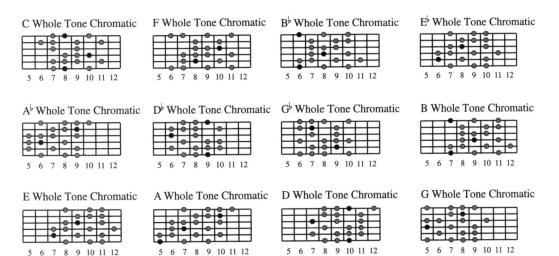

C Whole Tone Chromatic F Whole Tone Chromatic B♭ Whole Tone Chromatic E♭ Whole Tone Chromatic

A♭ Whole Tone Chromatic D♭ Whole Tone Chromatic G♭ Whole Tone Chromatic B Whole Tone Chromatic

E Whole Tone Chromatic A Whole Tone Chromatic D Whole Tone Chromatic G Whole Tone Chromatic

Two-Note-per-String Fingering

E Whole Tone Chromatic

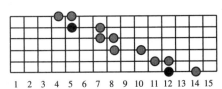

C Whole Tone Chromatic Vamp

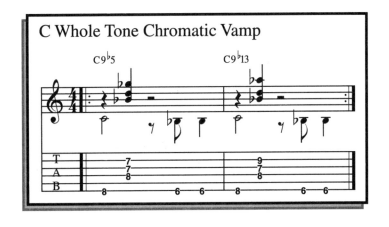

Yo (1 2 ♭3 4 5 ♭7 8)

Yo is a traditional six-note Japanese scale. In a Western context, it resembles the *Dorian mode* (page 231, the 2nd mode of the *major scale*, page 272) but does not include the 6th scale degree. Yo can be applied in Dorian and other minor 7 chord situations. The exclusion of the 6th scale degree calls more attention the other featured tensions of this scale, the 9 and 11. The chord outlined in the vamp at the bottom right corner of the page is the min11.

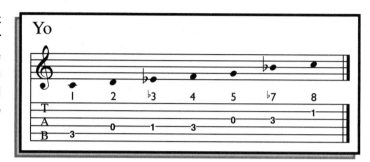

Yo

Open Position

C Yo

Single-String Fingering

C Yo

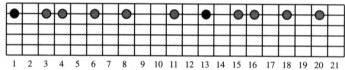

Position Fingerings Through the Circle of 4ths

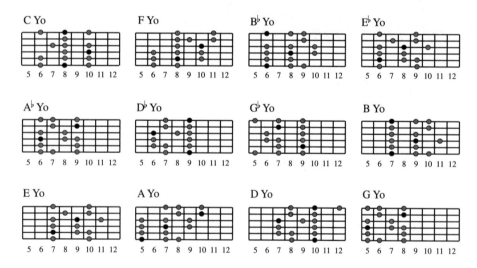

C Yo   F Yo   B♭ Yo   E♭ Yo

A♭ Yo   D♭ Yo   G♭ Yo   B Yo

E Yo   A Yo   D Yo   G Yo

Two-Note-per-String Fingering

E Yo

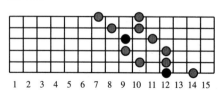

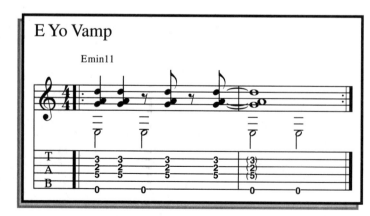

E Yo Vamp

Emin11

Zirafkand (1 ♭2 ♭3 4 ♭5 ♭6 7 8)

Zirafkand is a seven-note Arabian scale. When used in a superimposed context, Zirafkand, like the *Todi* scale (page 312), can be substituted for the *Mixolydian* mode (page 293, the 5th mode of the *major* scale, page 272) or the *minor pentatonic blues* scale (page 291). If the ♭6 scale degree is emphasized, Zirafkand takes on a dominant sound. For example, with the focus on the A♭ in C Zirafkand, the scale could be interpreted as: 1-#9-3-11-5-13-♭7-8. The vamp at the bottom right corner of the page explores this superimposed dominant application. Play C Zirafkand over the A♭7.

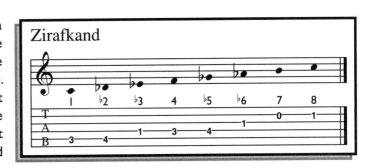

Zirafkand

Open Position

C Zirafkand

Single-String Fingering

C Zirafkand

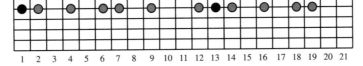

Position Fingerings Through the Circle of 4ths

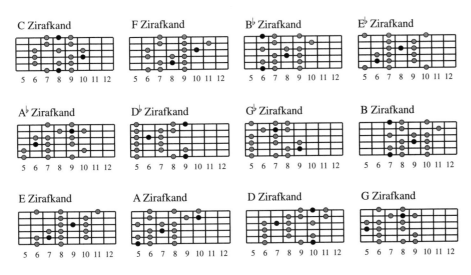

C Zirafkand F Zirafkand B♭ Zirafkand E♭ Zirafkand

A♭ Zirafkand D♭ Zirafkand G♭ Zirafkand B Zirafkand

E Zirafkand A Zirafkand D Zirafkand G Zirafkand

Two-Note-per-String Fingering

E Zirafkand

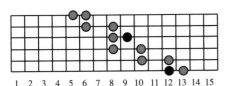

C Zirafkand Vamp

A♭7

Zokuso (1 ♭2 4 ♭5 ♭6 8)

Zokuso a traditional five-note Japanese scale. In a Western context, it can be thought of as a pentatonic version of the *Locrian* mode (page 251, the 7th mode of the *major* scale, page 272) or the *Phrygian* mode (page 297, the 3rd mode of the major scale). This scale can be applied in min7♭5, altered dominant or Phrygian contexts. The exclusion of the 3rd scale degree makes Zokuso an interesting alternative choice. The vamp at the bottom right corner of the page is the same as for Locrian. Zokuso is an excellent substitution for any Locrian-type application.

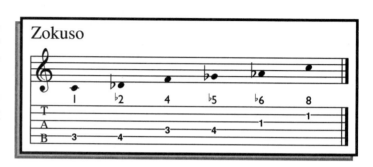

Open Position

C Zokuso

Single-String Fingering

C Zokuso

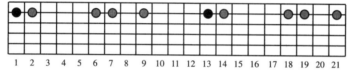

Position Fingerings Through the Circle of 4ths

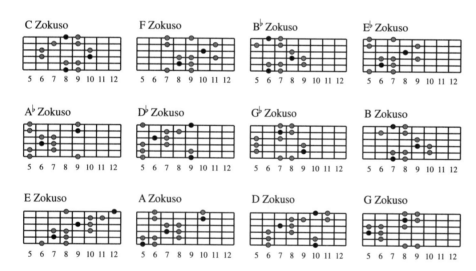

Two-Note-per-String Fingering

C Zokuso

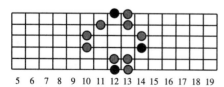

Appendix A—Theory and Improvisation Concepts

This book is a resource for improvisers rather than a method. To get the most out of this book, you should have a good working knowledge of music theory and improvisation. The next few pages will provide some theory background and review, as well as some interesting concepts for improvisation. For a more thorough exploration of the topic, check out *Theory for the Contemporary Guitarist* by Guy Capuzzo and *The Complete Jazz Guitar Method* by Jody Fisher, both published by The National Guitar Workshop and Alfred.

THE MAJOR SCALE

The major scale is built with the following sequence of whole steps (two frets) and half steps (one fret):

W-W-H-W-W-W-H

Here is a C Major scale:

W = Whole step

H = Half step

THE CIRCLE OF 4THS OR 5THS

Knowledge of the twelve *keys* is essential. A key is the tonal center of a composition. The keys can be arranged in a circle (or *cycle*) of ascending *4ths* or ascending *5ths*. 4ths and 5ths are *intervals*. An interval is the distance between two notes. If we go around the circle, building major scales in each successive key, a new flat or sharp is acquired for each key.

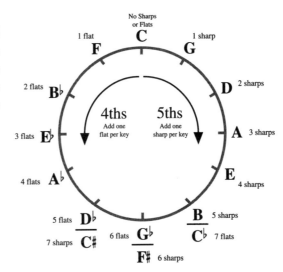

The Notes in All the Sharp and Flat Major Scales								

Sharp Keys								
G —	G	A	B	C	D	E	F♯	G
D —	D	E	F♯	G	A	B	C♯	D
A —	A	B	C♯	D	E	F♯	G♯	A
E —	E	F♯	G♯	A	B	C♯	D♯	E
B —	B	C♯	D♯	E	F♯	G♯	A♯	B
F♯ —	F♯	G♯	A♯	B	C♯	D♯	E♯	F♯

Flat Keys								
F —	F	G	A	B♭	C	D	E	F
B♭ —	B♭	C	D	E♭	F	G	A	B♭
E♭ —	E♭	F	G	A♭	B♭	C	D	E♭
A♭ —	A♭	B♭	C	D♭	E♭	F	G	A♭
D♭ —	D♭	E♭	F	G♭	A♭	B♭	C	D♭
G♭ —	G♭	A♭	B♭	C♭	D♭	E♭	F	G♭

COMPARING A SCALE/MODE TO ITS PARALLEL MAJOR SCALE

To define, name and determine the character or "flavor" of a scale, we compare it to its *parallel major* scale. The parallel major scale is simply a major scale starting on the same root as the scale in question. For example, the parallel major scale of C *Lydian* ♭7 (page 257) is C Major. In the example to the right, the C Lydian ♭7 (the one on top) has a ♯4 and a ♭7 when compared to a C Major scale because the 4th note has been altered upward one half step with a sharp and the 7th note has been altered downward one half step with a flat.

DIATONIC HARMONY

Diatonic means belonging to the key or scale. A *diatonic chord* is a chord that exists within the scale. In the following example, the C *Harmonic Minor* scale (page 239) has been *harmonized* by stacking 3rds on each note in the scale. This creates minor, diminished, augmented and major *triads* (three-note chords). These comprise the unique *diatonic harmony* of the harmonic minor scale.

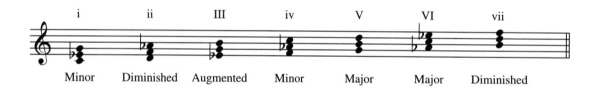

Notice that *Roman numerals* are used to indicate each harmony, Lower case numerals are used for minor and diminished chords; upper case numerals are used for major and augmented chords. Here is a quick review of Roman numerals:

I ......i 1	V ......v 5
II .....ii 2	VI .....vi 6
III ....iii 3	VII ....vii ... 7
IV ...iv 4	

7 CHORDS AND TENSIONS

A 7 chord is a four-note chord built by stacking 3rds. If you stack an additional 3rd on a triad, you have a 7 chord. For each particular kind or "flavor" of 7 chord, there are additional notes that can be added above the 7th called *extensions* or *tensions*. The following example shows four common 7 chords and their acceptable tensions. The first four notes comprise the 7 chord. The higher tones—9s, 11s and 13s—are the tensions. Notice that tensions can be altered with a flat ♭ or sharp ♯. Also notice that the numbers are used to express the flavor of the chord just as they are used to express the flavor of a scale—by comparing the tones to those of a major scale (this is true of the tensions, too: 9=2, 11=4, 13=6).

Maj7 = Major 7 (CMaj7)	
Dom7 = Dominant 7 (C7)	
min7 = Minor 7 (Cmin7)	

This list is not set in stone, but it does reflect common usage. Remember:
- There are other possibilities. Let your ear decide.
- A chord can have more than one tension (for example, C7♯9♭13).
- Tensions can occur anywhere in the chord *voicing* (arrangement of pitches in the chord) but tensions in the bass may completely change the name of the chord and its function.

DIATONIC SCALE SUPERIMPOSITION

Improvising musicians will often use a scale other than the root-based scale prescribed for a chord. For example, jazz players dealing with a non-altered dominant 7 sound might think *Dorian* (page 231) a 5th above the root of the chord (e.g. D Dorian over G7). The more typical scale would be G Mixolydian, but by thinking in D Dorian, important chord tensions are naturally stressed.

The Relationships of D Dorian Pitches to a G7 Chord

This is called *diatonic superimposition*. This technique helps us get away from too much root-oriented thinking.

DIATONIC CHORD SUPERIMPOSITION

A great way to develop melodic ideas is to organize scale material into chord arpeggios. You can superimpose an arpeggio of any chord from the key you're in over the chord of the moment. For example, G7 is V in the key of C Major. You may use any of the other 7 chords in the key of C Major (Dmin7, Emin7, F, Amin7 and Bmin7♭5) as an arpeggio over G7. This concept is an excellent "melodic springboard," or device to help inspire ideas for improvisation.

The Relationships of Tones of Diatonic Chords in C Major to G7

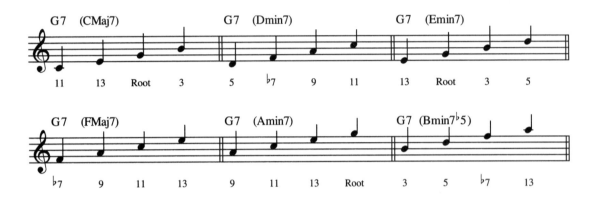

NON-DIATONIC SUPERIMPOSITION

You can superimpose a scale or arpeggio from a different key over a chord. This will create an altered or more tension-oriented sound. For example, to create an altered sound over G7, you can superimpose the E♭ *Lydian Augmented* scale (page 260). This reinforces certain chord tones and stresses certain altered tensions of G7.

The Relationships of Tones of the E♭ Lydian Augmented Scale to G7

Appendix B—Scale Study

There are many ways to practice scales. Ultimately, as a result of studying scales, you will develop a greater understanding of chord/scale relationships, which will enable greater expression in your improvisation. Following are some guitaristic approaches to learning the scales.

SINGLE-STRING STUDIES

Practicing a scale along the length of a single string is an extremely effective approach to learning the fretboard. At first, practice at a slow tempo with a simple, consistent rhythm and with strictly stepwise movement. As you gain confidence, begin to vary the tempo, melodic shapes and rhythms. Every scale in the book is presented on one single string. Learn each scale you practice on all six single strings.

Next, try changing keys, scales or modes within the exercise. For example, the exercise below is entirely on the 3rd string. It switches from A *Dorian* (page 231) to A *Mixolydian* (page 293).

Single-String Study—Switching Modes

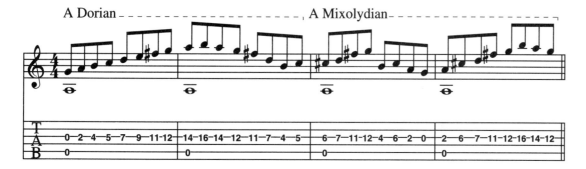

ADJACENT-STRING STUDIES

You can learn a lot about how the scale lies on the fretboard by restricting yourself to two adjacent strings. This can be approached as a *melodic* (single note) or *intervallic* (two simultaneous notes) exercise. Interval practice will heighten your sense of harmony. Explore one kind of interval for a while (adjacent string study will limit you to just a few technically practical intervals), then move on.

The next exercise explores the *Mixolydian mode* (page 293) on the 2nd and 3rd strings with an added A drone in the bass. It begins melodically and then switches to 3rds in the third measure. As with the single string exercise, start slowly and simply and then speed up and add variations later.

NON-ADJACENT STRING STUDIES

Now try restricting yourself to two non-adjacent strings (a two-string combination where the strings are not next to each other, such as the 2nd and 5th strings). This can also be approached melodically or intervallically. The next exercise uses only the 2nd and 5th strings. The scale is E Lydian (page 255). Try different string combinations, different scales and switch keys and flavors.

MINI-POSITION STRING STUDIES

Using small areas of the fingerboard ("mini positions") is another very useful exercise for practicing scales. Restricting the amount of fingerboard you use adds an excellent challenge to your practice. Always be conscious of the notes you are playing—don't just rely on patterns! In the following exercise, D Dorian is practiced on the 1st, 2nd and 3rd strings in 5th position (5th through 8th frets).

The following exercise also begins with D Dorian, once again in a mini-position on the top three strings, but it soon *modulates* (changes keys) to E♭ Dorian. To accommodate the key change, the mini-position is expanded by one fret on either side to include the 4th and 9th frets. Notice that there are some common tones between the two keys, and other notes that are changed. Try practicing over a Dmin7 to E♭min7 vamp.

THE ENTIRE FRETBOARD—STEPWISE STUDIES

This idea is a great fretboard exercise and a great ear training workout as well. The concept is to play the scale in a stepwise manner (in half and whole steps, or the smallest intervals present in the scale) over the entire length of the fretboard. When you run out of frets, descend in the same manner. Practice slowly and always be aware of the note you are playing. The style of fingering—how many notes per string, when to shift, etc.—is up to you.

Here's a stepwise exercise for practicing the F Major scale over the entire length of the fretboard:

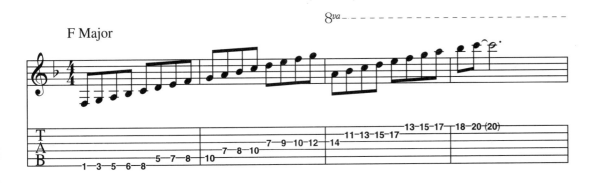

For an additional challenge, try ascending with one scale and descending with another. The exercise below ascends with F Major and descends with F *Lydian* ♭7 (page 257). Again, always keep track of which note you are playing. Try combining other scales, keeping in mind that fingerings will change.

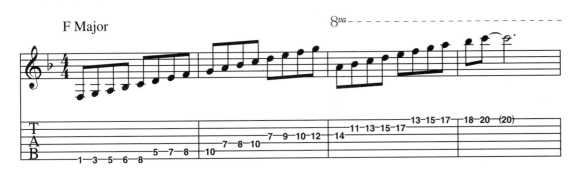

MELODIC HARMONY

Remember that as you improvise melodies you are not restricted to single-note lines. As guitarists, we can explore scales by combining intervals with our single-note expressions. This is called *melodic harmony*. The harmonies move with a melodic sense of flow. In the next example, EMaj7 is expressed by harmonizing parts of its chord scale, which is E Major. The intervals used are 6ths and 7ths.

Below, the same concept is illustrated, but with intervals and single notes combined. The example uses the E *Mixolydian mode* (page 293).

CREATING VAMPS

Creating vamps to practice over is an essential part of your practice. This book provides a two-measure vamp for each scale, but you will discover much more about the scale by creating your own.

Start by including a *pedal tone* (repeated note) or *ostinato* (repeated accompaniment pattern). Next, try to emphasize the distinctive characteristics of the scale. For example, to make a B♭ Lydian vamp sound Lydian, emphasize the ♯4. The ♯4 alone, however, tells us very little. But, if you combine the ♯4 with essential tones from the scale, such as 3 (which tells us whether it's a major or minor sound) and 7 (which gives the flavor of the 7 chord), you will have a much more defined tonality. Simply combine elements. Also, the vamp has to provide *groove*! Keep your rhythmic ideas simple and repetitive.

Here is the B♭ Lydian mode:

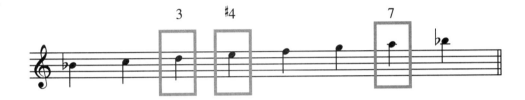

Here is vamp for the B♭ Lydian mode that combines a B♭ pedal and the other defining elements, 3 (D), ♯4 (E) and 7 (A):

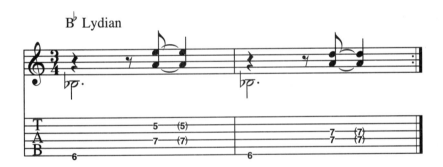

More Titles from the NGW/Alfred Catalog

To order any of these titles, call:
(860) 567-6083
Or visit us online at:
https://www.guitarworkshop.com/store/home.php

Shred Boot Camp • Hurwitz/Smolover
30283 • $19.95 • 80 pg Book & CD

**The Book of Six Strings: The Six-Fold
Path of Zen Guitar** • Sudo/Hurwitz
07-1135 • $19.95 • 128 pg Book & CD

**Sing Your Best: Seven Vocal
Exercises That Really Work**
• Smolover/Bertoli
07-1095 • $17.95 • 48 pg Book & CD
07-1096 • $24.95 • 48 pg Book, CD & DVD

Beginning Guitar for Adults
• Vecchio
07-1001 • $19.95 • 96 pg Book & CD
07-1087 • $23.95 • 96 pg Book & DVD
07-1088 • $19.95 • DVD

**Matt Smith's Chop Shop
for Guitar** • Smith
07-1033 • $20.95 • 96 pg Book & CD

**Guitar for the Absolute Beginner
Book 1** • Mazer
14976 • $17.95 • 48 pg Book & Enhanced CD
20421 • $23.95 • 48 pg Book & DVD
20422 • $19.95 • DVD

Intelli-Shred • Dillard
28027 • $19.95 • 96 pg Book & CD

The Total Blues Guitarist • McCumber
24420 • $19.95 • 128 pg Book & CD

The Total Jazz Bassist • Overthrow/Ferguson
26063 • $19.95 • 128 pg Book & CD

The Total Jazz Drummer • Jain
24429 • $19.95 • 128 pg Book & CD

The Total Acoustic Guitarist • Natter
24426 • $19.95 • 128 pg Book & CD

The Total Jazz Guitarist • Fisher
24417 • $19.95 • 128 pg Book & CD

The Total Rock Bassist • Bennett
30238 • $19.95 • 128 pg Book & CD

The Total Rock Guitarist • Hurwitz
24423 • $19.95 • 128 pg Book & CD

The Blues Guitar Experience • Natter
32650 • $16.95 • 48 pg Book & CD

The Jazz Guitar Experience • Dempsey
32656 • $16.95 • 48 pg Book & CD

The Rock Guitar Experience • Slone
32653 • $16.95 • 48 pg Book & CD

Blues Licks Encyclopedia • Riker
18503 • $19.95 • 96 pg Book & CD

Chord Progression Encyclopedia • Wallach
17868 • $12.95 • 96 pg Book only

Fingerpicking Pattern Encyclopedia • Manzi
19399 • $19.95 • 96 pg Book & CD

Guitar Chord Encyclopedia • Hall
4432 • $19.95 • 320 pg Book only

Guitar Mode Encyclopedia • Fisher
4445 • $19.95 • 224 pg Book only

Guitar Technique Encyclopedia • Various
19381 • $19.95 • 224 pg Book & CD

Jazz Licks Encyclopedia • Fisher
19420 • $19.95 • 96 pg Book & CD

Rhythm Guitar Encyclopedia • Fisher
14838 • $27.95 • 96 pg Book & 2 CDs

Rock Licks Encyclopedia • Cataldo
19417 • $19.95 • 96 pg Book & CD

World Beat Encyclopedia • Marshall
22594 • $19.95 • 96 pg Book & CD

Blues Guitar for Beginners • Giorgi
14973 • $17.45 • 48 pg Book & Enhanced CD

Classical Guitar for Beginners • Gunod
14083 • $17.95 • 48 pg Book & Enhanced CD

Folk Guitar for Beginners • Howard
14970 • $17.50 • 48 pg Book & Enhanced CD

Songwriting for Beginners • Davidson/Heartwood
14840 • $7.50 • 48 pg Book only

Guitar Atlas: Africa • Eyre
20450 • $14.95 • 48 pg Book & CD

Guitar Atlas: Brazil • Newman
20453 • $14.95 • 48 pg Book & CD

Guitar Atlas: Celtic • Ernst
22708 • $14.95 • 48 pg Book & CD

Guitar Atlas: Complete • Various Authors
30903 • $29.95 • 288 pg Book & CD

Guitar Atlas: Cuba • Peretz
26069 • $14.95 • 48 pg Book & CD

Guitar Atlas: Flamenco • Koster
20456 • $14.95 • 48 pg Book & CD

Guitar Atlas: India • Mishra
22851 • $14.95 • 48 pg Book & CD

Guitar Atlas: Italy • Manzi
26073 • $14.95 • 48 pg Book & CD

Guitar Atlas: Jamaica • Green
33486 • $14.95 • 48 pg Book & CD

Guitar Atlas: Japan • Speed
26076 • $14.95 • 48 pg Book & CD

Guitar Atlas: Middle East • Peretz
22711 • $14.95 • 48 pg Book & CD

The Versatile Bassist • Overthrow
28237 • $19.95 • 96 pg Book & CD

The Versatile Drummer • Sweeney
28240 • $19.95 • 48 pg Book & CD

The Versatile Guitarist • Green
28243 • $19.95 • 48 pg Book & CD

Guitar Roots: Bluegrass • Howard
20435 • $14.95 • 48 pg Book & CD

Guitar Roots: Swing • Howard
20438 • $14.95 • 48 pg Book & CD

Guitar Roots: Chicago Blues • Riker
18483 • $14.95 • 48 pg Book & CD

Guitar Roots: Delta Blues • Jackson
21928 • $23.95 • 48 pg Book & DVD
21917 • $19.95 • DVD

COMPLETE ACOUSTIC GUITAR METHOD
Beginning Acoustic Guitar • Horne
19335 • $20.95 • 96 pg Book & CD
23134 • $25.95 • 96 pg Book & DVD
22888 • $19.95 • DVD

Intermediate Acoustic Guitar • Horne
19338 • $21.95 • 96 pg Book & CD

Mastering Acoustic Guitar • Horne
19341 • $20.95 • 96 pg Book & CD

COMPLETE ACOUSTIC BLUES GUITAR METHOD
Beginning Acoustic Blues Guitar • Manzi
22866 • $19.95 • 96 pg Book & CD
26146 • $25.95 • 96 pg Book & DVD
25762 • $19.95 • DVD

Intermediate Acoustic Blues Guitar • Manzi
24203 • $19.95 • 80 pg Book & CD

Mastering Acoustic Blues Guitar • Manzi
24206 • $19.95 • 80 pg Book & CD

COMPLETE BLUES GUITAR METHOD
Beginning Blues Guitar • Hamburger/Smith
8230 • $20.95 • 96 pg Book & CD
20419 • $24.95 • 96 pg Book & DVD
20420 • $19.95 • DVD

Intermediate Blues Guitar • Smith
8233 • $20.95 • 96 pg Book & CD

Mastering Blues Guitar • Smith/Riker
8234 • $27.95 • 144 pg Book & CD
22860 • $33.95 • 144 pg Book & DVD
22861 • $19.95 • DVD

COMPLETE JAZZ GUITAR METHOD
Beginning Jazz Guitar • Fisher
14120 • $20.95 • 96 pg Book & CD
20423 • $25.95 • 96 pg Book & DVD
20424 • $19.95 • DVD

Intermediate Jazz Guitar • Fisher
14123 • $20.95 • 96 pg Book & CD

Mastering Jazz Guitar: Chord/Melody • Fisher
14126 • $19.95 • 64 pg Book & CD

Mastering Jazz Guitar: Improvisation • Fisher
14129 • $19.95 • 64 pg Book & CD

COMPLETE FINGERSTYLE GUITAR METHOD
Beginning Fingerstyle Guitar • Manzi
14099 • $20.95 • 96 pg Book & CD
22909 • $25.95 • 96 pg Book & DVD
22891 • $19.95 • DVD

Intermediate Fingerstyle Guitar • Manzi/Gunod
17825 • $20.95 • 96 pg Book & CD

Mastering Fingerstyle Guitar • Eckels
17814 • $20.95 • 96 pg Book & CD

Beginning Fingerstyle Arranging and
Technique for Guitar • Johnson
22869 • $19.95 • 96 pg Book & CD

COMPLETE ROCK GUITAR METHOD
Beginning Rock Guitar • Howard
14199 • $20.95 • 96 pg Book & CD

Beginning Rock Guitar: Lead & Rhythm • Howard
21934 • $25.95 • 96 pg Book & DVD
21916 • $19.95 • DVD

Intermediate Rock Guitar • Howard
14093 • $20.95 • 96 pg Book & CD

Mastering Rock Guitar • Halbig
14096 • $20.95 • 96 pg Book & CD

BASIC BLUES GUITAR METHOD
Book 1 • Giorgi
19438 • $15.95 • 48 pg Book & Enhanced CD

Book 2 • Hamburger
19441 • $15.95 • 48 pg Book & Enhanced CD

Book 3 • Hamburger/Smith
19444 • $16.95 • 48 pg Book & Enhanced CD

Book 4 • Smith
19447 • $16.95 • 48 pg Book & Enhanced CD

Beginning Guitar for Adults • Vecchio
07-1001 • $19.95 • 96 pg Book & CD
07-1087 • $23.95 • 96 pg Book & DVD
07-1088 • $19.95 • DVD

Beginning Theory for Adults • Gunod
07-1077 • $19.95 • 96 pg Book & CD

Jazz Chops for Guitar • Brown
07-1036 • $19.95 • 80 pg Book & CD

Blues Chops for Guitar • Brown
07-1042 • $19.95 • 80 pg Book & CD

Rock Chops for Guitar • Hurwitz
07-1039 • $19.95 • 80 pg Book & CD

THEORY FOR YOUNG MUSICIANS
Book 1 • Mazer/Gunod
18514 • $17.95 • 48 pg Book & CD

Book 2 • Mazer/Gunod
18517 • $17.95 • 48 pg Book & CD

Notespeller • Ulbrich
18512 • $5.95 • 32 pg Book only

Composition for Young Musicians • Wilson
22913 • $17.95 • 48 pg Book & CD

30-Day Guitar Workout • Fisher
17867 • $7.95 • 48 pg Book only
22894 • $23.95 • 48 pg Book & DVD
22893 • $19.95 • DVD

7-String Guitar • Hurwitz/Riley
21892 • $14.95 • 48 pg Book & CD

Art of Solo Guitar, The: • Fisher
Book 1 • 07-1053 • $20.95 • 96 pg Book & CD
Book 2 • 07-1056 • $20.95 • 96 pg Book & CD

Beginning Blues & Rock Theory
21962 • $15.95 • 48 pg Book & CD

Beginning Delta Blues Guitar • Jackson
21928 • $23.95 • 48 pg Book & DVD
21917 • $19.95 • DVD

Beginning Electric Slide Guitar • Kelley
21937 • $24.95 • 32 pg Book & DVD
21915 • $19.95 • DVD

Big Book of Jazz Guitar Improvisation • Dziuba
21968 • $24.95 • 144 pg Book & CD

Blues Grooves for Guitar • Fletcher
21895 • $19.95 • 96 pg Book & CD

Blues Lead Guitar Solos • Riker
21939 • $16.95 • 96 pg Book & CD

Chord Connections • Brown
16754 • $14.95 • 96 pg Book only

The Complete Studio Guitarist • Clement
22544 • $19.95 • 96 pg Book & CD

Cutting Edge Blues Guitar • Dziuba
17839 • $17.45 • 48 pg Book & CD

Cutting Edge Rock Guitar • Dziuba
17822 • $17.45 • 48 pg Book & CD

Ear Training for the Contemporary Guitarist • Fisher
19370 • $19.95 • 96 pg Book & CD

Easy Chord Idea Book • Donnelly
19368 • $19.95 • 80 pg Book & CD

Electric Bass for Guitarists
22602 • $17.95 • 48 pg Book & CD

**Fretboard Knowledge for the
Contemporary Guitarist** • Clement
21955 • $11.95 • 96 pg Book only

Guitar Chord & Scale Finder • Fisher
14148 • $9.95 • 96 pg Book only

Guitar Made Easy • Hogg
07-1025 • $17.45 • 48 pg Book & CD

Guitar Theory Made Easy • Gunod
07-1028 • $9.95 • 48 pg Book only

Guitar Shop: Getting Your Sound • Hurwitz
18424 • $15.95 • 56 pg Handy Guide & CD

Guitar Shop: Setup and Maintenance • Carruthers
18479 • $5.95 • 48 pg Handy Guide only

Guitar Shop: Tricks and Special Effects • Fiks
18427 • $15.95 • 48 pg Handy Guide & CD

Guitar Styles: Classic Jazz • Dempsey
14863 • $14.95 • 48 pg Book & CD

How to Succeed as a Female Guitarist • Clement
26052 • $19.95 • 96 pg Book & CD

I Just Bought My First Guitar
22705 • $14.95 • 48 pg Book & CD
22704 • $6.95 • 48 pg Handy Guide

Intelli-Shred • Dillard
28027 • $19.95 • 96 pg Book & CD

I Used to Play Guitar • Fisher
22683 • $19.95 • 96 pg Book & CD

Jam Guitar: Rock • Riley
23230 • $12.95 • 48 pg Book & CD

Jazz for the Rock Guitarist • Brown
14195 • $17.95 • 48 pg Book & CD

Jazz Guitar Christmas • Fisher
14869 • $18.90 • 48 pg Book & CD

Jazz Guitar Master Class • Fisher
14827 • $5.95 • 48 pg Book only

Jazz Guitar Harmony • Fisher
20440 • $20.95 • 96 pg Book & CD

Jazz Lead Guitar Solos • Buono
21956 • $16.95 • 96 pg Book & CD

**Jazz Skills: Filling the Gaps for
the Serious Guitarist** • Fisher
07-1012 • $19.95 • 96 pg Book & CD

Like Red on a Rose • Castleman
07-1134 • $3.95 • 8 pg Sheet Music

Learn How to Transcribe for Guitar • Hurwitz
14948 • $19.95 • 96 pg Book & CD

Martin Simpson Teaches Alternate Tunings
20415 • $23.95 • 48 pg Book & DVD
20416 • $19.95 • DVD

Matt Smith's Chop Shop • Smith
07-1033 • $20.95 • 96 pg Book & CD

Multi-Instrumental Guitarist, The • Horne/Phillips
21901 • $19.95 • 96 pg Book & CD

Pentatonic Improvisation • Halbig
23208 • $19.95 • 96 pg Book & CD

Pro Guitarist's Handbook • Lidel
19426 • $19.95 • 96 pg Book & CD

Progressive Rock Guitar • Riley
22547 • $18.95 • 96 pg Book & CD

Quick Start Blues Guitar • Giorgi
22692 • $9.95 • 48 pg Book & CD

Shortcuts for Beginning Guitar • Halbig
07-1090 • $17.95 • 48 pg Book & CD

Shred is Not Dead • Syrek
19324 • $14.95 • 48 pg Book & CD
21936 • $24.95 • 48 pg Book & DVD
21914 • $19.95 • DVD

Sight-Reading for the Contemporary Guitarist • Dempsey
21954 • $12.50 • 112 pg Book only

Some Towns and Cities • Verdery
4490 • $21.95 • 48 pg Book & CD

Teaching Guitar • Fisher
22916 • $19.95 • 96 pg Book & Enhanced CD

Teach Yourself Guitar Repair & Maintenance • Carruthers
22854 • $9.95 • 80 pg Book only
22856 • $29.95 • 80 pg Book & DVD
22855 • $19.95 • DVD

Theory for the Contemporary Guitarist • Capuzzo
16755 • $9.95 • 96 pg Book only
24208 • $25.95 • 96 pg Book & DVD
24207 • $19.95 • DVD (Dempsey)

Ultimate Guitar Scale Bible, The • Dziuba
07-1009 • $14.95 • 144 pg Book only

Ultimate Guitar Chord Bible, The • Brown
07-1083 • $15.95 • 128 pg Book only

Zen and the Art of Guitar • Peretz
21907 • $19.95 • 96 pg Book & CD

Zen Guitar • Philip Toshio Sudo (Simon & Schuster)
068483877X • $13.00 • 206 pg Book only

Easy Blues Guitar Licks • Riker
23225 • $14.95 • DVD

Easy Chords and Strums for Acoustic Guitar • Natter
26058 • $14.95 • DVD

Metal Guitar Licks • Steiger
23224 • $14.95 • DVD

Blues Guitar for the Absolute Beginner • Hinman
22872 • $17.95 • 48 pg Book & CD

Guitar for the Absolute Beginner Book 1 • Mazer
14976 • $17.95 • 48 pg Book & Enhanced CD
20421 • $23.95 • 48 pg Book & DVD
20422 • $19.95 • DVD

Guitar for the Absolute Beginner Book 2 • Mazer
14979 • $18.95 • 48 pg Book & Enhanced CD

Guitar for the Absolute Beginner Complete • Mazer
27815 • $29.95 • 144 pg Book & DVD

Jazz Guitar for the Absolute Beginner • Monaco
22875 • $17.95 • 48 pg Book & CD

Keyboard for the Absolute Beginner • Rodman
20432 • $17.50 • 48 pg Book & CD
22617 • $23.95 • 48 pg Book & DVD
22616 • $19.95 • DVD

Rock Guitar for the Absolute Beginner • Hinman
22878 • $17.95 • 48 pg Book & CD

GUITAR FIRST STEPS:
Chords, Strums and Licks • Manzi
07-1097 • $19.95 • 32 pg Book & DVD

Melody • Manzi
07-1109 • $19.95 • 32 pg Book & DVD

Strums, Fingerstyle and Soloing • Manzi
07-1138 • $19.95 • 48 pg Book & DVD

PLAY ACOUSTIC GUITAR:
Getting Started • Mazer
07-1113 • $19.95 • 32 pg Book & DVD

**Beginning Chords, Strums
and Fingerstyle** • Mazer
07-1125 • $19.95 • 32 pg Book & DVD

PLAY BLUES GUITAR:
Getting Started • Bihlman/Smith
07-1105 • $19.95 • 32 pg Book & DVD

Chords, Strums and Solos • Smith
07-1121 • $19.95 • 48 pg Book & DVD

PLAY ROCK GUITAR:
Getting Started • Hurwitz
07-1101 • $19.95 • 64 pg Book & DVD

Beginning Chords, Strums and Riffs • Nolan/Quick
07-1117 • $19.95 • 32 pg Book & DVD

Basic Lead and Rhythm Techniques • Quick
07-1129 • $19.95 • 32 pg Book & DVD

Scott Tennant's Basic Classical Guitar Method 1
19487 • $15.95 • 48 pg Book & CD

Scott Tennant's Basic Classical Guitar Method 1
22613 • $22.95 • 48 pg Book & DVD

Scott Tennant's Basic Classical Guitar Method 1
22612 • $19.95 • DVD

Scott Tennant's Basic Classical Guitar Method 2
19490 • $15.95 • 48 pg Book & CD

Scott Tennant's Basic Classical Guitar Method 3
19493 • $17.95 • 48 pg Book & CD

Easy Soloing for Acoustic Guitar • Mazer
28249 • $16.95 • 48 pg Book & CD

Easy Soloing for Blues Guitar • Bihlman
30257 • $16.95 • 48 pg Book & CD

Easy Soloing for Jazz Guitar • Dempsey
28246 • $16.95 • 48 pg Book & CD

Easy Soloing for Rock Guitar • Kokoszka
30254 • $16.95 • 48 pg Book & CD

4-Chord Songs for the Absolute Beginner • Mazer
30265 • $17.95 • 48 pg Book & CD

Guitar for the Absolute Beginner 1 • Mazer
14976 • $17.50 • 48 pg Book & Enhanced CD

Guitar for the Absolute Beginner 1 • Mazer
20421 • $23.95 • 48 pg Book & DVD

Guitar for the Absolute Beginner 1 • Mazer
20422 • $19.95 • DVD

Guitar for the Absolute Beginner 2 • Mazer
14979 • $18.95 • 48 pg Book & CD

Guitar for the Absolute Beginner Complete • Mazer
27815 • $29.95 • 144 pg Book & DVD